A History of
Musical Americanism

Studies in Musicology, No. 19

George Buelow, Series Editor
Professor of Musicology
Indiana University

Other Titles in This Series

A History of
Musical Americanism

by
Barbara A. Zuck

RESEARCH PRESS

Produced and distributed by
UMI Research Press
an imprint of
University Microfilms International
Ann Arbor, Michigan 48106

Library of Congress Cataloging in Publication Data

Zuck, Barbara A
    A history of musical Americanism.

    (Studies in musicology ; no. 19)
    Bibliography: p.
    Includes index.
    1. Music, American—History and criticism.   I. Title.
II. Series: Studies in musicology ; ser. 2, no. 19)
ML200.Z8   781.773   80-24050
ISBN 0-8357-1109-9

In Memory of Charles Seeger

Contents

Preface

As a graduate student at the University of Michigan in the early 1970s, I attended a discussion with Roger Sessions, then on campus for a performance of his opera *Montezuma*. As part of Sessions's presentation, a recording of his cantata *When Lilacs Last in the Dooryard Bloom'd* was played. With the brazenness only a student possesses, someone asked the composer how his setting "compared" to Hindemith's. Sessions commented on the two works' diverse styles, firmly concluding that only an American could treat the poem appropriately because only an American could understand it. No one challenged his response. I had not given much thought to what it means to be an "American" composer. Sessions's book, *Reflections on the Musical Life in the United States*, became my introduction to the subject.[1]

As the history of the composer of art music in America began to unfold before me, I realized that the title "'American' composer" held profound significance to many of our nation's musicians long before Sessions's remarks. Sometimes the term was a source of pride, sometimes of anguish. But most consistently, especially before around 1930, "'American' composer" represented a kind of socio-artistic discrimination that discouraged the development of a vital American creative musical culture.

The reaction to this discrimination yielded musical Americanism. Musical Americanism has its roots in the nineteenth century, when American musical culture was just becoming active enough to manifest a conflict between native and foreign ideals. As a movement, it sputtered on and off throughout the 1800s, gathered momentum in the early 1900s, and came to full flower between 1929 and 1945.

The period leading up to World War II was an eventful one in American musical history. The turbulent years of the Great Depression, especially, created an unexpectedly stimulating backdrop against which American art music developed as never before. Virgil Thomson has called the 1930s the "definitive decade" in American music.[2] In those

years, American composers brought themselves and native art music out
of isolation and into the American musical world at large.

The 1930s and early 1940s also were the last years in which a group
of composers — practically the entire generation born around 1900 — was
concerned with the common goal of composing specifically "American"
music. Not all of them manifested Americanism in their works. But
most revealed other facets of the concept through their writings or
activities. Sessions himself clearly displays the separate tendencies. His
works do not draw upon pre-existent musical Americana; in fact, his
remarks sometimes are used in this study as a counterpoise to those
advocating the use of native materials to create an "American" style. But
Sessions's preoccupation with the idea of an "American" music is
apparent in his writings from the period as well as later, such as in his
book mentioned above. It is this preoccupation that is at the heart of
musical Americanism.

The present study does not propose to cover musical Americanism
in all its guises. The topic is simply too broad. Chapter II, the survey of
the movement leading up to the 1930s, sometimes relies on other studies,
and more research is needed to clarify musical Americanism before this
century.

In the decade and a half of primary concern here, several
limitations — consciously or unconsciously — were imposed upon the scope
of the study. With the principal exception of the WPA, most of the
organizations and composers considered in detail were active primarily in
New York City.[3] Although probably no more representative then of the
entire nation than it has ever been, New York was surely the musical
capital of the United States at this time.

Several significant topics receive only cursory treatment. Howard
Hanson and the Eastman School of Music, important Americanist forces
from the mid-20s, warrant a separate, detailed examination. The League
of Composers, while not a specifically Americanist organization, played
an important role only touched upon in these pages. Similarly, the
influence of Henry Cowell and his *New Music* press is not adequately
explored here.

In essence, I chose in Parts II and III to focus upon those
organizations, activities, and trends relating to musical Americanism that
were special to the period between 1929 and 1945: the political leftism
of the Depression years, the patriotism of the war period,
Gebrauchsmusik, the Composers' Collective, the WPA and its Composers'
Forum-Laboratories, and the other groups and ideas which originated
and then declined in these years.

Even with these limitations, huge amounts of materials were

consulted. The magazines, newspapers, and much of the music are available, and many of the period's significant participants are still active, sometimes even willing to recount their lives in years past. Such a wealth of information is both the joy and the curse of the student of modern history.

Research for the study involved many people and resource centers. My work was greatly assisted by Richard Jackson of the Music Division, New York Public Library at Lincoln Center and Diette Baily, then at the same institution; Jon Newsom and Wayne Shirley of the Music Division, Library of Congress; Michael Goldman of the National Archives; Wallace Bjorke of the Music Library, University of Michigan; Ruth Watanabe and Mary Montean of the Sibley Library, Eastman School of Music; John Behrens of the Department of Program Information, CBS; Vivian Perlis of the Oral History Project in American Music, Yale University; and the staffs of the Wisconsin State Historical Society and the Music Libarary at the Ohio State University. Mary Montean, Wallace Bjorke, and Diette Baily must be specially thanked for providing materials when travel to their libraries was impossible.

I am grateful for permission granted for the use of letters or musical selections from Robert Russell Bennett, the late Roy Harris, the late Charles Seeger, Elie Siegmeister, the family of Henry F. Gilbert, and the Chappell Music Company.

Ross Lee Finney, Elie Siegmeister, Virgil Thomson, and Charles Seeger were kind enough to grant me personal interviews, and Aaron Copland graciously answered inquiries pertaining to my research. From them I gained insights into American music that are unavailable elsewhere. Mr. Seeger volunteered to read large sections of the study. His informative suggestions and good will were invaluable.

I extend heartfelt thanks to my doctoral committee members from the University of Michigan: Frank Rossiter (now at the University of Texas at Dallas), Charles Trinkaus, Glenn Watkins, William Albright, and William Malm. The choice of my chairman, Richard Crawford, was fortunate. I benefited from his extensive knowledge and experience as a music historian, and from his wise counsel on many facets of research and writing.

For their assistance in the preparation of this edition, I wish to thank Robyn Fritz, Production Editor, Richard T. Wood, Publisher, and George Buelow, Series Editor, of UMI Research Press. I am also grateful to my mother, who helped complete the index.

Finally, I wish to thank my family, without whose encouragement and assistance my work would have been thrice as difficult and a lot less fun.

Part I

Americanism in American Musical History

I

Americanism as a Concept in Music History

The human instinct to categorize is not limited to the visible and the objective but extends to the world of ideas. One of our many efforts to classify patterns of thought has resulted in a group of terms identified by the common suffix "-ism." According to the *Oxford English Dictionary*, "-ism" denotes "forming the name of a system of theory or practice, religious, ecclesiastical, philosophical, political, social, etc., sometimes founded on the name of its subject or object, sometimes on that of its founder"; words ending in "-ism" may also be "more of the nature of class-names or descriptive terms, for doctrines or principles."[1] Significantly, while this verbal order has existed since the time of ancient Greece, it burgeoned only with the sixteenth century, as though the age of exploration demanded a new mode of graphic expression. Indeed, so prolific has this category proven that the suffix itself has become free-standing. The noun "ism," then, refers to—or identifies—a specific type of descriptive noun.

While isms originate as simplifying agents, their meanings often seem to expand with use. Words once having very special definitions become general headings under which a number of related ideas are lumped. The "classic" example is "classicism," which has moved with astounding flexibility from the world of ancient Greek art to touch numerous cultural areas. When one term becomes too crowded with definitions and sub-definitions, a new category breaks off and takes a meaning of its own. There is now "neo-classicism," for instance, to denote the persistence or revival of certain ideas in different times and settings.

Something of both these trends—the simplifying and the expanding—can be seen in the evolution of the word "Americanism."[2] Initially, "Americanism" was used to denote a figure of speech peculiarly American, a meaning it maintains today.[3] As such, the term generally is preceded by the indefinite article, an "Americanism," or is found in the plural, "Americanisms." Originating in the eighteenth century, "Americanism" was coined by the British in derisive reference to their new-world offspring's seeming misuse of the mother tongue. A little of that contempt, although usually playful, continues today among Britishers who insist that they are the ones who speak English, and that their cousins speak another language.

More important to the present discussion is the persistence of the original meaning of "Americanism" in an expanded definition denoting anything peculiarly American. The second sense of "Americanism" refers to something brought from another country—a word, an idea, a person—that becomes "Americanized," using here a related term which implies that the changing process itself is American. "Americanism" can also infer something originally but identifiably American. In this enlarged meaning, "Americanism" has broad significance to American culture, not least of all the arts. It recalls our roots in other places. But it also points up the acculturation process that has led to the creation or recreation of things uniquely our own.

The last dictionary definition of "Americanism," used without the indefinite article and with no plural form, is altogether different from the others, for it has to do with emotions: "attachment to, or political sympathy with, the United States."[4] In this sense, "Americanism" is closer to "patriotism," meaning "zealous devotion to one's country,"[5] or to "nationalism." The *Oxford English Dictionary* offers four definitions of "nationalism," one corresponding roughly to the emotional component of "Americanism." "Nationalism" is "devotion to one's nation, national aspiration, or a policy of national independence."[6] As an allegiance to one's country, "Americanism" might be said to be a specific type of "nationalism."

One might wonder why the term "Americanism" in its emotional sense evolved, when comparable words for other individual countries have not. No "Francism" nor "Britainism" exists. There is "Frenchy" and "Briticism," but these terms are essentially one-dimensional and hardly have the same weight as "Americanism." The very evolution of the term "Americanism" implies a uniqueness, a separateness from "nationalism"; "Americanism" implies America's separateness from other nations.

Both "nationalism" and "Americanism" have acquired connotations that have given each a distinct aura not readily obtained from a dictionary. Because of excesses in national feeling in modern times, "nationalism" has accumulated negative associations that conjure up an ugly picture of chauvinist belligerence.[7] These connotations do not seem to have been carried over to the actual use of "Americanism," at least not in quite the same way. Americanism, meaning the concept of an accentuated attachment to the United States, seems to be a quality that one group of Americans claims for itself, as though boasting a greater or truer American allegiance than other groups. For example, a frequently-seen phrase from the 1930s comes immediately to mind: Earl Browder's slogan "Communism is Twentieth-Century Americanism," which was employed—even exploited—by Communist sympathizers during that period.

Perhaps a deeper understanding of "Americanism" results from considering its use by the American Legion, a veterans' group founded in 1919 by Theodore Roosevelt, Jr. The American Legion has been a strong promoter of patriotism through an organized "Americanism" program including civic training, school awards and contests based on citizenship, and citizenship classes for aliens. The Legion also has been, in the words of one historian, "one of the country's chief defenders against 'un-American' influences."[8] In essence, "Americanism" has come to be associated with groups trying or claiming to be more American than others.

A more isolated but nonetheless revealing use of the term in a musical context is that of John Tasker Howard. He injects "Americanism" into a discussion of folk music and its value to American art music.

> Some of us are not as yet agreed as to who are Americans. A writer has told us that in a foreign district of one of our large cities a social worker once visited a public school classroom and questioned the children upon their various nationalities. He asked all the Bohemian children to raise their hands. Quite a number responded, and he went on through the list of Russians, Armenians, Italians, and the rest. Finally he asked for the Americans, and one little Negro girl raised her hand.
>
> Are we to infer that the Negro is the only true American? We trust not, but there are those who say that because the black man came to our shores unwillingly, and since he himself can remember no ancestry of other than American birth, his claim to the only real Americanism is well founded. These same people will further hold that even the American Indians are not indigenous to the soil. . . . It is indeed an unhappy state of affairs if none of us are Americans.[9]

Used here almost as an equivalent to American nationality, the specific meaning of the word "Americanism" is no more significant than the context in which it is found. Trying to decide who are the "true" Americans—and assuming there are such things—has been a persistent attempt in American history. Almost as persistent has been the attempt to determine what or whose music is "truly" American.

The connotations surrounding "Americanism," then, are quite different from those of "nationalism." If nationalism is something expressed in opposition to another nation, then Americanism would seem to be the reverse. For Americanism appears to be the manifestation of internal aggression, or perhaps abrasion, as opposed to the externally directed vigor of nationalism. Americans have tended to be "at war" with themselves over the issue of national identity rather than with other nations. This is an important distinction. "Americanism" reflects a concern over a self-image that is, by virtue of American history, multiple and therefore difficult to define.

"Americanism" as used by music historians and other musicians at first would not seem to carry quite these same overtones. However, many of the original (that is, non-musical) meanings and associations do persist in the term's adaptation to music history, an adaptation considerably more recent than that of nationalism. Paul Rosenfeld's use of "Americanism" in 1940 is broad:

> The dream in certain American musicians of "expressing national experience," "representing American life," "achieving an American style," in fine the wish to attain what might be termed "Americanism" in music, much censored today and equally much acclaimed, is generally assumed a recent one. Actually it is rich in background.[10]

Rosenfeld equates "Americanism" with the expression and representation of American life in music, as well as with creating an indigenous national musical style. Thus, he has adapted one of the original meanings of the word "Americanism" — something identifiably American — to music history by giving the term an active quality. Rather than using "Americanism" to describe a musical element peculiarly American, Rosenfeld employs it to describe American composers' attempts to imbue their music with something peculiarly American.

A more contemporary and specific adaptation of "Americanism" is that of Gilbert Chase. Chase has moved the evolution of the word in its musical context a little further by using "Americanist," the personal derivative of "Americanism," to describe a composer "trying hard to be 'American.'"[11] Here is the accentuated nationality of the original meaning. Furthermore, Chase's elaboration of how "Americanists" have gone about becoming American incorporates the idiomatic portion of the standard definition.

> Some composers turned to the tribal chants of the Indians, some were attracted by the Negro spirituals, others drew on the tradition of Anglo-American folk music,

and others found material in the songs of the cowboys. A few composers . . . were tapping the resources of current popular music.[12]

According to Chase, then, the incorporation of native American idioms, styles peculiarly American, in art music is a manifestation of "Americanism," musical "Americanism." H. Wiley Hitchcock, in his survey of American music, employs the term in much the same manner.[13]

The similarities between the adaptations of the words "Americanism" and "nationalism" to music history are immediately noticeable. Yet, as with the original meanings of these terms, there are important differences. The following, from a popular music history textbook, may be taken as a standard definition of "nationalism" as currently used in a musical context.

> Musical nationalism refers specifically to a nineteenth-century movement, particularly in Russia, Bohemia (Czechoslovakia), and Scandinavia, that sought to put an end to the domination of foreign importations, especially from Germany and Italy, to encourage native composers and native folk music, and to emphasize themes drawn from national history and legend. The impetus for these developments came partly from the Romantic movement that idealized the importance of folk materials and partly from political events in the nineteenth century that encouraged national aspirations everywhere.[14]

Musical nationalism, therefore, is generally associated with two historic trends: nineteenth-century European Romanticism, and a larger-scale political-cultural nationalism experienced by several European countries. The American musical world did participate peripherally in these tendencies, as is discussed in the subsequent chapter.[15] But the motions toward a national music in the United States before 1900 were hardly of the scope of those in countries abroad. More importantly, America's long drive for a specifically American art music did not reach its peak until well into this century, in a period and milieu quite removed from either the European Romantic or nationalist movements. Musical Americanism, particularly in this century, appears to have been a homegrown phenomenon, the result of societal and cultural occurrences peculiarly American.

Hitchcock has developed a useful terminology to describe a basic division which evolved in nineteenth-century music in the United States: the "cultivated" and the "vernacular" traditions.[16] Music in the "cultivated" tradition is that sometimes known as "art," "fine art," or "classical" music, usually created by trained composers to be interpreted by trained performers. The "vernacular" tradition comprises music "understood and appreciated simply for its utilitarian or entertainment value," such as the numerous varieties of American folk and popular music.[17]

Extending Hitchcock's terminology, it would seem that there really have been three traditions, because the "cultivated," itself, has long been split. The two components of the "cultivated" partition might be called the tradition of "cultivated music in America" on the one hand, and the tradition of "American cultivated music" on the other. "Cultivated music in America" may be described as that perpetuated through the major teaching, performing, and recording institutions in the United States: in short, until recently, the "Great Masters" of European music. "American cultivated music" simply refers to the composition of new music by American composers.

The historic imbalance in sponsorship and recognition between these two cultivated traditions is no secret. Neither is the past isolation of American composers from many of the organizations founded for the perpetuation of cultivated music. In essence, musical "Americanism" has been the American composer's attempt to break down this distinction, to create but one cultivated tradition in which he participates fully in America's major music-making institutions.

Here is the point at which connotations of the non-musical meaning of "Americanism" as internal national abrasion finally fit into a musical context. For in breaking down the distinction between the two strands of cultivated music in the United States, the Americanist has had to do battle with other Americans. The pro-American-music utterances of frustrated composers in the "American cultivated tradition" were the first stirrings of musical "Americanism," aimed at the perpetuators of the "cultivated tradition in America."

Musical "Americanism" has manifested itself, then, in two basic ways. One, which might be called "compositional" Americanism, is the musical use of native elements, as suggested by Chase. The other, as described above, might be termed "conceptual" Americanism, denoting a pro-American-music stance expressed in lectures and writings or through activities in behalf of American music. The second type of "Americanism" initially might not seem to mesh with the first. Yet, they may be seen as different expressions of the same impulse. The two components of musical "Americanism" frequently co-exist in American history as well as in the writings and music of the same composers, particularly after 1900 and most completely in the 1930s and 40s. Both aspects of musical "Americanism" are reactions to the fundamental division in the cultivated tradition.

In a significant essay, Charles Seeger traced American art—or cultivated—music in its relationship to class structure.[18] Seeger noted that as America developed a sizeable wealthy upper class in the nineteenth century, a movement took shape within this class to identify itself with the finer things of life. One of these "finer things" was art music. It is a fact of American musical history that when support for art music first coalesced, that support went not to Americans but to Europeans.

Various reasons may be offered to explain why America's nineteenth-century upwardly-mobile failed to identify Americans with art music: the widespread fame of European art music; the influx into the United States of Germans familiar with and skilled in the Austro-German musical heritage; the low social regard in which professional musicians in the United States were held; the lack of a fully-developed and immediately recognizable American compositional "genius"; the exotic appeal of Europe; the persistence of Puritanical views toward music; and so forth. Nevertheless, as Seeger noted:

> From about 1830, a small vanguard of private citizens, allied with some European musicians who had emigrated to the New World, set themselves with almost religious zeal to "make America musical" in the exact image of contemporary Europe.[19]

This was an American-initiated movement. Americans, usually the wealthy and those who sought to be identified with them, were chief among the spokesmen and organizers. Thus the split in the cultivated tradition had its origins in American class separation. Furthermore, as "cultivated music in America" became more exclusively the province of the upper-class, it became less associated with the vernacular tradition.[20] Or looking at it another way, the supporting class disassociated itself more and more from the classes practicing the vernacular tradition.

In a basic misunderstanding of European art music, the "make America musical" initiators failed (or chose not) to recognize, it seems, the importance of native folk and popular elements as an inspirational source for the very composers they revered. Albeit persisting in a refined or distilled state, the vernacular music of European countries long had been incorporated consciously and unconsciously into European cultivated music. Not seeing this, many Americans also did not realize the significance of a vital intercourse between the cultivated and vernacular traditions in their own country. The fine—or "high"—art of European music was, to them, just that: "above" the vernacular. At the same time, American composers attempting to imitate European composers often felt themselves ignored, and were generally considered unworthy practitioners of a high art identified exclusively as European.

American composers, therefore, were for a long time confronted with what might be called a "no-win" situation. Not really able to beat the Europeans at their own game, neither did they associate with their own vernacular musical heritage, at this time surely more indigenously American in quality than the cultivated. Musical Americanism was, in its first stage, merely a recognition of this situation. Later, Americanists began an active, if sporadic, campaign in several ways: by forming organizations for the performance and publication of their music; and by making up for lost time, so to speak, in seeking out identifiably American sources. These are the subjects of the remainder of this study.

A further point should be made about the significance of "compositional" Americanism. The conscious incorporation of native vernacular sources in art music is certainly not extraordinary in the history of music. Yet it was something relatively new to American composers in the late-nineteenth century. The "cultivated tradition in America" had almost precluded any serious interest in either vernacular music or its possible use in developing an identifiably "American cultivated tradition." Thus when Americanist composers drew upon the wealth of native vernacular sources about them, they were making more than a purely musical statement. They were making a social statement as well, whether or not they recognized it as such. For in drawing upon Negro or Indian melodies, by incorporating ragtime, jazz, or folksong, they were acknowledging both the existence and the worth of the people who had created this music.

In a small way, therefore, Americanist composers were contributing to and reflecting the on-going democratization characteristic of the United States.[21] The compositional Americanist outlook affirms both the diversity of American culture and the oneness of mankind, an appropriately "Americanist" viewpoint in all senses of the word. The following excerpt from the writings of Elie Siegmeister, despite an overlay of sociopolitical language from the 1930s, exemplifies the idealism underlying compositional Americanism:

> With the growth of a new world democracy, people's music will no doubt develop its own distinctive forms, just as religious, aristocratic and middle-class music has done in the past. These forms are already growing out of the use of music as an instrument of democracy, and out of the specific ways in which music serves a people's society. In the past ten years, signs of a new style, in which "popular," "folk" and "serious" elements are mingled, have begun to emerge. . . . There is a certain strength, an emotional directness, a freshness and simplicity that have come from close contact with the broad democratic audience and a profound belief in the greatness and power of the people.[22]

It is fitting and not surprising that musical Americanism (including compositional Americanism) reached a peak during the years of the Depression and World War II. In the first period, American artists of all types experienced a tremendous outpouring of social concern. In the second, most Americans perceived the Allied war effort as necessary for the survival of democratic principles. Particularly in this decade and a half, many Americanist composers took seriously their role as members of a national — or even international — society. They sought to make their music meaningful, and in some cases serviceable, to the general public.

But perhaps the most important ingredients of musical Americanism as a concept are really two assumptions, both arguable. One assumption made by Americanists is that the road to an identifiably American art music is through identifiably American, particularly vernacular, sources. This conviction has been controversial throughout American musical history, and is yet unsettled. The other is the assumption that the people (meaning all social classes and the musically literate and illiterate) actually desire an art music that they can understand, that appeals to them both as Americans and as human beings. Americanist composers have also assumed that audiences want something more than a purely vernacular musical life; they acted as if a caring public was out there waiting and that all the composer had to do was reach it. Since the end of World War II, however, these assumptions have eroded.

One final aspect in the discussion of "Americanism" as a concept needs to be mentioned: the problem of defining "American." A dictionary definition is straightforward and simple: "belonging to the United States," or "a citizen of the United States."[23] It is obvious, however, that "American" has held and continues to carry a greater range of meanings and connotations than any dictionary can provide, and certainly when the word has been used by composers. In 1915, Henry F. Gilbert wrote that there were as yet no "*American* composers" and that, even if there were, American music was unwanted especially if it happened to be "*American music.*"[24] Henry Cowell stated in 1933 that Roy Harris was only at his best compositionally when he was "his rugged American self."[25] And in 1943, Charles Wakefield Cadman wrote to Charles Ives that he hoped to meet Ives and be able to "shake his American hand."[26] Such uses of "American," only a few of many which could be cited, reveal the importance if not the exact meaning of the term to earlier American composers.

In discussing "American," it might be instructive to briefly consider another people traditionally beset with identity problems. The Jewish philosopher Mordecai M. Kaplan, in response to often-asked questions about Judaism, has written simply that Jews are a people with a common history and a common destiny.[27] It is the "common history" portion of this description that is pertinent to the present discussion. Now two hundred years after the birth of the United States, Americans have a common history as a nation. But they remain widely disparate in their ethnic, religious, and cultural backgrounds.

The lack of a common cultural past — or perhaps usable past — on which to construct American art music has frequently been noted by native composers in the cultivated tradition. Aaron Copland has said that during the 1920s he was not aware of appropriate past source material from which he could draw. In the vernacular tradition, he knew Stephen Foster's music.[28] In the past Americanist tradition, he knew that of Henry F. Gilbert.[29] Thus even into the present century, it was unclear to Copland, and seemingly to his colleagues as well, from what previous American music they could learn. Of course, with the "discovery" of jazz, folksong, and — in another sense — the music of Charles Ives, this situation changed rapidly.

In a conversation with a composer active in the 1930s and 1940s, the term "Americanism" was mentioned. There was an instantaneous reaction. "Why do you use that word?" he demanded. "It sounds like a disease. One is either an 'American' composer or he isn't."[30] The question of how to distinguish one from the other was not brought up.

Yet it would seem that this very question — "what is an 'American' composer?" — has been asked repeatedly in the past. From the moment it was realized that an identifiably "American" art music was not an inevitable result of the creation of the United States, nor was it a necessary corollary of achievements in the other arts, the issue has been at the root of musical Americanism. It seems that each generation of American composers answered the question in its own way, finding its own meaning of "American." How succeeding generations responded to "what is an 'American' composer?," how Americanist composers identified what was "American" in the culture about them, is really the history of musical Americanism itself.

"Americanism" and Related Terms

The fundamental types of musical Americanism, as discussed above, are "conceptual" Americanism and "compositional" Americanism. Within these two types further distinctions may be made according to degrees: degrees of commitment to a cause, as in conceptual Americanism; degrees of penetration in music, as in the case of compositional Americanism.

Conceptual Americanism involves a concern with problems of

American composers: access to performances, recognition—both socially and financially, and creating an "American" musical style. Conceptual Americanism also may be manifested by founding organizations for the performance or publication of American music, and is by no means limited to composers. Critics, performers, conductors, even music historians sympathetic to American art music sometimes have helped create an atmosphere which encourages the establishment and development of American music. For instance, the critic/historian Paul Rosenfeld vigorously supported American composers in the 1920s and 1930s. Similarly, the foreign-born conductor Serge Koussevitzky's support for American music was shown by his eagerness to perform the works of native composers at a time when it was unfashionable to do so.[31] Throughout American musical history, conceptual Americanism creates a fairly consistent pattern and is readily identifiable. However, compositional Americanism is more difficult to assess.

Strictly speaking, there is no such thing as "Americanist" music. There can only be music reflecting the particular attitude of its creator. Composers indicate an Americanist outlook in their works by various means. Frequently, pre-existent American vernacular music has been incorporated into newly-composed art music, as suggested by Chase. Yet there are various ways—various degrees—to which pre-existent music can affect the style of composition.

One of the best-known folklorist/composers of all times, Béla Bartók, addressed himself to this issue. On the subject of incorporating pre-existent native material into new music, Bartók has written:

> We may, for instance, take over a peasant melody unchanged or only slightly varied, write an accompaniment to it and possibly some opening and concluding phrases. . . .
>
> Another method by which peasant music becomes transmuted into modern music is the following: The composer does not make use of a real peasant melody but invents his own imitations of such melodies. . . .
>
> There is yet a third way in which the influence of peasant music can be traced in a composer's work. Neither peasant melodies nor imitations of peasant melodies can be found in his music. In this case we may say, he has completely absorbed the idiom of peasant music which has become his mother tongue.[32]

Bartók's statements are helpful in understanding Americanist music which draws upon vernacular sources. His observations reveal the varying levels on which pre-existent materials can be a force in composition, from the mere setting of a melody to the ultimate recasting of the composer's musical language.[33]

There is yet a separate category of Americanist music, including that composed in a patriotic or nationally-inspired fashion, which makes no attempt to incorporate pre-existent music. But Americanist inclinations have spilled over from rhetoric into an aspect of the composition such as the title, program, or subject matter. The composer may seek to evoke the aura of a geographical region or pay tribute to a historical occurrence or national hero. Since there is no use of identifiably American musical elements, the degree of penetration compositionally is only at the surface level. As shown in the following survey, much music composed by Americanists reveals no obvious influence from native musical styles. However, it does reflect Americanist leanings in this other, extra-musical manner.

A discussion of native materials as sources for art music opens up a rather complex area of related descriptive terms. One of these, "nationalism," has already been discussed. At least two other words common in music history intersect this sphere of interest. These are "folklorism" and *"Gebrauchsmusik."*

Curt Sachs has written that "folklorism" is the study of folk music and the use of folk materials in art music; it may, but does not necessarily, indicate a composer's nationalism.[34] *Gebrauchsmusik*, meaning literally music for use, stems from the desire to "bridge the gap between supply and demand," according to Sachs.[35] Usually written for a specific commission or event, *Gebrauchsmusik* may be technically appropriate for amateurs, and sometimes results in the incorporation of familiar or popular elements.[36] These definitions suggest that folklorism and *Gebrauchsmusik* may be the similar consequences of two different, but related, causes. Neither of these two terms, however, necessarily indicates an effort to create a national music, a definite tendency of Americanism. Therefore, folklorism, *Gebrauchsmusik*, and Americanism, in their strictest senses, are related only by the like manifestations of differing intentions. Nevertheless, the three concepts have sometimes co-existed and overlapped historically, such as in the period between 1929 and 1945.

A distinction between folk music (associated with folklorism) and popular music (associated with *Gebrauchsmusik*) is helpful for an understanding of Americanism. Bruno Nettl, acknowledging that folk music is defined by several criteria, has written that "the main one is the transmission by oral tradition; . . . folk music is not, in its native setting, written down."[37] What Americans generally refer to as popular music originally is written down, but its transmission is also primarily oral. Thus, the difference between folk and popular music must be more fundamental.

Folk music has been associated traditionally with a specific cultural segment, a group isolated by occupation, geographical location, or ethnic origin. Popular music also may be indigenous to a particular ethnic or class subdivision, but it is a subdivision fairly evenly dispersed throughout the nation in which it is found. The gradual disappearance of folk music and its replacement by popular music in the United States has followed two trends: the development of media technology, allowing for rapid dissemination of music; and the increasingly transitory living patterns of most Americans. The term "popular" music bespeaks a widespread appeal. It is only natural that composers in the "cultivated" tradition should turn to popular as well as to folk styles in hopes of creating an indigenous American art music.

The manifestations of Americanism in the world of music in the United States have been diverse. Americanism reached a climax between 1929 and 1945. Yet Americanism in this period was not without precedent. In fact, Americanism has had a long history, in the course of which nearly every type of American vernacular material has served as a source for native composers in the cultivated tradition.

II

A Survey of Musical Americanism
Through the 1920s

Introduction

From its disparate racial, ethnic, religious, and national backgrounds, the United States has forged an unprecedented power. Yet the pastimes of a society distinguish it at least as much as politics and economics. Despite the power of the United States, American cultural life has long been the subject of debate at home and abroad alike. Many intellectuals in the nineteenth century, for instance, believed that the United States possessed no distinctive culture of its own. They felt that America had achieved world leadership in every field except artistic creativity, and that the American arts remained in the shadow of European traditions. American inferiority in this area was a real, often consuming problem only aggravated by foreign opinion. Perhaps as a result of American political insolence and independence, Europe reacted by calling attention to our weak spot.

Sidney Smith (1771–1845), an English critic, published an article in 1820 sparking a literary controversy in the United States that raged for the next several decades. "In the four quarters of the globe," Smith asked disdainfully, "who reads an American book? Or goes to an American play? Or looks at an American picture or statue?"[1] Ralph Waldo Emerson, in a well-known address of 1837, responded by directing Americans to strike out on their own intellectual paths.

> We have listened too long to the courtly muses of Europe. The spirit of American freedom is already suggested to be timid, imitative, tame. . . . We will walk with our own feet; we will work with our own hands; we will speak our own minds.[2]

Emerson's challenge was met quickly by American writers. By the middle of the nineteenth century, Thoreau, Hawthorne, Melville,

Whitman, and others had established a foundation for American literary achievement.

In the other arts, particularly music, independence from Europe and self-identity were longer in coming. Music, it will be noted, remained unmentioned by Smith in his blast at American culture. But at least some entertained the possibility of creating a distinctive American musical character. Not surprisingly, composers were most concerned with the problem. In 1852, following a vein similar to Emerson's, the American composer/critic William Henry Fry also lectured:

> It is time we had a Declaration of Independence in Art, and laid a foundation of an American school of Painting, Sculpture, and Music. Until this Declaration of Independence in art be made—until American composers shall discard their foreign liveries and found an American School—and until the American public shall learn to support American artists, Art shall not become indigenous to this country.[3]

Fry's Declaration of Independence initiated a tradition of musical Americanism that was to span almost a century.

The cry for musical independence was influenced by factors peculiar to the history of music in the United States. The division in American cultivated music took shape in the 1800s. During the first half of the century, increased and changing immigration patterns brought large numbers of continental Europeans to the United States for the first time. With these immigrants came vital musical practices, stronger–at least in art music–than the previously prevalent British heritage. In the Colonial and Revolutionary War periods, the British tradition had been dominant in both secular and sacred music. American psalmody was a development of English models. Secular songs, instrumental works, and theatrical productions–most notably the ballad opera–were either imported or directly related stylistically to corresponding British genres. Although an Anglo-American offshoot had taken root, the level and scope of native composition and performance was not sufficiently strong to resist the influx of continental European music. Many well-trained immigrant musicians were eager to capitalize on their abilities in fresh territory, forcing native Americans to compete with musicians better trained than themselves.

Prior to 1800, few opportunities existed for professional musicians in the United States. But as the expanding American economy gradually opened up positions for performers, conductors, and teachers, Europeans–particularly Germans–stepped into the most desirable of them. As a result of this growing professional dominance, naturally it was European music that was published, taught, and performed. Thus, cultivated music grew so identified with Europeans that being European became a symbol of quality for both performance and composition. In the mid-nineteenth century, with foreign domination of American music obvious, a few native musicans began to articulate their musical Americanism. But by no means did they all, for many travelled to Europe in hopes of acquiring the proper musical background, thus beginning a long, one-sided tradition of cross-Atlantic musical dialogue.

The several related issues touched upon by Fry in his Declaration of Independence – public support for American artists, an American school of the arts, discarding "foreign liveries" – became chronic problems for native composers of art music in America. By calling attention to these concerns, the musical Americanist often stirred controversy with his solutions. As will be shown, it was the very uniqueness of America – its multiplicity of origins – which presented native composers with their trickiest question: what might be the basis for an indigenous American music?

The following survey of Americanism in American musical history is sometimes an interpretation of previous research by others. Much basic study remains to bring to light Americanist activities and personalities only mentioned below, and to uncover others as yet unknown. One thing does seem clear. Musical Americanism has been a fairly consistent presence from the earliest rhetoric of Fry through the close of World War II. Not always did the movement find an outspoken leader such as Fry, Farwell, or Copland. But Americanism appears to have a long, if vacillating, history in American music.

Early Americanists: Fry, Heinrich, and Bristow

In the "Prefatory Remarks" to his opera *Leonora*, William Henry Fry (1813–65) expressed awareness of a problem which, in 1845, was just beginning to concern American composers: the lack of a national proto-type for American music. Fry explained why neither the setting nor the music of *Leonora* was American:

> A scene laid in ancient Greece or Rome would preclude a national style of music now lost, if it ever existed. The action laid in this country, also, could not be illustrated with national music, since the original type is wanting.[4]

Whether or not one agrees with Fry's thinking about the correspondence between operatic setting and musical style, his is a telling statement. It is also open to interpretation.

Precisely what Fry meant in his remarks by "wanting" is unclear. He could have meant either that American "national" music was simply non-existent, or that this music was unsuitable to his purposes. Fry also gave no indication here what he considered to be "the original type" of "national" music. Was he referring to cultivated or vernacular music, or perhaps both?

It is difficult to believe that Fry could have been completely unaware of the lively tradition of vernacular music common in his own period. For instance, the spirituals and folk and camp-meeting hymns of both whites and blacks were current. Black-face minstrelry was well underway to becoming a nationwide fad, and the genteel parlor song was a staple of the booming sheet music industry.[5] Rather, Fry probably found this music unacceptable as a source. In his own eyes, at least, he was a composer with only the loftiest aims. Of *Leonora*, Fry wrote:

> This Lyrical Drama was produced on the stage with a view of presenting to the American public a *grand opera* originally adapted to English words. The class of opera technically so designated, is, on the continent of Europe, employed for works of serious or tragic character. . . . This is essentially the high, complete, and classic form to give to the opera.[6]

Leonora was a serious musical undertaking, one which, to Fry's thinking, excluded the use of everyday music. A composer who considered operatic spoken dialogue "wretched and vulgar"[7] surely would have frowned upon simpler, perhaps less pretentious music; Fry, like many musicians after him, looked down upon vernacular music as unworthy of the composer of art music. In fact, Fry's attitude indicates how clearly a division between American cultivated and vernacular music was recognized in the 1840s.

Regardless of his attitude toward vernacular music, it probably never occurred to Fry that these genres could be a route to "national" music. After all, Fry was writing long before European nationalism's major period of folk interest; there were only limited precedents for the conscious use of folk or popular music as a major source either at home or abroad.[8] The dearth of an "original," "national" music which Fry referred to, it seems safe to assume, meant a lack of native-composed art music.

Fry definitely considered it desirable to compose art music with a national character.

> It is a clear proposition that no Art can flourish in a country until it assume a genial character. It may be exotic, experimentally, for a time, but unless it become indigenous, taking root and growth in the hearts and understandings of the people generally, its existence will be forced and sickly, and its decay quick and certain.[9]

Fry's interest in establishing and calling attention to native art music became an increasing interest, almost an obsession with him.[10] Indeed, today he is remembered more for his Americanist writings and lectures than for his music.

Leonora was premiered in Fry's native Philadelphia at the Chestnut Street Theatre on June 4, 1845. Although fairly well-received at the time,[11] it was not produced again until thirteen years later. In a revised version, *Leonora* was performed in New York at the Academy of Music in 1858. This time, to Fry's displeasure, it was presented in Italian. According to Irving Lowens, the operatic troupe then in New York was "incapable of mastering the intricacies of the English language,"[12] a perfect illustration of the Italian domination of opera in America during the mid-nineteenth century.

Fry's "Prefatory Remarks" to *Leonora*, especially that section quoted above regarding "American" music, may well be seen as an *apologia*. In the opinions of many of his contemporaries as well as later music historians, the first American grand opera was unmistakably modeled on the Italian style. Considering the musical world of Philadelphia during Fry's formative years as a composer, this is not surprising. A review of the 1858 New York production, the second and last complete staging of *Leonora*, included the following evaluation:

> At the time when Mr. Fry composed this opera, Donizetti and Bellini were the most popular composers for the stage, and evidently he wrote under their influence. He ends his phrases just as they do, and unfortunately he also commences like them. There seems to be no attempt on his part to mix the common ingredients of a very common dish in such a way that they may not seem *too common* – a most surprising fact.[13]

Commenting on the operatic scene in Fry's Philadelphia, William Treat Upton has written:

> If we were to be transported back into the operatic world that Fry knew in Philadelphia in the 1840's, we should find ourselves strangers indeed. . . . Rossini, Bellini and Donizetti dominated the world's operatic state.[14]

In accordance with Italian operatic structural conventions of the time, Fry's *Leonora* begins with the characteristic one-movement, sectional overture, followed by three acts. The plot is a love story involving intrigues and disguises. Musically, both recitative and aria styles are Italianate, with several of the arias containing as much coloratura as Rossini's. The *da capo* aria (see Example 1) – "My Every Thought, My Every Word" – reveals the Italian derivation in style and form.

Example 1
"My Every Thought, My Every Word," *Leonora,* William Henry Fry.

In light of the exoticism also common to much nineteenth-century musical subject matter, it should not seem unusual that Fry's opera is set in Spain in the remote period of the early sixteenth century, and is based on a nineteenth-century novel by an English writer.[15] Although Fry did consider his success at setting English speech to musical recitative an important step toward achieving a native musical theatre, he could not pride himself on a similar breakthrough in musical content.[16]

Considering his job as a journalist (first as foreign correspondent from 1846, then as music editor from 1852 of *The New York Tribune*), Fry's musical output was sizeable. Among his major works are: three operas *(Aurelia the Vestal*, 1841; *Leonora*, 1845, rev. 1858; *Notre Dame of Paris*, 1864); two oratorios (*Stabat Mater*, 1855; *Moses in Egypt*, incomplete, n.d.); two large-scale choral works *(Crystal Palace Ode*, 1854; *Hallelujah Chorus*, n.d.); numerous orchestral works (including *Santa Claus: Christmas Symphony*, 1853; *Niagara*, 1854; and two overtures); a *Kyrie Eleison* (n.d.); and a *Mass in E-Flat* (1864).[17]

Fry apparently had some trouble in getting performances for his works, particularly the larger orchestral pieces. Since many of his works were for full orchestra, such difficulty is not surprising. However, lack of interest by the few local organizations capable of performing large scores undoubtedly was one of the principal contributing factors to his vociferous verbal Americanism. Not until the Frenchman Louis Antoine Jullien (1812-60), maestro of the touring Jullien orchestra, took an interest in Fry's compositions did many of them receive their premieres.[18]

The derivativeness of Fry's compositions probably was their most consistent feature. Upton attests to a definite stylistic refinement in Fry's development as a composer, but there was evidently no real tendency to break away from European models.[19] In one work, the symphony *Niagara*, Fry obviously referred to a natural phenomenon already an American national landmark. But this is apparently the closest Fry came to seeking inspiration for his music in this country.

Fry's place as an early Americanist rests, therefore, on his rhetoric, not his music. His Americanism was articulated primarily in his lectures of 1852, and the New York Philharmonic Society incident of the following year.[20]

In his series of lectures (Metropolitan Hall, New York; beginning November 30, 1852), Fry attempted to cover the entire art and history of music as he interpreted it. Several local newspapers and periodicals publicized the series well in advance of the autumn starting time. Even *Dwight's Journal of Music* in Boston foreshadowed the event by carrying an announcement from *The New York Tribune*:

Wm. Henry Fry, Esq., proposes a course of lectures upon the Science and Art of Music, and upon a most colossal scale. Yet imposing as is his programme, it does not seem to us impossible, and of the very great benefit and actual necessity of such an undertaking there is no doubt.[21]

These apparently were well-anticipated lectures.

Fry was assisted by current Italian Opera Company soloists, the Philharmonic Orchestra, and the Harmonia Society Chorus.[22]   All performers as well as additional expenses were paid by Fry himself. Originally billed as a series of ten, Fry added an eleventh lecture in which he discussed American music.   It was in this lecture that Fry called for the "Declaration of Independence" of the arts which was cited earlier in this chapter.   He also reportedly chastised his countrymen both for a lack of musical taste and a lack of support for American artists.[23] The subject and tone of Fry's eleventh lecture did little to enhance his popularity.   However, Fry apparently felt that if he enlightened the public to the problems of recognition faced by the American composer, he might also somehow improve that situation.

Judging from his "Prefatory Remarks" to *Leonora*, the duality of his own stance with regard to Americanism does seem to have concerned Fry.   He noted the desirability of an "indigenous," thriving American musical culture.   Yet he did not elaborate in these "Remarks" or elsewhere about the specific subject of an "American" style for art music. Nor did Fry, like later Americanists, break out on his own stylistic path or seek the foundation for an American musical style in the popular sources of his day.   The reasons why, though conjecture, have been suggested.   To Fry, the composition of a grand opera in English was his contribution to the creation of an American musical theatre, and an event to be regarded as a major achievement.   Considering the lack of precedents for such a venture, and the infancy of the American cultivated tradition, one is inclined to agree with him.

To varying degrees, Fry addressed himself to the different yet related issues comprising musical Americanism: gaining recognition for American cultivated music, and creating music of an indigenous character.   The first is essentially a socioeconomic problem, while the second is an aesthetic one.   These themes, given their earliest articulation by Fry in the 1840s and 50s, remained uppermost among concerns of many American composers of art music.   Indeed, they comprised the issue of American music for nearly a century.

Before continuing a chronological discussion of Americanism, it might be well to consider briefly just what precedents Fry had in native-composed art music.   While religious works–hymns, anthems, and

America's own fuguing tunes–comprise the major output of native composers in the late eighteenth century, Oscar Sonneck's *Early Concert-Life in America* reveals an active interest in secular art music as well.[24] Still, much of the concert music performed in these years, as might be expected, was European. The native-composed secular music of this period tends toward the smaller genres, such as songs and piano or other keyboard music, and could provide no model for Fry's full-scale opera. The growth of orchestras and orchestral music as well as operatic organizations was just beginning in the first half of the nineteenth century.[25]

As for Americanist composers known before Fry, there is really only one, Anthony Philip Heinrich (1781–1861). As previously mentioned, Americanism relating to music and the other arts did not become an issue until the nineteenth century. The patriotism and national pride of some of America's better-known eighteenth century composers, most notably William Billings (1746–1800) and Francis Hopkinson (1737–91),[26] bear only partial relationship to Fry's concerns about American music and American composers. The Americanism of these earlier composers was "Americanism" in the original, non-musical definition of the term. Neither Billings nor Hopkinson was concerned with the more specific Americanism related to music because the conflict between native-born and foreign composers did not yet exist. Heinrich, chronologically approximately midway between these Revolutionary period composers and Fry, is a somewhat special case.

Anthony (*né* Anton) Philip Heinrich is a delightful character to discuss because of his personal eccentricities, expressed both musically and extra-musically. He is in some ways an archetypical Romantic figure. A millionaire in youth, he quickly lost his fortune and spent most of his remaining life trying to make ends meet. His romantically bombastic outlook is obvious in the titles and programs of his compositions (for example, an orchestral movement entitled "Destruction of the Bivalves" . . . *vulgate* "Clam Bake"[27]) as well as in his letters and forewords to works. Whatever Americanist propensities he had, however, are qualified by his nationality. He was born in Bohemia and came to this country as an adult. Still, Heinrich was frequently attracted to patriotic themes and other Americana. As one of the better-known composers of art music in the United States before the Civil War, his music may have set a precedent for other such works.

To the extent that it was performed, Heinrich's music was apparently warmly received; the title given him of "Beethoven of America" now is well-known.[28] The extent of his regard and influence among other musicians at the time is revealed by his selection as chairman of the committee to guide into being the newly conceived Philharmonic Society of New York.[29]　Yet Heinrich's idiosyncracies certainly were recognized in his own day.　John Hill Hewitt related an amusing incident of Heinrich's presentation of a composition dedicated to then United States President Tyler.　Heinrich labored long and hard in performing the work for the president, after which the Chief Executive's only remark was a request for an old Virginia reel.　Hewitt, who himself called the piece "complicated," then listened to Heinrich furiously exclaim that the president knew no more about music "than an oyster."[30]

Heinrich began composing late in life, near the time he came to the United States.　He arrived in the Kentucky wilderness in 1818, around the age of thirty-seven, and lived there for a time in a log cabin.　In his first collection of compositions, *The Dawning of Music in Kentucky*,[31] Heinrich already revealed what would become of his life-long interest in American subject matter in essentially light works like "Hail Columbia (Minuet)," "Yankee Doodle Waltz," "The Birthday of Washington," and "Yankee Doodliad."[32]　Such pieces in this collection — comprised primarily of songs, piano works, and other instrumental music — though often demanding a virtuosic technique, are similar in concept to the various arrangements of patriotic songs and marches burgeoning in the late eighteenth century.

Heinrich rapidly moved on to the larger genres, a tendency which continued throughout his life until, as in some of Berlioz's music, the size and scope of a few works approached the gigantic.[33]　He also discovered the program symphony, to which he sometimes applied his personal yet grandiose conception of America.[34]　For example, the following scenario accompanies his *Grand Overture to the Pilgrim Fathers*:

> **Adagio Ottetto.** – The Genius of Freedom slumbering in the Forest shades of America.
> **Adagio Secundo** – FULL ORCHESTRA – She is awakened into life and action by those moving melodies with which Nature regales her solitude.
> **Marcia** – The efforts of power to clip the wing of the young Eagle of Liberty.
> **Finale Allegrissimo** – The joyous reign of universal Intelligence and universal Freedom.[35]

Some of Heinrich's compositions were inspired by the lives and music of the American Indian.　Although it is unclear, at least to this writer, whether he incorporated actual Indian tunes into his own scores, these works reveal a very early interest in Indian subject matter by a composer of art music.[36]　The earliest of his several Indian-inspired works is apparently the orchestral fantasy *Pushmataha: A Venerable Chief of a Western Tribe of Indians*, completed around 1831.　The piece also provides further evidence of Heinrich's eccentricity.　To conclude a work devoted to an American Indian, the composer presents "God Save the King," a quotation made more unusual by its highly chromatic setting.[37]

By no means did Heinrich compose only Americanist music; several pieces are dedicated to his native Bohemia.[38] One composition, "The Hickory, or Last Ideas in America,"[39] reveals a variety of national allegiances and a good bit of practical forethought on the part of Heinrich. Composed in England but with an eye toward his return to America, the work includes fantasies on both "God Save the King" and "Yankee Doodle." The piece is dedicated to Heinrich's native Bohemia, where he was to travel just after leaving England.[40] The "Coda" to the composition — the "Yankee Doodle" fantasy — is an example of Heinrich's lively pianistic style.

To determine the exact extent of Heinrich's verbal Americanism requires further study of letters and other written documents, many of which were unavailable to this author. Howard writes that Heinrich "fought fiercely for the hearing that he felt all American composers were entitled to have,"[41] but he does not cite precise incidents. Still, it is clear from the oft-quoted "Preface" to *The Dawning of Music in Kentucky* that Heinrich experienced difficulties being a composer in the United States in the first half of the nineteenth century. His remarks also reveal his obvious pride as an early composer of art music in America.

> The many and severe animadversions, so long and repeatedly cast on the talent for Music in this Country, has been one of the chief motives of the Author, in the exercise of his abilities; and should he be able, by this effort, to create but one single *Star* in the *West*, no one would ever be more proud than himself, to be called an *American Musician.* — He however is fully aware of the dangers which, at the present day, attend talent on the crowded and difficult road of eminence; but fears of just criticism, by *Competent Masters*, should never retard the enthusiasm of genius, when ambitious of producing works more lasting than the too many *Butterfly effusions* of the present age.[42]

One might also add that the above quote indicates a certain lack of modesty on the part of Heinrich.

Heinrich addressed himself less to the problems verbally articulated by Fry than to a Romantic vision of America expressed musically. His importance as an early composer of large ensemble music lies in his stress on American themes and his success, relatively speaking, at getting these works performed. Heinrich freely drew upon musical and extra-musical Americana. Patriotic tunes and Indian subjects comprise most of the vernacular material incorporated in his pieces. Heinrich's interest in American sources, however, did not seem to result in a musical style different in essential content from European music of similar scope, at least in the minds of his contemporaries. Indeed, one of the reasons for his success with critics, notably the venerable John Sullivan Dwight, is apparent from the following:

> This eccentric, noble-hearted man, now quite advanced in years, whom it was the fashion to call music-mad, until further acquaintance with the great music of Germany taught us to suspect our own taste rather than his genius, is at last reaping some reward for a life of disinterested, ill-appreciated devotion to Art and to all kindly sentiments.[43]

The yardstick for measuring musical excellence in the United States at this time was decidedly German.

Perhaps because he was foreign-born, Heinrich was not particularly concerned with the question of an "American" music, at least in style and content.   As a European, Heinrich naturally viewed the American musical scene from a different angle than Fry, who commented on America's lack of an "indigenous" music. One native composer of mid-century, George Frederick Bristow, did move his own music away from European inspiration, even if he had little to say on the subject.

William Henry Fry serves as a good model and starting point in the history of Americanism because of his strong verbal stance on the issues confronting American composers.   In contrast, Fry's contemporary and fellow Americanist George Frederick Bristow (1825-98) tended less toward verbal and more toward compositional Americanism.   Although Bristow made rare use of vernacular sources, many of his works reveal an interest in and inspiration from extra-musical Americana.

George Frederick Bristow was a versatile and active participant in the musical world of his native New York City. Gilbert Chase has called him a "typical professional composer of art music in the United States."[44] His multifaceted career indicates how one made a living as a musician in the United States at this time. Bristow was a performer, conductor, and teacher as well as being a composer. A pianist, organist, and violinist, he learned the rudiments of music from his father. He later studied with Henry C. Timm, a German who helped found the New York Philharmonic Society, and an English composer, G. A. MacFarren.

Bristow joined the New York Philharmonic Society Orchestra at its inception in 1842 and remained a violinist in the group for nearly forty years.   In 1851, he became the conductor of the Harmonic Society of New York, the chorus that sang in Fry's lecture series of 1852-53. Bristow's position with the Harmonic Society was reflected in his compositions, for after 1851 he wrote more works for large chorus.[45] Later on, he also was to help found another group, the short-lived

American Music Association (1856-58), which evolved from his own and others' Americanist feelings.[46]

Bristow began composing at a young age and was quite prolific. By his thirtieth birthday, he had already written forty chamber music, choral and orchestral pieces, and his most famous work, the opera *Rip Van Winkle*. America's second grand opera was premiered at Niblo's Garden by the then well-known Pyne and Harrison Troupe on September 27, 1855, with the composer conducting.[47]

A three-act opera with brief orchestral introduction, *Rip Van Winkle*[48] is stylistically lighter, less sophisticated, and less Italianate than Fry's *Leonora* of ten years before. Despite the presence of a few arias with coloratura decoration, the vocal style is on the whole simple — even simplistic — particularly in the choruses. A perusal of the score suggests that the work is as much influenced by eighteenth-century English comic opera as by the more recent influx of Italian operatic styles. This is given further weight by Bristow's intermingling of spoken dialogue with recitative.

The plot of *Rip Van Winkle* is based on Washington Irving's story, then popular in a variety of dramatic versions on New York stages.[49] Bristow's librettist, J. W. Shannon, introduced a romance, about which the opera centers, between Rip's daughter and a Continental army officer. The love interest allows for several duets, while the presence of the Continental army leads to operatic favorites such as a drinking song and a soldiers' chorus.

Rip Van Winkle was warmly received by the public in New York in 1855, and ran for eighteen performances. Critical reaction was mixed. One writer, noting the lightness and gaiety of the work, also commented on its musical style:

> The composer evidently aimed at producing a popular, and not a classical work. The melodies are light resembling those of Auber, sometimes reminding one of the better class of native compositions, by some miscalled Ethiopian. Simple and graceful themes, set in stirring, strongly marked rhythms, keep the public feet in motion, and the public heart pounding with delight.[50]

Another critic added:

> In the treatment of his subject Mr. Bristow has evidently consulted the popular appetite for light and cheerful music, with a leaning at times towards the sentimental and martial school. He has succeeded in garbing some slight ideas in an agreeable manner, but has not, we think, given birth to any strikingly original ones. The character of the music may be described in a single word — it is pretty.[51]

Rip Van Winkle is historically significant as our first native-composed grand opera on an American topic. From the author's study of the score (admittedly not as satisfactory as also hearing it) and from contemporary evaluations, *Rip Van Winkle* appears to be something of a stylistic newcomer in the United States. Not really a ballad opera, not Italianate either, the work succeeds in being distinctive in its simple, congenial manner of setting English text. Current reviewers did not find fault, as they had in the case of *Leonora*, with a musical language too obviously based on European models. One reviewer of *Rip Van Winkle*, as cited above, even noted a similarity between the opera's musical style and contemporary "Ethiopian" – presumably minstrel – tunes. It would be too much to say that Bristow's *Rip Van Winkle* was a major breakthrough toward creating an indigenous American operatic style. Still, the work achieved some distinctiveness in a musical landscape otherwise dominated by European models and idioms.

Several of Bristow's other major compositions reveal an interest in Americana similar to *Rip Van Winkle*. Some, in fact, are blatantly patriotic. Like Fry, Bristow also wrote a symphony inspired by Niagara Falls. Subtitled a "Symphony for Grand Orchestra, Solos and Chorus," *Niagara*, Op. 62, is a multi-movement, mostly instrumental work with voices used sparingly.[52] The vocal sections are quite elementary, and are frequently homorhythmic and chorale-like. Another work, the symphony *The Pioneer ("Arcadian")*, Op. 49 (1874), quotes an Indian melody, according to Hitchcock probably the first such incorporation in American music.[53]

One of Bristow's most obviously patriotic works is *The Great Republic, An Ode to the American Union*, Op. 47.[54] The poem of the same name on which this cantata is based was written by William Oland Bourne in 1861 in response to current pronouncements that the United States, due to the Civil War, was "no more"; the poem's author hoped to express "the spirit and enthusiasm of the people, and to resent the premature utterance of the nation's dirge."[55] In the musical setting of this poem, Bristow followed the mood of the text, beginning with a dirge-like section, as shown in Example 2, and later breaking out of this mood to a jubilant indication of national confidence.

It would seem to be part of Bristow's personality for him to express his feelings musically rather than verbally. Delmar Rogers has written:

> He seldom gave vent to his opinions in public. . . . The comments about and by him show that at best he was ill at ease in situations where he was not involved as a performer. . . . Upon meeting the new president of the New York Philharmonic Society, George Templeton Strong, Bristow addressed him in a curt

Example 2
Opening of *The Great Republic, An Ode to the American Union*, George
Frederick Bristow.

fashion: "Mr. Strong, I believe? I'm Mr. Bristow. Strong, Bristow; Bristow, Strong. Know one another." And he thereupon vanished abruptly.[56]

In light of his normal reticence, Bristow's outspoken involvement in the controversy initiated by Richard Storrs Willis and Fry is all the more significant in revealing the intensity of his Americanist sentiments. Unlike Fry, who was ready—even eager—to enter rhetorical battle, Bristow's public statements are limited.

The lengthy episode began early in 1854 with an unfavorable review by Willis, editor of the New York *Musical World and Times,* of Fry's *Santa Claus: Christmas Symphony.* Willis refused to take the work seriously, a view which brought an angry response from the composer. Fry's letter was met with a counterattack by Willis, followed by rebuttals of rebuttals in which both parties aired their ideas and feelings on a wide range of musical topics.[57] Bristow joined the fight with comments on a related subject: the alleged favoritism of the New York Philharmonic Society toward European music and its corresponding disregard of American music. Although portions of Bristow's remarks are reprinted in several sources,[58] it seems worthwhile to recall the letter here.

> As it is possible to miss a needle in a haystack, I am not surprised that Mr. Fry has missed the fact, that during the eleven years the Philharmonic Society has been in operation in this city, it played once, either by mistake or accident, one single American composition, an overture of mine. As one exception makes a rule stronger, so this single stray fact shows that the Philharmonic Society has been as anti-American as if it had been located in London during the revolutionary war, and composed of native born English Tories. Your anonymous correspondent who is not worthy of notice except that you endorse him says that a symphony of mine, also, was rehearsed, and not played in public. So Uncle Toby says—"Our army swore terribly at Flanders"—but that army did not fight. It appears the Society's eleven years of promoting American Art, have embraced one whole performance of an overture by an English man stopping here—Mr. Loder—(whom your beautiful correspondent would infer is an American) who, happening to be conductor of the Philharmonic here, had the influence to have it played. Now, in the name of the nine Muses, what is the Philharmonic Society—or Harmony-lovers' Society—in this country? Is it to play exclusively the works of German masters, especially if they be dead, in order that our critics may translate their ready-made praises from German? Or, is it to stimulate original Art on the spot? Is there a Philharmonic Society in Germany for the encouragement of American music? . . .
>
> It is very bad taste, to say the least, for men to bite the hands that feed them. If all their artistic affectations are unalterably German, let them pack back to Germany and enjoy the police and bayonets and aristocratic kicks and cuffs of that land, where an artist is a serf to a nobleman, as the history of all their great composers shows. America has made the political revolution which illumines the world, while Germany is still beshrouded with a pall of feudal darkness. While America has been thus far able to do the chief things for the dignity of man,

forsooth she must be denied the brains for original Art, and must stand like a beggar, deferentially cap in hand, when she comes to compete with the ability of any dirty German village. Mr. Fry has taken the right ground. Against fearful odds, he has, as a classical composer, through you and your journal challenged all Germany to meet him before the audiences of the Philharmonic and Mr. Jullien; and the challenge has not been accepted.

Mr. Dwight, too, the editor of *Dwight's Journal of Music*, published in Boston, has found my "forms" in symphonic writing "odd": – I beg to tell him they are not quite so odd as his critical forms when he gave an opinion on my music, as he now acknowledges "hastily" and without having heard a note of it.[59]

Bristow's angry letter indicates obviously hurt feelings at having his works ignored by the very orchestra in which he was a long-time member. Still, his letter goes beyond mere self-pity, expressing some of the same concerns more frequently voiced by Fry: support of American composers in general, and America's seeming inability to create an "original Art."

Bristow resigned from the Philharmonic Society, but only until the end of the 1853–54 season. After his return, the orchestra did make some effort to perform more American works, including Bristow's own *Symphony #2* in 1856 and *Symphony #3* in 1859. Bristow helped found the American Music Association in 1856, an organization devoted to bringing the works of resident composers before the public.[60] *Dwight's Journal of Music* carried the following announcement from New York City:

There has recently been organized in this city [New York] a new Musical Association which though as yet in small numbers and of limited influence, promises in time to become a mighty level in raising the standard of musical appreciation in this country. It is called the "American Music Association," and its fundamental principle is the fostering of native talent and the production of native musical works. This object is more explicitly expressed in the first article of its constitution, which says: "The object of this society shall be to further the interest of musical composers residing among us, by having their works effectively presented to the public, in order that they may be fairly criticized and impartially judged."[61]

Although the Association never fulfilled its promise, having gone out of existence early in 1858, it did premiere compositions by Bristow, Fry, Willis, William Mason, and other Americans, and was perhaps the first organization of its kind.

Bristow's Americanism, then, was expressed verbally and compositionally as well as by his efforts to create an Americanist musical association. Although his compositional Americanism was primarily limited to the surface level – that of subject matter and title – his *Rip Van*

Winkle, even if inconsistent and not always distinguished, seems to have been on a path away from European models. In light of the strength of Americanist feelings expressed by Bristow and Fry, it is difficult to believe that no one immediately followed their lead. The Civil War may be a major reason for the apparent absence of musical Americanist pronouncements in the 1860s. However, after the war and its immediate recovery period, musical Americanism again became increasingly important to musicians in the United States. In fact, in some quarters of the American musical world, particularly that of music education, Americanism seemed to be less the exception and more the rule than in the period of Fry and Bristow, perhaps explaining the lack of contemporary focus on one or two individuals. Still, in the 1860s, the business at hand was the Civil War.

The Civil War Years

Early in the Civil War years, *Dwight's Journal of Music* expressed the enthusiastic hope that the current turmoil would result in profound national musical statements.

> Who shall say that the wonderful scenes through which we are now passing, shall not give birth to nobler inspirations of undying love of country, greater sacrifice for its good, calling forth our heart's most ardent praise in poetry and in song? . . . It is of the higher forms of composition we would speak; forms, which shall exercise (as they always have) a powerful influence upon the cultivation of musical taste of the nation.[62]

Although the war was divisive rather than cohesive, as it would have been against an external foe, northern intellectuals viewed it almost as a religious test for the nation. Democracy was at stake. To many, the conflict was seen as but a stepping stone to "national perfection," as one historian has put it,[63] and only heightened their patriotism. Bristow's idealistic *Great Republic*, although not published until 1880, exemplifies this stance.

The major musical manifestations of the war, however, seem to have been popular songs. These songs proliferated on both sides, expressing and accentuating the opposing views of the two halves of the nation. Periodicals of the era reveal a variety of attitudes about this burgeoning repertory. For instance, *The Musical Review and Musical World*, a New York publication, compiled a list of songs related to the war. Acknowledging the musical simplicity of these works, the writer stated:

> If we go over the many songs which have been written in relation to the war since its first outbreak, we find again a justification of the old truth, that the songs of a nation are a mirror of its virtue as well as its shortcomings. . . . they have proved to be apt to stir the hearts of hundreds of thousands and cause the deepest emotions even among those who are able to judge music in its loftiest aspirations.[64]

Others were less kind. One writer, noting the dearth of "good" music expressing the sentiments of a country in war, could not overlook the tawdriness of some of these songs:

> There is something fit in these mouthings of commonplace, this ringing of the charges on stars and flags, and mothers and brothers; these platitude counterfeits purporting to be true poetic gold, which is worthy the theme. A boastful patriotism has boastful singers; a shameful war is recorded in ignoble strains.[65]

The war years were marked as well by a general decrease in musical activity that is the inevitable result of any such disruption. Several soldiers, for instance, complained of the dismissal, presumably as an economy measure, of army bands.[66] Others noted the diminishing concert life. Speaking of the previously active summer months, one writer noted:

> There is an absolute dearth of any kind of musical culture. . . . Alas! the war shows again its hideous face as a warning not to indulge in such fancies. And yet who knows whether such a gathering for such a purpose could not be made to yield even something for the prosecution of the war; something towards sustaining the Government in its present struggle![67]

At least one composer of art music suffered greatly from the Civil War. The poet/musician Sydney Lanier (1842–81) entered the war as an enthusiastic Southerner, but returned to ill-health and poverty. He contracted tuberculosis in the early 1870s and left only a few compositions when he died at the age of thirty-nine. Among the uncompleted works was a *Symphony of the Plantation* which, according to Lanier, was to represent "the old and new life of the Negro, in music."[68] One writer has commented on Lanier's description of his *Symphony:*

> The latter suggests, as do occasional references in Lanier's book *Florida: Its Scenery, Climate, and History*, an interest that reveals Lanier as a pioneer in the appreciation of this genuine American music, balancing his interest in Negro dialect revealed in a number of dialect poems which are probably the first Negro dialect poems to be published.[69]

Had this work been completed as planned, the *Symphony* might have been a very early example of the use of Afro-American idioms in newly-composed art music.

Although some pieces were written on American subjects or patriotic themes, such as those by Silas Gamaliel Pratt (1846–1916)[70] or those composed for the Centennial Exposition in Philadelphia,[71] no one composer was consistently attracted to Americana. Compositional Americanism, when visible, was generally at the surface level. From the time of the Civil War, more and more native-born Americans chose to go abroad for their musical training, thereby perpetuating from within the European domination of American cultivated music.

Composers schooled in German music either abroad or with immigrants at home, along with foreign-born Americans, controlled the national musical scene. Americans such as John Knowles Paine (1839–1906), naturally a leader through his unprecedented teaching position at Harvard beginning in 1875, and Dudley Buck (1838–1909) were of the first generation of those travelling to Germany for their music education. After them George Chadwick (1854–1931), Horatio Parker (1863–1919), Arthur Whiting (1861–1936), and others perpetuated the European traditions and schools of musical thought. Edward MacDowell, although German-educated, cut a somewhat separate figure and will be discussed in more detail below. Yet while this group of Germanic-Americans was still maturing as composers, verbal Americanism again was taken up in the 1870s and 1880s, and with new vitality in the 1890s as a result of the catalytic presence of Antonin Dvořák.

At least one American in the mid-nineteenth century defies the generalization about a lack of interest in native American sources: Louis Moreau Gottschalk (1829–69). Gottschalk's music and general biography are by this time well-known enough that they need be mentioned only in relation to Americanism.

Gottschalk's piano works incorporate a wide variety of American vernacular sources, from patriotic and plantation tunes ("The Union" [1862]; "Le Banjo" [c. 1851], to hymns and New Orleans Creole dances ("The Last Hope" [1854]; "La Bamboula" [c. 1845]). His ingenuity at recasting and recreating this vernacular music pleased audiences of his time and continues to do so today, as the revival of interest in his works shows. But Gottschalk was not limited by national boundaries; he drew heavily upon many other national and ethnic sources, among them Cuban, Spanish, and West Indian music. Gottschalk compiled virtually a musical travelogue in his lifetime as a touring virtuoso. Robert

Offergeld, in his Introduction to the *Centennial Catalogue of the Published and Unpublished Compositions of Louis Moreau Gottschalk*, has written:

> We can be certain that in all his globe-trotting he at no point lost his expertise at topical or reportorial music, a faculty he possessed from the first. As a youth of nineteen, for example, Gottschalk spent the revolutionary summer of 1848 in the French countryside, where robust peasant women worked the fields as seen in the paintings of Millet. He returned to Paris with *La Moissonneuse,* which we have, and *La Glaneuses,* which has been lost. It is as if almost anything that interested or amused him might provide him the nudge from reality that set him to writing a *piece d'occasion.* The prospect of visiting an unfamiliar country (or even the unexpected availability of a good brass band) seems to have been pretext enough—.[72]

There is little indication in the writings of Gottschalk that his quotations of American popular or patriotic tunes were done out of Americanist tendencies any more than his elaborations of the Brazilian national anthem were a measure of Brazilian nationalism.

> My fantasies on the national anthem of Brazil, of course, pleased the emperor, and tickled the national pride of my public. Every time I appear I must play it.[73]

The editor of Gottschalk's *Notes of a Pianist,* Jeanne Behrend, has written that "an appeal to their patriotism, Gottschalk discovered, was infallible."[74]

Gottschalk was known and loved not only as a composer but as a virtuoso who composed works for popular consumption, and his audience was—of necessity—constantly changing. Gottschalk himself admitted that he had to cater to the taste for light, salon music of the day to please his audiences.[75] Moreover, as a virtuoso first and a composer second, Gottschalk may not have had to face—at least not on a continuous basis—the same kind of discriminating criticism of the more sober circles in which Fry and Bristow moved.[76] For this reason, perhaps, there was less of a stigma attached to his use of vernacular material than had Fry or Bristow done the same thing. Also, this partly may explain the lack of influence that Gottschalk's music had on contemporary composers of art music. He was a "matinee idol,"[77] not the successor to Beethoven.

But Gottschalk was familiar with the classics, played them for private audiences, and later began to include them more frequently on his programs. The trend in concertizing in the late 1850s and 1860s was shifting away from the display pieces popularized by Gottschalk and toward European art music. While virtuosity certainly never lost its appeal, the growing interest in loftier music eventually lessened the demand for the lighter repertory associated with Gottschalk.[78]   Anton Rubinstein (1829–94) and Hans Von Bulow (1830–94), foreign successors to Gottschalk as touring pianists, consolidated the change in the 1870s.

Gottschalk had a deep and lasting affection for the United States. In his *Notes of a Pianist*, he spoke of his "national pride"[79] and his belief in and allegiance to the Union during the Civil War despite his Southern origins.[80]   He occasionally despaired at the seemingly low level of aesthetic judgement on the part of many American audiences.[81] However, Gottschalk was not an Americanist in the sense of his contemporaries Fry and Bristow or later composers such as Farwell and Gilbert.   The only Americanist activity with which it is possible to associate Gottschalk is the American Music Association founded by Bristow and others, and this connection is tenuous.   According to *Dwight's Journal of Music*, Gottschalk agreed "to give it hearty co-operation," but the extent of his support is unknown and probably never went beyond the nominal.[82]

The problems to which Americanist composers addressed themselves — public support, access to performances, etc. — were not Gottschalk's concerns.   He had publicity and, of course, was regularly performing his own pieces.   Furthermore, Gottschalk was a man of the world in the sense of many national loyalties.   Born in cosmopolitan New Orleans, trained in France, and a constant traveler, he spent the last years of his life in Latin America.   As Jeanne Behrend has written, "Gottschalk was of a world tripartite: North America, Latin America, and Europe."[83]   His personal and musical interests extended far beyond the land of his birth.

Americanist Activities in the Late Nineteenth Century:
The M.T.N.A., Novelty Concerts, and the Manuscript Society

Activities which could be termed "Americanist" during the 1870s through the early 1890s are somewhat difficult to evaluate for two reasons: the need for further research of this period in general, and the lack of one outstanding Americanist personality on whom to focus.   Neither verbal nor compositional Americanism found a strong leader until the late 1890s.   Still, there was definite concern for the issues of Americanism in some circles, principally those comprised of music educators and some native composers.   Americanism seems to have been expressed in this period chiefly through rhetoric or efforts to attain performances for American cultivated music.

Among indications of a growing interest in native-composed art music in the 1870s and 1880s were the activities of the Music Teachers National Association. Although not generally recognized today for its nineteenth-century Americanism, the M.T.N.A. provided perhaps the earliest significant forum for American composers. Sumner Salter, a composer, writer, and early member of the M.T.N.A., charted the Association's efforts in behalf of native music in the 1880s, and stated emphatically:

> A fairly careful survey of the development of musical composition in America unquestionably leads to the conclusion that the M.T.N.A. is entitled to the credit of the first organized effort and the most effective early influence in promoting the interest of American musical composition, or what has often been called the 'Cause of the American Composer.'[84]

The M.T.N.A. was founded in 1876, and held its first meeting in Delaware, Ohio in December of that year.[85] Although the organization met annually after 1876, records are available only from 1884. The surviving proceedings of the M.T.N.A. show that the organization was clearly Americanist in its outlook.[86]

While the central interest of the M.T.N.A. was the teaching of music, some of its members were composers who turned to teaching as a livelihood. Among the charter members, only three are known to have been composers: George W. Chadwick, William Henry Dana, and George F. Root.[87] Also, the Association appears to have taken no special interest in American music in its formative period.[88] But membership increased rapidly in these early years. From a nucleus of 70 attending the first meeting on December 26, 1876, the M.T.N.A. attracted 304 by 1881 and 575 by 1884, and had added such notable composers as Arthur Foote, William W. Gilchrist, Frederick Grant Gleason, Silas G. Pratt, Frederick W. Root, Sumner Salter, and Arthur Whiting to its roster.[89]

The banner year for American composers associated with the M.T.N.A. was 1884. Acting on a proposal made at the 1883 convention,[90] the Association, at its annual meeting July 2, 3, and 4, 1884 in Cleveland, initiated a program to stimulate interest in and the creation of American music. The effort was two-pronged. Convention speakers addressed themselves to problems and trends in American composition, and members planned and sponsored the first of what was to become an annual concert series of American works.

The originator of this Americanist platform was Edward M. Bowman (1849–1913), a well-known organist/choir director and president of the Association in both 1883 and 1884. Although not a composer himself, Bowman had taken a strong interest in the problems of American composers. And because he was an influential member of the

M.T.N.A. (he was to serve as president five times), he was in a position to keep the issue of American music alive before the group.   So significant did the M.T.N.A.'s efforts and Bowman's role in them seem to Frederick Grant Gleason that in 1890 he dubbed Bowman "the Father of the American movement."[91]

An announcement circulated before the 1884 meeting set the tone for the M.T.N.A.'s new activities, and revealed the impetus behind them.

> Art life has reached that state in this country where it begins to take on character worth conservation and support.
>
> There are a number of composers who understand the higher forms of composition, and are capable of doing work which will compare favorably with foreign compositions, and there are many more who need only to feel that their work would find appreciation and sale to cause them to make use of their talents. . . . Why should we not have creative as well as interpretative [sic] musicians, composers as well as sculptors, actors, scientists, and poets? That we have not had them in due measure has been owing to a variety of causes, but chief among them has been, and still is, the apathy and want of encouragement on the part of the whole musical and publishing fraternity.
>
> We have not fully outgrown that snobbish, toadyistic sentiment that foreign works are as a matter of course superior to the homegrown article. Teachers use the compositions of foreign writers in preference to those of their American brethren without giving them a fair trial side by side. They will use careless, indifferent reprints of foreign rather than domestic compositions, which latter have the advantage of the personal revision of the composer. The publishers do all they can, as a matter of business, to stimulate this preference, and the idea that European composers are of necessity superior to Americans does the rest. The result is that our native and resident composers are indifferent, and the cause of American composition languishes or has never really thriven as it might and will do when the proper copyright law goes into operation, which will make it desirable for publishers to issue the works of American composers, and when our teachers and artists do their part by using more freely the works of their American brethren. When this time begins to dawn and to show signs of permanence there will be no dearth of American composers, and the day of an American School of Composition will not be far distant.[92]

"An American School of Composition," an ideal in music roughly equivalent in significance to "the Great American Novel" in literature, was a phrase used frequently by commentators on American music well into this century. Indeed, George E. Whiting delivered a lecture by that title at the 1884 meeting which, according to Salter, engendered considerable discussion.[93]

The M.T.N.A.'s self-perceived role, however, was not to decide such weighty matters as what constituted an American School, but to help provide an atmosphere in which native composition might thrive. And members apparently regarded this role as appropriate to the larger purposes of American music education. In an essay entitled "Musical

Art-Creation in America, and the Relation of Music Teachers Thereto,"
Willard Burr, Jr. of Boston challenged teachers to encourage more
American musical creativity.

> The teachers of America . . . have been, and are today, the vanguard in the
> progress of true art and art appreciation.
> We as a body of teachers throughout the country have already achieved great
> successes, but there are far greater ones yet to achieve. We have used our success
> and influence as teachers for the promotion of art . . . by the formation and
> perpetuity of various musical organizations throughout the land, by which the
> works of art of all ages and nationalities can be performed. This has had and is
> having a strong educational influence upon the people, and such service to art
> reflects credit upon ourselves. . . .
> Can we not serve art and ourselves equally well, if not better, by giving the
> same encouragement to art creation?
> That art would be served equally well, no one would hesitate to affirm, for
> such encouragement would tend directly toward the creation of art.[94]

In his "President's Address" at the 1886 annual M.T.N.A. convention,
Calixa Levallée summed up the importance of the performance of
American works to composers and to the Association itself.

> In carrying out our broad conception of how the Association should subserve
> most effectually the purposes of its existence, the production of AMERICAN
> COMPOSITIONS is a feature which must commend itself to every intelligent
> musician. It is a legitimate outgrowth of our fundamental purpose. It must be
> an incentive to the earnest student to feel that a society like our own stands
> pledged to grant him every advantage for the production of meritorious work.[95]

One concludes from these remarks that M.T.N.A. members regarded
the progress of American music education and musical composition as
parallel and mutually reinforcing.

As revealed from the 1884 announcement cited above, a problem
confronting American composers which particularly irritated the
M.T.N.A. was the lack of equitable international copyright practices. At
that time, foreign composers had no means of retrieving royalties from
the sale of their music in America. Thus, American publishers naturally
favored reprinting foreign works. In an intense mood of "musical
chauvinism," as Salter put it, at the 1884 meeting, the Association drafted
a petition to Congress demanding the creation of an international copyright law.[96]

> Believing that the promotion of musical art-creation in America would
> materially benefit us as a nation, and would enable us to command greater respect
> of other nations, and that such art-creation has not developed proportionately with
> the other arts on account of very serious impediments, one of the most important

of which is the want of an international copyright law, whereby our own art-creators are placed at a marked disadvantage before those of foreign nations through the permission of reprints of foreign musical works. Therefore,

We, members of the Music Teachers' National Association, in convention assembled at Cleveland, O., this 3rd day of July, A.D., 1884, and all others whose names are hereunto subscribed, do most respectfully and earnestly petition you, the Honorable Members of the Senate in Congress Assembled, that you will take active measures toward the speedy establishment of an international copyright law, and to this end pray that you will favor the passage of the so-called Dorscheimer bill, or any similar bill, whereby the creative interests of the art of music in America will receive the encouragement so much needed at the present time.[97]

Although the first International Copyright Union was established in 1886 at the Berne Convention in Switzerland, the United States did not enter it. Nevertheless, reciprocal copyright unions with individual countries were begun in 1891.[98]

Additional excerpts from papers read at the annual M.T.N.A. conventions of this era reveal another aspect of the Association's musical Americanism. At the 1890 meeting in Detroit, John S. Van Cleve of Cincinnati spoke on the "fitness of the American life for artistic expression":

First, then, of American music we may say, as of American literature, it is vain to ask for '*the one* American typical novel' till we have *the one* typical American people. So, also, why ask for the one American symphon [sic] so long as there is not the one American life? Yet, there has been good literary work produced in this country, good novels, excellent dramas, and above all, poetry which seems to have the life-blood of eternity in it, and perhaps, the same may be, in a certain limited degree, claimed for American music of the present and the past. . . .

Patience, patience, brother American composers, we are not faring worse than our greater ancestors.[99]

Van Cleve then presented a historical rationalization for what he termed American music's imitative nature, pointing out that great composers generally based their music on that immediately before them. If Van Cleve's remarks reveal a certain inferiority complex about American music, other comments are even more to the point.

The status of creative art in our country merits our most careful consideration. . . . We have but very few native artistic works of importance in the market, and no demand worthy of the name. (American musical art-creation has yet gained no foothold of any kind in this country.)

Our American poets are universally admired here, and quite extensively abroad; and so are our painters and sculptors to a considerable degree; but our native American composers are not only very little known here but are absolutely without recognition elsewhere.

Not a single oratorio or symphony of theirs, to my knowledge, has ever been performed outside of America. In art-creation we rank even below England, Denmark and Russia.[100]

One senses from these proceedings that the M.T.N.A.'s musical Americanism may have been stimulated considerably by Americanism in its non-musical sense. Burr spoke idealistically of American composers and musicians eventually travelling abroad and winning "victories for American art."[101] Calixa Levallée thought that composers should be a "credit to their nation."[102] The thrust of these and similar statements seems to be that the United States—self- and world-recognized as prosperous and powerful—should have an equally outstanding musical culture. It was expected. And "great" American music, measured by the standards of European masterpieces, also was expected. Indeed, some M.T.N.A. members seem to have believed that American music was about to burst forth toward genius at any moment. With the establishment of American performing and educational organizations of all varieties, only one thing seemed to be missing—native music of distinction and excellence.

In 1837, Ralph Waldo Emerson had challenged American artists and intellectuals to free themselves from the "courtly muses of Europe" and speak their "own minds." [103] A half-century later, Burr, Bowman, Van Cleve, Levallée and others in the M.T.N.A. noted how the other American arts had met that challenge and hoped that music would soon do likewise.

While Edward Bowman may have been the prime mover behind the M.T.N.A.'s Americanist efforts, considerable credit must be given to Calixa Levallée for organizing the Association's first American concerts. Levallée (1842–91) was a Canadian pianist, conductor, and composer who, after studies in Paris, settled in the United States.[104] He planned and performed a good share of the 1884 recital, including pieces by Gilchrist, Foote, Pratt, Chadwick, Dudley Buck, and John Knowles Paine.[105] According to Salter, who attended the 1884 meeting, the M.T.N.A.'s first American program was greeted very warmly.

The intense enthusiasm aroused by Mr. Levallée's program and its excellent performance reached a climax that was nothing short of thrilling at the close of the Gilchrist trio, which created a veritable furore [sic]. As one of the cheering audience at the time the writer can testify to the stir and excitement of applause, bravos, hat-waving, *et.cet.* which made a rare scene for a gathering of usually sedate and critical music teachers.[106]

So positive was the response that for the 1885 meeting in New York

City, the musical portion of the meetings was considerably expanded. In fact, from 1885 through 1890, the regular entertainment fare was at least two major concerts, often with both orchestra and chorus, as well as smaller programs interspersed throughout the discussion sections.

Levallée was responsible for the concerts in 1884, 1885, and 1886. Because he was elected president of the Association for 1887, other help then was needed. The M.T.N.A. engaged Frank Van der Stucken (1858-1929), a native Texan who was a composer and the conductor of New York City's Arion Society. Van der Stucken's sympathy for American music probably was known to the Association. In 1884, he had produced a series of what were called "Novelty Concerts" at New York's Steinway Hall.[107] Each concert included several pieces by Americans, with the final one devoted entirely to native compositions. Thus, Van der Stucken was a logical choice to participate in the American series offered by the M.T.N.A.

At the 1888 meeting in Chicago, the well-known conductor Theodore Thomas led three major concerts for the Association. Contrary to past M.T.N.A. policy, however, Thomas liberally mixed European pieces with those by Americans. A large concert and a shorter orchestral program comprised the principal offerings for 1889. Plans were expanded again for the 1890 meeting in Detroit, and Theodore Thomas was engaged a second time. Edward MacDowell, the best-known American composer of the period, performed his D minor Piano Concerto at the first of two major concerts, and considerable chamber music was performed by the Detroit Philharmonic Club.[108]

The 1890 convention was the most elaborate to that point in M.T.N.A. history and, as it turned out, for a considerable time afterward. Besides the regular concerts and meetings, a substantial social calendar also had been planned. A visit to a nearby organ factory, a steamboat ride up the Detroit River, a lavish banquet on board the boat, and a grand reception at Philharmonic Hall were just part of the extracurricular activities.[109] The grandiose social program, added to the costs of sponsoring conductor Thomas and his orchestra, incurred unprecedented expenses. It may have been partly for this reason that no meeting at all was held in 1891, and that the 1892 convention was far below the extravagant standards set in 1890. Salter has noted that in 1891, the Association entered a "depression period."[110] Although American concerts were sponsored again in 1892 and 1899, the M.T.N.A. never regained the Americanist enthusiasm of the six years beginning in 1884.

The fervor of the Association's interest in American music also may have been diminished by the formation of the Manuscript Society of New York City in 1889, an organization devoted solely to the performance of new American music.[111]   Many of the same people involved with the pro-American activities of the M.T.N.A. founded or participated in the new Society: Foote, Gilchrist, Gleason, Pratt, Salter, and Whiting.[112]   With a group specially geared to the interests of the American composer, perhaps the M.T.N.A.'s role as a patron of native works seemed less important.   Nevertheless, the Manuscript Society might well be seen as an outgrowth and extension of the Americanist ideas first explored in the M.T.N.A.

The M.T.N.A.'s Americanist attitudes and activities may seem insignificant by latter-day standards. But just how unusual they were at the time clearly is shown by a brief look at other current commentary on American music. Probably the most influential music periodical of the 1870s and early 1880s was Boston's *Dwight's Journal of Music*.[113]   The year after the founding of the M.T.N.A., *Dwight's* attempted a survey of the status of American musical life.

> Our musical progress is a subject of interest to all lovers of art and country . . . . We will remember what music and musical art was in this country, only 22 years ago, and rejoice to say that the art has made gigantic steps in the advance, without wishing thereby to imply, that we are the most musical people in the world.[114]

The survey thus began positively. In the course of the article, however, there is not one mention of an American musical composition. Rather, the growing popularity of European art music in the United States was viewed as the principal evidence of American musical advancement. Likewise, in a sequel entitled "Our Music, Past and Present," the status of opera and concert life was discussed, again ignoring American contributions to these endeavors.[115]

The standard music periodical of the era seems to have been devoted almost exclusively to cataloguing musical activities at home and abroad which featured European composers and performers. Interest in specifically American musical culture usually was restricted to the extent to which it kept pace with European developments. While in some publications concern was expressed over the progress of American musical life, this progress appears to have been measured largely by the numbers of concerts given and orchestras founded, and only rarely by the performance or the creation of American music. Referring to increased hearings of contemporary European works in the United States, one writer stated enthusiastically:

Thus Americans may stay at home and get a pretty good idea of what is going on in the musical world, at the same time that they have abundant opportunities to keep up their knowledge of the masterpieces of the past.[116]

American music apparently did not figure into this "musical world."

The contrast in attitude is clear between many standard music periodicals and the M.T.N.A. *Proceedings* and *Official Reports* of this era. In a way, though, the unsympathetic view toward American music common outside the M.T.N.A. may also be regarded as a manifestation of a cultural, if not specifically a musical, Americanism. Finding current American music not up to their expectations, writers—generally non-composers—criticized it bitterly or just ignored it. Exemplary of such a stance was the remark of one commentator who stated that Americans should "be a little timid in calling [themselves] a genuine musical people" until the nation remedied its failures in achieving the "glorious art."[117] From such statements, it almost would appear that anything less than superb native music was not worthy of the nation—in short, un-American.

Such a contrast in pros and cons on the subject of American music is entirely feasible, though, when considered in the light of an era of intense political nationalism. In many Western countries during the nineteenth century, nationalism replaced religion and the family as a principal object of allegiance, and patriotic symbols such as flags and national anthems evolved.[118] Viewed against this backdrop, music—like any other aspect of society—could be held up as a source of national pride and as an example of national superiority. Although the United States already was politically unified and did not participate in the revolutionary outbreaks occurring in Europe throughout the 1800s, American cultural nationalism was strong. And Europeans still set the artistic standards which Americans had to meet.

While many musical commentators impatiently dismissed American music as unworthy of the United States, however, the M.T.N.A. in the late 1880s adopted a more understanding and realistic stance. The M.T.N.A. may not have been wholly satisfied with the current status of American composition. But it recognized the difficulties involved in forging a musical culture from a nation of multiple ethnic origins barely a century old and still largely wilderness. "Great" American music would come, but it had to have the proper atmosphere for doing so.

Reflecting upon the M.T.N.A.'s early help for American composers, Arthur Foote wrote in 1932:

As to the help the M.T.N.A. gave to us, it was invaluable *at the time*, in those important concerts. . . . A great debt is owing to the M.T.N.A. . . . The M.T.N.A.

gave a chance to composers to show what they could do, and made their names known far and wide. I personally feel that I owe a great deal to it, and think it was fortunate that *just at that time* the Association went so heavily into the concert business.[119]

In an environment essentially hostile to American music, the Association offered composers a forum for their ideas and their works. By doing so, the early M.T.N.A. encouraged what many of its members believed to be the crowning achievement of good music education and a healthy musical society — the creation of new music.

One of the principal sources documenting Americanist efforts in the 1880s and 1890s is "Early Encouragements to American Composers" by Sumner Salter.[120] Salter cites Frank Van der Stucken, mentioned above in conjunction with the M.T.N.A., as an important champion of American music. Van der Stucken worked as a composer and conductor in several American cities, principally New York and Cincinnati.[121] Although trained in Europe (Brussels, Leipzig, and briefly with Liszt in Weimar), he frequently conducted American works. In 1884, on his return from studies abroad, he became conductor of the Arion Society of New York, a men's chorus, holding this position until 1895. Also in 1884, Van der Strucken undertook the production of his "Novelty Concerts" at Steinway Hall to feature American music, although the presentations included European pieces as well.[122] As a result of the apparent success of these programs, Van der Stucken was invited to conduct two similar concerts of American compositions in Paris. Among the composers represented on the Paris programs were George Chadwick, Edward MacDowell, and John Knowles Paine. One writer in Paris, Charles Darcourt, used a review of one of these concerts for an unfavorable evaluation of American music as a whole:

> American music is not yet born. . . . It cannot be said that there are not among the citizens of the United States good musicians, who know as many notes as any one else in any country, but they have not yet discovered the art of amalgamating sounds in a manner even slightly personal. . . . The American composers oscillate between the French and German Schools; they have, at times, expression, but never originality.[123]

Over the next fifteen years, Americanists were to make similar criticisms of the music of many prominent native composers in the European tradition.

Van der Stucken's concerts were, however, better received at home, and the first Novelty series was followed by another in New York in the fall of 1887. This time, all the concerts were devoted to American compositions. The prospectus for the series, which took place at Chickering Hall, was given by Van der Stucken as follows:

> In announcing a series of concerts to be devoted exclusively to the compositions of musicians born in America, Mr. Van der Stucken believes that he is consistently carrying out the principles which have characterized his efforts in behalf of musical progress since he came to New York. The purpose of his Novelty Concerts, of which the first was given in October, 1884, was to give a hearing to the young writers who had been left unconsidered in the schemes of established concert organizations. To acquaint the public with the styles of all schools, he made up his programs from the works of the younger German, Italian, French, Russian, Flemish, and Scandinavian writers. His last concert of the first season he surrendered to his countrymen, the Americans. In all his subsequent concerts Mr. Van der Stucken made it a point to give American composers a hearing, and he has had the satisfaction of seeing his example followed in a measure by the conductors of New York and other cities.[124]

Salter reported that H. E. Krehbiel, then music critic of *The New York Tribune*, greeted this second series with enthusiasm.[125] Although this author has no additional statements by Van der Stucken himself, his concerts and the comments written about him indicate that he had a strong commitment to the performance of American music. His Novelty Concerts were Americanist in intention. However, the music performed on these programs—by Chadwick, Paine, MacDowell, and others—was not Americanist music; compositional Americanism was yet another decade and a half in the future.

Perhaps the most active and controversial organization encouraging the performance of American compositions in New York City at this time was the Manuscript Society. Sumner Salter was for some years associated with this group and consequently had a more than passing interest in its history. The Manuscript Society was organized in August, 1889. According to Salter, the Society was initially the idea of Addison F. Andrews (1857–1924), a musician and journalist residing in New York City.[126] The term "manuscript" was suggested by Andrews to reflect the group's intention of performing only newly-composed works as yet unpublished. Thus the Manuscript Society was planned as a forum for the presentation of the most recent American compositions. Gerrit Smith (1859–1912), an organist/composer, was elected the first president of the organization, which grew to include a total of nearly 1,000 members during its twelve years of existence. The original New York Society eventually fathered two associate groups in other cities. The Philadelphia Manuscript Society was founded in 1892, with composer William W. Gilchrist (1846–1916) as its first president, and the Chicago branch was organized in 1896 under the leadership of Frederick Grant Gleason

(1848–1903), also a composer. Both originally had been members of the New York Manuscript Society.

While the early records of the Manuscript Society of New York have been lost, it is still possible to determine that the purpose of the group was to further the performance of specifically American music. *The New York Times* critic W. J. Henderson, reporting on the organization's first public concert, wrote:

> Now the American composer certainly deserves a hearing. His work may not always be of a lofty or inspiring kind, but it is only fair that the public should have a chance to decide upon its merits. . . .
>
> The Manuscript Society is formed of musicians who are interested in the development of American art. Most of them are composers, and last year they held a number of interesting private meetings. This year they have gained courage, and their enterprise was rewarded last night by the presence of a large and interested audience.[127]

Henry E. Krehbiel of *The New York Tribune*, in a review of the same concert, noted:

> If there were not a corrective in the methods of the two organizations [Manuscript Society and the American Composers' Choral Association] which have sprung up into exceedingly active life within a year, for the purpose of giving a hearing to the American composer, one might be tempted to say that individual, after long suffering neglect, now seems to be in imminent danger of being coddled to death.[128]

Further indication of the purpose of the Manuscript Society is revealed through its concert programs. Although it did not sponsor public concerts in its first year, after December, 1890 the organization held regular programs of American works, usually at New York's Chickering Hall. *The Musical Record* carried the following announcement of the first series:

> The Manuscript Society, an association of American composers, announces concerts to be given in Chickering Hall, New York, Dec. 10, Feb. 4 and April 15. The society started in August, 1889. Last year several meetings were held, the society gaining in power and influence at each meeting. To-day it claims among its members some of the best known composers in the country. Among New York members are Gerrit Smith, president of the society; Rheinhold S. Herman, Henry Holden Huss, Bruno Oscar Klein, George William Warren, and S. B. Mills. George W. Chadwick and Arthur Foote, Boston, W. W. Gilchrist, Philadelphia, Frederick Grant Gleason, Chicago, and T. Y. Flagier, Auburn, are among non-residents. The first concert will claim interest from the fact that every work presented will be heard for the first time, and will be conducted, if an orchestral or choral work, by the composer. At the first concert Mr. Chadwick will conduct an overture, and Mr. Foote works for string orchestra. Mr. Mills will play an

original piano concerto, and original songs for contralto and baritone, by Homer N. Bartlett and Henry Rowe Shelley, will be sung.[129]

Among composers represented in other concert programs sponsored by the Manuscript Society in the 1890s were Edgar S. Kelly, Frank N. Sheppard, Addison F. Andrews, Silas G. Pratt, Sumner Salter, Ethelbert Nevin, and Horatio Parker. Indeed, the works of many of the prominent American composers at this time were performed at the Society's concerts. The name of one important composer, however, is conspicuous by its absence from this group: that of Edward MacDowell.

The Manuscript Society flourished until the late 1890s, when internal bickering among members and greater emphasis on socializing at meetings obscured its original purpose.[130] Ironically, it was in these later years that the Society probably received its greatest public attention, particularly when the most highly-regarded American composer of the day, Edward MacDowell, joined. But after a brief and stormy association with the Society, MacDowell resigned, in effect dealing the group its death blow. The principal bone of contention between MacDowell and the Manuscript Society was the Society's very purpose: the performance of exclusively American works.

The Society, as it began to founder in the late 1890s, repeatedly requested MacDowell to join in hopes of his adding stature and breathing new life into the organization.[131] Long before this, MacDowell had formulated his own ideas about the Society and its purpose. In a letter to Frederick Grant Gleason, MacDowell stated that such an organization should be national—not local—in scope, and should not be "a mere mutual-admiration society."[132] In a drastic measure to obtain MacDowell's membership, the Society changed its name to "The Society of American Musicians and Composers" in May, 1899. MacDowell agreed to join and simultaneously was named the next president of the reorganized group.

The change in scope of the organization is noticeable in the first *Prospectus* issued under MacDowell's leadership:

> As far as conditions in this country allow, the new Society is based upon the methods of the Allgemeine Deutsche Musik-Verein of Germany and the Societé des Compositeurs Français of France, which in their respective countries have effected such important results in the introduction and development of native composers. . . .
> The purpose of the Society . . . is to advance the cause of musical composition in America, by offering to every composer an opportunity for the performance of his or her works under the best conditions. . . . the Society will be at liberty to present any composition which will add to the value of the programmes, or which it will profit American musicians to hear.[133]

The content of musical programs was soon affected by these new goals; the first private concert of the organization under MacDowell included works by Handel and Hummel along with American selections, while the next program featured only European works.[134]   After this second concert, which went against the very grain of the original Society's purpose, support from the older members of the organization reached a low ebb.[135] Thus, early in his reign, MacDowell found himself with very little backing from the group of which he was now head.

Lowens suggests that MacDowell's "patience with people who could not agree with him — after what he considered a reasonable time had elapsed — had diminished greatly over the years,"[136] and that this may have contributed to his problems with the group.   His disdain for what he considered amateurish about the older, original organization is apparent from a letter to William Henry Humiston:

> The club you mention as desiring a manscript [sic] from me, little knows my savage habits when I hear "Manuscript Club" — or "manuscript concerts" mentioned. They suggest to me the very topmost pinnacle of mediocrity.[137]

Salter presents a portion of a letter by MacDowell which seems to pinpoint the composer's sentiment:

> If our musical societies would agree never to give concerts composed exclusively of American works, but on the other hand, would make it a rule never to give a concert without at least one American composition on the program, I am sure that the result would justify my position in the matter.[138]

MacDowell's reasoning for this view is best explained by an excerpt from a subsequent letter to Frederick Grant Gleason:

> As it is now, whenever an exclusively American concert is given, the players, public, and press seem to feel obliged to adopt an entirely different standard of criticism from the one accepted for miscellaneous concerts.   Some people would run down an American concert before hearing the music — and others would praise it (also before hearing it).[139]

MacDowell feared a double standard of evaluation would result from presenting concerts of only American pieces. An acclaimed composer in his day, he spoke from a decided position of strength. His works were known and were performed side by side with those of European masters. For the second rank of American composers, the situation was somewhat different. MacDowell, however, apparently felt that the universal set of standards proper to judging music would be put off balance if concerts were weighed in one way or another at the outset.

MacDowell submitted his resignation as president of the Society of American Musicians and Composers on January 4, 1900 after less than six months in the position.   In addition to his own resignation, MacDowell demanded that the Board of Directors also step down *en masse*.   At first the membership declined to accept his withdrawal and allowed the Board to remain in office, although some did resign. MacDowell requested that he be allowed to choose his own board, a request which was also denied.   The *Musical Courier* carried the following report of the proceedings:

> E. A. MacDowell, president of the Society of American Musicians and Composers, has resigned that office.   His statement for so doing is simple: The society declared itself incompetent to authorize him to choose his own board of directors for the balance of the season in place of those who resigned, recommending a recall of the old board.   This Mr. MacDowell refused to do, and resigned.   Thus far neither the Manuscript Society nor the S.A.M.C. has been alive to its responsibilities. What will be done?[140]

The details of the next months of the Society's history are blurred, but apparently the matter was left unresolved until the completion of the 1899–1900 season.   MacDowell, however, never returned to the presidency.

In May of 1900, the membership of the Society voted to return to its original name, the Manuscript Society of New York, and under that title it continued for several years. The organization never recovered its original fervor of purpose. Salter wrote:

> It had already become evident that the society's hold on life was very precarious, successive administrations of oxygen having failed in their effects, so that the final cessation of its functions may be simply stated as happening at an unknown time from various unknown causes.[141]

Whether the Manuscript Society was merely a "mutual-admiration" society for a clique of like-thinking composers, as MacDowell suggested, is difficult to determine.[142]   Nor is it simple to assess the extent of public interest generated by the Society's concerts.   The fact that MacDowell, the foremost American composer of his day, eventually did concede to become president of the Society does argue for its potential importance. Nevertheless, it is certain that the Manuscript Society, despite its internal problems, succeeded in bringing to performance many new works by American composers.   In doing so, it was part of a growing awareness of native-composed music occurring in several circles of the American musical world during the 1890s; it was also one of the first battlefields, if a minor one, for the issues of Americanism.

The Impact of European Nationalism: Dvořák, MacDowell, Farwell, Cadman, and the Issue of "American" Music.

> Moszkowski the Pole writes Spanish dances. Cowen in England writes a Scandinavian Symphony. Grieg the Norwegian writes Arabian music; and, to cap the climax, we have here in America been offered a pattern for an "American" national musical costume by the Bohemian Dvořák – though what the Negro melodies have to do with Americanism in art still remains a mystery. Music that can be made by "recipe" is not music, but "tailoring."[143]

According to Edward MacDowell, "national musical costume" in the guise of folk music could be worn by any composer, whatever his origin or artistic goal. MacDowell's feelings about musical nationalism corresponded to his opinions about all-American concerts. Music must be judged only according to quality, not nationality. The issue of musical nationalism became a hotly contested one in the United States around 1895. And as MacDowell's statement indicates, it was prompted largely by a specific instigator.

The most significant Americanist event of the 1890s was the arrival in the United States of the Bohemian nationalist composer Antonin Dvořák (1841-1904). His presence from 1892 to 1895, his music, and his ideas precipitated a flood of controversy about American music that continued long after his departure. Whether intentionally or not, Dvořák stimulated an unprecedented discussion in which nearly all prominent American musicians of the day took part. The issues articulated a half-century earlier by Fry and Bristow were brought up and argued with renewed vigor. More important, however, were the new elements in the debate: American folk and popular music and their relationship to art music. As Arthur Farwell recalled some years after the fact:

> Anton Dvořák stepped into the scene, to teach students who could not go to Europe and to send out his call to American composers to strike into the musical folk-sources of their own soil.[144]

Dvořák came to New York at the invitation of Jeannette M. Thurber, founder and president of the National Conservatory of Music of America, to teach composition there. When Dvořák arrived in the United States, he was an established, world-renowned composer, honored in several countries in addition to his own. Therefore, his presence was a major musical event in the United States, and although he came here primarily to teach, his influence extended far beyond the classroom.[145] In the three years of his visit, Dvořák altered the course of American music in two principal ways: by his composition of works on American themes, most importantly his famous *Symphony No. 9 (From the New*

World); and by his interviews and writings concerning the state of American music.[146] In both these areas, Dvořák stressed the importance of American vernacular music, particularly that of Indians and Negroes, to the creation of an indigenous American art music.

Soon after his arrival, Dvořák began to acquaint himself with American folk music. According to Jeanette Thurber, he had earlier read Longfellow's *Hiawatha* and wanted to write an opera based upon it.[147] Although the opera was never completed, Dvořák apparently did study some unspecified Indian songs.[148] Around this same time, he was also introduced to Harry T. Burleigh (1866-1949), the young black composer who soon became one of Dvořák's pupils. Dvořák encouraged Burleigh to sing Negro spirituals for him, and he is said to have been impressed immediately with their beauty.[149] However, Dvořák had only limited contact with and superficial understanding of American folk music, a fact substantiated by his continual linking of Negro and Indian music. In an interview for *The New York Herald*, Dvořák referred to the relationship between American folk music and his own *'New World' Symphony*:

> Now, I found that the music of the Negroes and of the Indians was practically identical. I therefore carefully studied a certain number of Indian melodies which a friend gave me, and became thoroughly imbued with their characteristics.
> It is this spirit which I have tried to reproduce in my new symphony. I have not actually used any of the melodies. I have simply written original themes embodying the peculiarities of the Indian music, and using these themes as subjects, have developed them with all the resources of modern rhythm, harmony, counterpoint and orchestral color.[150]

Although it is often assumed that Dvořák quoted from specific spirituals in his *'New World' Symphony*, his themes apparently were simulated.[151] And according to Dvořák, the *'New World' Symphony* was meant to suggest Indian tunes just as much as Negro spirituals.

The real importance of Dvořák's *'New World' Symphony*, however, lay not in the sources of its themes, but rather in the association of Indian and Negro music with the symphonic genre by a major European composer. No such association had been made before in the United States.

The *'New World' Symphony* was first performed in New York by the Philharmonic Society orchestra under the direction of Anton Seidl on December 16, 1893. The response was immediate and electric. In its December 20 issue, the *Musical Courier* carried seven full columns of analysis and commentary on the work. Excerpts are given below, and well indicate the prevailing concern and confusion about art music and nationality:

Dr. Dvořák is primarily a symphonist. This symphony embodies his impressions of the New World. Dr. Dvořák is a Bohemian. His new symphony in E minor is not American. . . . Who knows but that the Bohemian came to America to rifle us of our native ore! . . . But why American? Is there such a thing yet as native American music, music racy of the soil? . . .

It may be American but it sounds very Celtic or very Scandinavian. It also contains a curious touch of the "Venusberg music." . . . The American symphony, like the American novel, has yet to be written.[152]

Of importance equal to Dvořák's music were his ideas on American musical life expressed through interviews and articles.[153] His most complete statement was presented in an article for *Harper's* entitled "Music in America."[154] On the economic status of the arts in the United States, Dvořák had these comments:

Only when people in general . . . begin to take as lively an interest in music and art as they now take in more material matters will the arts come into their own. Let the enthusiasm of the people once be excited, and patriotic gifts and bequests must surely follow. . . .

Art, of course, must always go a begging, but why should this country alone, which is so justly famed for the generosity and public spirit of its citizens, close its doors to the poor beggar? . . .

The great American republic alone, in its national government as well as in the several governments of the States, suffer art and music to go without encouragement. . . Another thing which discourages the student of music is the unwillingness of publishers to take anything but light and trashy music. European publishers are bad enough in that respect, but the American publishers are worse. Thus when one of my pupils last year produced a very creditable work, and a thoroughly American composition at that, he could not get it published in America, but had to send it to Germany, where it was at once accepted. The same thing is true of my own compositions on American subjects, each of which hitherto has had to be published abroad. . . . Such a state of affairs should be a source of mortification to all truly patriotic Americans.[155]

This admonishment of American composers' neglect at the hands of the public, the government, and the publishing industry must have been a vicarious steam-letting for many who felt wronged. The most significant remarks, however, were yet to come:

A little while ago I suggested that inspiration for truly national music might be derived from the negro melodies or Indian chants. I was led to take this view partly by the fact that the so-called plantation songs are indeed the most striking and appealing melodies that have yet been found on this side of the water, but largely by the observation that this seems to be recognized, though often unconsciously, by most Americans. . . .

It is a proper question to ask, what songs, then belong to the American and appeal more strongly to him than others? . . . The most potent as well as the most beautiful among them, according to my estimation, are certain of the so-called plantation melodies and slave songs, all of which are distinguished by unusual and subtle harmonies, the like of which I have found in no other songs but those of old Scotland and Ireland. . . .

It matters little whether the inspiration for the coming folk songs of America is derived from the negro melodies, the songs of the creoles, the red man's chant, or the plaintive ditties of the homesick German or Norwegian. Undoubtedly the germs for the best of music lie hidden among all the races that are commingled in this great country.[156]

Dvořák had touched upon what soon became the major issue of American music. Although he acknowledged the problem of choice, it was unimportant to Dvořák which vernacular music was really to be considered "American"; what was important was the use of these sources for the foundation of American art music. The American musical world did not dismiss the question quite so easily.

The significance of the change in Americanist attitudes at this time can hardly be stressed enough. The history of Americanism thus far has revealed little interest in American folk or popular music. From the 1890s on, however, a variety of vernacular sources thought to be representatively "American" were taken up successively by a number of prominent American composers. The first World War interrupted this process, but only briefly. The musical Americanist movement and the stress on compositional Americanism — once discovered — were enduring, lasting from around 1895 to 1945. And side by side with compositional Americanism continued a stormy controversy.

Oddly enough, it was Edward MacDowell who — contrary to his own wishes and philosophy — became identified with one segment of the pro-folk music faction, the "Indianists."[157] MacDowell, whose thoughts on Americanism have already been discussed briefly, began composing an orchestral suite based on Indian subjects in 1891, two years before Dvořák's *'New World'* Symphony. When his *Second (Indian) Suite* received its premiere in 1896, the issue of musical nationalism was much in the air.

Somehow, the important fact that MacDowell had begun the Suite as an experiment got lost in the process. His work was henceforth cited as the leading American specimen of what could be accomplished with American source materials, and he, as its creator, became unwittingly associated with the Indian faction.[158]

The source of MacDowell's Indian themes in the *Indian Suite* was probably Theodore Baker's *Über die Musik der nordamerikanischen Wilden,* mentioned in footnote 148 of this chapter. Henry F. Gilbert, a pupil of MacDowell's, had these recollections about the composition of the *Suite*:

> MacDowell became interested in Indian lore and curious to see some real Indian music.   He asked me to look up some for him, so I brought him Theodore Baker's book, *Die Musik der Nordamerikanischen Wilden* [*sic*].   "Oh, yes," he said, "I knew of this book, but had forgotten it."   From Baker's book the main themes of his Indian Suite are taken. . . . Although all the themes have been changed, more or less, the changes have always been in the direction of musical beauty, and enough of the original tune has been retained to leave no doubt as to its barbaric flavor.[159]

That MacDowell's themes were not direct quotes from Indian tunes is also substantiated by his prefatory remarks to the score: "The thematic material of the work has been suggested for the most part by melodies of the North American Indians."[160]

MacDowell disliked musical nationalism of any kind, and denied any Americanist intentions on his own part. In the following remarks, he referred specifically to Indian music in what seems like an effort to justify his own use of it. The earlier part of his lecture on nationalism was cited above, and it will be remembered that MacDowell described the use of folk music in an effort to establish national identity as "tailoring."

> To be sure, this tailoring may serve to cover a beautiful thought; but – why cover it? and worst of all, why cover it (if covered it must be: if the trademark of nationality is indispensible, which I deny) – why cover it with the badge of whilom slavery rather than with the stern but at least manly and free rudeness of the North American Indian?[161]

If taken alone, these comments would seem agreeable to those in favor of Indian music. MacDowell continued, however:

> If what is called local color is necessary to music (which it most emphatically is not), why not adopt some of the Hindoo *Ragas* and modes? . . . But the means of "creating" a national music to which I have alluded are childish. No: before a people can find a musical writer to echo its genius it must first possess men who truly represent it – that is to say, men who, being a part of the people, love the country for itself: men who put into their music what the nation has put into its life; and in the case of America it needs above all, both on the part of the public and on the part of the writer, absolute freedom from the restraint that an almost unlimited deference to European thought and prejudice has imposed upon us.   Masquerading in the so-called nationalism of Negro clothes cut in Bohemia will not help us.   What we must arrive at is the youthful optimistic vitality and the undaunted tenacity of spirit that characterizes the American man.   That is what I hope to see echoed in American music.[162]

One senses the anger MacDowell must have felt at having the outsider Dvořák's music held up by some as an example of what American music should be. If anyone was going to write "American" music, he should at least be American.

MacDowell was the most eminent American composer of his day. Admittedly he was German-educated and unashamedly an admirer of the German musical tradition. If his interest in Indian music stemmed from any "ism," it was most assuredly Romanticism. But MacDowell had succeeded to some extent in achieving a personal style,[163] probably the first American composer of art music, with the exception of the then unknown Charles Ives, to do so. And MacDowell regarded artistic personality — not nationality — as an aesthetic quality.

> So-called Russian, Bohemian, or any other purely national music has no place in art, for its characteristics may be duplicated by anyone who takes a fancy to do so. On the other hand, the vital element of music — personality — stands alone.[164]

He therefore did not recognize the need and desire of other American composers to free their music consciously from what seemed to them a slavish imitation of European music; in particular, he objected to a liberation via American vernacular sources. That Dvořák, the model, was also European seemed to matter little to the Americanists. Dvořák had directed them toward America, even if his doing so was founded on the current European conception of musical nationalism. As Gilbert Chase has written, "it was Dvořák, and not MacDowell, who proved to be the man of the hour."[165]

The most immediate positive response to Dvořák's ideas was that of Arthur Farwell (1872–1952). Farwell was a mid-westerner, born in St. Paul, Minnesota and living there throughout his late teens. His early musical exposure and training were limited, although he did study the violin to some degree. Heading first in the direction of an electrical engineering career, he graduated from the Massachusetts Institute of Technology in 1893. Music, however, soon became his consuming interest. After studies with Homer Norris, George Chadwick, and encouragement from MacDowell, he travelled to Germany for further education. There he continued his studies with Humperdinck and Pfitzner, and before returning to the United States in 1899, he stopped in Paris to work briefly with Guilmant.[166]

Farwell, later in life, acknowledged that Dvořák had decidedly affected his musical direction.

I had taken Dvořák's challenge deeply to heart, and worked in the field of Indian music, not with the idea that this or any other non-Caucasian folk music existing in America was the foundation of a national art, but because it existed only in America and its development was part of my program to further all unique and characteristic musical expression that could come only from this country.[167]

In essence, Farwell accepted the notion of musical nationalism as it was occurring in Europe at the end of the nineteenth century. Dvořák was an influence, but Farwell's travels and studies in Europe were also formative. The current reaction against German domination of music in Europe was re-echoed in Farwell's words on the state of American music. Although he was an admirer of German musical accomplishments, he saw America's emulation and imitation of German traditions as the first obstacle to overcome in achieving an American musical language:

> The first correction we must bring to our musical vision is to cease to see everything through German spectacles, however wonderful, however sublime those spectacles may be themselves.[168]

In reference to France, Russia, Norway, Bohemia, and Spain, Farwell recalled "I had particularly observed that the countries which were gaining a national individuality of their own, . . . were doing so through their own folk music."[169]   It was in America's folk music, then, that Farwell saw the future of American art music.

In transplanting European nationalism to the United States, Farwell recognized this country's composite nature. And he understood that although Indian music was his own particular interest, it could not wholly represent the varied character of America. He therefore directed his fellow American composers to all folk music he felt to be indigenous to the United States, "notably, ragtime, Negro songs, Indian songs, cowboy songs."[170]   Written in 1903, this directive proved prophetic. It was these folk musics — together with jazz, at this time unknown — which dominated compositional Americanism for its remaining forty years.

Farwell held what might be called a "total vision" of Americanism. When he spoke of his "program to further all unique and characteristic expression," he meant precisely that. On returning from Europe, Farwell immediately recognized the lack of social status of American composers, with the exception of those who continued the conventions of the German tradition. As he wrote to Edward N. Waters, "I was just plain mad, and vowed I would change the United States in this respect; I was not willing to live in a country that would not accept my calling."[171]

Farwell also held the firm conviction that American music at the turn of the century was finally on the road toward a style of its own.

> It is certainly suicidal, and would be fratricidal—were not our brothers so strong—to deny that we have a worthy and distinctive musical life of our own, when already many persons are joyously living that life to the end of their fingertips. All American composition needs is publicity.[172]

It was to this latter end—publicity—that much of Farwell's energies were devoted. Although there is as yet no one definitive historical study of Farwell and his music, many of his musical activities, particularly the Wa-Wan Press, are discussed in detail elsewhere.[173] Through his writings, his music, and his unceasing efforts to get a hearing for American music, Farwell emerged as the most eloquent spokesman for Americanism in the early years of this century.

As an Americanist composer, Farwell's principal interest was the music of the North American Indian. His total compositional output was, however, large and varied. Farwell's music is currently the most neglected aspect of his career. Brice Farwell, the composer's son, estimated that within the elder Farwell's own lifetime, only one-fifth of his works were published.[174] Today his music is mostly out of print, except for the pieces in the Wa-Wan Press series, now re-issued.

Many of Farwell's Indian pieces were piano settings of tribal melodies. Farwell usually included the legend or rituals accompanying each song to enable the performer to better understand and interpret the music. Farwell had this to say about the musical content of his pieces:

> It must be understood that these songs are entirely dependent upon mythical or legendary occurrences, which they qualify or interpret, or upon religious ceremonies of which they form a part. The writer realized that if the musical imagination could be fired by a consideration of the particular legend pertaining to a song, it would give rise to a combination of harmonies far more vitally connected with the song's essence, its spiritual significance, than any which should be a mere consideration of the melodies' tonal structure.[175]

In other words, Farwell did not always underpin the original tunes with conventional harmonies. He attempted to add creatively to them through an understanding of their original place in religious ceremonies. On this same subject, he continued:

> The harmonic color-scheme is purely the outcome of the melody and its specific religious significance and is merely an aid to its more complete expression. Without this significance, the melody would never have been born; without the melody, the harmonic combination (the joint result of the significance and the melody) would never have been the consequence of a trained intellect seizing

upon, and expressing in a mode comprehensible to its kind, a feeling already fully developed in a race whose mode of expression is more primitive, or perhaps merely different.[176]

In achieving his understanding of Indian ritual, Farwell was greatly aided by the continuing research of a number of early ethnomusicologists. In his introduction to the *American Indian Melodies*, he frequently acknowledged the aid of scholars interested in Indian life and music. The first serious study of Indian music was German, Theodore Baker's *Über die Musik der nordamerikanischen Wilden* (1882). Several American works were in progress during Farwell's time, such as Frederick R. Burton's *American Primitive Music*,[177] Alice C. Fletcher's *Indian Story and Song from North America*,[178] and Natalie Curtis's *The Indian's Book*.[179] *The American Indians and Their Music* by Francis Densmore[180] came somewhat later. The interest in Indian music by Americanist composers at this time was facilitated considerably by this research.

The simultaneous attraction of both composers and scholars to Indian music suggests a fad. Perhaps in part this was because the independence of the North American Indian at the turn of the century was at last completely defused. No longer a threat to American society, the Indians for the first time could be viewed with appreciation for their individuality, an individuality fast diminishing. In later years, Farwell recalled that his Indian music served as a drawing card in his promotional campaign for American music.

> Between 1903 and 1907, I made four trips to the Far West, stopping everywhere across the country, at towns large and small, drawing audiences by playing my Indian music, and discovering new composers. The Indian music, because of its novelty, became a powerful weapon of propaganda; it enabled me to reach large numbers of people. Indeed, I could not have made this national campaign without it.[181]

The difficulty of finding a publisher for his first Indian pieces led Farwell to found the Wa-Wan Press in December, 1901. In doing so, he hoped to provide an outlet both for his own music and for any American music which tended toward "native distinction, however broad and all-embracing that distinction may be."[182] In his "Letter to American Composers," which prefaced an early Wa-Wan Press issue, Farwell addressed

> all composers who feel the pulse of life that marks the beginning of an era in American music, and who will see in this movement a definite hope for their own artistic future and a reason for their entire devotion to their highest ideals.[183]

There can be no question of Farwell's devotion. He established the Wa-Wan Press, a purely non-profit venture, and ran it almost single-handedly. The Wa-Wan Press originally printed two volumes per quarter for subscribers, one each of vocal and instrumental music, at eight dollars per year. Many of the volumes contained introductory essays by Farwell and others, providing a forum for current Americanist ideas. Later, separate publications of sheet music were also issued, and beginning in January, 1907, volumes occurred monthly, alternating between vocal and instrumental collections.[184] The monthly issues were short-lived, however. Farwell joined the editorial staff of *Musical America* in 1909, and with his subsequent relocation in New York, it became increasingly difficult to oversee both operations. In 1912, the Wa-Wan Press became part of the G. Schirmer publishing house.

Over the course of its ten years, the Wa-Wan Press published the compositions of thirty-seven different American composers, including ten women. Among them were the principal Americanist composers of the period: Henry F. Gilbert, Arthur Shepherd, Frederick Ayres, Louis Campbell Tipton, Edgar Stillman Kelly and Harvey Worthington Loomis, the latter two pupils of Dvořák.[185] As such, the Press left a permanent historical document of the Americanism and American music of its period. Though many became involved in the Wa-Wan Press, it was really the inspiration and creation of one man.

Arthur Farwell's Americanism was unprecedented. In addition to composing, lecturing, writing, and publishing music, he promoted public singing programs and founded nationwide Americanist organizations.[186] One such group, the New Music Society of America (1905; New York), for a time presented concerts of the most recent American works.[187] Farwell was clearly an exceptional personality. Prolifically creative in composition, he was also an effective leader and organizer. Perhaps no single composer, with the exception of Aaron Copland, embodies the spirit of Americanism as completely as Farwell, for his Americanist efforts extended to nearly every facet of his own and the nation's musical life.

Several of Farwell's contemporaries also were interested in Indian music as a source for their own compositions. Among them were Arthur Nevin (1871–1943), Harvey Worthington Loomis (1865–1930), Charles Sanford Skilton (1868–1941) and Charles Wakefield Cadman (1881–1946). The most important of these was Cadman, an ardent Indian enthusiast and Americanist. His compositions on Indian themes range from the smaller genres frequently printed by Farwell to orchestral pieces and even operas. His best-known composition was *The Robin Woman (Shanewis)*,[188] probably the most adventuresome of all Indian works except perhaps for MacDowell's *Indian Suite*. *Shanewis*, subtitled "An American Opera," was produced by the Metropolitan Opera in 1918.

Like Farwell, Cadman relied heavily on the scholarship of current Indian researchers and used authentic Indian music in his works. In *Shanewis* he incorporated Omaha, Cheyenne, and Osage melodies, and based dance scenes on Indian ceremonies.[189] Cadman toured the West in 1909 with Francis La Flesche to study the music of the Omaha tribe.[190]

In his "Foreword" to *Shanewis*, Cadman makes this statement about the nature of his opera, and clearly reveals his Americanism:

> The composer does not call this an *Indian* opera. In the first place the story and libretto bear upon a phase of present-day American life with the Indian in transition. As it is not a mythological tale nor yet an aboriginal story, and since more than three-fourths of the actual composition of the work lies within the boundaries of original creative effort (that is: not built upon native tunes in any way) there is no reason why this work should be labeled an Indian opera. Let it be an opera upon an American subject or if you will – an American opera![191]

Cadman wanted his opera to appeal to a larger portion of Americans than only those sympathetic to Indians. To give the opera added historical and national significance, Cadman suggested that in the "musicale" portion of Part I, the principals and chorus be dressed in the costumes of "characters representing the various phases in America in the making."[192] However contrived, even ludicrous, it may seem to us today to have Pocahontas, John Alden, and Evangeline sharing the stage with Abraham Lincoln, Sir Francis Drake, Susan B. Anthony, and others, Cadman's opera contains such a scene.[193]

The plot of *Shanewis*, however, is not ludicrous. Although based on the common love triangle, the story (libretto by Nelle Richmond Eberhardt) transcends a purely romantic view of Indian life to achieve a certain degree of realism. This is apparent in the libretto's emphasis on the Indian's bitterness toward white American civilization. The story ends tragically, not in the death of the Indian maiden, but in the murder of the white hero at the hands of a tradition-conscious and resentful young tribesman.

Contemporary reaction to *Shanewis* was quite enthusiastic. Premiered at the Metropolitan Opera House by an all-American cast (a mixed blessing; an all-American cast at this time meant no stars), it was hailed by some as the best American opera to date. The *Musical Courier* carried extensive and highly favorable coverage of the opening:

> The *Musical Courier* is glad to state without hesitation that Mr. Cadman's opera is the best American work which the Metropolitan has yet produced. . . .

> The most important point from the standpoint of success was the very evident fact that the public genuinely liked the work. . . .
> It is the best evidence we have had yet that there will one day come the truly American school in music.[194]

Despite its seemingly positive beginning, *Shanewis* was produced only twice more, once each in 1924 and 1926.[195]

The realism of *Shanewis* reflects Cadman's respect for authenticity in using elements of Indian culture. His philosophy about the significance of Indian songs to American art music was presented in an article, "The 'Idealization' of Indian Music," for *The Musical Quarterly.*[196] In this article, Cadman explained his and others' interest in the music of North American Indians:

> The little hand [of Indianists] is not trying to express *itself* so much as it is trying to express, in terms of tone, the spirit of the land in which it lives. . . .
> The folk-song that we *have* attempted to idealize has sprung into existence on the American continent. It is as much the heritage of America and Americans and of the musicians who live in America as the music of the barbaric hordes of Russia is the heritage of cultured Russians and Russian musicians.[197]

To Cadman's mind, Indian music represented America, a view somewhat narrower than that of Farwell.

Regarding the musical treatment of Indian melodies by composers of art music, Cadman responded to the "chief objection of those who oppose the harmonizing and idealizing of Indian themes," the use of harmony.[198] Cadman believed that the Indians may have had an embryonic harmonic sense despite the purely monophonic tradition of their musical culture. Citing a report on the Omaha tribe by Alice C. Fletcher and Francis La Flesche, Cadman wrote that authentic melodies given simple four-part harmonies and played for the Indians in this manner repeatedly evoked a positive reaction.[199] The need to justify the use of Indian music by implying that Indians liked their songs in this new manner suggests a certain insecurity on the part of Cadman, probably warranted by the amount of unfavorable criticism of the Indian movement as a whole.

The success of Farwell, Cadman, and their fellow Americanists at publicizing their own brand of American music is clearly evidenced by the attention of contemporary writers to the relationship between American folk and art music.[200] This was particularly true in the 1910s through the early 1920s, when jazz replaced folk music as the major interest of both Americanist composers and their opposition. In "Our

Folk-Music," John Tasker Howard presented an evaluation of current
concern about American folk music:

> We are not as yet agreed as to what is really American in this folk-music of
> ours. We know that the Africans, for instance, are a musical race; but how much
> of the American Negro's song is African and how much of it is in imitation of
> the white man is another matter. Some of us are not yet agreed as to who are
> Americans.[201]

Howard did not feel that Indian music was representative of the United
States, and of its current popularity among composers he said:

> It is not probable that the impress of the Indian music will be strongly felt.
> The race itself is dying out, and the exotic flavor of their wild songs and dances
> is too far removed from the comprehension of the rest of us to ever become vital
> to our artistic expression.[202]

Howard's forecast for Indian music did prove correct, because even then
(1921) the Indian movement among American composers was in its final
stages. Equally prophetic was Howard's assessment of the significance of
black American vernacular music, which he found considerably more
accessible than Indian music.

> The music of the American Negro, as we know it, is nearer to us and closer to
> our own conception of musical expression. The Negro has been more among us
> than has the Indian, and although the racial distinction has been strongly
> emphasized, the black people have not been put on reservations by themselves.
> By intermingling, our musical expressions have found common ground.[203]

Regarding American music in general, Howard did not agree with
Farwell about the status of American composition. Farwell, in 1903, had
noted that indigenous American art music was already being written.[204]
Here, in 1921, Howard emphatically disagreed. He felt that American
music still was emulating European styles.

> At present the great majority of American composers are following the steps of
> various foreign schools. . . . None can deny, however, that we are slowly
> becoming an American people, and that the day is coming, far distant though it
> may be, when we shall be a distinct race with characteristics, and, it may be,
> peculiarities. . . .
> Time alone will answer these questions. There are, without doubt,
> contributions from these folk-tunes that will leave their mark on the worthy
> American music of the future.[205]

Although Howard was not strongly opposed to folk music incorporated
into art music, he did not share the view common among Americanists

that vernacular music was the natural foundation for an indigenous American musical style. Indeed, Howard believed that truly "American" art music was a good deal further in the future.

Clearly the leader of the opposition to compositional Americanism at this time was Daniel Gregory Mason (1873–1953). Daniel Gregory Mason was the most prominent of the third generation of the eminent Mason family; he was the son of Henry Mason of the piano company Mason and Hamlin, and grandson of Lowell Mason, hymnodist, organizer, and leader of the drive for music in the public schools. He firmly represented the "Official voice" of music in America, to use Farwell's term,[206] because it was in his blood. Educated at Harvard, he studied there with John Knowles Paine, then with George Chadwick, Percy Goetchius, and finally with Vincent d'Indy in Paris.[207] Mason was among those American composers who began to seek their training in France rather than Germany, demonstrating that German domination in the United States was lessening at the turn of the century. Mason became the MacDowell Professor of Music at Columbia University in 1910, holding that position until 1940.

Although he was a composer, Mason probably was more influential in his own time as a writer. Today this is his principal legacy. Among his numerous books were a four-volume critical-historical series on music completed in 1918: *Beethoven and His Forerunners, The Romantic Composers, From Grieg to Brahms,* and *Contemporary Composers*.[208] As the discussion of American composition became heated, Mason contributed numerous articles on the subject, as well as *The Dilemma of American Music* and *Tune In, America*,[209] in which he evaluated the past and present trends in American music and speculated about the future.

In his article "Folk-Song and American Music," significantly subtitled "A Plea for the Unpopular Point of View," Mason addressed himself to the current rash of compositional Americanism based on native vernacular music.[210] Mason came out strongly against the contemporary interest in Indian music:

> That the crude war dances and chants of the red aborigines of this continent should be in any way representative of so mixed a people, compounded of so many European strains, as we who have exterminated and displaced them, is thought more worthy of savages who believe that the strength of their enemy passes into them when they eat him, than of our vaunted intelligence, fortified by ethnological science. We should hardly entertain it if we were not misled by the interest that attaches to anything unusual or outlandish, and tempted by certain idiomatic peculiarities of these monotonous strains to exploit "local color."[211]

However, Mason also spoke against the similar concern with Anglo-

American folk music, just then gaining attention, and even more intensely against ragtime.   Recognizing the complexity of American society, Mason questioned how any one folk music could represent the whole.   This is, of course, a well-founded observation, but one must remember that Farwell recognized the same issue.   Mason's dislike for compositional Americanism seems based on something more than this argument.

Mason apparently could not accept art music which incorporated folk songs unless the composer succeeded in lifting these sources above their everyday origins.   In his denunciations of folk-based compositions, one senses that Mason regarded vernacular sources too commonplace to be used in art music.   Mason wrote that the national "aesthetic" was founded on basic misconceptions:

> It often mistakes the conception of the average for that of the ideal type, and supposes that the man in the street represents the best taste of America.   Above all, it condemns any attempt at universalizing artistic utterance as "featureless cosmopolitanism" or "flabby eclecticism," and suggests that the musician who speaks, not a dialect but a language understood over the civilized world (as Tchaikowsky did, for example, to the disgust of the Russian nationalists), has "lost contact," as the phrase goes, "with the soil."[212]

As a composer, Mason did make at least one notable venture into the realm of folk music, his *String Quartet on Negro Themes* (1919).   It would seem, then, that Mason believed the use of folk music acceptable if it was properly elevated — or "civilized" — to the level of what Mason felt was "universal" art music.   Americanism, in his mind, meant moving in the other direction; it was lowering art music because Americanists sought the identity of vernacular music.   As examples of the successful treatment of folk songs in art music, Mason noted only European scores, such as Brahms's *Academic Festival Overture* and — Dvořák's *'New World' Symphony.*   One need not emphasize the irony here.

The "universal" in music was clearly Mason's ideal; and the universal, according to Mason, was achieved by that artist who could "understand the ordinary man through sympathy, and interpret for him his own deeper, and usually unconscious, values."[213]   Citing Schopenhauer, Mason wrote that the majority of mankind was capable only of the "stamp of commonness," and the "expression of vulgarity."[214] Charles Ives, like Mason, believed a universal expression of mankind was the artist's highest achievement.   Also like Mason, Ives did not condone musical Americanism.   Yet there were significant differences in their essential artistic philosophies.

One of America's major composers of this period—although not recognized as such at the time—had strong feelings about the relationship between vernacular and art music. Charles Ives (1874–1954) is a special case for a variety of reasons. Certainly a patriot, not a musical Americanist, and surely not a mimic of Europe, Ives succeeded in creating a uniquely varied and bafflingly complex musical language. A musical recluse, he isolated himself from many of the problems which troubled Farwell, his almost exact contemporary. Although Ives had his musical likes and decided dislikes, he followed the progress of contemporary music only from a distance. Due to Ives's taste for Americana and his Yankee personality characteristics, he commonly is thought of today as the most "American" of American composers. It is Ives, not Farwell, who holds this title. In light of this, and because of his musical style, it is worthwhile to examine Ives's thoughts on Americanism.

Portions of Ives's *Essays Before a Sonata* (c. 1916), his philosophical *magnum opus*, reflect the current concern with folk and national music. In the following passage, Ives touches on the two folk styles—Indian and Negro—which were most popular among Americanists at this time:

A composer born in America, but who has not been interested in the "cause of the Freedman," may be so interested in "negro melodies" that he writes a symphony over them. He is conscious (perhaps only subconscious) that he wishes it to be "American music." He tries to forget that the paternal negro came from Africa. Is his music American or African? That is the great question which keeps him awake! But the sadness of it is that if he had been born in Africa, his music might have been just as American, for there is good authority that an African soul under an X-ray looks identically like an American soul. There is a futility in selecting a certain type to represent a "whole," unless the interest in the spirit of the type coincides with that of the whole. . . .

Again, if a man finds that the cadences of an Apache war-dance come nearest to his soul—provided he has taken pains to know enough other cadences, for eclecticism is part of his duty; sorting potatoes means a better crop next year—let him assimilate whatever he finds highest of the Indian ideal so that he can use it with the cadences, fervently, transcendentally, inevitably, furiously, in his symphonies, in his operas, in his whistlings on the way to work, so that he can paint his house with them, make them a part of his prayer-book—this is all possible and necessary, if he is confident that they have a part in his spiritual consciousness. . . . In other words, if local color, national color, any color, is a true pigment of the universal color, it is a divine quality, it is part of substance in art—not of manner.[215]

Ives, like Mason, admired the "universal" in music, for both composers' ideas about music were essentially an outgrowth of their deep roots in nineteenth-century transcendentalist thought. Their definitions of musical universality differed considerably, however. In his essay

"Democracy and Music," Mason had lamented what he felt was the lowering of musical values resulting from the nineteenth-century democratic movement in Europe. The concert halls had been invaded by "masses of . . . childlike listeners" who wished to have stories instead of music.[216]   Composers, in an effort to reach the new audiences, had compromised their art by writing program music. Such music was

> at the expense of the subtler, more highly organized effects of art — on sensation as against thought, on facile sentiment as against deep feeling, on extrinsic association as against intrinsic beauty.[217]

The ears of the masses were continuing to be coddled, felt Mason, by impressionism.[218] The masses should not be talked down to by a simplified aesthetic, but uplifted to an appreciation of higher musical achievements.

Ives also developed categories of musical quality – those of "substance" and "manner."[219]   Music of "substance" was the higher value, possessing universal spirit and truth, while "manner" was the lower, consisting of form alone and lacking conviction. But Ives liked to point out that musical training and technical achievement had nothing to do with creating music of substance, that substance spoke directly from the soul. Therein lies the essential difference between Ives and Mason, for Mason seemed to feel that the composer's technique was required as an intermediary between the common man and universal expression.

To Ives, therefore, as long as music transcended its "local color" to speak to the universal soul of mankind, it was music of substance. If it was truly "American" music it would also be truly "African" music, because it would be an expression of humanity, not nationality. Ives even supported, if in a back-handed manner, Mason's criticism of the current interest in ragtime as a truly "American" music. Mason has written:

> If indeed the land of Lincoln and Emerson had degenerated until nothing remains of it but a "jerk and rattle," then we at least are free to repudiate the false patriotism of "My country, right or wrong," to insist that better than bad music is no music, and to let our beloved art subside finally under the clangor of the subway gongs and automobile horns, dead, but not dishonored.[220]

Ives responded:

> It is better to sing inadequately of the "leaf on Walden floating," and die "dead but not dishonored," or to sing adequately of the "cherry on the cocktail," and live forever?[221]

Earlier, however, he had written that "ragtime has its possibilities. But it does not 'represent the American nation' any more than some fine old senators represent it."[222]

That Ives thought all music of substance to be of the same essential quality, no matter what its origins, may partially explain his mingling of diverse musical styles in his own compositions. Henry and Sidney Cowell have written that "to the Transcendentalist, music is not separate from the rest of the universe but permeates and is in turn permeated by all that exists."[223] Ives was not a musical Americanist; nowhere in his writings does one find the expressed desire to write "American" music, so frequently found in Americanist rhetoric. Frank R. Rossiter has written:

> Ives was no narrow patriot or local colorist in his music; but he believed that if a composer attempted to reflect in his art the spirit of the universal people as expressed in music, it was natural that he should turn to the popular music that he knew most intimately.[224]

Ives's interest in Americana stemmed from, in addition to Transcendentalism, a profoundly nostalgic feeling for the New England of his youth, and a good memory of its music. His use of vernacular materials was essentially natural because he drew primarily upon the music with which he was intimately acquainted, the native music of New England.

In contrast, the Indian melodies and to a lesser degree the Negro spirituals which interested Farwell and others were essentially foreign to their own backgrounds – almost as much as to Dvořák. Farwell spoke of consciously "working in the field" of Indian music, as did Cadman. Ives did not need to study the music of camp meetings and small-town bands; he had absorbed it from boyhood. It might be suggested that Dvořák identified Indian and Negro music as "American" precisely because it was the music most foreign to a European visiting the United States at this time. What was overlooked, at least for a while, was that this music was also foreign to most Americans.

Due to his reclusive habits, Ives's music had only restricted influence among his contemporary American composers or on those of the next generation. By the time his music was widely known, musical Americanism as a movement was over. It would be interesting to speculate, of course, on the path of American music had his works been known earlier. As perhaps the first American composer to create a truly distinctive musical language, he achieved what Farwell called "the spontaneous introduction of national spirit into music through independent musical thought."[225]

Americanism and Afro-American Music

Thus far the discussion about folk music and Americanism in this century has centered primarily on the interest in music of North American Indians. The Indianist movement of Farwell, Cadman, Skilton, et al., reached a peak in the late teens, with Cadman's *Shanewis* probably the major contribution to the larger genres. After 1920, the concern for art music based on Indian sources gradually faded. This may have been, as Charles Seeger wrote, because the "traditional Indian music was more interesting" than the newly-composed music incorporating it.[226]

In 1895, Dvořák had noted another type of folk music in addition to Indian songs as a potential source for American composers of art music. This was the music of black Americans. At the time of Dvořák's directives, Afro-American music meant principally Negro spirituals, and to some extent minstrel songs, largely white-composed but imitating elements of black practice. In the period roughly between 1890 and 1920, Afro-American music underwent the crucial development which eventually led to jazz, whose precise roots and history continue to bewilder musicologists. This development took black music from the realm of "folk" to "popular" music, categories which are nebulous but nevertheless decidedly different in connotation.[227]

In essence, Afro-American music in the guise of ragtime and finally jazz became increasingly visible and attractive to America as a whole. Thus, it became more interesting to American composers. Jazz was a musical rage in the 1920s, despite its seedy associations and the stigma of racism. The contrast is clear: Indian music was purely folk music, music of a people separate and unassimilated into the larger American society; ragtime and jazz, on the other hand, were the products of a cross-pollination. And although the Euro-American tradition had nothing in it which alone could have produced jazz, its influence on black music was enough to make the resultant hybrid accessible and appealing to the mainstream of America. Jazz in the 1920s became recognized as the "American" music for which many had been waiting and looking.

The trends in compositional Americanism to a large degree parallel the development of Afro-American music in the first three decades of the 1900s. In the early years of this century, a few white American composers incorporated Negro spirituals and minstrel tunes into their compositions, a practice which continued sporadically throughout the entire Americanist period—that is, until around 1945.[228] But on the whole, the first compositional Americanists concerned themselves with Indian music, perhaps in an effort to lessen direct comparison with Dvořák, whose *'New World'* Symphony was commonly thought to be based only on spirituals. However, as the newer Afro-American music grew more widely known, it, and not Indian music, gained the attention of Americanists. John Tasker Howard had been correct in his prediction that the influence of black music on American art music would prove more lasting and significant than that of Indian sources. Compositional Americanism followed the lead of Afro-American music, and as the original black music moved farther into the spotlight, so did the newly-composed works of compositional Americanists.[229]

No one composer better represents this progression of musical styles and interests in his compositions than does Henry F. Gilbert (1868-1928). Gilbert was among those who drew upon the earlier Afro-American styles, such as Negro spirituals, as well as the spicier music of Gottschalk's Creole New Orleans. But Gilbert was also the first American composer to incorporate ragtime consistently in newly-composed art music, doing so primarily before 1920.[230] Although Gilbert later used jazz in the 1920s, such an interest then was less of a novelty than had been his ragtime pieces in the previous period.

Just before Henry Gilbert's *Comedy Overture on Negro Themes* was premiered by the Boston Symphony Orchestra in 1911, the conductor Max Fiedler considered removing the work from the program. The inclusion of ragtime in the opening theme, he feared, might offend his audience. That the work was performed as written was found to be "undignified" – and worse – by some;[231] but others, including some of Boston's most discriminating critics, felt the *Overture* "stirred the blood of the audience who rejoiced in hearing a new voice."[232] Even H. T. Parker of the *Boston Transcript* praised the work, saying that Gilbert's *Comedy Overture* was "music of American folk-tunes that meets every musical taste, . . . that keeps the matter, the voice, and the spirit – the difficult item – of its origin."[233] Thus Henry Gilbert started American art music down the road toward jazz that would climax in the louder furor attending Gershwin's *Rhapsody in Blue* thirteen years later.

Gilbert's music is little known today. The 1920s jazz works of a few others, primarily Gershwin and Copland, live on, in part as examples of the daring, carefree mood which has come to be associated with this era.[234] Few presently realize that well over a decade before Gershwin's landmark work, Gilbert set the precedent. In the early teens, Gilbert was experimenting with ragtime when it was just becoming fashionable to do so.

Henry Gilbert epitomized what many feel to be the true "American" personality: the nonconformist.[235] Perhaps this had something to do with his unusual physical appearance. A rare heart condition left him brightly and permanently red-faced, and probably shortened his life. When it was currently *de rigueur* to travel to Europe for musical training, Gilbert stayed home. And when Harvard was the second choice after Europe, he went to the New England Conservatory. When Gilbert finally did go abroad, it was to hear an opera he understood to be about everyday people, Charpentier's *Louise*. In some ways, Gilbert and Charles Ives were similar, for the music of the common man attracted both.[236] However, it was Gilbert who really experienced this life, one of poverty, odd jobs, and travel in exploration of the folk music of many countries.

Henry Franklin Belknap Gilbert was born in Somerville, Massachusetts into a family of musicians. He was MacDowell's first pupil, studying with him for nearly three years. After a series of occupations including real estate agent and silk worm farmer, he travelled in 1893 to the Chicago World's Fair, where he acquainted himself with the music of visiting orientals. On the money from a small inheritance, he managed to go to Europe in 1895. Inspired by a performance of *Louise*, he decided to devote his life completely to music.

After Gilbert's return to America in 1902, he became the associate and close friend of Arthur Farwell. Like Farwell, Gilbert experimented at first with the music of North American Indians. However, soon he found the various musical expressions of Afro-Americans more interesting.[237] Although Gilbert admired all the world's folk musics,[238] he had strong feelings about the specific relationship of American vernacular sources to American art music. Also like Farwell, he felt that American composers could best establish a native school of music different from the prevalent, imitative European style by founding their works on indigenous American folk or popular music.

In "The American Composer," an article for *The Musical Quarterly*, Gilbert voiced his concerns about American music in relation to society. He also expressed his Americanism. Gilbert wrote that there were "as yet no real American composers," in the sense that the great French, German, and Italian composers represented their own nationalities. He theorized that the American population was still a "hodge-podge of almost all conceivable elements," and that until these were amalgamated there could be no "American" race and therefore no "American" music. Still, there was, Gilbert said, an "American *spirit*," the spirit of youth, whereas Europe's was the spirit of age.[239]

Re-echoing and elaborating on the concerns articulated by William Henry Fry sixty years earlier, Gilbert wrote of the frustrations of being an American composer in a society which seemed to care little about art music, particularly about an "American" art music. Somewhat more enthusiastically, he noted:

During the last quarter of a century or so there may be observed a slight tendency on the part of our composers to kick over the traces of European tradition, and to treat American subjects, to use fragments of melody having an American origin as a basis for musical structure. . . . It seems to indicate that our composers are gradually beginning to realize that we cannot arrive at a distinct adulthood in our music until we have left the home nest of European tradition and struck out for ourselves.[240]

And Gilbert, like Farwell and Cadman, was among those who treated American subjects.

Gilbert's Americanist music drew upon a wide variety of Afro-American styles. As Elliott Carter wrote:

All kinds of Negro music aroused Gilbert's interest—minstrel, spirituals, Creole songs and dances like the cake-walk—because that music seemed closely related to the spirit of all America. Its national popularity testified to that.[241]

Among Gilbert's more important works were: the *Comedy Overture on Negro Themes* (1911), which drew upon riverboat songs and spirituals as well as ragtime;[242] *Negro Rhapsody, 'Shout'* (1915), which included spirituals; and *The Dance in Place Congo* (1918), based on a description of New Orleans Creole dances by George W. Cable,[243] the same dances which had inspired Gottschalk's *La Bamboula*.

The Dance in Place Congo was premiered the same day and same place as Cadman's *Shanewis*. Originally a symphonic poem, the work was rejected by Karl Muck, conductor of the Boston Symphony Orchestra, when the composer submitted it for performance shortly after its completion. Muck viewed the piece, its source material, and its composer with contempt, according to Gilbert.[244] Failing to get a hearing for the score as an orchestral work alone, Gilbert wrote a scenario. The work was performed as a ballet, and although more attention was paid to Cadman's opera, Gilbert's work was greeted with general enthusiasm. An anonymous critic in the *Musical Courier* noted:

Mr. Gilbert's inspiration is fresh, and interest never flags from beginning to end; and there is the magnificent "Bamboula" theme, which returns time after time with its tantalizing rhythm. . . . The audience received this work, too, with much enthusiasm, calling Mr. Gilbert repeatedly before the curtain.[245]

Others of Gilbert's works incorporated the more recent Afro-American developments: *American Dances in Ragtime Rhythm* (1915), five *Negro Dances* (19 ?) also using ragtime idioms, and *Jazz Study* (1924).

More widely recognized as a composer in his own day than Farwell, Gilbert was also probably the first native to be hailed specifically as an "American" composer. As early as 1914, the *Boston Post* carried the following:

> There has been no more typically and creditably American composer than Mr. Gilbert. I say "American." He is genuinely American . . . His equal has yet to appear among the younger composers to-day.[246]

Likewise, in 1918 Olin Downes wrote:

> Let me say at once, in discussing the significant accomplishment of a composer only now coming into his own, that by "American composer" I do not mean here an individual born or long resident in this country, who composes. I mean a composer whose music is essentially and distinctively American.[247]

It could very well be that Gilbert's use of the increasingly popular Afro-American sources, the first time it was done consistently, had something to do with his recognition as an "American" composer.

One might think from the favorable comments about Gilbert's music that he would have been the natural model for the next generation of American – or at least Americanist – composers. This was not the case. Although Copland acknowledged an awareness of Gilbert,[248] younger composers on the whole paid little attention to him and his contemporaries of the period before 1920. Elliott Carter suggested that Gilbert's ragtime and other Afro-American pieces began to sound old-fashioned in comparison with the jazz-based works of the twenties.[249] Gilbert's *The Dance in Place Congo,* along with Copland's *Music for the Theatre* (1925), was selected to represent the United States at the 1927 International Festival of Contemporary Music in Frankfurt. According to a review by Adolph Weissmann, *The Dance in Place Congo* already sounded dated and naive, causing the audience to laugh at what the composer had intended to be serious.[250] Although Gilbert did write one jazz-oriented piece, *Jazz Study,* most of his compositional experimentation with Afro-American materials was done before the 1920s; he was to die before the end of this decade.

The title of "American composer" was given to a variety of Gilbert's Americanist successors in the 1920s and 1930s. Most prominent of these were George Gershwin, Aaron Copland, and Roy Harris. Gilbert, however, first received this title, and he was perhaps the earliest American composer to discover the great appeal of Afro-American music. In his own words, he was "a pioneer in American music – and that fellow usually has a hard time."[251]

The decade of the twenties in American musical history was a complex and active one. It is easy to think of the period solely as F. Scott Fitzgerald's familiar heading "the Jazz Age," overlooking the many other styles and influences coming together in the United States at this time. European "modern" music, as it was known, was becoming increasingly recognized and emulated in America through a continued cross-Atlantic intercourse which had been interrupted only briefly by World War I. Edgar Varèse, who came to the United States in 1915, represented the experimental and progressive European point of view here, and provided a rallying point for those interested in the newer trends. New organizations devoted to the performance of modern music were founded. Chief among them were the International Composers' Guild (1921–27) founded by Varèse, and the League of Composers, sponsor of the important periodical *Modern Music* (1924–46).

Perhaps more significant to American art music in the early twenties was the presence of many younger composers in Paris. As H. Wiley Hitchcock has written, Paris at this time was artistically a "cauldron of ferment."[252] The persistent American habit of seeking musical training abroad had not diminished, although its locus had changed from Germany to France. The new generation of American composers (those born c. 1900) who were attracted to Paris at this time were exposed to the latest music of the European moderns. The various styles of those known as "Les Six," the witticisms of Satie, and the developing neoclassicism of Stravinsky and others were all current. It is no wonder that the music of Farwell, Cadman, and Gilbert seemed hopelessly provincial by comparison. One of the most important European stimuli of American music was the discovery of the unusual teaching abilities of Nadia Boulanger (1887–1979). The establishment at Fountainebleau of the "Boulangerie" (c. 1921), as the school was affectionately known, produced the leaders of American music for at least two generations, among them Aaron Copland, Virgil Thomson, Walter Piston, Randall Thompson, Roy Harris, William Schuman, and Elliott Carter.

Still, it was jazz that created the dominant musical mood of the decade.[253] Not long before 1920, jazz was an isolated genre practiced by American blacks primarily in southern cities. By the second half of the 1920s, jazz was a commercially successful national craze danced and listened to by millions, and performed by both blacks and whites. With the help of the radio and the phonograph, it had become "popular" music.

It must be noted that the "jazz" which music historians presently associate with the 1920s – the music of Louis Armstrong, Jelly Roll Morton, and others – was not wholly what the term "jazz" described at the time. "Jazz" encompassed a wide variety of styles which evolved mainly along racial lines. To most white Americans, for instance, "jazz" meant the vigorous, syncopated dance style popularized by Paul

Whiteman and other band leaders, who arranged and laundered the material of their black contemporaries. This music, later sometimes called "pseudo-jazz," de-emphasized the traditional black jazz technique of improvisation and achieved a more polished, sophisticated sound.[254] For this reason, perhaps, cultivated composers drew upon other idiomatic jazz elements like rhythm and instrumentation rather than improvisation, although the problems improvisation present to any musical style were surely important.

Jazz quickly became known abroad as well as in the United States. And for the first time in the long history of Euro-American musical dialogue, America made a substantial contribution. Ironically, European composers first recognized jazz as a viable and vital musical language.[255] As Marc Blitzstein commented about this period, "we seem unable to have even our own authentic chauvinism."[256] While it is true that Gilbert had cleared the way with his ragtime pieces in the teens, American composers did not really follow his lead with jazz until the mid-1920s. At least two early-1920s works revealed some jazz influence: John Alden Carpenter's *Krazy Kat* (ballet, 1921) and George Gershwin's little-known *Blue Monday* (one-act opera, 1922; later retitled *135th Street,* 1925).[257] However, it was Darius Milhaud's *La Création du Monde* (ballet-pantomine, 1923) which gave jazz its legitimate and international status.[258] Jazz was becoming fashionable among the Parisian *avant-garde* composers just at the time many young Americans were studying there.

What finally fastened the interests of American composers of art music on jazz was *Rhapsody in Blue* (1924). Gershwin's first major attempt to move from Tin Pan Alley to the concert hall created an uproar, and the work was proclaimed a masterpiece by many. *Rhapsody in Blue* was an unprecedented event; it was the first major journey by an American popular composer toward "serious" music, a route usually travelled in the other direction. Jazz idioms, therefore, became the meeting ground—the common denominator—in the 1920s, for they were used by both popular and cultivated composers alike.

With the success of Gershwin's *Rhapsody in Blue,* and with European sanction, jazz became the first native vernacular music to attract large numbers of American composers. The nature of compositional Americanism thus far, with its emphasis on North American Indian and early Afro-American styles, had been removed from the mainstream of American music. Jazz, however, was hardly limited to esoteric tastes. In addition to its transcontinental popularity, jazz was also "American." For the younger generation of American composers, jazz became the logical solution to establishing both modernity and Americanism in their music; it also seemed to hold the key to a wider audience than ever before possible for the American composer of art music.

There can be little question that jazz was regarded as "American" by many in the 1920s. George Gershwin, undoubtedly the composer most commonly identified with jazz in the concert hall, stated:

> A national musical identity is basically a matter of rhythm. This it stresses, and it becomes identified with the nation. In America this preferred rhythm is called jazz. Jazz is music; it uses the same notes that Bach used. When jazz is played in another nation, it is called American. . . . One thing is certain: jazz has contributed an enduring value to America in that it has expressed ourselves.[259]

Another writer of the period with a different outlook, Edwin Stringham, expressed the music educator's point of view toward jazz. Stringham voiced concern about the questionable moral origins of this music, and wrote that it was up to music educators and American composers to mold jazz. To Stringham, jazz was only a raw material out of which a more sophisticated musical language might be created:

> What we now need is the proper guidance of the jazz germ. . . . It is for the open-minded American musicians and music educators to discern, preserve, and develop the worthy elements of jazz.[260]

Still, Stringham gave a positive assessment of the "American" quality of jazz: "I share the view that jazz is the most distinctive contribution America has made to the world-literature of music."[261]

Not everyone was convinced about the value of jazz. One well-known commentator came out in the strongest terms against this music: "American music is not jazz; jazz is not music," stated Paul Rosenfeld in 1929.[262] Rosenfeld, usually an ardent supporter of American musical developments, felt that the real "American" music was a "body of sonorous work . . . compositions rooted in the American soil; exploiting the material of sound in characteristic ways, and releasing a typical pathos."[263]

In addition to being called "American" in the 1920s, jazz as cultivated by native composers was associated with an ultramodern movement in music. This was in part, perhaps, because of the attention paid to jazz by European contemporary composers. But it was also due to the sudden and seemingly shocking departure made by younger American composers from the previous traditionalism of the mainstream of American art music. "America is struggling in the throes of a musical rebellion. . . . The musical atmosphere is highly agitated," wrote one observer in 1924.[264] Looking back upon this decade, Aaron Copland noted that it was in the 1920s when the United States experienced the full impact of the contemporary music movement.[265]   Some musicians seemed to consider their predecessors stodgy conservatives. One writer commented disparagingly on the older generation of Americans:

> Nothing new and nothing different from what we already have is now to be expected, we suppose, from the Chadwicks, the Loefflers, and Converses, or even the Masons, the Hills and Carpenters of America. . . . The older American music was a labored and generally weary reiteration of thoroughly alien forms and styles.[266]

The younger generation by contrast, said this same author, showed in their music a new "virility" and "robust spirit."[267]

Perhaps no one single musical event so sums up the mood of daring ultra-modernity, Americanism, and jazz as they were associated together in this period as the now-famous Aeolian Hall concert of 1924. At this concert Paul Whiteman and his orchestra premiered George Gershwin's *Rhapsody in Blue*. Billed as an "Experiment in Modern Music," the program also included such seeming incompatibles as Zez Confrey's "Kitten on the Keys," Edward Elgar's "Pomp and Circumstance," and an adapted version of Edward MacDowell's "To a Wild Rose."[268]   The exciting atmosphere of the evening is best revealed by Hugh C. Ernst's opening address. Ernst, acting as Whiteman's spokesman, began by stating that the concert was intended to educate the public to the great strides being made in the use of popular music. Then Ernst gave what seemed like a pep talk to American composers:

> American composers should be encouraged to not only maintain the present standard, but to strive for bigger and better things. Eventually there may evolve an American school which will equal those of foreign origin or which will at least provide a stepping stone which will make it very simple for the masses to understand and therefore enjoy symphony and opera. That is the true purpose of this experiment.[269]

There seemed to be no middle ground in the reception given Gershwin's *Rhapsody*. Some of the press found the piece "empty passagework and meaningless repetition"[270] or comprised of "trite and feeble and conventional tunes."[271]   On the other hand, many of New York's most influential critics outdid themselves in praise of the work. Olin Downes of the *Times* compared Gershwin's "unconscious attempt to rhapsodize" with Franz Liszt; *Rhapsody in Blue*, said Downes, was "fresh and new and full of promise."[272]   W. J. Henderson of the *Herald* wrote:

> If this way lies the path toward the upper development of American modern music into a high art form, then one can heartily congratulate Mr. Gershwin on his disclosure of some of the possibilities.[273]

Rhapsody in Blue set the American precedent for the use of jazz in art music.

Although the spirit of the Aeolian Hall Concert was clearly one of Americanism in the sense of self-conscious awareness of creating an "American" music, the degree of Americanist commitment—at least of Gershwin as the most important figure—demands closer inspection. Gershwin has not left the historian a great store of letters and essays filled with pertinent remarks about his music and the music of his time. Actually, this alone is somewhat revealing, because the Americanists studied so far frequently gave vent to their frustrations and expressed in writing their vision of an "American" music. Gershwin does not fit this pattern. Certainly his compositional Americanism—jazz in the 1920s and other Afro-American styles in the 1930s exemplified by *Porgy and Bess* (1935)—is beyond question. Indeed, the closest thing we have to an Americanist statement by Gershwin is something he wrote about *Porgy and Bess*. Referring to the Negro story and musical idioms of his opera, Gershwin wrote: "First of all, it is American, and I believe that American music should be based on American materials."[274] Nowhere, however, does Gershwin insist on ending European domination of American music, on creating opportunities for American composers, on getting American music performed and published, etc., all common to other Americanist writings. The strong verbal commitment associated with the Americanism of Fry, Farwell, and Gilbert is missing from Gershwin's writings. And this lack is easily explained.

Gershwin simply did not have the problems common to many American composers of art music. When he turned his attention to the concert hall in the 1920s, he was an extremely popular composer. His concerns were not those of seeking performances and publishers, or enduring seemingly prejudiced critics and lack of public support. He was not on the outside looking in. Gershwin was the best-known American composer of his period, despite his nebulous status in the concert world. In a way, his situation is somewhat analogous to that of Gottschalk seventy years earlier. Both men were popular national idols. Both wrote music delightful to listen to with seemingly little effort. Both delved freely into vernacular Americana. And both defy our standard classification as to what is "serious" and what is "popular" music.

Gershwin was not trained abroad, and therefore did not need to shake off the foreign influences by which others felt constricted. Although he was an ardent follower of developments in modern art music, he was rooted in American vernacular styles. But he did possess the ability—some think genius—to transcend the mere "popular" in a way which many of his concert-hall colleagues found difficult.

Gershwin's Americanism, therefore, was essentially non-verbal, concerned with music alone. His position simply did not demand rhetoric, and neither his interests nor his abilities lay in this direction.

The majority of other American composers interested in jazz idioms in the period approached this popular style from the more traditional direction, from the vantage point of the composer of art music drawing on lighter vernacular materials. Among these were, in addition to the aforementioned Gilbert and Carpenter, Randall Thompson, Louis Gruenberg, William Schuman, Morton Gould, and Aaron Copland.[275] Copland is certainly the most important, and is also the most clearly Americanist in his intentions. Although the entire matter of Copland and Americanism will be discussed in greater detail in Chapter XI of this study, it will be useful here to consider briefly his role in the 1920s.

Copland was one of the younger generation of American composers who studied with Boulanger in France in the early 1920s. As mentioned above, jazz interested European composers in Paris, and Copland and the others were no doubt aware of this. In Copland's history of contemporary music, he discusses the influence of ragtime and jazz on the works of Stravinsky, Milhaud and others.[276]

One of Copland's most frequently quoted statements has come to serve many writers as the key to understanding the 1920s. Copland, reflecting on the circumstances of his *Music for the Theatre*, stated:

> I was anxious to write a work that would immediately be recognized as American in character. This desire to be "American" was symptomatic of the period. It made me think of my Symphony [*Symphony for Organ and Orchestra*, 1924] as too European in inspiration. I had experimented a little with the rhythms of popular music in several earlier compositions, but now I wanted frankly to adopt the jazz idiom and see what I could do with it in a symphonic way.[277]

Although we may certainly accept Copland's authority in describing widespread Americanism in the 1920s, it is still difficult to determine the movement's precise extent. As has been noted, jazz was considered "American" and it was very popular among American composers of art music in this period. If all interest in jazz in the 1920s can be taken as indicative of Americanism, then the amount of Americanist activity in the decade was considerable.

Perhaps the safest assessment is simply that every composer approached jazz in the 1920s for his own reasons. As in the cases of Gilbert, Gershwin, and Copland, each had a different and separate route which led to jazz. For Gilbert, jazz was the next logical step in his attraction to a variety of Afro-American materials; for Gershwin, popular idioms were more his native tongue than the art music tradition in which he incorporated them; for Copland, jazz was the most "American" music at the time, and he wanted his own compositions to sound "American."

To what extent Americanism was the motive behind the widespread interest in jazz can probably never be determined. Jazz was popular, and Americanist composers had continually despaired about their invisible status in American society. Perhaps jazz was seen as the irresistible force leading out of obscurity; it certainly served as such. Equally important, however, was the very appeal of jazz; composers drew upon it simply because they liked it.

Americanists' interest in jazz was primarily concentrated in the 1920s. By the end of the decade, their fascination with this music had lessened, at least in part because of the growing change in the country's mood. However, unlike Indian and other ethnic sources previously of passing interest, jazz has found some adherents among nearly every succeeding generation of American composers. Moreover, jazz has had a lasting impact on the art music of the United States. The influence of jazz idioms on American art music is discussed in several studies. Among them are Copland's "Jazz Interlude,"[278] and the aforementioned Baskerville dissertation, probably the most complete attempt to date. Gershwin briefly discusses this subject in his "Composers in the Machine Age," cited above. Most opinions on the effect of jazz on art music agree that, of the various stylistic features comprising jazz, rhythm is the most significant. Here Copland's remarks might serve as most representative. Copland quite emphatically stated that:

> By far the most potent influence on the technical side was that of rhythm. . . . It is safe to say that no living composer has been entirely unaffected by the revitalized rhythmic sense we have all gained through contact with the peoples of the Dark Continent.[279]

The stock market crash in 1929 marked the end of the "Jazz Age." Jazz was of the here-and-now, it spoke of today, it was modern; that is what had made it so attractive. After 1929, the here-and-now no longer seemed as pleasant. The arts in the 1930s endured a corresponding change, in some cases taking up the causes of the poor, in others initiating what may possibly be America's first period of national nostalgia. The political leftism rampant among artists and intellectuals in the Depression period was an intense expression of a desire for social change. On the other hand, nostalgia—the idealization of what seemed the simpler, more secure American past—exemplified a nation reassuring itself. Both trends were apparent in the arts, and both led American composers to a more simplified musical language.

Merle Armitage has written of George Gershwin:

The fact that Gershwin was a Jew, and that many of his musical sources were Negroid confirms his basic Americanism. For this is not a country of race, it is a country of races.[280]

Some American composers, like Gershwin, continued to focus on Afro-American materials in the 1930s. The majority of Americanists, however, gradually moved to the principal national heritage in the United States, the one lineage essentially overlooked until this time: the Anglo-American tradition, that of the prevalent and dominant segment of the American population. It was this more subdued and less modern sound that proved most appropriate to the turbulent 1930s.

Part II

Musical Americanism
and American Society, 1929–1945

III

Introduction

In the decade and a half between 1930 and
1945, Americans twice were forced to re-
examine their assumptions about their
country in order to face the crises of
depression and war.

David D. Van Tassel, Preface to *Nationalism
in American Thought, 1930–1945*, by Charles
Alexander

Many periods in American history evoke a set of images through a kind
of collective national knowledge. The 1930s, the decade of the Great
Depression, is certainly one of these. Pictures of bread lines, apple
sellers, and Hoovervilles are so etched in Americans' minds that they
symbolize the era. But while such symbols identify a national mood,
they do little to explain its causes and issues. Perhaps until Studs
Terkel's recent *Hard Times; An Oral History of the Great Depression*
(New York: Avon Books, 1970), popular images have sufficed, as though
any further explorations of the 1930s would be distasteful.

Surely the period is painful to recall for many Americans.
Joblessness, losing a home, or going on the "dole," as public financial aid
was known in those days, are not happy memories. The government's
struggle to solve Depression problems led to bitter political divisiveness.
Civil violence also marred these years. Labor strikes turned into battles,
and confrontations exploded between the unemployed and local officials
in numerous cities. The Great Depression was a low point in American
history.

With its immediacy past, however, discussing the Depression is no
longer avoided. By contrast, the subject of World War II has generally
been welcomed, for the United States' role in that war has been a source
of national pride. War movies and novels abounded even before the
conflict ended. Contrary to the Depression, World War II evokes images

of heroism, national unity, and strength. The two eras seem light years apart, the first marred by civil disturbance and the second joined by patriotism. Yet they are chronologically contiguous.

The simplest explanation for the move from turmoil to unity is explained by the external threat against which the United States rallied. In fact, the progression took considerable time. The 1930s were characterized by a political isolationism that many reluctantly laid aside only after the Japanese invasion of Pearl Harbor. Perhaps fundamental to both periods was a faith in the nation that, if shaken by the Depression, had to be accepted almost unquestioned during the war. Indeed, many Americans' fervent patriotism in the 1940s suggests a need for a reaffirmation of national ideals.

American composers' concern with current events between 1929 and 1945, like that of other artists, was unprecedented and remains unique in American history. In the 1930s, the principal national issues were social and economic. The theatre critic John Mason Brown has written that the two most important phenomena for the American stage in those years were not openings but closings — the stock market crash of 1929 and the banking "holidays" of 1933.

> Closings these events may have been, yet with all that they symbolized and all that was to come after them, they set free America's conscience and pried open the American mind to new vistas of thought no less surely than they left locked and bolted forever the doors leading to our old ways of life and our old habits of thinking.
>
> The boom days were gone; their assumptions discredited. . . . Starvation in the midst of plenty was food for thought.[1]

Brown's comments may well apply to all the arts, for economic concerns engendered aesthetic ones. Many artists were attracted to Marxism as a solution to national difficulties, and proletarian art became common in the mid-1930s. But whatever their political sympathies, artists were preoccupied with America and her internal problems, particularly those affecting the poor and the unemployed. In one way or another, America's writers, visual artists, and composers sought to give the troubled times an appropriate expression. Specifically Americanist music ranged in subject matter from nostalgia to communism — from Copland's *Billy the Kid* to Blitzstein's *The Cradle Will Rock*. By the late 1930s, war preparations replaced the Depression as the country's first priority. Patriotic or war-theme music, such as Robinson's *Ballad for Americans* and Thompson's *The Testament of Freedom*, reflected apprehension about the expanding war in Europe.

In addition to composers' heightened sociopolitical involvement, the years from 1929 through 1945 incorporated many other changes in the musical world: the development of mass media, expansion in the fields of American dance and theatre and their increased association with American music, the artistic maturation and increasing influence of the American students of Nadia Boulanger, the reaction to and retreat from modern compositional techniques developed during the 1920s, the assimilation of Anglo-American folk-song into many streams of American music, and a comprehensive government program for the arts. Interacting with all these was a movement which had been gathering momentum for nearly a century. The final flowering of musical Americanism in all its aspects occurred between 1929 and 1945.

The type of Americana chosen by Americanists as source material in these years is significant. Often in the 1930s and 1940s, composers ignored America's ethnic and racial multiplicity—even their own particular origins—to concentrate on one musical heritage to represent the United States. This trend had precedents earlier in the twentieth century, when Indian and then Afro-American materials each were exploited with enthusiasm. The vernacular musical materials associated with the "American" image between 1929 and 1945 were most frequently Anglo-American. The use of such materials, generally consonant and rhythmically uncomplicated, often resulted in an art music considerably less "modern" in sound than current European music or even previous American music. Thus, while the 1930s were politically leftist and activist, they were musically reactionary and traditional. The conservative compositional trend carried through the early 1940s, as Hitchcock has noted:

> With the approach and onset of World War II, the political and cultural isolationism of America faded but, in music at least, it was replaced by a no less conservative tendency to emphasize national and patriotic themes and materials. Thus the 1930s as an era in American musical history actually extended through the early 1940s, to the end of World War II.[2]

The composers also organized,[3] and with considerably more effectiveness than ever before. Groups devoted to the performance of contemporary music had been formed in the 1920s, most notably the International Composers' Guild (1921) and its offshoot, the League of Composers (1923). The League was at its peak of activity during the 1930s and 1940s, and was responsible for bringing much American music before the public. With the formation of the American Composers' Alliance in 1937, there was an organization completely devoted to attaining economic returns for American art music.

Paralleling the growth in composers' organizations was the

establishment of several festivals specializing in the performance of American cultivated music. Prototypical of these were the American Composers' Concerts begun by Howard Hanson in May, 1925, shortly after he assumed the directorship of the Eastman School of Music. Hanson's series, later called the Festivals of American Music (1931–71), continued for nearly half a century, probably making Hanson directly responsible for the performance of more American music than any other individual.[4] The Eastman Festivals were complemented in the late 1920s and 1930s by several other concert series primarily sponsoring American music: the Copland-Sessions Concerts (1928–31), the Yaddo Festivals of American Music (beginning in 1932), and several series in various cities sponsored by the WPA Music Projects, including the Composers' Forum-Laboratories (beginning in 1935).

Harold Clurman had dubbed the 1930s the "fervent years."[5] Similarly, John Mason Brown has called the period those "full lean years," indicating the wealth of American creativity amid general material poverty.[6] In fact, the 1930s marked a shift in artistic focus from Europe to the United States, with New York as the center. Symbolic of this change was the return of many American expatriate artists from their self-imposed, principally Parisian exile. As Europe moved closer to war, many foreign artists and intellectuals also moved to this country. Among composers, Bartók, Eisler, Hindemith, Krenek, Milhaud, Schoenberg, Stravinsky, and Weill were all living in the United States by 1940. In most cases, the influence of these important immigrants was not felt in American music until after World War II.

The United States for a long time had been on the receiving end of musical culture, always in the position of reacting to foreign influence. Even the interest in jazz by American composers of art music in the 1920s was stimulated initially by European treatment of this music. At a time of national unrest in the 1930s, American composers returned both literally and figuratively to their native soil.

IV

Anti-Modernism and Gebrauchsmusik

In a series entitled "Music in the Changing Social Order" given at the 1935 Biennial Meeting of the National Federation of Music Clubs, *The New York Times* music critic Olin Downes outlined some of the principal musical issues of the Depression period. Downes began by sketching the changing origins of support for art music in Europe.

> We all know that music was provided largely by the aristocrats in the seventeenth and eighteenth centuries, and we know of the democratic currents that swept across Europe in the nineteenth century; and we know about the fall of the monarchies and about the gradual emergence of what the Bolsheviks call "the rich bourgeoisie class"; and now, in the tremendous catastrophe which came upon the world since the war, and in the immense economic depression, we see something more. And that is that the wealthy patrons of music are growing fewer and fewer in number, less and less willing or able to support musical enterprises; and that music, having gone from the aristocrats down to the plutocrats, let us say, is now going from the plutocrats down to the people themselves.[1]

In some ways, Downes echoed Daniel Gregory Mason's "Democracy and Music" from the late 1920s. Downes, like Mason, felt that European music had not successfully adapted to these socioeconomic changes, and that the art was in decline.

> If we go back to the period of Wagner, Brahms and Liszt and their contemporaries, and then on to that of Strauss and Debussy, and then from Strauss and Debussy to the Sibeliuses and the Stravinskys, and then on to the Yehudi Menuhins, etc., of today, we see a constant decline in the significance and the character and the figure of the creative offering.[2]

While pessimistic about European music, Downes, in contrast to Mason, was very optimistic about American music. Downes observed that American musical life was blossoming at last, as audiences for art music were just developing. It was time in the United States to "unlearn . . . European precepts and fashion a new method, a new point of view."[3] Downes suggested that the United States had the chance to forge a new musical culture appropriate to its people.

> We should not be specialists writing music for musicians, but should be writing
> for the public. . . . We in America must cast aside our inherited mental snobbery
> and smartness and talk of art for art's sake, as a means of communication from
> man to man and from woman to woman, taking it as a reality, being honest with
> ourselves by casting out fear and being original and creative in our own right.[4]

In two sentences, Downes encapsulized Americanism, social conscience,
and, though understated, a musical anti-modernism.

Roy D. Welch's comments at the annual M.T.N.A. meeting the
same year affirmed Downes's opinions.   Welch noted a fundamental
change in the relationship between the composer and the public in recent
years.   And like Downes, he suggested that it was the composer who
must change.

> The musician in the modern world cannot fail to be aware that there is a crisis in
> music.   He is easily deceived about the causes of the crisis.   The teacher, I
> observe, attributes his difficulties largely to the financial debacle. . . . For the
> composer, it is a crisis between feelings of the past and of the present, one that
> seems limitlessly new. . . . We may be conservative about every aspect of music,
> we may shut our eyes to all of the readily apparent differences between music of
> the last two decades and that which preceded it, but we cannot afford to be
> unaware that in these last years a radical change has occurred in the relation
> between musician and society.   The musician, like other workers, survives either
> because he supplies something society wants, or, in fewer cases, because he is
> forceful enough to compel society to want what he has to give. . . .
>   Now the moral of this, if there be a moral, arises directly from the fact that in
> human life and human society, nothing survives that is not truly functional, that is
> not seen to have a necessary part in the business of life.   Since old institutions
> either are gone or seem to be in the way of dying, we should be worse than
> blind were we to withhold cooperation from any undertaking that promises to
> make the arts an integral factor in the society that is to come.[5]

Conflicting socioeconomic and musical trends came face to face in
the 1930s.   European art music had undergone sweeping changes in the
first three decades of the twentieth century.   As discussed in Chapter II
of the present study, American composers in the 1920s were familiarizing
themselves with new European practices, and American music was on the
verge of becoming "modern."

Both Downes and Welch commented on the dilemma of American
contemporary music during the Depression.   New compositional
techniques had exceeded the comprehension and appreciation of general
audiences at a time when their support was crucially needed.   Both
Downes and Welch implied that a retreat from these advances was
necessary for the survival of art music.   Both were essentially anti-
modernist.   Key phrases and terms found in their writings — such as "art

for art's sake," "communication," "functional," and the concept of composers as "workers" — became clichés of the period.

Downes and Welch were touching on what Virgil Thomson succinctly has called "the economic determinism" of cultivated music. Thomson noted that composers who worked on commissions wrote differently from those who were teachers or those who supported themselves at non-musical employment.[6] But during the Depression, the economic determinism of music was considerably more fundamental. Oscar Levant has written that much of the moneyed private support for music and musical organizations was eliminated in the 1930s. Therefore, musicans and music groups had to rely more heavily on the general public, and their repertories were ultimately affected. For instance orchestras, the most revered performing institutions in America, experienced declining attendance in the early Depression. Thus they could not afford to alienate audiences with unfamiliar, dissonant, or complex music. As a result, according to Levant, the "insinuating" of new American music into orchestral programs slowed, and

> perhaps as a reflex of this there came a gradual recession in the excesses of the music that was being written, an attraction to simplicity, a reverence for clarity as opposed to the former adoration of complexity. . . . The simple life became an ideal in a composer's music as well as in his personal habits.[7]

Levant accurately described an important trend among many composers in the 1930s. Those who wanted commissions or wished their works performed by major musical organizations had to make their music understandable and pleasing to general audiences. One way Americanist composers hoped to achieve this end was to use native vernacular source materials. But also in the 1930s, it became "modern" to simplify.

Americanist composers always had been concerned about their place in American society, and their attempt to build a popular audience in the 1930s was partly a result of this older, continuing Americanist cause. What seemed new during this period was the wider concern among the general musical community about the status of American art music and the fundamental aesthetic issues in question. The extent to which socioeconomic and artistic aims intertwined between 1929 and 1945 was new to musical Americanism.

While many of the traditional institutions of cultivated music were threatened by the Depression, other arenas for new composition emerged. In the 1930s, American composers for the first time found patronage — not in the European sense of the aristocracy — but from organizations which simply needed music for specific purposes. Copland has commented on the expanding possibilities for commissions in the 1930s, and the effect they had upon musical style:

> Suddenly, functional music was in demand as never before, certainly as never before in the experience of our serious composers. Motion-picture and ballet companies, radio stations and schools, film and theatre producers, discovered us. The music appropriate for the different types of cooperative ventures undertaken by these people had to be simpler and more direct.[8]

According to Copland, functional music written in the Depression was geared largely toward musical amateurs or the general public. Thus stylistic simplicity was further required by the newer areas of support for art music.

Tracing all the media Copland mentioned in relation to American art music is beyond the scope of this study. Still, noting some of the more important developments is significant to an understanding of the period.

Gilbert Chase has used the term "workaday" music to describe Copland's commissioned pieces in the late 1930s.[9] Similarly, Julia Smith labelled these works *Gebrauchsmusik*,[10] roughly the German equivalent of Chase's term. The concept represented by *Gebrauchsmusik* and the term itself are associated with the German composer Paul Hindemith.

In the mid-1920s Hindemith, like American composers in the 1930s, became troubled by the growing isolation of contemporary composers from their audiences. Recalling the earlier period, Hindemith wrote in 1951:

> A quarter of a century ago, in a discussion with German choral conductors, I pointed out the danger of an esoteric isolationism in music by using the term Gebrauchsmusik.[11]

To remedy the situation, Hindemith decided to write works for "use" among students and amateur musicians that were also of sufficient artistic quality for public performance. Other *Gebrauchsmusik* was composed for specific events or for a particular performance medium lacking a repertory in contemporary music. Sometimes this music drew upon national folk or popular sources.

The term *Gebrauchsmusik* was familiar to American composers before Hindemith's emigration to the United States in 1937.[12] For instance, Blitzstein used the term in two articles in the mid-1930s, but scorned the idea's lack of political relevance.[13] Smith noted that at the time of Copland's commission to write an opera for the Henry Street Settlement, *Gebrauchsmusik* by both Weill and Hindemith had recently been performed there.[14] A specific link between the German concept and American composers is difficult to make, however. Therefore, although the term *Gebrauchsmusik* has come to be associated with certain American music in the 1930s, its use does not seem to be the result of a direct German influence. Rather, there is a similarity in premise between some German music in the 1920s and some American music in the 1930s. American composers in the 1930s, like their earlier German counterparts, were reacting to the vast technical changes occurring in art music since the turn of the century. Furthermore, American works referred to as *Gebrauchsmusik* frequently drew upon musical Americana or native subject matter, matching German *Gebrauchsmusik's* incorporation of folk or popular idioms. However, *Gebrauchsmusik,* workaday music, or functional music in the United States during the Depression was also a response to fresh needs for music in areas rarely or never before opened to American composers. Thus, the term *Gebrauchsmusik* has a somewhat wider application in American music than originally indicated by Hindemith.

As Copland suggested in the quote cited above, the number of commissioned pieces proliferated in the 1930s. Copland's *The Second Hurricane* (1936), the opera written for the Henry Street Settlement, was his first in the newer, simpler style. Straightforward and folk-like, *The Second Hurricane* is musically appropriate to its rural subject and setting.[15] Douglas Moore also chose an American subject for his school opera, *The Headless Horseman* (1937), based on Washington Irving's well-known *Legend of Sleepy Hollow.*[16]

Opportunities to compose theatre or ballet music expanded considerably in the 1930s. Incidental music for dramatic works—often WPA Federal Theatre Productions after 1935—was provided by composers such as Copland, Thomson, and Paul Bowles.[17] This music was probably less important to musical Americanism than that written for the ballet, which allowed for considerably more compositional flexibility.

American ballet's development in the 1920s and 1930s paralleled that of American music, with the number of native-born dancers and choreographers increasing dramatically. The interaction between American music and dance grew when both composers and dancers found themselves attracted to jazz. The combination of jazz rhythms and dance was obvious, frequently leading to ballets on contemporary American subjects. John Alden Carpenter's *Krazy Kat* (1922) and *Skyscrapers* (1924), both jazz-based, were commissioned by the choreographers Adolphe Bohm and Serge Diaghileff respectively.[18] Bohm requested William Grant Still's *La Guiblesse* (1926), which is based on Creole tunes.[19] Still also composed the jazz-influenced *Lenox Avenue* (1937) for

CBS Radio.[20] Although originally an orchestral work, a ballet scenario was added later. Other jazz ballets were written for specific dancers. For instance, *The Legend of John Henry* (1930) by Lamar Stringfield was composed for the black dancer Hemsley Winfield.[21]

Collaborations between American composers and dancers continued in the 1930s and 1940s. Although jazz had ceased to be a principal inspiration, it was replaced by other American vernacular sources. Again, ballet subjects generally paralleled trends in American music, shifting from contemporary jazz to older folk or historical themes. Copland's first commissioned ballet, a spoof of American politics entitled *Hear Ye! Hear Ye!* (1934), was rooted in jazz idioms. But his later, better-known ballets were based on rural, regional subjects and drew upon native sources accordingly. *Billy the Kid* (1938) was composed for Lincoln Kirstein's Ballet Caravan and choreographed by Eugene Loring.[22]   In 1942, Copland and the choreographer Agnes de Mille were commissioned by the Ballet Russe de Monte Carlo to create another cowboy ballet, *Rodeo*.[23] The culmination of Copland's works for ballet was *Appalachian Spring* (1944), written for Martha Graham as a commission from the Elizabeth Sprague Coolidge Foundation.[24] The quality and success of Copland's contributions to American dance are without equal, and the music of these works is performed in the concert hall as well as in the theatre.

Lincoln Kirstein's Ballet Caravan commissioned several other scores dealing with Americana in the late 1930s and 1940s: Virgil Thomson's *Filling Station* (1937), a work drawing on various American vernacular sources,[25] Henry Brant's *City Portrait* (1940), and Elliott Carter's *Pocahontas* (1939), one of his few pieces on an American subject.[26] Paul Bowles, a composer whose music is almost exclusively for the theatre or the dance, wrote *Yankee Clipper* for Kirstein in 1937.[27]

The newest frontiers for American music in this period were radio and the recording and film industries. Of these, the recording industry seemed slowest to recognize the American composer. The first recording of an American work in the cultivated tradition, Roy Harris's *Concerto*, was not made until 1933.[28] Around this same time, the music critic Irving Kolodin stated:

> If the attention devoted to so salient a figure as Schönberg is a mere two works out of a lifetime's production, it is apparent that native American composers can expect little consideration in the ordinary channels of commercial recording.[29]

Kolodin also noted, however, the first release of *New Music Quarterly Recordings*, an offshoot of Henry Cowell's *New Music Quarterly* organized to record contemporary music. And, in 1939, Howard Hanson and the Eastman School of Music began recording expressly American music for RCA,[30] demonstrating the commercial industry's increased interest in native composers.

Charles Alexander has commented that radio in the 1930s held great promise for American cultivated music.[31]   CBS Radio began broadcasting Saturday evening concerts featuring the New York Philharmonic as early as 1930.   In 1931, NBC initiated its Saturday afternoon Metropolitan Opera presentations and programs of light classical music by the Detroit Symphony Orchestra.   When Toscanini became conductor of the NBC Symphony Orchestra in 1937, radio programs of art music had found their biggest star.[32]

The growing importance of art music in radio broadcasting in the 1930s is revealed by CBS's published statistics.   Between 1933 and 1937, the number of hours devoted to art music nearly doubled.[33]   The amount of specifically American art music broadcast also increased during this period.   The League of Composers helped by sponsoring programs of contemporary music, including many works by Americans.   Broadcast over both the NBC and CBS networks, the League's presentations often included interviews or discussions with the composers.[34]   Through the League — CBS association, commissions of the new works by Americans resulted in many radio premieres during the late 1930s and early 1940s. In 1937, the first year of the commissions, Still's *Lenox Avenue*, Hanson's *Third Symphony*, Harris's *Time Suite*, and Copland's *Music for the Radio* were presented.   Copland's work has since become known as *Saga of the Prairie*, a title suggested by a radio listener.[35]   Three operas commissioned by CBS were Louis Gruenberg's *Green Mansions* (1937), Vittorio Giannini's *Blennerhasset* (1939), and Randall Thompson's *Salomon and Balkis* (1942).[36]   NBC also premiered American operas, of which the most significant was Gian-Carlo Menotti's *The Old Maid and the Thief* (1939).   A purely Americanist series of commissions was "Folk-Music of America" sponsored by CBS during the 1939–40 season.   One new work based on American folksongs was premiered each week.[37]

With the addition of sound to filmmaking in 1927, another outlet for *Gebrauchsmusik* was created for composers.   Films, as much as any other medium, reflected the reassessment of American life stimulated by the Depression.   Government-sponsored documentaries, funded by a variety of federal departments, provided numerous composers with commissions in this period as well as during the war.   These films, intended to give an accurate picture of American life, afforded composers opportunities to write music corresponding to the national scene.   Scores of varying quality and style were produced because, as Gail Kubik commented, no government policy or guidelines existed for documentary music.[38]   Kubik, Director of Music for the Office of War Information (domestic) Film Bureau during World War II, noted that some of the most significant contributions to government film literature were made by the cinematographer Pare Lorentz. Lorentz, with commissions from the Resettlement Administration, requested Virgil Thomson for music to his *The Plow That Broke the Plains* (1936) and *The River* (1937), two of the period's most outstanding documentary films.   Thomson's music employed regional musical materials, from the West and the South respectively.[39]   The Department of Agriculture sponsored *Roots in the Earth* (1940) with a score by Paul Bowles, who earlier had composed music for the Southern Tenant Farmers' Union documentary *America's Disinherited* (1937).[40]

Federal agencies were not alone in the attempt to portray American life during the Depression.   Numerous non-governmental agencies, foundations, and small or educational film studios commissioned scores for documentaries in the 1930s and 1940s. Among these were Copland's *The City* (1939) for Civic Films, Inc., David Diamond's *A Place to Live* (1940) for the Philadelphia Housing Association, Harris's *One-Tenth of a Nation* (1940) for Rockefeller Documentary Films, and Blitzstein's *Valley Town* (1940) for New York University's Film Institute. The last-named score by Blitzstein incorporated blues idioms for a film exposé of a company town gone bankrupt.[41]   Blitzstein composed music for the controversial *Native Land* (1941) sponsored by the leftist Frontier Films. The film depicted racial and religious intolerance in the United States among such groups as the Ku Klux Klan.[42] Blitzstein also wrote a score for the government's *Night Shift* (1942), a film concerning industrial production during wartime. Another war-related film sponsored by the government was *The Cummington Story* (1942) for which Copland composed music.

Commercial filmmaking suddenly needed the composer in the 1930s. As a result, many composers who normally lived on the East Coast responded to Hollywood's beckoning and headed west. Among the better-known composers who were writing for major studios in the mid-1930s were George Antheil, George Gershwin, and Oscar Levant. Somewhat later, Louis Gruenberg and Aaron Copland also were commissioned by West Coast filmmakers.[43] Copland's brief stay produced music for *Of Mice and Men* (1939) and *Our Town* (1940). Later visits resulted in scores for *North Star* (1943), *The Red Pony* (1948), and *The Heiress* (1948), the last receiving an Academy Award for music in 1949.[44]

Composers' reactions to the increased demand for their music were generally favorable, if only because such demand was so new. Copland observed that American composers felt "needed" in the 1930s for the first time.[45]   Similarly, Thomson wrote that the period was "a time of fulfillment for musicians of my age because we were ready for that, and also because our country was ready for us."[46]   Surely the requests for new music by dance and theatre companies as well as the media contributed to this feeling of acceptance.

By the early 1940s, however, some composers' enthusiasm for these new sources of patronage was dampened.   The film industry, in particular, attracted criticism despite the uncharacteristically high salaries it offered composers in the cultivated tradition for their work.   Film-making was a business as well as an art form, and composers had to adapt to business requirements.   For instance, David Diamond observed that commerical film studios preferred bland music. "Hollywood assumes that background music is never heard," he wrote, and "as a result, we have a banal and inconsequential music which negates itself."[47]   According to Diamond, music confused and frightened film producers, who therefore treated it as an accessory.   Copland complained that after the composer completed his score, he lost control over it.[48]   Thus the sound track might be considerably different than he intended.   To the composer, the artistic statement of his score was inviolate; but to the filmmaker, music was but one part of a complex product whose popularity determined his future.   The conflict between the "cultivated" composer and the commercial studio was inevitable.

Surely not all demands for new music were as limiting for composers as those from commercial film studios.   However, the problems of composers in Hollywood were merely exaggerations of those found in other fields as well.   Composers gradually became aware that the special requirements for much commissioned music hampered their artistic freedom.   By the end of the 1930s, composers realized that *Gebrauchsmusik*, while a solution to the practical problem of income for new music, was sometimes a two-edged sword.

Gebrauchsmusik was a partial answer to finding a place in society for new American cultivated music.   To some composers in the 1930s, political commitment seemed like another.   The radicalism stimulated by the Depression took musical Americanism in another new direction, leading to a brief flourishing of proletarian music and eventually to a recognition of native folksong by the American musical world as a whole.

V

Americanism Takes a Left Turn

Then let us praise this heritage, this humble lot
Revere this God, this flag, this tommyrot.

Kenneth Patchen, "American Heritage," *New Masses*, April 10, 1934

Introduction

Marxism has never been welcomed by most Americans, despite a continuing if fluctuating appeal to each generation. The political historian Louis Hartz has theorized that the initial absence of a feudal structure in America rendered democratic and social revolution unnecessary.[1] Furthermore, the long-prosperous and relatively stable American economy produced a faith in its financial and social systems that has carried the nation through even the hardest economic times without really disturbing its capitalist roots. Where there has been the chance for upward mobility and even the hope of wealth, socialism has seemed an unattractive compromise.

The stigma against Marxism also has stemmed from its foreign origins and its aura of negativism toward American society. In some quarters, Marxists have been viewed as the American people's enemies, their beliefs tantamount to treason. That view flourished especially in the late 1940s and early 1950s, when the label "communist" became an indiscriminate weapon of those claiming a superior patriotism. The movement known as "McCarthyism," after Wisconsin's Senator Joseph R. McCarthy, pitted a few self-appointed national protectors against real or imagined communists from all walks of life. McCarthyism made it unwise if not unsafe to be identified with any leftist philosophy.[2] It is small wonder that the attraction of Marxism to America's intelligentsia during the 1930s and 1940s has been downplayed, particularly by former sympathizers themselves.

It seems necessary, therefore, to recall the relative openness of leftist expression during the pre-World War II period. Before various unsavory revelations about Soviet life, the advent of the Cold War, and American anti-communist legislation, Americans – especially intellectuals – participated blatantly and often naively in Marxist activities. Not surprisingly, the heyday of intellectual radicalism coincided with the Great Depression, American capitalism's lowest point. While most Americans moved left out of social dissent rather than ideological conviction, Marxist concepts touched the world of arts and ideas in the United States, leaving behind an identifiable creative legacy.

Socialism was nothing new to the United States in the 1930s. American socialist parties date back to the 1870s, and the impact of Marxism had been increasing before World War I. After 1919 there was a temporary respite. Unlike the economies of several European countries devastated by the First World War, American business flourished. Capitalism seemed never healthier, and the resulting prosperity generally bred indifference to socialist ideas except among the die-hard few. Yet when the prophecies of doom appeared to be coming true in America late in 1929, socialism seemed outdated.

Several things distinguish leftist economics and politics in the 1930s from previous years. One was the spectacular growth of interest in communism. Although the American Communist Party was founded in 1919 from several small extreme socialist factions, its expansion in the 1920s was marred by ideological infighting.[3] More unified by the time of the 1929 Stock Market Crash, the American Communist Party actually benefitted from the Depression, for the unprecedented severity and urgency of these years encouraged radicalism. Socialism did not disappear. In fact, the American Communist Party never equalled the size of the older Socialist Party.[4] Yet communism had a special fascination for the intelligentsia and therefore made a more significant impact upon American culture. Symbolizing this directional change, *New Masses* (1926), successor to the earlier Socialist periodical *Masses*, became a forum of the Communist Party. Under the editorship of Michael Gold during the Depression years, *New Masses* attracted many important creative Americans.

Furthermore, the American Communist Party, unlike its Socialist parents, was essentially Russian-controlled. In this way, American Marxist politics followed the trend toward extremism and Soviet domination that was occurring internationally. Almost from its inception, the American Communist Party was directly supervised by the Moscow-based Comintern (Communist International), founded by the Bolsheviks in 1919.[5] And the top priorities of the Comintern were an all-out war against capitalism and the expansion of communism under the strict supervision of Moscow. Not until the International Party platform known as the "Popular Front" was created in summer, 1935 did this hardline approach soften.[6] In the face of growing European fascism, the Comintern sought to enlist support among foreign countries through an appeal to patriotism and nationalism and a lessening of their anti-capitalist stance.

Of greatest importance to the American arts, however, was the influence of Soviet culture and ideas upon American intellectuals, who were generally more enamored of the concept of communism than actually active in Communist politics. Members not directly involved in Party mechanisms and fellow travelers as well considered the Soviet Union virtually a model society.[7] Developments in Soviet cultural life and news of successes of the Soviet "experiment" were studied and analyzed diligently by American sympathizers. For many Americans who were disillusioned by the current state of their own country, Russia provided an ongoing example of a new system at work. As Richard Pells has noted, "socialism in its Russian form represented a compelling substitute for their own decaying society."[8]

Perhaps the most striking aspect of American leftism in the 1930s was its prominence. The Party held rallies and meetings, supported labor strikes and pickets, published its own newspapers such as the *Daily Worker*, and organized numerous cultural societies. In a growing tide of leftism, the presidential election of 1932 netted an unprecedented number of votes for both the Socialist and Communist candidates.[9] The Communist nominee, William Z. Foster, was publicly endorsed by an impressive array of intellectuals.[10]

Communism drew its support in America mainly from three overlapping groups: certain segments of the working class, ethnic minorities, and the intelligentsia.[11] For workers and minorities, the Communist Party offered immediate support on issues directly affecting their economic and social well-being. The Party became a rallying point for labor in the violent right-to-organize disputes of mid-decade. Discrimination against America's blacks, Italians, Irish, and Jews, as well as other ethnic groups, was condemned repeatedly in Communist publications. As the only political organization actively to champion America's minorities in these years, the Communist Party capitalized on its appeal to America's social outcasts.[12]

For intellectuals as well as the poor economic classes, radical politics were manifestations of an intense desire for social change. However, many intellectuals were from middle or upper-middle class backgrounds and had not, generally speaking, experienced the worst sufferings caused by the Depression. Nor had they been, with the exception of the rather large number of Jewish intellectuals, the object of ethnic discrimination. Therefore, theirs was more an ideological attraction, an outgrowth of disillusionment with an America they considered adrift.

Communism provided intellectuals with answers, direction, and an enemy. Capitalism was seen both as the cause of the apparent collapse of the American economy, and as the oppressor and corruptor of the American people. Many Americans seemed to take Marxist doctrine beyond the political realm to something bordering on a religion. As portrayed repeatedly in leftist plays of the period, capitalists were seen as the very embodiments of wickedness. The American interpretation of communism, therefore, had strong moral overtones. As if taking seriously the Biblical dictum "the love of money is the root of all evil," communism versus capitalism became a battle of good and bad. With communism seen as a way of righting the wrongs of America, leftist intellectuals seemed to suggest that the United States, if not human nature, could be perfected.[13]

Furthermore, communism was not viewed as opposed to American democracy, as it was by non-sympathizers. Rather, it was thought to be a means of making democracy truly equitable, economically as well as legally. Earl Browder, whose guarded image was that of a small-town Kansan, coined the well-quoted "communism is twentieth-century Americanism," mentioned previously.[14] This phrase well might be taken as a summary of what communism meant to the American intelligentsia during this period.

For American artists and intellectuals, specifically Russian communism had another attraction, more directly related to their economic identity. Particularly in the years just before the WPA Arts Projects, huge numbers of American artists were employed or working at jobs unsuited to their training and aspirations. Kenneth Patchen's poem "American Heritage," cited at the opening of this section, expressed the bitterness felt by many artists as their traditionally precarious place in society grew even shakier. Throughout the late 1920s and 1930s, leftist sympathizers traveled to Russia to view firsthand the Soviet system of state-supported arts. This only aggravated the discontent. Harold Clurman, founder of the Group Theatre, was one who observed the renowned Moscow Art Theatre. Upon his return to the United States, he wrote that he was even more keenly aware of "the weight of the American burden, the difficulty of the artist's task in America."[15] The question many asked was why the United States could not do something comparable for its artistically gifted. In 1935, the WPA provided a partial and temporary answer to this plea. In the meantime, communism as observed in the Soviet Union offered the vision of comprehensive support for the arts, something that capitalist America seemed unable or unwilling to provide.

There was a certain stylishness about being a communist in the 1930s which made it almost *de rigueur* to sympathize, if not become a Party member. Political radicalism was an intellectual fad of the Depression, fitting into a nonconformist lifestyle long associated with the artistic community. For instance, the poet Maxwell Bodenheim, a Greenwich Village bohemian in the 1920s, became an enthusiastic communist.[16] Marc Blitzstein, in artistic exile on the Mediterranean, felt the need for involvement and came home, eventually becoming very active in leftist activities.[17] Paul Bowles recalled that he and his wife joined the Party at the urging of friends but afterwards found much of the dogma unpalatable.[18] Disinvolving oneself from the Party was more difficult than joining, noted Bowles. Yet many sympathizers dropped communist ties in the late 1930s as quickly as they had been "converted" in earlier years.

Still, the faddish aspect of communist interest does not negate the sincerity of social concern for many involved. Blitzstein was one of several who found a life-long artistic credo in sociopolitical causes. For the most part, though, American intellectual radicals were not political animals. Neither did they have an exclusive claim to sympathy for human suffering. However, as Bowles has noted, the Communist Party had an important sociopolitical function at this time in its organized agitation against groups fostering discrimination and racial hatred.[19] Thus, political leftism in the 1930s simply became a common framework in which the American intelligentsia expressed their idealism and humanitarianism. Artists found in leftism a focus for social outrage, and their work increasingly reflected their concerns. By their hands, America underwent an intense self-examination which in the early and middle 1930s tended toward harsh criticism. The psychological burden of unemployment and the physical pain of hunger became artistic preoccupations. Photographers Margaret Bourke-White and Walker Evans, among others, captured the bleakness of Depression poverty.[20] As a contributor to *New Masses,* Erskine Caldwell reported continuing violence against blacks in the South.[21]

Art was not used merely as a reflective tool, however. Among ardent leftist sympathizers, the concept of art experienced a drastic change. Standards of criticism moved from aesthetics and personal taste to politics. In this case, the Marxist stricture of art "as a weapon in the class struggle" became the basic criterion. Indicative of this change was the cold reception given F. Scott Fitzgerald's *Tender is the Night* amid cries for "social relevancy." According to Jerre Mangione,

Tender is the Night was published at the height of the proletarian cult in 1934, and dismissed by the book reviewers as socially insignificant because instead of dealing with workers and the class struggle it dealt with "superficial Americans living on the Riviera."[22]

The "class struggle" did find creative expression in the 1930s, resulting in what might be termed the "proletarian period" of the American arts. Leftist plays abounded, of which those by Clifford Odets were among the best-received. The visual arts frequently featured idealized versions of the American worker or everyday American activities. The bigger-than-life face of Lenin, pictured amidst an American labor dispute, stared down from a mural commissioned for Rockefeller Center.[23] Poets such as Genevieve Taggard and Richard Wright contributed their writings to *New Masses*.

Social purpose penetrated even the relatively shallow ground of American musical comedy. The tone was set by the Gershwins' *Of Thee I Sing* (1931), which satirized American politics and government. Irving Berlin and Moss Hart followed suit a year later with *Face the Music*, which placed a corrupt New York City police department against a Depression backdrop. The Gershwins attempted to match their 1931 success with a sequel, *Let 'Em Eat Cake* (1933). More biting than *Of Thee I Sing*, many critics thought *Let 'Em Eat Cake* was, to paraphrase the words of one, a triumph of hatred over humor.[24]

A grim outlook also pervaded *Americana (third edition)*, a 1932 revue. Brooks Atkinson called *Americana* "a little confused in its ideals."[25] J. P. McEvoy, author of the sketches, was in Atkinson's opinion "more sadistic than jolly" as a "jester of the depression."[26] The show's vacillating mood, said Atkinson, floundered on "the surface of a vast and dismal subject, merely reminding us of the suffering we are powerless to relieve."[27] *Americana* did have at least one memorable tune, but hardly in the traditional Broadway "catchy" sense. Atkinson prophetically called Jay Gorney's "Brother, Can You Spare a Dime?" an expression of the "spirit of our times."[28] As much as even the folk protest tunes growing directly out of the Depression experience, this song has survived as a symbol of the period.

Five years later, sociopolitical leftism had penetrated the musical theatre more deeply. By 1937, "the organization of the working man" had progressed sufficiently to be viewed by some as the solution to America's problems. Unionization was represented in that year by two notable New York productions. One was Marc Blitzstein's musical labor play *The Cradle Will Rock*, which made national headlines, theatre history, and a powerful social statement. The other was the very successful revue *Pins and Needles*, with music and lyrics by Harold Rome and sketches by several contributors including Blitzstein.[29]   *Pins and Needles* was a theatrical landmark for more than its leftist viewpoint and its barbs at American politics. It was sung, acted, danced, and produced exclusively by the members of the International Ladies Garment Workers Union, and thus exemplified the direct artistic participation of America's working class.

Despite the poverty and violence that marred the Depression decade, it was a period of exhilaration and challenge for most leftist artists. Some now look back upon those years as an era of great importance to the American arts, of unexpected and unequalled activity. One literary critic who grew up in the 1930s, Maxwell Geismar, has written that his first-hand knowledge of the period differed dramatically from the accepted versions.

> I wondered particularly why I had misunderstood the epoch of my own youth. I had always thought of the Thirties as a brilliant, lively, exciting, hopeful period; in my later thinking I saw it as the last true outburst of our social and literary creativity before the somnolence of the 1940s, the silence of the 1950s.[30]

Surely the social involvement of artists and their arts during the Depression was without parallel in American history. By taking up the causes of the disadvantaged, the intelligentsia furthered their direct interaction with other segments of American society. And the specifically "American" nature of this involvement was significant. Pells has noted that when Michael Gold lashed out at Thornton Wilder for his unwillingness to "confront contemporary realities," he was as much criticizing the author's lack of an "American voice" as his lack of radicalism.[31]   Conversely, when Philip Barr reviewed Blitzstein's *The Cradle Will Rock,* he praised not only its social statement but also its effective treatment of contemporary American life.

> *The Cradle Will Rock* by Marc Blitzstein is the American opera that many of us have waited for. It is like seeing the life of our times laid out on a line. . . . It has made me less nostalgic for other places, other times; all that seemed most contemptuously raw and unattractive in the modern American scene has become incandescent.[32]

The negativism fostered by leftists in the early and middle years of the Depression decade would seem to be the very antithesis of Americanism in its usual sense, that of exalting national life. Certainly in this period the focus was on the uglier aspects of American society. Yet while condemning American failures, radical artists and intellectuals at the same time urged the fulfillment—the perfection, perhaps—of the American promise of true equality. Their creative efforts manifested this goal through praise for the American common man, who was pictured as the seeker, the builder, and ultimately the beneficiary of America's promise. Particularly after the "Popular Front" platform, past or present Americans whose lives in some way had furthered or exemplified democratic principles were seen as the greatest heroes, the truest Americans. Jefferson, Lincoln, and Whitman were particular favorites.

There was, therefore, a certain irony to America's brand of Marxism in the 1930s — at least to the Marxism advocated by most of the intelligentsia. While Marxism is an international movement, American Marxism was nationally rather than internationally inspired and focused. Despite the foreign control and international aspirations of the Communist Party, the actual leftist movement among Americans encouraged a closer inspection of national life. Thus while political radicalism in the 1930s arose from disillusionment with the United States, it resulted in an increased artistic Americanism.

Although there were stalwart believers who remained associated with Party activities through its major and minor ideological crises in the 1930s and 1940s, the American communist movement was dealt several severe blows long before Senator McCarthy arrived on the scene. The first was the Nazi-Soviet Pact of August, 1939. In a seemingly incomprehensible about-face, Stalin signed a non-aggression agreement with Hitler, reversing the Soviets' previously vigorous campaign against fascism. Bowles recalled the bleak mood of leftist WPA members who, at news of the Pact, asked "where do we go from here?"[33] For many disillusioned idealists, even Russia's later staunch military defense could not remove the bad taste of political expedience. And revelations of Soviet discrimination against dissenters and minorities only furthered the retreat of intellectual sympathizers.[34] Seeing fundamental principles apparently abandoned by the only current Communist state, many Americans likewise deserted their leftist ties.

In the last years of the decade, as international problems overshadowed national ones, most Americans recognized an enemy more immediate and dangerous than capitalism. Growing concern over the threat of Hitler diminished the preoccupation with America's internal difficulties, and even those remaining in the leftist movement joined an all-out campaign against fascism. In the late 1930s, many artists seemed to seek refuge in an easier, less critical expression of traditional American values as if to present a strong, unified national image. And at this time, folklore, folk music, and rural American life increasingly became sources and inspirations for the arts, as is discussed below and in Chapter VI. The developing artistic awareness of rural America, along with the World War II patriotic period, are most commonly thought to comprise the roots of the period's Americanism; yet they came by way of an earlier, more controversial progenitor.

American Art Music to the Left of Center

For several reasons, the direct relationship between leftism and American art music in the Depression decade has been little discussed. Most important is the political problem. With the onset of postwar "witch-hunting," American composers were forced to conceal previous radical involvement, even when it had influenced their musical development. Few leftist musicians or other sympathizers were prepared for the quick turn of events following World War II. Today, more than twenty years after the "red scare," the McCarthy era is still a powerful reminder of how rapidly political winds can change.

Moreover, composers and historians have neglected the relationship between radicalism and art music because the "proletarian cult" – the leftist attempt to create a "people's art" – was not as readily nor as frequently adapted to cultivated music as to the other artistic genres. The surviving repertory of politically-oriented art music is not large, particularly when compared with the number of folk-protest songs which arose in the late 1930s and 1940s. Furthermore this music, with one exception, has remained almost completely unknown beyond the small number of contributing composers and their friends. Really only one leftist musical offering of extended scope, Blitzstein's *The Cradle Will Rock*, transcended its political origins to gain recognition among a wider audience. Even so, *The Cradle* has come to be regarded as a period piece, remembered more for its controversial slant than for its musical or dramatic worth.[35]

In retrospect, it is not surprising that American composers and other artists in the cultivated tradition found it difficult to maintain Marxist goals for very long, regardless of political pressure. The whole nature of cultural proletarianism imposed drastic limitations upon creativity. In fact, in the strictest sense, proletarianism seemed to go directly against the very traditions of "art" as generally understood in western civilization.[36] First, the Euro-American arts historically have found their support among the upper class, a chief object of Marxist hatred. More importantly, the very word "art" as comprehended in the West implies a substantial measure of creative freedom. The aspiring proletarian composer had the dual task of appealing to the American masses on an understandable level and converting them to Marxism as well. Not all American sympathizers were willing or able to subordinate their creative talents to sociopolitical purpose.

As it turned out, the "quest for proletarian music"[37] by classically-trained composers failed, at least in the eyes of the Communist Party. A "cultivated" solution to the problem of appropriate "mass" music was publicly rejected. Yet American composers' brush with communism, aside from producing a unique repertory of American music, seems to have had a significant influence on stylistic trends outside the realm of purely politically-inspired pieces. The parallels between the "quest for proletarian music" and the trend in art music toward compositional simplification in the mid-1930s seem far more than coincidence. And the same may be said for the upsurge of interest in folk music during the last years of the Depression decade. American composers' attraction to folk music has a long history. Nevertheless, the widespread recognition of folk styles as viable sources for American art music in the 1930s appears to have occurred first within some quarters of the American Communist Party, then among certain leftist composers, and finally among composers outside the realm of politics. Viewed in this light, the impact of American leftism upon American art music from the mid-1930s well into the 1940s and beyond is substantial.

It is difficult to determine precisely when American composers' attraction to Marxism began to affect their musical creativity. Carl Ruggles's name is listed among the editorial staff of *New Masses* in its premiere volume (1926), but not thereafter. In his discussion of the Depression decade, Cornelius Canon has noted the liberal philosophy of the New School for Social Research.[38] Aaron Copland, Elie Siegmeister, Wallingford Riegger, and Charles Seeger all taught there during the late 1920s and 1930s,[39] and Henry Cowell was its director of musical activities from 1930 to 1936.[40] Music courses at the New School stressed the social relevance of the art, and traced trends in modern composition.[41] The New School probably offered an atmosphere for the development of several composers' keen interest in the social place of the arts. Indeed, the New School was the location throughout the 1930s for a number of events sponsored by the Workers Music League and the Pierre Degeyter Club, both politically oriented groups discussed subsequently.[42] And the noted German revolutionary composer, Hanns Eisler, offered several courses there in 1935, including one in "mass song" composition.[43]

Yet it was a major step from the often latent liberalism of the 1920s to the radicalism of the 1930s—a step requiring a potent catalyst. Certainly it was the Depression that ignited the political interest of the majority of America's left-leaning musicians. "L.E. Swift" noted this when he wrote:

In this country music has been perhaps the last of the arts to break away from the 100 per cent reactionary art for art ideology. Only since the Depression, which has thrown tens of thousands of musicians out of work, closed down opera houses and concert halls and seriously devastated the possibilities of performances of new works by American composers, has the great rank and file of musicians and music lovers begun to feel that something is wrong somewhere.[44]

Charles Seeger, whose acquaintance with Marxism predated World War I, still vividly recalls winter in the depths of the Depression. The sight of freezing, homeless New Yorkers asleep on snowy streets was but one scene that intensified his sociopolitical concern. To Seeger, basic human compassion was fundamental to the American leftist outlook in those years.[45]

With American economic conditions worsening in the early 1930s, several musicians sought to put their abilities to direct humanitarian or political purpose. Earl Robinson, whom Bowles has called "the Communist Party's unofficial composer,"[46] came to New York City after graduating from the University of Washington. He was "looking for something like the left movement and a chance to write music that said something."[47] Similarly, Marc Blitzstein, who was in Europe in 1934, recalled:

My wife was writing a book. I was writing music. Practically in the middle of an eighth note I asked myself, "What the hell am I doing here?" I'd been getting periodicals from America. I left the beginning of a great people's movement and, further, felt the necessity for such a movement. Twenty-four hours after the question, we were packed and on our way back to the States.[48]

A commitment to political leftism, particularly communism, affected the entire creative outlook of those involved. Radical sympathizers learned that the development of an American proletarian culture was an important aspect of the communist movement at this time. To this end, several leftist musicians traveled to the Soviet Union to observe the model society at work. Subsequently, more than one aspect of Russian musical life under communism was transplanted to this country.[49] Sympathetic musicians joined fringe groups such as the Workers Music League (W.M.L.), the principal musical association connected with the American Communist Party through the mid-1930s. The W.M.L. was founded in New York City (1931) first as a publishing organization, but rapidly grew to include and oversee a large number of choruses, bands, orchestras, and other performing units including some in Boston and Philadelphia.[50]

The W.M.L., as the music section of the Workers Cultural Federation, is the cultural organization of all music forces connected with the American revolutionary

working class movement. Its aim is to coordinate, strengthen, and give both
ideological and musical guidance to these forces.[51]

Eventually, an educational branch known as the Downtown Music School
also was established.[52]

Applying propaganda to musical commentary, activists contributed
partisan reviews and essays to leftist newspapers and magazines, or
occasionally placed politically-slanted articles in non-political periodicals.
Elie Siegmeister's leftism in this period led to the most extended social
history of music by an American to that time, his *Music and Society*.[53]
The development of the American leftist composer's creative viewpoint
can be studied in the pages of the *Daily Worker* and *New Masses*. In
these publications, the composition of proletarian music was a lively and
frequent topic of consideration among musicians and non-musicians alike.

Creating proletarian music was an important goal. "Our movement
must learn to SING," urged Michael Gold, a columnist in the *Daily
Worker*, an editor of *New Masses*, and a major cultural spokesman for
the American Communist Party.[54] Taking seriously the slogan "art as a
weapon in the class struggle," the Party viewed music as an integral part
of its crusade.

> Music is of great importance to a people's movement. Songs have a positive
> value that can almost be calculated in watts and volts of mass energy and mass
> morale.[55]

Recognizing the voice as the universal instrument, the creation of
proletarian or "mass" songs was the first priority. Over and over in
his column "Change the World!" Gold emphasized the significance of
singing to the cause.

> Songs are as necessary to the fighting movement as bread. A song is really a
> slogan that has been dramatized, given emotional depth that makes it sink into the
> bones. We need more songs in the revolutionary movement of America.[56]

As an example of a song with "positive value," Gold cited "The
Internationale." "You can hear it in a thousand cities on May Day," he
wrote, and "Chinese workers have gone to be beheaded with this great
proletarian anthem on their lips."[57] American songs of a similarly stirring
quality were urgently needed, Gold felt.

The importance of song to American communism and the relative
technical accessibility of singing are reflected in the large number of
choruses associated with the Party. Choruses composed of Party mem-

bers and sympathizers formed the very backbone of the Workers Music League. Oldest and best known of the singing societies was the *Freiheit Gesang Farein* founded by Jacob Schaefer. Schaefer, a German immigrant, was one of the first professional musicians to align himself with the American communist movement.[58] His chorus was called the "finest workers' choral organization in the United States."[59] Additionally, there were Lan Adohmyan's New Singers, the Brooklyn *Arbeiter Saengerchor*, and other ethnic choruses comprised of Lithuanians, Yugoslavs, Finns, Ukrainians, and Italians.[60]

It is significant that when the *Daily Worker* Chorus, initially directed by Adohmyan and later by "Swift," gave its premiere in January, 1934, it was hailed as the "first English singing aggregation of its kind" in New York City.[61] Schaefer's chorus, for instance, was composed almost entirely of German Jews, and the group's insistence on performing in Yiddish or German engendered harsh criticism.[62] This lingual and old-world cohesiveness, however, accurately reflects the makeup of the American communist movement at the time, particularly in urban centers. Foreign-born and Jews comprised a high percentage of Party members or sympathizers.[63]

As the membership of the W.M.L. groups reveals, the communist movement in the early 1930s was isolated from the American mainstream by its new-immigrant and ethnic constituency as much as by its ideology. This explains, at least in part, the Party's emphasis on Americanism as the Depression decade progressed. In an effort to compensate for this isolation and to appeal for wider support among the American populace, the Party sought to identify itself with established American roots, traditional values, and cultural heroes. It is worth noting how closely that tendency parallels, in a different sense of course, the isolation and resulting Americanism of many native composers of art music over a much longer period of time.

The Composers' Collective

A number of leftist American composers charged themselves with the task of providing appropriate songs for what they regarded as a true people's movement in the early 1930s. For some who were unaccustomed to commissions, performances, or indeed to any significant acknowledgment whatsoever of their talents, the new commitment fostered an unprecedented feeling of purpose. Although certainly not an unrecognized composer, Copland expressed this—as well as the socio-political import of the task—when he wrote:

> To write a fine mass song is a challenge to every composer. It gives him a first-line position on the cultural front, for in the mass song he possesses a more effectual weapon than any in the hands of the novelist or even the playwright.[64]

Furthermore, leftist songs almost were guaranteed a performance by one of the numerous W.M.L. groups, and perhaps even publication. Thus, the leftist movement in the United States offered direction—both social and creative—to its composers of art music. It is small wonder that problems of politics and artistic freedom temporarily were overlooked in the simple joy of feeling wanted.

The need for proletarian songs declared by the Party, particularly in its association with the American labor movement, resulted in a group called the New York Composers' Collective. According to a 1936 article in the *Daily Worker*, the Composers' Collective was formed in 1932 by Charles Seeger (using the pseudonym "Carl Sands"), Henry Cowell, and Jacob Schaefer as a "seminar in the writing of mass songs."[65] Seeger, however, recalled that the group was minute but functioning when Cowell suggested he "come around" in 1932.[66] The members were familiar with similar current Soviet composers' societies, and Seeger dubbed the American group a "collective."[67] Cowell had been in Russia in 1929, and Ashley Pettis, music editor of *New Masses* and active in leftist circles, wrote about Soviet collectives after a visit in 1932.[68]

The Composers' Collective was an affiliate of the Pierre Degeyter Club of New York, an "organization of professional musicians having definite Leftist tendencies . . . [which] developed an orchestra, a chorus, study courses, lectures, concerts, etc."[69] The Club was the official musical organization of the American Communist Party, and was named for Pierre Degeyter (1849-1932), the French woodcarver who had composed the "Internationale."[70]

The principal purpose of the Composers' Collective was to create proletarian music, particularly mass songs suitable for labor rallies or Party meetings. To this end, members' pieces underwent a Collective criticism session, in which works were read through and discussed before publication.[71] As of the winter of 1934, the Composers' Collective was comprised of

> about twenty-four men and women . . . representing every shade of musical opinion from the conservatism of Jacob Schaefer, veteran conductor of the Freiheit Gesang Farein, to the restless radicalism of Lahn Adohmyan.[72]

Schaefer, mentioned above, and Adohmyan, another immigrant, both were conductors as well as composers. They appear to have been early influences in Collective activities, and may have been at least partly responsible for familiarizing American leftists with European communist music.

There seems to be no complete listing of Collective membership. Despite the continual presence of several stalwarts, the Collective's constituency appears to have been mostly a function of meeting attendance. Even at the time, estimates of the group's size differed. In reporting a ceremony honoring Hanns Eisler, "Sands" noted the "sixteen members and associates" of the Collective,[73] in contrast with the above reference to twenty-four. The *Daily Worker* and *New Masses* frequently carried notices or reviews dealing with the Collective, listing names of participant composers. Important sources on the Composers' Collective are two small notebooks kept by Marc Blitzstein, who recorded activities of the group's meetings during late 1934 and 1935. Apparently serving as secretary, Blitzstein registered those in attendance, even clarifying a few of the pseudonyms used by members, probably for his own benefit. Some composers, like Seeger ("Carl Sands") and Siegmeister ("L.E. Swift"), regularly employed protective names during the early and mid-1930s while engaging in communist activities, although Siegmeister dropped his later on. Seeger recalled that he used "Sands" because of the Party's tendency to exploit sympathizers' names in its press. Consequently, he did not want to endanger either his family or his musicological career.[74]

From the Blitzstein notebooks and the other above-named sources, it is possible to determine that the following were active in Collective functions during the 1930s: Seeger, Cowell, Adohmyan, Schaefer, Pettis, Siegmeister, Wallingford Riegger (sometimes using the pseudonym "J.C. Richards"), Norman Cazden, Hanns Eisler (when in the United States), Earl Robinson, Marc Blitzstein (after his return from Europe), Alex North, George Maynard, Herbert Haufrecht (sometimes "Herbert Howe"), Henry Leland Clarke (sometimes "J. Fairbanks"), Janet Barnes, Julius Keil, and Harold Brown.[75] According to Seeger, Ruth Crawford also attended Collective meetings occasionally.[76] Two others associated with the Collective were Isidore Freed and Mitya Stillman, although there is no confirmation that they were regular constituents.[77] One Collective member was cited as stating that George Antheil and Aaron Copland had just joined their "ranks."[78] Copland did participate in some leftist activities during this period, but did not belong to the Collective.[79] Antheil, on the other hand, apparently had little or no connection with the Collective or political leftism, and was rarely in New York during those years.[80]

The Composers' Collective confronted several obstacles in its attempt to create American proletarian music. One was a dearth of appropriate song texts in English. In an effort to remedy this situation, the W.M.L. sponsored a contest in the spring of 1934. Alluding to this cause in his column, Michael Gold contributed a new poem.[81] Not long after, "L. E. Swift" wrote to Gold complaining that there still were not enough good lyrics, noting that leftist songs suffered from the "stiffness, the inadequacy, the labored quality" of the poetry.[82] "Swift" suggested a number of timely American topics, including the "N.R.A., Unemployment Insurance, . . . brain trusters, liberals," and "labor skates."[83]

Gold rejoined the discussion by commenting that free verse was the traditional American poetic style.   Here he evoked the figure of Whitman, as he so often did, stating that the great poet's style was symbolic of "Jeffersonian anarchism."[84]   He also praised the current Whitmanesque character of the works of Carl Sandburg. The implication was that new American songs for the people should have poetry as "American" as that of Gold's literary heroes.

The lack of suitable texts in English for proletarian songs was but one creative difficulty the Collective faced in the early 1930s. Even more problematical was the absence of an American musical prototype. Perhaps the songs closest in spirit to the current leftist goal were those of the "Wobblies," the International Workers of the World founded in the early years of the twentieth century. Although Gold frequently held up as models the songs of the Wobblies' singing leader, Joe Hill, the Collective apparently did not consider them seriously at this time, though some former members found them more attractive later.[85] The simple folk or popular origins of Wobbly tunes were one of their major attractions to Gold, but among their detractions for the Collective in its early years. According to Seeger, Collective members took their role as composers very seriously; they wanted to create a new type of music, not copy labor songs of the past.[86]

A natural place for the Collective to look for its proletarian musical model was, of course, the Soviet Union. American leftists were familiar with Russian mass songs, such as those in the multi-lingual *International Collection of Revolutionary Songs.* This anthology, which appeared in the United States in late 1933 or early 1934, included pieces from several countries.[87]   Furthermore, at least one Collective member and another well-known leftist musician, Siegmeister and Pettis respectively, visited Russia in the Collective's formative years between 1932 and 1934, and recorded their impressions of the new socio-political order.

Both noted immediately the lack of unemployment among musicians, a sharp contrast to the current American situation. Yet neither writer was able to identify a coherent trend in contemporary

Russian composition.   Pettis, for instance, commented that Soviet composers were consciously eliminating all "bourgeois" stylistic tendencies.[88]   This involved forsaking folk music, which was associated with pre-revolutionary Russia, as well as contemporary foreign compositional characteristics.   Instead, Soviet composers were trying to deal with "the realities of life in a worker's state," and to build a "new Russian school free of all . . . pseudo-Russian influences."[89]   The turning away from the traditional generators of musical development, as well as such an age-old inspirational source as religion, had left recent Russian composition in a state of flux.

Seigmeister seems to have defined the ideal of American Collective members when he described the new role of the Soviet composer as he saw it in 1934: "a highly-skilled and hence socially valuable worker."[90] Yet he noted that this role was only beginning to be realized by Russian composers, and that the new generation was searching for fresh stylistic sources.

> Many of the young composers study their thematic material and their audience in this way — on collective farms, new construction projects (such as Dnieprosty, Matnitigorsk), on travels in the various Soviet republics.[91]

It is significant that Siegmeister recognized Shostakovich as "by far the best-known and best-loved of all Soviet composers" at this time.[92] Shostakovich maintained popularity in Russia, wrote Siegmeister, in spite of his "advanced" musical language.[93]   This aspect of Shostakovich's music apparently was one at least some members of the Collective wished to emulate.

Shostakovich soon gained greater renown and favor among American leftists with the New York premiere of his *Lady Macbeth of Mzensk* on February 5, 1935.   "Sands" and other sympathizers hailed Shostakovich's opera, at the same time denouncing New York critics such as Olin Downes and Lawrence Gilman for their "scurrilous and superficial" unfavorable reviews.[94]   In fact, it was less than a year later that *Lady Macbeth* was banned in its homeland, where not long before it had been praised.   A stinging article in *Pravda* in January, 1936 called the work a "mess instead of music."[95]   An inkling of changing tides, this commentary included derogatory labels such as "petty-bourgeois" and "formalist" which became common in later years.[96]   As shall be seen, the tightening grip on creative freedom in the USSR was paralleled by un-favorable American communist criticism leveled at sympathetic com-posers in the United States.

In effect, American composers looking to Russia for a model really were confronted with a nebulous state in Soviet proletarian composition.

Although Shostakovich and a few others were admired and studied, a more direct foreign influence upon the Collective appears to have come from another source. Not only were the works of the German Communist composer Hanns Eisler known to American leftists, but Eisler himself spent considerable time in the United States during the Depression years. Exiled from his native Germany in 1933 and his music banned there, Eisler was to make America his home base until 1948, despite extensive travels elsewhere.[97] A few of Eisler's songs, such as "Comintern" and "On Guard," were already well-known among fringe groups in this country, as were his pro-Communist activities.[98] Thus his reception by leftists in New York was like that given a conquering hero. During a visit early in 1935, events were organized in his honor, he made speaking and concert tours, and the *Daily Worker* music column followed his every move and pronouncement. No American composer, with the possible exception of Earl Robinson in the late 1930s, ever received the amount of leftist press coverage as did the German Eisler. He was hailed as the prototypical revolutionary composer for the proletariat, and American composers naturally looked to him for guidance.

> Hanns Eisler is not only the foremost composer in the workers' movement of the world, but is also the ideological leader and organizer of that movement.[99]

His arrival in the United States was the "great event" for the Collective.[100]

Eisler's own musical style ran the gamut from tonal mass songs to atonal abstract compositions.[101] In music especially for the proletariat, he advocated simplicity, but claimed that it was no excuse for music of poor quality. Eisler, who had been a pupil of Schoenberg, believed that a revolutionary composer could serve his social purpose only with thorough training, and particularly schooling with contemporary "masters."[102] Seeger recalled that Eisler was greatly opposed to folksong as a conscious source for proletarian music, perhaps partially explaining the Collective's disinterest in it in the fact of the American Communist Party's criticism. What so amazed Seeger was the way in which Eisler's own proletarian works so amiably and unconsciously combined folk, popular, and art components. Such a style, Seeger believed, was the result of centuries of German musical development, and was impossible in the United States of the 1930s.[103]

Eisler made an extended visit to New York City beginning in October, 1935. At this time, he offered two courses at the New School for Social Research. In one class, Eisler taught "choral writing as well as . . . Mass Song" composition.[104] The second course, open to anyone regardless of musical ability, covered modern music in relation to current social conditions. This latter course, "The Crisis in Music," presumably led to an essay of almost identical title published by the Downtown Music School in 1936.[105]   Scholarships to Eisler's classes were sponsored by the W.M.L. and the magazine *Music Vanguard.*[106]

While it is difficult to gauge directly Eisler's impact upon the American Collective, it is certain that he was well-known to the group and was present in New York City through much of the mid-1930s. Eisler's influence may well have been to reinforce the Collective's tendency to persist in an essentially international style infused with certain characteristics of "advanced" modern techniques, as opposed to a "national" style in the image of Joe Hill.   By 1936, the American Communist Party already was embarking on its trek toward the American folk, leaving music founded on the "masters" beyond the realm of American proletarian needs.[107]

"On Proletarian Music"

In the discussion of proletarian music in the early 1930s, the chief spokesman from the American composer's standpoint was Charles Seeger (1886-1979).   Through his column in the *Daily Worker* and his contributions to other publications, Seeger examined the musical needs of a revolutionary American society, and expressed the philosophy of the Collective and the Communist Party.[108]   His statements about the compositional aims of the Composers' Collective are instructive.

Seeger repeatedly insisted that proletarian music must reflect a new revolutionary order. He criticized current American leftist music, noting that "even in most of our present songs the musical ideology conflicts with the political."[109]   Primarily, he wrote, "there must be a revolution in the very system of music if it is to further, and not betray, the revolution in the system of society."[110]   Seeger believed that revolutionary content (communist propaganda or social meaning) should be matched by revolutionary style. But how this was to be achieved, indeed, what this meant in composition were the problems.   "We cannot," he stated, "simply invent a new musical style."[111] He admitted that true proletarian music in the United States would only result "from revolutionary tendencies persisted in over a considerable length of time."[112]

Seeger's most extended exposition on the needs of revolutionary America was the article "On Proletarian Music."[113]   This essay is significant on several counts. First, it was written close to the height of Seeger's and other American "cultivated" composers' interest and influence in Marxist circles. Within two years' time, favorable notice of folk-protest music more frequently appeared in the *Daily Worker,* and

Seeger himself left the Collective. Secondly, Seeger's commentary appeared in a non-communist periodical, and thus explained and justified leftist positions more than it might have otherwise. Seeger summarized the leftist viewpoint, as well as the specifically American outlook, on the social place of music.

For the most part, Seeger presented the characteristic arguments for cultural proletarianism: music was a "weapon in the class struggle"; art was "always and inevitably a social function"; the composer who did not recognize the social value of music was in an "ivory tower," unwilling to write music with a positive view toward a better life.[114] Because all art was propaganda, either positive or negative, the composer must choose from one of three possible paths:

> fascism, which means positive propaganda for the older order; isolation, which means negative propaganda [tacit approval] for it; and proletarianism, which means propaganda for the new order.[115]

But Seeger also expressed a primary incentive for the cultural outlook characteristic of the American intellectual's communist association: humanitarian idealism.

> The humanizing of humanity is regarded as a thing that is happening simply because an increasing number of people cannot help striving to make it happen. Creative minds and abilities especially, tend to desire its happening "as soon as possible."[116]

Seeger viewed intellectuals, "including musicians and other artists," as members of what Marx and Engels had called the "superstructure" of society. They were also part of the Proletariat–the "virtually propertyless members of modern industrial society"–as were the workers (the "structure").[117] It was the duty of the "superstructure" to inform the "structure" of the "facts of life."[118] Clearly, in the early stages of this "social evolution," the superstructure, the intellectuals, bore the major burden.

On the more specific issue of proletarian songs, Seeger emphasized the creation of a new, "revolutionary" style. Here he equated "revolutionary" style with advanced compositional techniques. Seeger noted that twentieth-century "bourgeois" art music had achieved definite revolutionary tendencies, not in content but in "technic."[119] Current proletarian music, on the other hand, exhibited the reverse characteristics. Leftist composers needed to combine the two revolutionary trends of technique and content, while eliminating all the bourgeois traits. In revolutionizing music, Seeger advocated a step-by-step approach: "content first, technic second."[120]

Clearly, in the beginning, the bulk of the fabric of new compositions for the proletariat must be in idioms not unfamiliar to it. Into this can be introduced more and more of the newer technical resources.[121]

As exemplary of this cautious approach, Seeger praised "L.E. Swift's" three-part round appearing in a W.M.L. publication.[122] The round employed alternating meters at a brisk tempo. but was within a tonal framework (see Example 1).[123]

Example 1
"Onward to Battle," "L.E. Swift," *Workers Song Book, No. 1.*

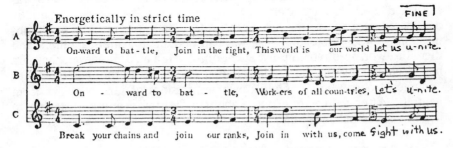

Into this exposition on style, Seeger introduced a catch-phrase frequently found in communist discussions of American leftist songs and presumably describing the ideal American proletarian music. "The slogan is," wrote Seeger, "national in form: revolutionary in content."[124] Considered against the background of his comments on "advanced" technique, this slogan does not quite fit. Though not necessarily opposed, "national" style alone (and Seeger did not elaborate) does not conjure up a picture of revolutionary music. Yet if one takes this slogan as the Collective's own condensed expression of its goal, it is significant. The Composers' Collective apparently felt it necessary to give an "American voice" to its music within the framework of a universal Marxist movement.

In another article, Seeger criticized a leftist composer's songs as not American, but European.[125] Yet in the same article, Seeger wrote that the top priority was making leftist songs identifiable as such, giving them a trademark which would set them apart from "bourgeois, patriotic or religious songs on the one hand and from the conventional, easy going, subservient folksong on the other."[126] In other words, the preceding musical genres had little to do with being "national" – or "American" – in Seeger's opinion at this time, at least as far as new composition was concerned.

This negative view toward American traditional music, especially the folksong, is telling, particularly when compared with the "national in form" slogan. It seems all the more remarkable because the Collective had heard Southern protest songs as early as 1933.[127] Moreover, Seeger, a musicologist as well as a composer, embarked on folksong collecting tours of the South in 1935,[128] and thereafter became a strong advocate of American folk music. Yet he and other Collective members regarded folksong as an inappropriate basis for American proletarian music, despite suggestions for that direction by Party represesentatives, especially Gold; the Collective itself offered no other "national" music as a stylistic model.

For instance, jazz – a likely potential source in the early 1930s – was suggested and rejected early on in the "quest." Jazz was briefly considered as a source for American proletarian music in Gold's columns in 1933. Gold wrote that jazz was "important in American life," and therefore worthy of communist attention.[129] He noted, however, that jazz had been banned in the Soviet Union, where it was thought typical of "bourgeois corruption." Gold's own impressions of jazz were far from neutral. After a free-verse poem about a "wasted evening" listening to jazz in a dance hall, he remarked:

> I do not always hate jazz! I think it has some merit as a source of new rhythms. Jazz may be good also to dance to but on the whole it is fairly cheap and tawdry.[130]

In addition, jazz represented the "Broadway crook," all the evils of capitalist Tin Pan Alley, and it had no roots in anything except the "Broadway pavement."[131]

After his initial thoughts on this music, Gold admitted that letters on the subject had been numerous. Indeed, his column on jazz had netted more response than any previously.[132] In light of Gold's strongly-worded views, though, it is little wonder that comments from readers cited in his column continued the condemnation. One response quoted at length was from Siegmeister. Although generally agreeing with Gold on the unattractive bourgeois connotations of jazz, Siegmeister pointed out that jazz in its original, noncommercial strain had been a "fresh, spontaneous invention of a number of Negro and white composers."[133] These composers had succeeded in setting down the "peculiar rhythms and significant twists of the voice which mark off the American dialect from the English."[134] Jazz was distinctly American. It was the problem of aspiring proletarian musicians to eliminate "all that is false, cheap, sexy, hysterical in this music and yet retain the essential American note."[135] Calling upon the Collective's slogan for proletarian music, "national in form, revolutionary in content," Siegmeister asked: "What other really national music have we in this country beside jazz?"[136]

It is apparent from these discussions that, in the crucial years of 1934 and 1935, the Composers' Collective was undecided on what native style to base their American proletarian music. Jazz was viewed as inappropriate. Folksong was barely considered. Thus despite their goal of a "national form," Seeger, Siegmeister, and presumably other Collective members remained vague about how to create an American music of mass appeal. A brief examination of the musical output of the Composers' Collective reveals that generally only the texts, not the music, held direct ties to current American experience.

Books with Red Pages

The major compositional achievements of the New York Composers' Collective, as one might expect, occurred in the field of mass songs or choruses.[137] These were published in two songbooks by the W.M.L. at the height of the Collective's activities in 1934 and 1935. Leftist songbooks were hardly unprecedented in the United States. The Wobblies had had such collections, and the W.M.L. had published a *Red Song Book* in 1932. There were also imported anthologies, such as the aforementioned *International Collection.* Unlike the *International Collection*, comprised almost entirely of foreign works,[138] the *Red Song Book* contained a few pieces by American immigrants as well as some familiar tunes set with new texts. Examples of the latter are the conversion of Beethoven's chorale from the *Ninth Symphony* into the "Red Marching Song," and "My Bonnie Lies Over the Ocean" into the "Soup Song." The text of the "Soup Song," as opposed to the majority of others in the *Red Song Book*, was distinctly an outgrowth of the American Depression.

> I'm spending my nights at the flophouse
> I'm spending my days on the street.
> I'm looking for work and I find none
> I wish I had something to eat.
>
> Chorus:
> Soo-up
> Soo-up
> They give me a bowl of soo-oo-up
> Soo-up
> Soo-up
> They give me a bowl of soup![139]

Among the other works included in the *Red Song Book* was one song each by Schaefer and Adohmyan, one by Ella May Wiggins, and one by Aunt Molly Jackson. The *Workers Song Book, No. 1* (1934) and *Workers Song Book, No. 2* (1935) are unique in that they are almost exclusively the work of the Composers' Collective. The first collection was edited by Adohmyan and "Sands." According to the "Foreword," all of the pieces included were written by Collective members, and all but four composed in 1933.[140] The editors noted with pride that the volume was the "first collection exclusively of original revolutionary mass, choral and solo songs with English texts to be made in America."[141] In accordance with the practices of the Collective, the songs had come through a "critical fire" from members:

> All of the works have been tested in rehearsals and most of them, in performance by mass organizations in New York City.[142]

The "Table of Contents" of *Workers Song Book, No. 1* is as follows:

1. "Mount the Barricades" – "Carl Sands"
2. "The Scottsboro Boys Shall Not Die" – "L. E. Swift" (text by Abron)
3. "Hunger March" – Jacob Schaefer (text translated from the Yiddish by Abe Little)
4. "Song to the Soldier" – Lan Adomian [*sic*] (text by Rose Pastor Stokes)
5. "Three Workers' Rounds" – words and music by "L. E. Swift"
6. "Strife Song" – Jacob Schaefer (text translated by V. J. Jerome)
7. "Lenin – Our Leader" – Jacob Schaefer (text translated from the Yiddish by I. Rontch)
8. "Song of the Builders" – "Carl Sands"
9. "Red Soldiers Singing" – Lan Adomian [*sic*] (text by Joseph Freeman)
10. "God to the Hungry Child" – Janet Barnes (text by Langston Hughes)
11. "A Negro Mother to Her Child" – Lan Adomian [*sic*] (text by V. J. Jerome)
12. "Pioneer Song: Who's That Guy?" – "Carl Sands"[143]

This premiere collection was reviewed by George Maynard in the *Daily Worker* and by Aaron Copland in *New Masses*. Both writers were associated with the Collective although neither's music was included in this volume. Maynard called the *Song Book* "handsome" and "practical," noting that it represented a "year's work on the part of the league [W.M.L.] and members of the Composers' Collective."[144] Copland hailed the *Song Book* as the "first adequate collection of revolutionary songs for American workers."[145] Little notice seems to have been made of the volume, however, by important leftist non-musicians such as Gold.

Most of the music in *Workers Song Book, No. 1* was praised by Maynard and Copland. Singled out by Maynard was "Swift's" "The Scottsboro Boys Shall Not Die," a song based on a current American controversy and already popular among workers' groups and choruses.[146] Even Gold commended this work, perhaps due to its straightforward, rousing march style, particularly in the "Refrain" (see Example 2).

Example 2
"The Scottsboro Boys Shall Not Die," "L.E. Swift." *Workers Song Book, No. 1.*

Copland applauded "Swift's" "Workers' Rounds" and the three pieces by
"Sands." "Who's That Guy?" by "Sands" was an amusing attack on
policies of the Roosevelt administration, while one of "Swift's" rounds
was a satire on "Poor Mr. Morgan" unable to "pay his income tax" (see
Examples 3 and 4). Janet Barnes's "God to the Hungry Child," although
composed to American revolutionary poetry, seems more in the character
of an art song (see Example 5). These and a few other pieces attempted
to relate to American experiences by picking familiar subjects or issues of
current importance among leftists. Others, such as Schaefer's "Hunger
March" and Adomian's [sic] "Song to the Worker," reveal their European musical origins and make no attempt to reflect the specifically
American leftist movement.

   Workers Song Book, No. 2 was a larger volume and, more
significantly, contained works by a greater number of composers. This
Song Book consisted of twenty pieces and three workers' rounds (as

Example 3
"Pioneer Song: Who's That Guy?" "Carl Sands," *Workers Song Book,*
No. 1.

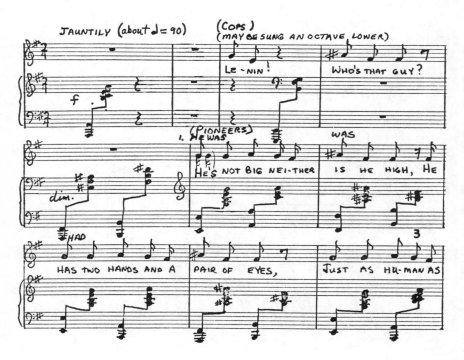

Example 3
(continued)

Example 4
"Poor Mister Morgan," "L.E. Swift." *Workers Song Book, No. 1.*

Example 5
"God to the Hungry Child," Janet Barnes. *Workers Song Book, No. 1.*

compared to the first collection's ten songs and three rounds) written or
arranged by twelve composers (as compared to five previously). Eight of
the composers were Americans and six were Collective members. Again,
the "Foreword" brimmed with enthusiasm, stating that the published
selections were only a few "chosen from among dozens submitted."[147]
The "Table of Contents" of *Workers Song Book, No. 2* is as follows:

1. "United Front" – "J. Fairbanks" (music and text)
2. "War Is Murder" – Lan Adomian [sic] (text by Barney
    Conal)
3. "Into the Streets May First!" – Aaron Copland (text by
    Alfred Hayes)
4. "Song of the Pickets" – Earl Robinson (text by Stephen
    Karnot)
5. "Forward, We've Not Forgotten" – Hanns Eisler (text by
    Bert Brecht, translated by Henry Jordan)
6. "Comintern" – Hanns Eisler (English text by V. J.
    Jerome)
7. "Our is the Future" – Stefan Volpe
8. "Stop in the Tracks" – Lan Adomian [sic] (text by
    Michael Quin)
9. "Look Here Georgia!" – Lan Adomian [sic] (text by Don
    West)
10. "The Ballad of Harry Sims" – Lan Adomian [sic] (text by
    Harry Alan Potamkin)
11. "We Toil We Work" – Karl Vollmer (English text by "L.
    E. Swift")
12. "I went to 'Tlanta" – arr. by "L. E. Swift"
13. "Sistern and Brethren" – arr. by "L. E. Swift"
14. "We Want the World" – "L. E. Swift"
15. "The Red Banner" – arr. by "J. C. Richards" (English
    text by M. L. Korr)
16. "Chinese Red Soldier Song" – arr. by "J. C. Richards"
    (English text by M. L. Korr)
17. "The First Red Cavalry" – A. Davidenko (English text by
    Del Ruskin)
18. "John Reed Our Captain" – George Maynard (text by
    Michael Gold)
19. "The Flying Squadron" – Oscar Saul, Peter Martin, and
    Earl Robinson (music and text)
20. "Three Workers' Rounds" – one by "L. E. Swift" and two
    by "Carl Sands"[148]

The editors presented their own estimation of the volume's
accomplishments:

Particularly noteworthy in the present collection are: 1) the publications, for the
first time, of two original Negro songs of protest revealing the rising discontent

and militancy of the oppressed Negro people; 2) songs dealing with the struggles for the United Fronts and against war and fascism; 3) songs commemorating American class war heros, fallen in battle (John Reed, Harry Sims, Sperry and Coundorakis); 4) satirical songs in the American folk style aimed at the "best" personalities of American Capitalism; 5) popular workers' songs from Germany (including Eisler's famous "Vorwärts und nicht vergassen" from "Kühle Wampe" as well as songs by Vollmer and Volpe); 6) outstanding fighting songs from the Soviet Union, Mongolian People's Republic and Red China.[149]

The inclusion of the German pieces probably reflected an increasing concern with German fascism, as well as the presence of several exiled German composers in the United States.   All of the foreign songs appeared with English texts, either as translations or as in the originals.

    The majority of the pieces in this second *Song Book* (thirteen of twenty-two) were newly-composed by Collective members or associates, while an additional four were arranged by group members. A significant new source was Lawrence Gellert's *Negro Songs of Protest,* from which "Swift" had chosen and arranged two melodies.[150] Other composed songs related directly to the American working class struggle, such as "John Reed Our Captain" by Gold and Maynard, "Stop in Your Tracks," by Quin and Adomian [*sic*], and "Song of the Pickets" by Karnot and Robinson.   It was probably the rounds by "Sands" and "Swift" which the editors referred to as "satirical songs in the American folk style."[151] "Swift's" "The Three Brothers," for instance, poked fun at the wealthy Dupont family (see Example 6). As in the first volume, Adohmyan,

Example 6
"The Three Brothers," "L. E. Swift." *Workers Song Book, No. 2.*

"Swift," and "Sands" are each represented by more than one work apiece. American composers whose leftist music appears here for the first time are Copland, Robinson, Maynard, "Richards" (Riegger), and "Fairbanks" (Clarke).

Copland's piece, "Into the Streets May First!," originally had been published in *New Masses* as the winner of a song contest sponsored by that magazine.[152]   Contestants, including Collective members and a few other sympathizers, each had submitted a setting of Alfred Hayes's poem "Into the Streets May First!" All twenty-four composers convened to select the winner. They agreed without difficulty that Copland's music was the best. Seeger, however, who thought his own work the worst compositionally, asked whether Copland's song could be sung at any time, by any people regardless of musical training, or with make-shift instrumentation.[153]   Although Seeger and the other composers believed the song well-written, they were less certain about its appropriateness to its purpose.

Styles of individual pieces in the two *Workers Song Books* vary greatly. Yet the question of appropriateness might be asked of many of them. A few were simple, completely tonal rounds. Others were settings of pre-existent revolutionary songs. Much of the contents of the *Workers Song Books*, though, was newly-composed in a style more suited to trained choruses than amateurs or random groups of picketers. Copland's song, with its melodic leaps of an octave and unconventional harmonies, may be taken as an extreme example of the Collective's attempt to maintain certain characteristics of "advanced" musical language within the framework of "revolutionary" content. Its singability by the musically illiterate was very doubtful.[154]   Furthermore, the Collective's music bore little obvious resemblance to American folk or popular styles. The principal exceptions here are the two "Swift" settings of Negro protest songs. These may be taken as an indication of one Collective member's growing awareness of American traditional music. On the whole, however, there was little conscious effort compositionally to fulfill the "national in style" portion of the Collective's slogan despite the stated intent to do so.

Seeger has since remarked that he felt Gold was correct and more prescient than the Collective in recognizing folksong as a proper vehicle for leftist protest in the United States.[155]   Certainly time has borne out Gold's inclinations on this subject. Yet Seeger noted that the Collective members felt themselves above such things as rewriting folksongs, at least in 1934 and 1935. To classically-trained composers like Seeger and the others, this naturally seemed a vastly limiting task.   Probably the influence of Eisler and the Collective's clouded view of the Soviet musical world only contributed to this stance. Nevertheless, whatever support or encouragement the Collective had received from the Party was halted early in 1936 when the group, their music, and especially "Sands" were attacked by Gold in the *Daily Worker*.[156] Thus it is not surprising that *Workers Song Book, No. 2* was the final joint compositional effort of the Collective. They had reached a dead end.

The New York Composers' Collective was an experiment in writing art music of mass American appeal with a specifically leftist message. As a group, the Collective reflected the ethnic makeup of much of the American Communist Party during this period. Excluding Seeger and Cowell, the remainder of the Collective largely was comprised of foreign-born or urban Jews attracted to the leftist movement for the same reasons as many others with like backgrounds. Thus in the context of sociopolitical radicalism of the mid-1930s, the Composers' Collective represented the characteristic merger of Marxism and Americanism: Marxism growing from a disillusionment with current American life; and Americanism emerging from a love of country, but also as compensation for a political philosophy, a lineage—and, in this case, a profession—not immediately identified as "American." Reduced to the simplest terms, the Collective simultaneously was protesting and attempting to belong to American society. This mixture of goals was tipped in favor of Americanism for many Collective members after the dissolution of the group and with the growing popularity of rural Americana, specifically folk material, as an inspirational source in the late 1930s.[157]

The Composers' Collective is significant within the context of general music history as well. Despite the special nature of its origins— the turbulent sociopolitical atmosphere of the early 1930s—the group addressed larger compositional questions of art music in general and American art music in particular. Seeger joined the Collective because of his political stance, but also because the organization was tackling the greater issue of music in relation to modern society.[158]

Many of the difficulties still confronting contemporary composers first came to a head in the 1930s: a revolutionized Euro-American musical language leaving the general audience uncomprehending, loss of a wealthy supporting class, and new forms of entertainment encroaching on the traditional place of art music. These problems, combined with the long-standing lack of interest in American cultivated music, were all well-known to members of the Collective. The basic questions were: for whom did one write music, and how? Furthermore, the Collective continued the long historical concern with giving an "American voice" to their music. Their uncertainty about a native source for American proletarian music was indicative of a preoccupation among current American composers in general. In effect, the Collective proposed a compromise in its songs, a combination of some technical trends from contemporary art music and the wider appeal of American subject matter. Other Americanists and other modern composers have proposed different solutions.

The idea of a cross-section of American composers—both well-known and little-known, native-born and immigrant, technically advanced and conservative—jointly confronting these numerous issues is an engaging one. It was the idealism (Seeger said "innocence"[159]) of this effort which remains extraordinary.

The Emergence of the Folk-Protest Song as Proletarian Music

The conflict in compositional ideology between the Composers' Collective and the cultural wing of the American Communist Party led by Michael Gold came to a head early in 1936. It took the form of Gold's open criticism of the group in his *Daily Worker* column, singling out "Sands" for a personal attack. While it is true that much of the fire had gone out of the Collective by late 1935, this was the final blow.[160] Individual members, however, were not unaffected by the decisive leftist affirmation of folk music which Gold's column signaled.

Michael Gold was an important formulator and spokesman of cultural policy in the American Communist Party during this period. While Reuss has noted that Gold was not uniformly admired within the Party, he was widely read.[161] His brand of Americanist Marxism characterized the Party's stance, especially in the late Depression years. On the one hand, his directives were predictably those of Marx and Lenin as interpreted by current Soviet leaders. On the other, he held up Whitman as the consummate American poet of the people, and Lincoln as the consummate statesman. Most importantly, he called for arts rooted in the American vernacular.

While Gold had not outwardly denounced the Composers' Collective and had even supported some of its activities in the early years, neither had he wholly endorsed the group. The Collective was not his answer to the "quest" for an American proletarian music and the search for a "communist Joe Hill."[162] Even before the discovery of Woody Guthrie, who for a time became that new Joe Hill, Gold recognized protest singers spawned in rural labor movements whose works were in the folk tradition.[163] Usually from the South, singers such as Huddy Ledbetter (Leadbelly), Aunt Molly Jackson, and Sarah Ogan had a rough-hewn quality which leftists associated favorably with earlier

American nonconformists. Being rural rather than urban in origin, their music differed strongly from the popular productions of capitalist Tin Pan Alley, and more truly represented the proletariat.

One of the first protest groups to be discovered and endorsed by Gold was the Auvilles. Giving them the ultimate compliment, Gold noted that "Comrades Ray and Lida Auville, two Southern mountaineers who are proletarian singers," had the same "folk-feeling" that Joe Hill had possessed.[164] Texts to songs by the Auvilles and other folksingers or poems by folk poets increasingly appeared in the *Daily Worker* in 1934 and 1935. A collection of songs by the Auvilles, *Songs of the American Worker*, was published by the John Reed Club of Cleveland in 1934.[165]

The Composers' Collective, however, did not wholeheartedly accept Gold's enthusiastic assessment of the Auvilles. It was an article by "Sands" which eventually became the specific issue around which Gold's refutation of the Collective was built. When "Sands" reviewed the Auville anthology in the *Daily Worker*, he praised the revolutionary content of the songs but criticized the musical idiom. "Sands" wrote that the style was that of "1890 or earlier," and was "old-fashioned and stodgy."[166] Furthermore, "Sands" believed that the melodies were not very good. Noting the popularity of this type of song among workers, "Sands" stated that popularity alone did not make it the correct music for the revolution.

> No one but a musician widely trained in the many musical fields of our day and thoroughly conversant with the history of music and its relation to general history can realize how low and how uncritical is the present level of American taste. The melodies of songs like these of the Auvilles are concentrated bourgeois propaganda of a peculiarly vicious sort. For every step forward in the verse one takes a step backward in the music. That one is unaware of it makes it all the more dangerous.[167]

The opposing stances were clear. "Sands" upheld the standards of the trained musician and composer, placing the responsibility for creation of proletarian music with them. Gold favored a readily accessible style, specifically music with a rural folk quality in the tradition of Joe Hill. What is somewhat surprising is that it took Gold nearly a year to publicly denounce "Sands's" review. One might speculate that in that time the Party formalized its cultural direction, or attempted a conversion of the Collective. Nevertheless, when Gold did respond, he scorned the Collective and singled out "Sands" as representative of their elitist attitudes. It is worth quoting extensively from Gold's article for the innuendos in his comparison between the Collective and folk protesters such as the Auvilles.

Comrade Sands had some mighty harsh things to say about the songs of Ray and Lida Auville, among other comments. . . . They are a couple of southern mountaineers who for years had toured the country with their two kids and an old Ford, making a living out of singing mountain ballads.

Ray Auville fiddles; no, he doesn't play the violin, he fiddles with gusto and native style, as rousingly as any old moustached veteran of the Great Smokies in Tennessee. And his wife, lovely, soft-eyed Lida, she plays the guitar, and they sing together.

About two years ago this mountaineer couple ran smack into the working class revolution. Ever since they have devoted their talents to writing and singing songs of and for the American workers and farmers.

It is the real thing, folk song in the making, workers' music coming right out of the soil. I wrote about them in this column some time ago, and reprinted some of their songs.

But Comrade Sands called their work a "hybrid mixture of jazz and balladry," and bore down on it with all the heavy thunder of professional aestheticism. . . .

Really, Comrade Sands, I think you have missed the point. It is sectarian and utopian to use Arnold Schoenberg or Stravinsky as a yardstick by which to measure working class music.

What songs do the masses of Americans now sing? They sing "Old Black Joe" and the semi-jazz things concocted by Tin Pan Alley. In the South they sing the old ballads. This is the reality; and to leap from that into Schoenberg seems to me a desertion of the masses.

Not to see what a step forward it is to find two native musicians of the American people turning to revolutionary themes, converting the tradition to working class uses, is to be blind to progress. . . .

Would you judge workers' correspondence by the standard of James Joyce or Walter Pater? No, a folk art rarely comes from the studios; it makes its own style, and has its own inner laws of growth. It may shock you, but I think the Composers' Collective has something to learn from Ray and Lida Auville, as well as to give them. They write catchy tunes that any American worker can sing and like, and the words of their songs make the revolution as intimate and simple as "Old Black Joe." Is that so little?[168]

The anti-intellectualism of Gold's cultural outlook is apparent here, as is his anger at "Sands's" heavy criticism of the Auvilles, a group Gold himself had praised. In light of this now open refutation of "Sands," it is not surprising that references to the Collective all but disappeared from the *Daily Worker.*

Precisely how long after early 1936 the Collective functioned is unclear. In a November, 1935 article for the *Daily Worker,* "Carl Sands" announced W.M.L. plans for a new songbook. Significantly, "Sands" did not mention any specific role for the Collective in these plans, for the proposed book was to be a collection of existing songs in new arrangements.[169] In February, 1936, the *Daily Worker* reported the dissolution of the W.M.L., of which the Collective was a part, and its replacement by the American Music League (A.M.L.).[170] The A.M.L.'s range of activities was smaller than that of its predecessor, but one of its stated goals was to "publish and popularize American folk music."[171] According to Reuss, the Collective "lingered on for a time" within the A.M.L., and Collective members Earl Robinson, Elie Siegmeister, and Marc Blitzstein remained active in the new organization.[172] The Collective simply seems to have petered out.

What is certain is the Collective's loss of Party support in the face of mounting leftist enthusiasm for folksong as the vehicle for protest in the late 1930s and 1940s. Woody Guthrie, Pete Seeger, Leadbelly, and other now well-known personalities identified with folk music were already functioning to varying degrees by 1940 as singing spokesmen for the left. Of the three, Guthrie and Leadbelly were authentic "folk" figures in all senses of the word. Guthrie's remarkable life as a dustbowl "Okie," a hobo, and a victim of Huntington's Disease has become widely known. Leadbelly's experiences as a black in southern prisons and chain gangs made him more than a folksinger; he became a controversial symbol of an often forgotten segment of American life. The younger Seeger, an articulate Harvard dropout, wholly committed himself to sociopolitical protest in the late 1930s. Unlike his father, however, Pete Seeger immediately adopted folksong as his medium. Seeger's Almanac Singers, ancestors of the better-known Weavers, were composed of individuals with backgrounds both like his own and like Guthrie's. Woody was one of several occasional members of this group, which functioned as an adjunct to the Party in the early 1940s.

While the vitality of American communism ebbed in the late 1940s, that of the folk revival continued. Burl Ives, the Weavers, and others gradually softened their overt political message and increased their popularity. By the time the Kingston Trio tapped a growing audience in the late 1950s and early 1960s, folk music had become a multimillion dollar business. Yet in the hands of individuals such as Pete Seeger, Bob Dylan, and Joan Baez in the 1960s, the Anglo-American folk tradition remained a forum for social comment, although that comment was less tied to a specific political movement than it had been two decades earlier.

More pertinent to this study is the influence the popularization of folk music had upon the American cultivated tradition. The folk consciousness begun by the leftists in the mid-1930s helped to stimulate a similar awareness among American composers of art music in the late 1930s and into the 1940s. While folksong served as a vehicle for leftist protest, it simultaneously became a means for American composers to reach concert audiences, who in the 1940s generally remained unaware of traditional music's political adaptation.

VI

The Emergence of Folksong
as an Americanist Source

In 1934, Charles Seeger's essay "On Proletarian Music" appeared in *Modern Music*.[1] Seeger assessed the artistic development of the American people according to Marxist guidelines, taking the viewpoint that

> art . . . is always and inevitably a social function. It has social significance. It has social force. It is propaganda: explicit, positive; implied, negative. The better the art, the better the propaganda it makes; the better the propaganda, the better art it is.[2]

Five years later, Seeger's "Grass Roots for American Composers" appeared in the same periodical. Maintaining that American folksong of quality existed abundantly in the United States, Seeger lamented that this music was ignored by the country's professional musicians.

> The folk music of America [has] embodied for well over a hundred years the tonal and rhythmic expression of untold millions of rural and even urban Americans. Contrary to our professional beliefs, the American people at large has had plenty to say and ability to say it, so that a rich repertory has been built up – thousands of tunes each for the dance, for the ballad, the love song, and the religious song. . . . But American songs, hymns and dances were not, and still to practically all musicians and teachers, are not music at all.[3]

Furthermore, Seeger urged his fellow American composers to "discover America" by travelling through the nation and absorbing the music of the American people.

> The first thing, it seems to me, is for the professional composer to make up his mind that his place in world music will depend upon his finding his place in American music and in American life. . . . The second move is to discover America. . . . If, therefore, a composer is going to sing the American people anything new, if he is going to celebrate his oneness with them (not his difference from them) . . . he must first get upon a common ground with them, learn their musical lingo, work with it and show he can do for them something they want to have done and cannot do for themselves.[4]

   The sentiments expressed in Seeger's "Grass Roots" represent the culmination of the author's social outlook as well as his musical Americanism. Seeger's conversion to folksong, so strongly contrasted with his early Collective view of traditional music, is obvious. Yet his appreciation of folksong represents a recognition of musical language regardless of social class. Moreover Seeger's article, particularly in the last passage cited above, clearly illustrates the two assumptions of musical Americanism: that American source material will make American art music "American"; and that the American people desire such music.

   The expression of both social and Americanist concern in "Grass Roots" makes it a representative exposition of American art music from the late 1930s. On the one hand, the essay revealed the heightened sociopolitical awareness that proceeded from the American Depression. On the other hand, Seeger's "Grass Roots" harked back, however unintentionally, to an earlier type of Americanist declaration, such as that made by Farwell or Cadman, by prescribing native vernacular music as a source for native cultivated music. The music of principal interest to Seeger, however, was not Amer-Indian as in the early 1900s, or jazz as in the 1920s, but rural American folk music. "Grass Roots" reflected the move among Americanists toward white traditional sources to establish "American" music. Seeger's article, by its lack of Marxist rhetoric, also represented a considerable softening in the leftist approach toward music as a tool of social and political dissent.

   The change in attitude and direction in Seeger's two articles exemplifies a larger trend followed by many American composers. Realizing that a revolution in American society was not at hand, native composers once again turned their attention to their role as composers, rather than agents of social change, and to their own responsibility for addressing the American audience. To gain recognition, to become a part of American life, they must write "American" music. Folksong—especially folksong in the Anglo-American tradition—proved to be a natural means to this end, for such music reflected the prevalent American ethnic background. Composers seemed to believe that folksong would appeal to the heritage of much of their audience, even if many listeners were not personally familiar with traditional music.

   Other causes can be noted for the popularity of folksong as an Americanist source. The interest in folk music and folklore was part of an ongoing idealization of the common man that had accompanied the leftward swing in the early 1930s and had been heightened by the Popular Front's increased Americanism after 1935.[5] Now, late in the decade, this idealization became connected more specifically with America's "unspoiled" countryside. The American West and its inhabitants, especially, held a fascination as being untainted and ruggedly "American."

A striking demonstration of the social nature of the "discovery" of folksong can be observed among former Collective members. As the foremost exponents of early and mid-1930s proletarianism, several soon became fervent advocates of folk music. Probably the most deeply affected were Charles Seeger, Earl Robinson, and Elie Siegmeister.

When Mike Gold's critical column appeared in the *Daily Worker* in January, 1936, Seeger already had disassociated himself from both the Party and the Composer's Collective; he also had acknowledged his interest in folk music. At least a generation older than most of his Collective colleagues, Seeger acquired his musical training at a time when American composers customarily emulated European music. Seeger's friendship with the Americanist author Van Wyck Brooks in the early years of this century first led him to realize that cultures worthy of study and artistic expression existed in the United States.[6] As early as 1913, he had included Anglo-American folksongs in a concert of world folk musics at the University of California at Berkeley. At the time, however, he regarded the songs as "dying survivals" and was unaware of any current American rural musical cultures.[7]

Seeger's real introduction to Anglo-American folksong came in 1931, when the painter Thomas Hart Benton asked him to participate in the dedication of Benton's murals at the New School for Social Research. The entertainment was folk music, and Benton—surprised that Seeger was unfamiliar with American traditional music—began lending him his recordings.[8] Then in 1932, Seeger and Henry Cowell were hired by Macmillan Publishers to edit John and Alan Lomax's *American Ballads and Folk Songs.*[9] Seeger's association with the Lomaxes and his knowledge of George Pullen Jackson's *White Spirituals*[10] were important forces in his changing compositional/musicological outlook. Another influence was Michael Gold. Still another was Aunt Molly Jackson.

Aunt Molly, a Harlan County Kentuckian, was a ballad singer turned labor agitator. While striking with the miners of her native state, she began to alter the text of traditional songs to fit unionization and protest. She then came to New York and became active in leftist circles. Seeger himself recalled her adaptation of "Lay the Lily Low" to "Join the C.I.O.," resulting in what he called a "folk-popular" style.[11] The naturalness and success of Aunt Molly's fusion of old songs with contemporary messages convinced Seeger of both the inherent and social value of folk music. When Aunt Molly attended a meeting of the Collective in 1933, Seeger told her: "You are on the right track; we here are not."[12]

In 1935, Seeger gathered folk material in North Carolina while heading a folksong collecting project sponsored by the Special Skills Division of the federal government's Resettlement Administration. Thereafter, he was concerned with folk music as a musicologist, an editor, and as an administrator. In the last capacity he was responsible, among other things, for sending such former Collective members as Herbert Haufrecht into the field.[13] In 1938, Seeger became Assistant to the Director of the WPA Music Project and, with Writers' Project Chairman Benjamin A. Botkin, organized a massive research and recording campaign centered on American folk music.[14] The results of his undertaking are now part of the Archive of American Folk Song at the Library of Congress.[15]

By the mid-1930s others in Charles Seeger's family were beginning to be aware of folksong as well. In 1935, Pete Seeger, then sixteen years old, accompanied his father to a fiddle contest in Ashville, North Carolina.[16] The younger Seeger has since written that he saw his first five-string banjo during the trip, and that it was love at first sight.[17] Somewhat later, Charles Seeger's wife Ruth Crawford Seeger (1901–53), a composer in her own right, took an interest in folk music. She edited both her own folksong collections, such as *American Folk Songs for Children* (1948), and those of associates, such as the Lomaxes' *Our Singing Country* (1941).

Earl Robinson has been associated less with folklorist activities than with the performance of folksong and the composition of new music incorporating folk styles.[18] Robinson, a leftist stalwart even after the dissolution of the Composers' Collective, quite literally became the Party's troubadour of the working class. In the late 1930s, he frequently was pictured with his guitar on the arts page of the *Daily Worker*, sometimes leading groups of singing laborers.[19] An early example of his folk-based compositional style was "Joe Hill," a short strophic song to words by Alfred Hayes.[20] Of Robinson's many works using American subjects, by far the most famous from the 1930s is the "Ballad for Americans," originally composed for the Federal Theatre Project's production *Sing for Your Supper* (1939).[21] A cantata for baritone and chorus, the text by John Latouche traces highlights of American history, featuring the American Revolution and Abraham Lincoln's role during the Civil War. The "Ballad," harmonically consonant and tonal and with melodic lines indebted to folksong, celebrates America and the diversity of its people. Its first of many performances by the black leftist singer Paul Robeson was broadcast by CBS radio in 1939. It received a tumultuous response and started a long association, particularly among leftists, between Robeson and Robinson's "Ballad."[22] The "Ballad" was chosen to launch the 1940 Republican National Convention, although Robeson did not perform it there.[23]

All facets of Elie Siegmeister's career — as an editor, as a writer, as a performer, and as a composer — have been deeply affected by folk music. Siegmeister, like Seeger, also was influenced by Aunt Molly Jackson at a critical point in his creative life. While conducting a concert of new American music "for the people" in the mid-1930s, Siegmeister recalls that a sturdy and fearless-looking woman arose from the audience to demand "have you ever heard the music *of* the people?"[24] It was Aunt Molly, who thereafter proceeded to stop the show with her own ballad singing.

"I liked Aunt Molly and her music," Siegmeister has written.

> It seemed fresh and alive. When Lawrence Gellert invited me shortly afterwards to make notations of his collection of Negro folk music from the Deep South, I found that enjoyable, too. Charles Seeger and Henry Cowell played me more recordings of native American stuff at the New School (where I taught for a time) and roused my curiosity still more.[25]

Gellert's collection was the aforementioned *Negro Songs of Protest* (1936), for which Siegmeister made piano/vocal arrangements. In addition, Siegmeister was impressed by Carl Sandburg's *The American Songbag*, the first anthology of arranged folksongs of which he was aware.[26]

Siegmeister's sociopolitical outlook contributed strongly to his compositional stance. Like several other Collective members, his direct connection with Party activities had lessened by 1940, but his concern with the place of American art music in society had not. Early in his development as a musician, Siegmeister formulated an artistic philosophy that remains with him today.

> Art with a capital A is a menace; music is one of the elements of a normal American existence, not apart from it.[27]

Thus the phases of his compositional and literary output from the early to late 1930s were but different expressions of both his musical Americanism and his wider concern for American society. In the early and mid-1930s, his Collective songs and Marxist *Music and Society* reflected greater emphasis upon social problems.[28] By the late 1930s, his work in American folksong and compositions such as *American Holiday* exemplified a heightened musical Americanism. The two motivations of Americanism and social concern, as with Seeger, were rarely separate in this period.

Reflecting on the mid-1930s, Siegmeister has written:

> In the state of serious music in American about 1935 – that of a rather abstruse, over-dissonant, and intellectualized art – contact with the simple, human, quality of our folk traditon was a healthy, stimulating factor.[29]

Siegmeister could have been thinking of his own *Strange Funeral in Braddock,* a solo cantata to a text by Michael Gold, when he wrote this assessment.[30] The stylistic contrast between this dissonant, metrically-complex piece and his later works based on the folk genre could hardly be greater.

Siegmeister, a proud "Composer in Brooklyn," did everything he could to further his contact with rural American music in the late 1930s. For example, he founded the American Ballad Singers, a group of professional musicians specializing in folksong performance.[31] As the conductor and arranger for the Singers, Siegmeister traveled around the country for nearly four years. While on tour, people often came backstage after performances to give Siegmeister new songs or additional versions of ones the group had sung. In this way, Siegmeister was able to add to his growing collection, begun by setting down Aunt Molly's ballads. Many of Siegmeister's contributions to *A Treasury of American Song,* edited in collaboration with Olin Downes, were gathered in this manner.[32]

Siegmeister's experiences as conductor-collector with the Ballad Singers solidified his compositional outlook on folk music. He believed that the amalgamation of national influences in folksong gave a true picture of America's heritage.

> This real American folk music is as composite in origin as America itself. Its roots are English, Irish, Scotch, Negro, German, French, Spanish, and Dutch. Because of the predominance of British stock and of the English language, however, the British strains first formed the pattern. By about the time of the Revolution, however, we find these strains taking on a characteristic native flavor, and the humor, the strength, the feeling, and the vigor of the American temperament assert themselves in a distinctly American music.[33]

Like Seeger and other leftists, Siegmeister viewed folk music as at once "American" and representative of the universal common man.

> This folk music, I believe, is the living link between creative art and the people. I should like to see more and more Americans turning to it – although, as a matter of a fact, it has never waned. . . . I do not suggest that an interest in our folk music should replace the classics – far from it. The two types can develop together; indeed, they should, if America is to attain the full musical development of which she is capable.[34]

Finally, Siegmeister saw folk music as a means of bringing the American composer closer to his audience–both the mass audience of universal humanity and the specifically American portion of that audience.

> A closer acquaintance with our own folk music has many advantages, for it is a democratic music, one that reflects our tradition of freedom. It encourages the feeling that music is close to our common life; a means of expressing universal humanity through American accents. It brings the composer much closer to the people – that mass of the people for whom, after all, he must write. . . . I should like to see our composers study [folk song] as a means of learning what kind of music our people want to hear. Americans want American music![35]

Thus viewed, folksong was the obvious focus for Siegmeister's personal philosophy on the composition of American art music.

A natural outgrowth of Siegmeister's growing involvement with folk music in this period was the composition of a series of "American Legends" for performance by the American Ballad Singers. He has described them as songs "in a folk style to celebrate national heroes [such as Johnny Appleseed] who, for some odd reason, have never been included in the literature of folk-songs."[36] *American Legends* are but early examples of Siegmeister's long compositional concern with folksong. By 1944, he wrote approvingly of the impact of American traditional music on his own works.

> I know that my contact with folk music has influenced my composing style, and it is bound to do the same for others. I feel my music is clearer, more American, more easily understandable than before.[37]

Of his many other compositions affected in some way by folk music, two orchestral works similar in format and conception are *Ozark Set* (1943) and *Western Suite* (1945). Each piece evokes an aura of a distinct geographical and cultural region of the United States. The two suites differ, however, in their actual relationship to folksong. *Western Suite* incorporates authentic folk tunes, in this case cowboy songs, in each of its five movements. *Ozark Set*, on the other hand, is based on themes rooted in folk style but newly composed by Siegmeister.[38] Therefore, the suites illustrate the influence of folksong at two different levels of the composer's musical language.

While not all former Collective members were as deeply influenced as Siegmeister, Robinson, and Seeger, several have revealed more than a passing interest in folksong. Herbert Haufrecht, as previously mentioned, was introduced to rural American music when he began collecting songs as part of Seeger's Resettlement Administration project. His own compositions soon showed the influence of folksong, as in his *Square Set for String Orchestra* (1941).[39]   Haufrecht also has edited two folksong collections — *Folk Sing — A Handbook for Pickers and Singers* (1959) and *Treasury of Folk Songs* (1964) — and initiated the annual Folk Festival of the Catskills in 1940.[40]

Wallingford Riegger's compositions reveal no connection with folk music, although he edited and arranged folksongs, often under assumed names.[41]   Sidney Robertson Cowell collected folk material in the South in the late 1930s, and both she and her husband wrote about southern traditional music in the early 1940s.[42]   Henry Cowell's works frequently have incorporated American folksong, as in his *Tales of Our Countryside* (1940), or utilized themes composed in a folk style, as in *Old American Country Set* (1937).   Cowell's use of American folk music, however, seems more a reflection of his lifelong interest in many national musics than the specific result of the 1930s trend.

In the late 1930s, the popularity of folksong began to move from a coterie of leftist followers to American urban audiences and musicians in general.   Although as Siegmeister has recalled, anyone who was involved with folksong in those days was automatically considered a Communist by some,[43] folk music began to appear in politically neutral forums such as radio broadcasting and Broadway.   Commerical recordings of folksingers, which had begun to be made in the 1920s, had sold well in the South and other regional strongholds of traditional music.   But radio broadcasting of folk music on a national scale, either live or recorded, did not become significant until the late 1930s.[44]

Several folksingers who are now well-known appeared regularly on the CBS "American School of the Air — Folk-Music of America" radio series initiated in 1939.   Aunt Molly Jackson, Leadbelly, and Woody Guthrie all performed on these programs, which often were hosted by the folklorist Alan Lomax.[45]   Woody Guthrie almost had a show of his own over NBC but, as he has told it, found the air in Rockefeller Center's Rainbow Room too rarified.[46]   Burl Ives, billed as a "singer and storyteller," was the star of "Back Where I Come From" on CBS from 1940 through 1944.   Many of these personalities and others were featured on additional regular radio programs not specifically centered on music, such as Burgess Meredith's inspirational series "The Pursuit of Happiness."[47]

While *The Cradle Will Rock* stirred controversy in 1937 and 1938, several musical theatre productions reflected a growing fascination with rural American culture in the early 1940s.   Although not based on actual folksongs, Rodgers and Hammerstein's classic *Oklahoma!*, which opened with enormous success in 1943, indicated that nostalgia for the simple country life was no longer limited to the leftist intelligentsia. Folksong literally arrived on Broadway in 1944 with *Sing Out Sweet Land!*, whose music was a compilation of folksong and newly-composed pieces in a folk style by Elie Siegmeister.[48] Burl Ives's appearance in this show launched his career as a star performer.

As American audiences became more aware of folksong through su   pop   arizations, American composers in the cultivated tradition —   to apolitical — did so as well. The increased availability of   elped to spread a folk consciousness. Similar to the earlier   Farwell and Cadman, folklorist research preceded composers'   to native sources. Virgil Thomson summarized the effects of   scholarship upon American art music in the 1930s when he   nat this work "opened up a gold mine of nostalgic feelings   ies" to composers of his generation.[49]

'20, the study of southern American folklore had amassed a   literature, but little of the actual music was published.   lk music research began in the early years of this century,   path similar to that pioneered by Francis James Child, a   British folksong. Like the famous Child ballad anthologies,   rican collections generally contained only the poetry. John   itial edition of American cowboy songs in 1910 was among the   include both music and texts.[50] The first extensive scholarly   nglo-American folksong was done by the Englishman Cecil   eginning with *American-English Folk-Songs* in 1918, Sharp produced a stream of collections appearing throughout the 1920s.[51] Sidney Robertson Cowell noted that most were published in Sharp's native England, however, and thus were slow to become known in America.[52]

American composers who have acknowledged the influence of folksong studies upon their composition in the 1930s and 1940s are less likely to cite Sharp's than those by contemporary Americans. Siegmeister, as previously mentioned, recalled that his first acquaintance with folksong came through Carl Sandburg's *The American Songbag* (1927). Sandburg's collection was not a scholarly one, but a performing edition of folk music arranged and harmonized in a variety of styles by several American composers including Arthur Farwell and Leo Sowerby. Shortly after the publication of *The Songbag*, Robert Simon reviewed it in *Modern Music*, noting its importance as "source material."[53] Roy Harris drew themes for his *Folksong Symphony* (1940) from *The Songbag*, as well as from the Lomax collections of cowboy songs.[54] In his autobiography, Virgil Thomson acknowledged an indebtedness to both George Pullen Jackson and John Lomax in the composition of his score for Pare Lorentz's documentary film *The River* (1937).[55] Few composers interested in folk music could have been unaware of the collecting and editing efforts of the Lomaxes, Cowells and Seegers. The three families individually and jointly produced and inspired a voluminous amount of folksong scholarship in these years.

Although American composers' use of Anglo-American folksong in art music peaked in the late 1930s and 1940s, such incorporation was not new to American music. At least two composers of the generation maturing in the 1920s and early 1930s had shown an interest in traditional music before it became a trend. Douglas Moore's early compositions revealed both his Americanism and his interest in folk music. Not a contributor to the jazz-based art music of the 1920s, Moore quoted both spirituals and hymn tunes in the *Pageant of P. T. Barnum* (1924), and employed folk melodies in his *Overture on an American Tune* (1931).[56] Virgil Thomson's *Symphony on a Hymn Tune* (1928) was the earliest major work by a composer of that generation to exhibit the newer type of compositional Americanism. Thomson's *Symphony* was prophetic. Straightforward in its treatment of hymn and folk materials, the consonant, tonal language forecast the simplified approach common among Americanist works ten or fifteen years later.[57] Thomson, however, was not an Americanist in the sense of Seeger, Siegmeister, and others in this period. Rather, like Ives, he drew upon vernacular sources as an outgrowth of his familiarity with them since childhood.[58]

The folk-based music of one American composer from an earlier generation might have served as a model had it been better known. John Powell (1882–1963), who first achieved recognition as a pianist both at home and abroad, was more inclined toward composition. Although trained in Vienna, Powell never lost touch with his Appalachian roots nor the desire to portray them in his own pieces. As Chase has pointed out, Powell is one of America's few authentic regional composers, for much of his music was devoted to the traditional songs of his native Virginia.[59] In addition to being a composer, Powell was a collector and an organizer in behalf of folk music. He initiated the Virginia State Choral Festival and helped found the annual White Top Mountain Folk Festival.

One of Powell's first major works was *Rhapsodie Negre* (1917), a piece for piano and orchestra inspired by Joseph Conrad's *Heart of Darkness* and based on Afro-American musical idioms. Later compositions more frequently emphasized Anglo-American elements, such as *Natchez on the Hill* (1931) and *A Set of Three* (1935), both incorporating folk dance or folksong materials.[60] Powell's *tour de force* was the *Symphony in A*, commissioned by the National Federation of Music Clubs in 1932 but not premiered until 1947. Each of the *Symphony's*

ovements was founded on a folk music tradition native to
Virginia.[61] Charles Seeger maintained that Powell, of all American composers of art music, had the truest grasp of Anglo-American folksong.[62]

In 1932, Randall Thompson pointed to the use of jazz and Negro
spirituals as principal manifestations of the nationalist trend in the recent
American musical past. He wrote that "the actual quotation of folksong
is relatively rare; . . . the literal quotation of hymns is rarer still."[63] What
was rare in 1932, according to Thompson, became almost commonplace
by the end of the decade and the early 1940s. It seems as if nearly every
composer born between 1895 and 1910 produced at least one piece
drawing on American traditional sources. If leftist proletarianism had
not touched all American composers in the early and mid-1930s, the folk
consciousness of the late 1930s and 1940s certainly came close.

One group of commissions grew directly out of folksong's
popularity on radio. The CBS Music Library, in conjunction with the
"American School of the Air—Folk-Music of America" programs
mentioned above, sponsored a series of new works by American
composers. Each week from October 24, 1939 to April 2, 1940, a
different composer's piece was premiered on radio. The commission
requirements specified that the compositions be based on or be
arrangements of American folksongs, and the composers were encouraged
to make use of the Archive of American Folk Song at the Library of
Congress.[64] All of the pieces were designed for small orchestra, but the
results were stylistically various. Among the composers commissioned
were Roy Harris, who arranged cowboy songs; Aaron Copland, who
contributed a setting of "John Henry"; Jerome Moross, who wrote *A
Ramble on a Hobo Tune;* and Ruth Crawford Seeger, who composed
Rissolty, Rossolty for ten winds, strings, and percussion.[65]

The American West had a particular mystique for American
composers in this period. Pieces portraying western life, often quoting
cowboy tunes, were especially popular. Charles Ives's "Charlie
Rutledge" (1920?), based on a song from Lomax's collection,[66] became
familiar to some composers after its publication by Cos Cob Press in
1932 and subsequent performance at the first Yaddo Festival later that
year.[67] Ives's song was probably less influential upon stylistic treatment
of cowboy material than Virgil Thomson's score to the federally-funded
film *The Plow That Broke the Plains* (1936), the first large work by a
major American composer to incorporate cowboy songs.[68] In fact,
Thomson credits himself with giving the idea of such treatment of
American material to Copland, whose ballets *Billy the Kid* (1938) and
Rodeo (1942) also drew on music from the West. *The Plow, Billy the*

Kid, and Siegmeister's previously-mentioned *Western Suite* all quote versions of the cowboy tune "I Ride an Old Paint."[69]

Another composer who ventured musically across the Mississippi was Morton Gould.   His *Cowboy Rhapsody* (1940) incorporated a succession of tunes, including "Home on the Range."   The second movement of Roy Harris's *Folksong Symphony* is devoted to the West, and musically is based upon three cowboy songs.   Finally, Ross Lee Finney made choral arrangements of cowboy tunes, including *Oh Bury Me Not on the Lone Prairie* and *Trail to Mexico* (1940).

Although the songs of the American West were among the most frequently used folk sources in the late 1930s and 1940s, they certainly were not alone.   Various types of traditional music from other regions made their way into American cultivated music.   For instance, several composers set groups of folksongs from differing traditions.   Paul Bowles arranged *12 American Folk Songs* while employed by the WPA Music Project of New York City.   These songs also were published by the WPA (1939?).[70]   Copland's *Old American Songs, Sets I and II* (1950, 1952), although dated somewhat later, are among the best known folksong settings for solo voice.   Elie Siegmeister, apart from his book-length collections of folk music for voice and piano, arranged *Eight American Folksongs* (1940) for chorus.   As with some cowboy tunes, certain melodies were employed repeatedly.   The New England ballad "Springfield Mountain," for example, achieved considerable exposure through its incorporation in Copland's *A Lincoln Portrait* (1942) and Bernard Hermann's film score *The Devil and Daniel Webster* (1942).

The burgeoning interest in traditional Americana soon prompted a similar awareness of other types of old American music.   Songs associated with past American wars were rediscovered.   Perhaps most popular was the Civil War tune "When Johnny Comes Marching Home." Often thought to be of folk origin, this piece by Patrick Gilmore became the basis for Roy Harris's overture *When Johnny Comes Marching Home* (1934) and Morton Gould's later and better-known *American Salute* (1943).   Gould also portrayed revolutionary America in his orchestral setting of *Yankee Doodle* (1945).

The works of other earlier American composers were also re-examined, with Stephen Foster and William Billings particular favorites.[71] Foster's "Camptown Races," masterfully interwoven with "Springfield Mountain," was quoted by Copland in *A Lincoln Portrait*.   Robert Russell Bennett chose Foster's songs as the basis for his *Early American Ballade* (1932), while Gould drew upon several Foster melodies in his *Foster Gallery* (1941).   Roy Harris incorporated "My Old Kentucky Home" into his *Kentucky Spring* (1948).

William Schuman used the music of William Billings to great advantage in his *William Billings Overture* (1944). Billings's works also formed the basis for Schuman's later *New England Triptych* (1956) and *Chester* (1957). Beginning in 1942, Henry Cowell composed a series of *Hymn and Fuguing Tunes* based on Billings's melodies for various performing groups, an attempt by Cowell to update an older American compositional style.[72] Ross Lee Finney's *Hymn, Fuguing, and Holiday* (1945) was similarly conceived. Additionally, Siegmeister arranged a choral series, *Songs of Early America* (1940), which included settings of Billings's music.

The foregoing list of Americanist works notes only newly-composed music which actually incorporates preexistent melodic material. At least two more types of Americanist music deserve mention, if not enumeration: pieces whose themes are newly-written in a folk style, and programmatic works based on American subject matter or evoking American history or scenery. Lists of these categories would be enormous. Yet it is important to note that a particular kind of idea prevailed in such Americanist works, just as a specific kind of American musical material — namely Anglo-American folksong — dominated the previously-discussed class of compositional Americanism. If an American personality was selected, the most commonly chosen was Abraham Lincoln, followed in close order by Walt Whitman and Thomas Jefferson. The popularity of these figures in a United States at war during the 1940s will be discussed below. If a geographical area was the inspiration, rural America predominated. Again the West was popular (Siegmeister's *Prairie Legend*, 1945; Gardner Read's *The Plains*, 1940; Ernst Bacon's *A Tree on the Plains*, 1942), although other regions also were portrayed (Moore's *Down East Suite*, 1945; Gould's *Hillbilly*, 1935). Randall Thompson's choral work *Americana*, based on selections from the *American Mercury*, represents a general nostalgia for America's rural and small-town past. In essence, an attempt to be noncontroversial, to choose material of which every American could approve, pervaded all styles of musical Americanism in this period.

In retrospect, it is remarkable to discover the breadth of interest in traditional Americana during the 1930s and 1940s. Additional evidence of that interest, if the wealth of composition indebted to folksong was not enough, is the variety of writers who commented on folk music at this time. For instance, Otto Luening, a composer one would not associate readily with folklorism, grew excited about the traditional music he found in Arizona.

That here is a musical life of considerable importance in Arizona may surprise many. Let it be said, then, at the outset, that if the virile activity of the Southwest were universal in America our national scene would be greatly enriched.[73]

The New York critic Paul Rosenfeld, whose writings usually featured new music, was another who made his way to the country in the late 1930s. Rosenfeld related his impressions of a gathering of folk musicians in southwestern Virginia. For Rosenfeld, this was more than a mere get-together; the performers and their music had a powerful effect upon him.

It was the sense first of the quality of a life low-down by the soil, gritty with it, yet anything but primitive; adjusted to be sure to conditions of cold and discomfort; narrow, dour, without sensuousness, paroxysmic rather than passionate; possessed nonetheless of dignity, dominating animal existence, capable of religion, laughter, poetry. Pictures of soil in gaunt farmyards, beneath whitewashed little homesteads stilted on hillsides again and again invaded my mind.[74]

Although Rosenfeld's writing is characteristically elaborate and seems somewhat patronizing by present standards, one can sense that the meaning of his experience went far beyond the purely musical. This passage exemplifies the nostalgia for the "simple life" common in the late 1930s.

Not everyone was favorably disposed toward folksong nor its use by American composers of art music. As in previous periods of compositional Americanism, there was controversy about the necessity of establishing an American music and the advisability of doing so with folksong. In 1939, Elliott Carter noted the wealth of discussion on the subject of "American" music: "'The American composer should—' Here we are back in the middle of the fight with the exponents of American music talking through their hats."[75] Carter made specific mention of a discussion currently occurring in *The New York Times*, where the "American" quality of Samuel Barber's *Essay for Orchestra*—recently premiered by Toscanini—was being argued heatedly. Ashley Pettis called the work irrelevant to American life; Gian-Carlo Menotti accused Pettis of being passé.[76] If the incident reveals a division in the American compositional community, it also indicates the emotional strength with which the sides maintained their convictions.

Roger Sessions, never a compositional Americanist, believed that the tendency to reflect "the American scene" was a trend toward cultural isolationism.[77] He thought that this attitude forced people to set American music against European music, and Sessions, for one, felt that such a comparison was meaningless. Despite his personal admiration for folksong, Paul Rosenfeld wrote critical "Variations" on Seeger's "Grass

Roots." Rather than seek compositional origins outside oneself as Seeger proposed, Rosenfeld suggested that the American composer "be true to his soul, for there in his soul lie his evergreening grass roots and the source of his utility to men."[78] Somewhat later, Virgil Thomson affirmed Rosenfeld's opinions. Although Thomson himself partook of American vernacular materials, he did so because they were a part of his background. He disapproved of a self-conscious use of native materials in an effort to Americanize art music.

> The way to write American music is simple. All you have to do is to be an American and then write any kind of music you wish. There is a precedent and model here for all the kinds. And any Americanism worth bothering about is everybody's property anyway. Leave it in the unconscious; let nature speak.[79]

In a sense, all of these opinions were correct as far as they went. Surely no one could tell another how to compose. Americanism did, rightly or wrongly, foster a favoritism of American music. No one could argue with the admonition that American composers should be true to themselves. However, each viewpoint omitted an important fact, one admittedly easier to recognize in retrospect: in the context of American musical history, the compositional interest in folksong was but another coming to grips with a segment of American vernacular music and American vernacular life. Perhaps Roy Harris made the most candid appraisal of the folksong fad:

> America will have many folksong vendors in the next few years. Some city boys may take a short motor trip through the land and return to write the Song of the Prairies—others will be folksong authorities after reading in a public library for a few weeks. . . .
> But all this mushrooming exploitation of folksong will neither greatly aid nor hinder it. After the era has run itself out there will remain those composers who have been deeply influenced by the finest, clearest, strongest feelings of our best songs.[80]

Certainly by 1945, native folk music had been brought from relative isolation to assimilation in the larger sphere of American musical culture.

VII

Musical Americanism and the WPA

You wouldn't know a Depression was going
on.   Except that people were complaining
they didn't have any jobs.   You could get
the most wonderful kind of help for a
pittance.   People would work for next to
nothing.

Dr. David J. Rossman,
from Studs Terkel, *Hard Times*

Unemployment

Among the repercussions felt from the Stock Market Crash on October
24, 1929, none was more devastating to the American people than
unemployment. In March 1929, 2,860,000 Americans were out of work,
an economic danger signal that generally went unheeded.[1] After the
Crash, the number of jobless mounted rapidly: 4,340,000 in 1930,
8,020,000 in 1931, and 12,060,000 in 1932.[2] Estimates of those without
jobs at the bottom of the Depression in March, 1933, range from
13,300,000 to a staggering 17,920,000 out of a labor force of 51,000,000.[3]
    Statistics provide some focus on the early 1930s, but they reveal
only a part of the story. At first, unemployment merely caused cutting
back on extras for most people; but when continued over weeks and then
months, it meant doing without adequate clothing and heat, stretching
credit with the neighborhood grocer, pawning personal belongings, and
often the dislocating blow of losing a home. Eviction notices dissolved
families and helped create a new class of American citizen, the drifter.
At least one million people took to a road going nowhere in the early
1930s, and more than a quarter of them were under twenty-one years of
age.[4] At its peak, unemployment directly touched one-third of American
workers, but it meant distress for many more.
    While the Depression made the poor poorer and put working men
out of work, no socioeconomic class was completely immune.   The

traditionally hard-pressed artist found it especially difficult to support himself by his talents, and among artists in general, musicians appear to have been the hardest hit. In his dissertation on the WPA Federal Music Project, Cornelius Canon cites two factors contributing to the joblessness of American musicians in the early 1930s. One was the general financial malaise of the Depression. The other resulted from technological advances in communications that had a direct impact upon certain segments of the music industry.[5]

The 1930s have sometimes been called the "golden age" of radio, but many musicians had good reason to view the expansion of this medium as a profound threat.[6] Radio eventually proved a good disseminator of art music and even provided some composers with commissions. Yet according to Canon, its popularity as inexpensive entertainment had already cut into sheet music and piano sales by 1929.[7] The trend intensified in the 1930s, severely reducing employment in those areas.

The job situation confronting movie house instrumentalists was even worse. With the advent of sound films in 1927, live music in theatres quickly became obsolete. One study revealed that sixty per cent of theatre musicians in Washington, D.C. were out of work by 1931, while other surveys showed a similar national trend. Canon has noted that fear over even greater unemployment due to technological innovations led the American Federation of Labor to create a Music Defense League, using a symbolic "musical robot" in a campaign against the "mechanization of music."[8]

Other music professions were inevitably hurt by the plummeting economy of the early 1930s. Private teachers lost their students and thus their regular incomes. Public school instructors found their jobs cut as tax revenues evaporated. Performances, except in well-established organizations, also were caught in the downward spiral until by 1934, one survey estimated that sixty per cent of all American musicians were unemployed.[9] Large cities were drastically affected. So dire was the situation in New York, where four-fifths of the American Federation of Musicians were unemployed, that Walter Damrosch created a Musicians Emergency Relief Fund.[10] For several years beginning in 1931, Damrosch enlisted well-known artists to perform benefit concerts, with proceeds distributed to the neediest musicians.

The Depression and the hardship it caused were unprecedented in American history. Thus no models existed for the problems or for their solutions. At first, the federal administration relied upon charity and locally-sponsored direct relief to care for the homeless and the hungry. As the number of needy grew alarmingly in 1930 and 1931, a few larger-scale measures were considered. One plan directed poverty-stricken families to chop wood for surplus restaurant food gleaned from the plates of satisfied customers.[11] Another involved providing meals in particularly poor rural areas for all school children more than ten per cent underweight. This undertaking foundered when, in many schools, nearly all of the children were discovered to be eligible.[12] Jobless World War I veterans gathered in Washington from across the nation to demand a "bonus" for their military service.[13] After two months of camping within sight of the Capitol, they were driven out by Army regulars. Haphazard and demeaning, these actions attest to the government's unpreparedness, both organizationally and psychologically, in coming to grips with the social problems caused by the Depression.

The economy did not reverse itself, as President Hoover had predicted continually, and unemployment did not lessen. In 1933, the new Roosevelt administration confronted a national crisis; rumors of revolution were in the air. The effectiveness and legality of many New Deal policies have been and will be argued for years. As one commentator noted, however, most Americans were heartened that "something was being done."[14] One important program led to federally-funded jobs.

From the beginning of the "Roosevelt era"[15] the President's advisors on employment urged work rather than direct relief, insisting that the self-esteem of the jobless could be recovered only if they earned their pay. President Roosevelt, himself a firm supporter of government relief, implemented work programs in 1931 while governor of New York, the first governor to do so.[16] Thus after some months of the interim Federal Emergency Relief Administration (FERA), the initial federal employment project — the Public Works Administration (PWA) — got underway in fall of 1933. The PWA, headed by Harold Ickes, proved a good long-range economic stimulus. Because it involved complex construction projects, however, benefits were slow in coming, resulting more from large purchases of building supplies than from workers' salaries. With winter approaching and unemployment still severe, more jobs were urgently needed. The Civil Works Administration (CWA), with allocations from PWA, was created to put as many unemployed as possible to work during the cold-weather months. Under CWA, the first art program, the Public Works of Art Project (PWAP), found a home.

PWAP was the fulfillment of months of lobbying by two persistent and influential artists, George Biddle and Edward (Ned) Bruce, the latter also a lawyer/businessman who headed the Project.[17] Although small, PWAP brought the concept of federal funding for the arts before the Roosevelt administration, where it did not go unnoticed. A music program was added to CWA and, with art, eventually became a model for much larger arts agencies established almost two years later.[18]   No better tribute could be given to the government's employment of artists than the following description of opening day at New York City CWA offices.   The witness was George Foster, historian of New Deal music operations.

> The writer had the opportunity to sit behind a table in the bare storeroom of a music publishing house . . . as the first musicians came to register for jobs.   That picture will never be forgotten.   There were long lines of men and women – despair written in every face.   There were men on the verge of suicide. There were women who had sold everything but themselves and who did not know where the next meal would come from.   The last meal had come some days ago.   There were old men who had given up hope of ever working again.   Make no mistake, these people were not the musicians who had never had steady jobs. There were men from the Festspielhaus at Bayreuth.   There were men from La Scala, Milan.   The Metropolitan Opera and every major symphony orchestra in the nation was represented in that miserable line.   There were teachers who had studied with Liszt.   There were singers who had come over with Diaghileff and Chaliapin.   There were bandsmen who had played with Sousa and Pryor.   There were composers whose songs are regularly represented on Carnegie Hall programs. Looking over that line of hungry, desperate people it was hard to realize that in that cold bare room was assembled as much musical talent and reputation as had ever been gathered in one room in New York City.[19]

Even so, the CWA and other trial agencies proved to be only stopgap measures.   By the end of the 1934, it was apparent that unemployment remained high and that only more comprehensive programs could fully accommodate America's jobless.   With lessons learned from CWA and other relief organizations, the enormous federal bureaucracy known as the Works Progress Administration – the WPA – was legislated into existence on May 6, 1935.

The WPA

> Every time I go over to Central Park, I walk into the Children's Zoo.   This was built during the Depression by WPA workers. . . .   And I cannot help remembering – look this came out of the Depression.   Because men were out of work, because they were given a way to earn money, good things were created.
>
> As for the WPA, a picture comes to mind of men leaning on shovels.   (Herman Shumlin and Harry Norgard, from Studs Terkel, *Hard Times.*)

If any agency has come to represent both the good and the bad of Roosevelt's New Deal administration, it is the WPA.   According to one writer, the

WPA was an astonishingly vital, vulnerable, many-faceted operation. It was more than just a New Deal device for the jobless. It was a major phenomenon – the symbol and principal engine of the New Deal social revolution.[20]

Yet the WPA is a ghost from the past barely mentioned today. For even in the present, those who remember the WPA tend to regard it either as the saviour of America's unemployed or the worst government boondoggle in the nation's history.

The sheer size and scope of the WPA were revolutionary. Its immediate intent in 1935 was to employ 3,500,000 people in local projects nationwide.[21]   Still, it was the underlying premise of the organization that was new to the United States, for the WPA acknowledged that not all Americans stood equal in the national economic structure. The responsibility for the country's destitute was assumed for the first time by the federal government, where it has remained ever since.

If the concept of the WPA was new, it was also simple. Its architect was Harry Hopkins, a social worker, former head of New York State's emergency relief program under then Governor Roosevelt, and a major force in the New Deal administration. Hopkins's plan called for the federal government to put large numbers of unemployed Americans to work on projects ranging from construction to poetry.

Humanitarian concern pervades Hopkins's own account of relief during the Depression, *Spending to Save.* "We have turned over the American board and seen how many people live like slugs beneath its plenty," he wrote.[22] To eliminate further waste of diverse skills, Hopkins insisted that personal talents and work be matched in the job programs wherever possible. Hopkins's stress on this issue resulted in an innovation in American cultural history, the WPA Arts Projects.

The Arts Projects, like the entire WPA, were first and foremost employment programs, not patrons for artists or an arts education plan for the masses. Yet Hopkins viewed the possible contributions of the Arts Projects, which included Art, Music, Theatre, Writers', and the Historical Records Survey, as at least equal to the more tangible achievements in the other WPA programs.

It is said that the profit of business lies in the last 8 percent of its volume. The profit of our social experience certainly lies in the hands of a very small minority. That WPA has been the vehicle for this group to pursue their work, not for the privileged few alone, as they have been able to do in the past, but for the public benefit, establishing in some ways a new base for American life, is a fact of which we can be very proud.[23]

The Arts Projects would further the "democratization of culture,"

Hopkins believed.[24]   They were not to supersede existing artistic organizations, but to supplement them by bringing the arts to Americans who, either because of finances or geography, previously had been isolated culturally.   In other words, the Arts Projects were to disseminate cultural activity on a nationwide scale.   Thus while the Arts Projects, like all WPA agencies, were initiated as relief measures, they soon became imbued with far greater import than mere "make work."   To the artists, they symbolized a potential for purpose and financial stability never before offered them in American history.

Many Americans, however, did not view the WPA with comparable idealism, and within the massive WPA organization, the most debated programs were undoubtedly the Arts Projects.   At a time when the country seemed on the brink of ruin, many may have felt that public money should not be used for such activities as mandolin orchestras, outdoor sculpture, or poetry.   Moreover, the Arts Projects quickly became caught up in political factionalism.[25]   As the Depression decade progressed, the WPA cultural wing heard mounting accusations of promoting radical activities and harboring communists. The political controversy surrounding the Projects eventually helped snuff out America's sole experiment in comprehensive funding for the arts.

There was surely some validity to the complaints of sociopolitical dissent among Arts Projects' employees. Begun in the midst of America's leftist era, the WPA cultural programs naturally drew from the intellectually and creatively gifted, who comprised one of the largest groups of American Marxist sympathizers at this time.   Jerre Mangione, former National Coordinating Editor of the Federal Writers' Project, even suggested that mounting political radicalism in the early 1930s spurred the very creation of the Arts Projects. Fearing revolution, the government provided a sop to the left's ideological supporters.[26]   In fact, the left-leaning of American intellectuals never threatened America's internal order; but opponents of federal job relief had little trouble supporting their charges that many WPA artists were Marxist sympathizers.

Although each of the Arts Projects stirred its share of political bickering, the Federal Theatre Project, especially in New York City, was notorious.   John Houseman, head of two Federal Theatre projects in New York City in the 1930s, recalled the openness of WPA theatre workers' radicalism in those days by citing a flyer circulated when cutbacks jeopardized work programs.   The mimeographed sheet, headed "F.D.R. Juggles W.P.A." instructed its reader to detach a card on which was printed "I want more information about the Young Communist

League." The return address was "Y.C.L., c/o W.P.A." at the New York Theatre Project's headquarters.[27]

Of equal if not greater concern to government officials were the actual productions of the New York City Federal Theatre. Through its innovative *Macbeth*, its socially and politically caustic *Living Newspaper* series, and particularly its presentation of Marc Blitzstein's leftist opera *The Cradle Will Rock*, the Federal Theatre of New York City incurred the wrath of WPA critics and helped bring down the entire national theatre program. The Federal Theatre Project was terminated in 1939, the first WPA cultural program to end. Its demise had introduced but left unresolved the touchy subject of the government's role in federally-funded arts programs.

While the other Arts Projects received their share of criticism, they were less controversial than Theatre and thus longer-lived. Like the entire WPA, the music project lasted eight years under two names. The Works Progress Administration Federal Music Project (FMP), headed by the Russian-born conductor Nikolai Sokoloff, spanned from 1935 to 1939 when it was superseded by the Work Projects Administration (also known as WPA) Music Program. The second WPA, like the original, was nationwide but on a reduced scale and with greater administrative and financial input at the local level.[28] The WPA Music Program, directed by Earl V. Moore and subsequently George Foster, dwindled in the early 1940s until, with the rest of the WPA, it came to a complete halt in 1943. By then, the war effort took precedence over national concerns and reduced unemployment, the original cause for the WPA.

The "democratization of culture" was a lofty goal. Like the proletarianism of those more left than liberal, it characterized the social upheaval of the entire Depression decade. Further typifying the 1930s was an artistic Americanism already apparent as the WPA got under way. With the WPA in 1935, artistic Americanism was given official sanction.

Music in the WPA

The workings and accomplishments of the Federal Music Project and the WPA Music Program comprise a vast subject.[29] WPA music agencies were initiated in forty-two states. Although in several instances the FMP incorporated local music programs begun with federal loans under FERA (see above, p. 157), the FMP sometimes was placed in an administrative vacuum, literally appearing overnight where few organized musical activities had existed. The plan was to spread a musical awareness throughout the country.

The purpose of the Federal Music Project is to establish high standards of musicianship and to educate the public to an appreciation of musical opportunities, as well as to rehabilitate and retrain musicians so as to enable them to become self-supporting.[30]

In accordance with its stated aims, the principal division of labor in all Federal Music Project and WPA Music Program units was between performance and education. Each project sponsored performing groups which gave regular concerts, either free or for one dollar or less. Teachers were employed for group instruction in all musical subjects including instrumental and voice training, teacher training, and music therapy.

By July of 1936, one year after its creation, the FMP employed 15,000 musicians. Over one-third (5,700) belonged to the various concert orchestras which formed the backbone of both the FMP and the WPA Music Program. The remaining workers were assigned to other performing ensembles or to educational and administrative units.[31] Federal Project Number One, the bureaucratic heading of the Arts Projects, originally was to hire ninety per cent of its employees from the relief registers. This quota eventually was reduced to seventy-five per cent, allowing for some selectivity in leadership posts and, in music, selected professionals in key performance positions.[32] All FMP and WPA Music Program performers underwent auditions before assignment, and musically unqualified applicants were placed in other music units or shifted to other WPA projects.

While the goal of the present study is to show how the WPA music projects fostered musical Americanism, outlining a single local agency's activities yields some conception of the scope and structure of the national undertaking. The Federal Music Project of New York City is not completely representative due to its large size and ambitious programming. Yet some variation of the New York Project was going on concurrently in nearly every state, city and county across the country—impressive musical efforts indeed.

In May, 1937, the FMP of New York City filed the following report of its administrative structure: Chalmers Clifton, Director of the Project; George Crandall, Manager of Unit 1, Concert Division; Paul Haggerty, Manager of Unit 2, Chamber and Grand Opera; and Ashley Pettis, Manager of Unit 3, Social Music Education.[33] The Concert Division employed a total of 646 persons including twelve conductors, 558 performers, two tuners, and various support personnel. The Chamber and Grand Opera Division was comprised of 176, of which 72 were singers, 18 dancers, 39 stage hands, and the remaining in other technical positions. The Social Music Education Division employed 596, with 324 teachers, 123 concert artists, and others filling such posts as librarians or secretaries. Additionally, a business department consisted of 273 people. In all, 1,691 persons were employed by New York City's FMP in that particular month.

The types of presentations offered by the FMP of New York City, characteristic of all FMP agencies, ranged from solo performances for the indigent at welfare houses and in relief lines to full-scale symphony concerts and opera productions. Six WPA orchestras were active in New York City in May, 1937. The largest (93 members) was the Federal Symphony Orchestra, which gave weekly concerts to a total monthly attendance of 2,718.[34] The WPA's WNYC radio Concert Orchestra (27 members) made eighteen broadcasts during that same time. In addition to the orchestras, the FMP Concert Division included four concert bands, four dance orchestras, and eight chamber music ensembles of which three were designated "hospital units." Also in May, 1937, the Opera Division gave ten performances of a dual bill of Pergolesi's *La Serva Padrona* and the premiere of Frederic Hart's *The Romance of the Robot* to audiences totaling 4,388. With the closing of this production on May 25, opera workers began preparations for a June 22 opening of Offenbach's *The Tales of Hoffmann*. A sum of 288 performances, of which only 23 charged admission, was given by groups from all divisions to audiences numbering 132, 271.

The principal work of the Social Music Education Division was the group teaching of musical subjects at neighborhood locations throughout New York City. In this capacity, the FMP sponsored 13,063 class sessions at 123 designated music centers in May, 1937. Furthermore, this division trained musicians who had never taught and assisted foreign-born teachers with language or similar adjustment difficulties. While instruction and re-training were uppermost, other activities also were included in the education section. A recital bureau made performance arrangements for soloists "who could not be used in the division in any other way."[35] Other Education Division workers helped to establish community performing groups, such as youth bands and choruses, at local centers. Also, eight employees comprised a research department that gathered information about FMP teaching practices and assembled material on musical subjects for various FMP units. For instance, the researchers recently had compiled a bibliography of late Baroque-early Classical instrumental music as a teaching aid for education employees. Finally, the FMP Social Music Education Division of New York City created the first Composers' Forum-Laboratory, a public workshop for young composers which will be discussed subsequently.

Earlier in 1937, the FMP of New York City announced the opening of its Theatre of Music on West 54th Street.[36] Previously the Gallo, the Theatre became the headquarters of the New York City Project administration as well as the location for Project concerts and operatic productions.   Elsewhere around the City similar centers on a smaller scale, such as the Brooklyn Community Center, the Harlem Music-Art Center, and the Manhatten Children's Center, were founded in the hope of establishing neighboring roots for the Project.

Another step toward community involvement was the creation of a sponsors' bureau. All WPA agencies received federal orders in January, 1936 to recruit local sponsors for support of their programs.[37] The New York FMP enlisted volunteers to help publicize and promote Project activities and to supply information about the musical needs of individual neighborhoods. FMP sponsors also booked halls and located equipment for Project events and were allowed to share whatever profits accrued.[38] With the reduction of program funds under the WPA Music Program beginning in 1940, the sponsors' role was greatly enlarged.[39]

At first the national FMP received no support from the American Federation of Musicians, which feared that competition at budget prices would endanger existing musical institutions. FMP salaries were also a concern, for pay levels, if not munificent, were usually comparable to those of local private groups. However, as the FMP made known its intention to attract new listeners and as it provided work for unemployed AFM members, the Federation acknowledged and supported Project activities.

One measure of the acceptance of the New York FMP was the amount of publicity it generated. According to the Project's detailed data, eighty columns of material pertaining to the FMP appeared in New York papers in May, 1937 alone, with the majority of items carried by *The New York Times.*[40]   Notices also were found regularly in such diverse publications as the *Daily Worker* and the *Jewish Journal*, as well as standard city and neighborhood papers. Such statistics indicate that the FMP of New York quickly had made itself a recognized cultural force in a city rich in competing musical organizations. The FMP's success is particularly notable in light of its rather unorthodox programming.

A statement of purpose found in the New York City FMP *Monthly Report* for May, 1937 exemplifies the aims of the entire Project and reflects Hopkins's idealistic goal of national musical enlightenment.

> The Federal Music Project is not run in a haphazard manner. Its aim is not merely to present a series of free concerts and concerts at nominal prices and to provide work for unemployed musicans.   Beyond this is the thought that in educating the general public to an appreciation of the best in music, it will bring

about a heightening of the general cultural level. There is no doubt, also, that music helps many to maintain their morale, especially in depressing times. It pays the highest dividends in happiness, contentment and inspiration.[41]

Given the historical American tendency to consider "the best in music" to be works by well-known late eighteenth- and nineteenth-century European composers, it is noteworthy that many relatively unusual works found prominent places in FMP repertories. It seems that the FMP, released from financial dependence upon private sources, was free to be adventuresome, offering programs in counterpoise to those of existing organizations. For instance, the operatic choices of the New York City FMP for May, 1937 – Pergolesi's *La Serva Padrona* and Hart's *The Romance of the Robot* – were hardly standard fare at the Metropolitan Opera. Nor was it unusual to find works by Henry Hadley and Heinrich Biber[42] or Ernest Bloch and A.E.M. Grétry[43] gracing the same WPA programs. Specialized groups also added variety. Lehman Engel's Madrigal Singers, an FMP ensemble which achieved considerable acclaim in the late 1930s, unearthed and performed early music then little-known even to regular New York audiences.[44]

Furthermore, an examination of programs of the New York FMP reveals a consistently high number of American works. Included in the May, 1937 report of the New York City FMP was a catalogue of twenty-six American scores performed by FMP orchestras or chamber groups during that month. Music by John Knowles Paine and Charles Griffes was played as were pieces by younger composers such as David Diamond.[45] The focus on Americana was further emphasized by a seven-day Festival of American Music held at the Theatre of Music in observance of National Music Week (May 2 through May 8).[46] Early American popular and folk music as well as art music were performed. A panoramic view of American musical culture resulted from these nightly concerts, which featured many performing units from the WPA.

The regular programming of American music was not limited to the New York Project nor was it accidental. Musical Americanism, in the sense of a conscious favoritism toward performance of native works, was an FMP strategy formulated and articulated at the national level.

American composers have generally had so little chance to bring their music before the American public that the Federal Music Project has made provision to secure a hearing for them. Many composers have already had their compositions performed. Such a composition may have such success in St. Paul, for example, as to procure its performance in Boston, New York and Los Angeles. Some American composers who are better known to European audiences than at home have found in these new Federal orchestras the means of attaining audiences for the first time.[47]

Both Earl Moore and George Foster continued the WPA strategy under the Music Program beginning in 1940. Foster, however, was quick to point out that the partiality toward American works was not a specific rule but a general understanding, lest it be interpreted as a government imposition upon artistic freedom.

> From the beginning of the Federal Music Project, one of the objectives of the program had been to provide encouragement to American composers by the performance of their works.   While Dr. Sokoloff was careful to avoid any chauvinistic policies requiring the inclusion of any specified number of compositions on a program, it was understood by all State Directors of the Federal Music Project that they should be liberal in their programming of American works.   Practically all units of the Federal Music Project and WPA Music Program were consistent in regularly performing a large number of American works.[48]

Whether by formula or agreement, the performance of American works became standard WPA procedure for all music agencies.

So proud was the FMP of its musical Americanist efforts that it compiled lists of all American pieces played by WPA units. Shortly after its creation, the FMP began work on a nationwide *Index of American Composers*, a catalogue of musical facts gathered under four headings:

> 1) An alphabetical list of composers with notes and dates on performance, the performing units, conductors, and soloists.
> 2) An alphabetical list of compositions by form.
> 3) Program notes, excerpts from reviews by distinguished critics.
> 4) "Americana" noting derivatives of folk tune, legend, or landscape where these were ascertained accurately.[49]

The *Index* was never completed, for its funding was discontinued in 1940. Today it remains unpublished and essentially unused in its original file boxes at the Library of Congress. Yet despite the incomplete data, misspellings, and other inaccuracies, the *Index of American Composers* is a valuable resource. Among other information, it contains the only central record of American music performed, and in many cases premiered, by WPA units.

The *Index* reveals that as of March, 1940, more than 8,000 works by some 2,400 American composers had been performed by the FMP.[50] Not surprisingly, the most frequently played were older composers like Daniel Gregory Mason and Henry Hadley, or those who wrote popular or semi-popular music such as Victor Herbert, John Philip Sousa, Rudolph Friml, and George Gershwin.[51] Apparently not all FMP agencies were as bold as that in New York City. Although certainly an indication of tastes, these choices should be viewed in light of the overwhelmingly large number of "concert" orchestras, rather than full-scale "symphony" orchestras that made up FMP units. As Canon has noted, many of these smaller, sometimes make-shift groups lacked sufficient numbers or skills to perform the technically difficult modern or even standard art music repertories.

Despite limited resources the FMP gave world premieres of some 950 works by more than 500 American composers, according to the *Index*.[52] Some premieres were part of the Composers' Forum-Laboratory program, but many — like Roger Sessions's *Concerto for Violin and Orchestra* (Illinois Symphony Orchestra; January 8, 1940) and Elie Siegmeister's *Abraham Lincoln Walks at Midnight* (Negro Art Singers of New York; December 21, 1938) — were undertaken by regular WPA concert divisions.[53]

The "Americana" section of the *Index* documents the FMP's special fondness for works inspired by native materials, musical or otherwise. It also reveals a rather large number of American-related pieces by now obscure regional composers: Julian Edward's "My Own United States" (vocal solo, Oakland, California; 1936); Francesca B. DeLeone's *Indian Opera: Aglala* (Akron, Ohio; 1936); Carlton Colby's *Headlines, A Modern American Rhapsody* (Denver, Colorado; 1937), and others,[54] thus demonstrating that the WPA's interest was not limited to better-known professionals like Sessions and Siegmeister. There are also several patriotic pieces, even some dedicated to President Roosevelt (usually "F.D.R.") and the WPA itself.[55] Such information suggests that the WPA, besides stimulating a general appreciation of art music, spurred a compositional response as well. Canon has written that "local teachers, organists, and musical amateurs were encouraged to submit manuscript works for Project performance."[56] Thus the existence of WPA performing units receptive to American music appears to have prompted a "grass roots" creativity from composers who, under other circumstances, would have lacked a forum. Perhaps this is what one American composer, William Grant Still, had in mind when he spoke glowingly about the WPA in 1937. Still was so enthusiastic about the WPA that he saw it as the potential source of the long-sought American school of music.

> The value of the WPA to the American composer is increasingly apparent. Now he can actually hear his music, played on programs devoted solely to American compositions or, as MacDowell would have it, in the company of foreign composers, so that its relative merit may be discovered. Now there can be developed a real American school of music, for it is only in getting his product out to a responsive public that any artist can mature.[57]

Another Americanist action by the FMP was the creation of the Composers' Forum-Laboratories. Although limited to large cities, the Forums became the WPA's most significant contribution to American cultivated music.

The Composers' Forum-Laboratory

> Concerning the Composers' Forum-Laboratory I wish to go on record as follows: That such a project is indispensable to the growth of music in any society—and that if it can be undertaken from Government funds a double purpose is served—1) that of securing adequate performances of representative programs—and 2) of securing for the composer a social recognition in the body politic. (Roy Harris, Excerpt from Letter to Ashley Pettis, April 20, 1936.)

> No venture of the Federal Music Project has been more successful than the weekly concerts of the Composers' Forum-Laboratory. . . . It seems to me that no better way exists for aiding the creative talent of America. (Aaron Copland, Excerpt from Letter to Ashley Pettis, April 22, 1936.)

The FMP program that engendered the most enthusiasm from American composers was the Composers' Forum-Laboratory, the single WPA organization to involve composers regularly and actively as composers. The Forum did not provide funding for new compositions; rather, it gave composers an opportunity for the public performance and discussion of their music, primarily new works.

A part of the Music Education Division of the FMP, the Composers' Forum-Laboratory originated in the New York City Project in October, 1935. Thereafter, Forums were instituted in Philadelphia, Boston, Cleveland, Detroit, Chicago, Milwaukee, Oklahoma City, and Los Angeles.[58] The Americanist intent of the Forums appears to have been recognized quickly. A music correspondent in Los Angeles wrote:

> Let's go native seemed to be the slogan of a goodly number of concert goers who gathered zestfully in the auditorium of Federal Music Project headquarters last night to see what might be pulled out of the bag at the first meeting of the Project's newly created Composers' Forum.
> Dedicated to the proposition that native talent ought to be heard, the Forum, via Conductor Gastone Usiglio and the Federal Orchestra, last night fired the opening volley of what purports to be a permanent crusade in behalf of local composers.[59]

Although federal funding for the Forums stopped with the demise of the FMP in 1939 and no Forum was incorporated into the WPA Music Program, the New York branch was uprooted and removed to San Francisco. There it continued for two seasons under the auspices of the

San Francisco Conservatory of Music and the San Francisco Museum of Art.[60] After the interruption of World War II, the organization, renamed simply the Composers Forum, was reestablished in New York (1947) and has survived to the present with support from several sources, primarily the New York Public Library and Columbia University.[61]

The Composers' Forum-Laboratory was the idea of Ashley Pettis, a pianist and former music editor of *New Masses*, who became the New York City FMP Director of Social Music Education in 1935. Although Pettis did not broach the subject of the Forum to FMP Director Sokoloff until September, 1935, the concept of such an organizaton had been developing in his mind for some time. Pettis's musical Americanist views were manifest in his many writings during the 1930s. Though not a composer himself, he sympathized with composers' low status in American society — even American musical society.

> The plight of the American composer has long been known to those who are informed on the subject. With the exception of a very few well known names, he is practically an unknown quantity to the general musical public, even in the great cities which are supposed to be our "art centers."[62]

To Pettis, the performance and fair criticism of American art music was crucial for improving the position of native composers.[63]

Pettis's concern for the status of American composers was no doubt heightened in this period by his interest in sociopolitical leftism and its emphasis upon artist-audience interaction. Like Siegmeister and others, Pettis made a musical fact-finding tour of the USSR in 1932. Comparing the Soviet with American encouragement of musical activity, he found his native land lacking.[64] The Soviet Union, still in an experimental stage, was deeply committed to enlisting the arts in its society's conversion to Marxism. The Soviets provided a public forum for the "testing" of new art music, an innovation Pettis observed while in Russia.[65] Both musicians and lay people attended concerts devoted to the music of one or two composers. Following the performance, the audience was encouraged to comment or even question the composers, thus giving immediate public reaction to their works. While the Soviet forums had a specific Marxist purpose, however, Pettis seems to have been more impressed with the creative than the political benefits of such presentations. In essence, the forums aided both the composer and the listener: the composer gained a hearing and the listener gained a voice.

Several forerunners for the Composers' Forum-Laboratory existed on the American East Coast in the early 1930s, especially among the coterie of leftists with whom Pettis associated. The New York Composers' Collective was one. Yet the Collective was strictly limited to composers of a particular outlook, and their works were for a particular purpose. Nevertheless, the Collective's private and public presentations regularly included critique sessions, and Pettis was certainly familiar with them.[66] The Communist Pierre Degeyter Club occasionally sponsored apolitical one-man concerts followed by forums,[67] and several series of concerts featuring American composers were held at the New School for Social Research. Henry Cowell initiated one in 1931,[68] and Aaron Copland another in 1935.[69] Copland, probably the American composers' chief impresario in these years, earlier had helped create the Copland-Sessions Concerts (1928–31 in New York City) and the Yaddo Festivals of American Music (beginning summer, 1932 in Saratoga Springs, New York).[70] Canon has suggested the latter two series along with the larger-scale League of Composers Concerts as possible models for the Forums.[71] However, these did not all involve public discussions nor were they all devoted exclusively to American music.

It seems almost ironic that the United States government should sponsor a composers' group which had its roots in the intellectually popular leftism of the 1930s. Yet the Composers' Forum-Laboratories revealed little connection with their radical origins; the only remnant of Marxism was the forum idea itself and its potential for direct composer-audience interaction. In fact, the Forums garnered nothing but praise from federal WPA administrators. The opening of the New York City Forum's third season drew encouraging comments from Chalmers Clifton (New York City Director, FMP), Nikolai Sokoloff (National Director, FMP), and Ellen S. Woodward (Assistant Administrator to Harry Hopkins) respectively:

> I think it is an imposing and gratifying accomplishment for the present and future of American music.

> My best wishes for the continued success of the Composers' Forum-Laboratory . . . and my earnest appreciation for the Forum's contribution to the cause of American music.

> All thoughtful persons must recognize the significant contribution the Composers-Forum [*sic*] is making to contemporary American music.[72]

Much of the credit for the Forum's political neutrality belongs to Pettis himself, whose New York City Forum was the model for the other WPA units. Although Pettis was a Communist sympathizer, he sought to instill fairmindedness and an apolitical atmosphere in Forum presentations. One of his principal goals in initiating the Forums was to present a stylistic overview of all American cultivated music up to the late 1930s.

The aims of the WPA Composers' Forum-Laboratories are best represented by Pettis's opening statement at the October 30, 1935 inaugural presentation. Pettis's remarks demonstrate the musical Americanism which marked the Forum's foundation.

> The purpose of the Composers' Forum-Laboratory is manifold in its nature. Not only are we interested in the composer and his work, *per se*, but in the development of a more definite understanding and relationship between the composer and the public. . . .
>
> There have been numerous attempts to foster an interest in the work of the American composer, or more broadly speaking, the composer working in America. In spite of this fact, as far as the general public is concerned, the American composer is an unknown quantity. We are hoping that, through these evenings in intimate contact with composers, we may do our part in removing the barrier which has always existed between the composer and the people who are or should be the consumers of his goods.

Noting the mystique which has "enshrouded the composer," Pettis related an incident experienced by an earlier American composer:

> Rubin Goldmark tells a story of an occasion on which one of his works was performed in Carnegie Hall. Following the performance, in response to the applause of the audience, he arose in his box and acknowledged the acclaim. A woman was heard to say to her neighbor: "Who is that bowing?" Upon being told it was "the composer" she replied in astonishment, "I thought all composers were dead!"
>
> Naturally, not all have this *naive* misconception of creative musicians — but unquestionably, for most people, as a functioning, social being, the composer is non-existent. The result of this lack of inter-relation of composer and public is an unfortunate one for both. The composer, it is frequently observed, is driven perforce into his "ivory tower" (to use a favorite cliché of the day) and the general public is unconcerned with something which is, generally speaking, only a matter of hearsay.

Pettis hoped that the Forums would dispel this mystery by giving audiences a chance to come in contact with composers and composers an opportunity to discuss their works with listeners. The Forums would have varied programming.

> We will observe every type of music written by competent musicians — music expressive of every shade of thought and feeling peculiar to this moment in history. A panoramic view will be had of what is happening, in a musical way, about us.

Through education, the public would appreciate new American music and help create a vital musical society.

Above all, [the Forums] are designed for the stimulation, in direct contact with an intimate public of disinterested participants, of a strong, indigenous culture — far removed from the vitiated atmosphere which has been the realm of many composers of the day.[73]

As Foster has written, the Forums were run in "the spirit of a dress rehearsal."[74]   Although symphonic works occasionally were featured, budgetary limitations made smaller pieces the standard fare, with the composer sometimes performing. As in the Russian original, the concert portion of WPA Forums was followed by a discussion session at which the Forum supervisor, such as Pettis in New York City, presided. Usually, listeners wrote their questions on paper provided with the programs. These were collected after the performance and presented to the Supervisor, who then directed them to the composer.

While the Forums sought to pay most attention to native-born and young composers — in some cases college students — virtually every living composer in America had access to them.   During the WPA era, Forums were given on a regular basis. The New York City Forum, like the New York City FMP in general, was the most active, offering weekly programs for two years and a fortnightly series thereafter. At first, a single composer was afforded an entire evening. As funds diminished, however, two or more were placed on a single program. In accordance with Forum aims as expressed by Pettis, well-known and unknown, young and old, technically avant-garde and traditional composers were given a hearing. Composers presented by the WPA Composers' Forum-Laboratory of New York City from 1935 through 1939 were:

Astori, Alda	Chavez, Carlos
Baetz, Jessie	Cohn, Arthur
Balogh, Erno	Cole, Ulric
Bauer, Marion	Copland, Aaron
Beach, Mrs. H. H. A.	Cowell, Henry
Berezowsky, Nicolai	Crawford, Ruth
Beyer, Johanna M.	Creston, Paul
Binder, A. W.	de Brant, Cyr
Bingham, Seth	Delaney, Robert
Blitzstein, Marc	Diamond, David
Bloch, Ernest	Donovan, Richard
Bowles, Paul	Eisler, Hanns
Brant, Henry	Engel, Lehman
Brown, Harold	Freed, Isadore
Brunswick, Mark	Farwell, Arthur
Cazden, Norman	Filippi, Amadeo de

Finney, Ross Lee
Forst, Rudolph
Franco, Johan
Gallico, Paolo
Gardner, Mildred
Gerschefski, Edwin
Gershwin, George
    (In Memoriam)
Giorni, Aurelio
    (In Memoriam)
Griffis, Elliot
Gross, Robert
Gruen, Rudolph
Hadley, Henry
Hanson, Howard
Harris, Roy
Hart, Frederic
Haubiel, Charles
Haufrecht, Herbert
Helfer, Walter
Hier, Ethel Glenn
Hijman, Julius
Housman, Rosalie
Howe, Mary
Huss, Henry Holden
Inch, Herbert
Ives, Charles
Jacobi, Frederick
Johnson, Horace
Johnson, Hunter
Josten, Werner
Kennan, Kent
Kerr, Harrison
Koutzen, Boris
Kubik, Gail T.
Levenson, Boris
Lieberson, Goddard

Luening, Otto
McBride, Robert
Maganini, Quinto
Mamorsky, Morris
Mason, Daniel Gregory
Morgenstern, Sam
Morris, Harold
Naginski, Charles
Nordoff, Paul
Pimsleur, Solomon
Pisk, Paul Amadeus
Piston, Walter
Porter, Quincy
Rapoport, Eda
Riegger, Wallingford
Rogers, Bernard
Rozsa, Bela
Saminsky, Lazare
Schaefer, Jacob
    (In Memoriam)
Schuman, William
Sessions, Roger
Shepherd, Arthur
Siegmeister, Elie
Smith, David Stanley
Stillman, Mitya
    (In Memoriam)
Stillman-Kelley [sic], Edgar
Thompson, Randall
Thomson, Virgil
Tuthill, Burnett
Tweedy, Donald
Vrionides, Christos
Wagenaar, Bernard
Weinberg, Jacob
Wertheim, Rosy
Woltmann, Frederick

Wood-Hill, M.[75]

Due to a well-known practice of the federal bureaucracy — insistent record keeping — a lively and fascinating picture of American musical mores has been preserved with WPA materials: the Composers' Forum-

Laboratory transcripts. The discussion sessions after Forum concerts were faithfully transcribed by WPA staff secretaries and, when the WPA was dissolved, placed in the National Archives with other FMP materials.[76] While not every Forum from every city is represented, enough transcripts have survived to yield a remarkable account of unrehearsed remarks by both composers and their audiences.

Forum sessions were frequently heated, and how composers under fire handled questions is telling. Although Forum administrators attempted neutrality in selecting composers, listeners were not always so disinterested. Leftists, especially, seemed to comprise a regular and particularly vocal share of the audience. Their persistent questioning led Paul Bowles to call the Forum nothing but a "heckling session."[77] Others concurred. Elliott Carter noted the "pitiless questions from the audience."[78] One elderly, conservative composer was so put on the defensive that he finally exploded:

> I would like to have you people know that I believe in God. I believe in the sanctity of the home. I believe in the Constitution of the United States, and by thunder, I believe in the C major triad![79]

The Forums certainly revealed as much about the audience as about the composer. Commentators constantly demanded social relevance as well as comprehensibility from the music they heard. Elie Siegmeister was asked: "Do you think the Southern Negro or Pennsylvania steel worker would recognize the idiom of your music as their own?"[80] One questioner-turned-critic told Howard Hanson that his

> compositions are romantic in nature and do not reflect adequately the needs of our people. . . . Beauty in music means beauty for our people, music to awake them, to make possible greater participation in the making of music. . . . Let the events of the world and our country throb in every fibre of your great musical talent. Make your music serve our people in this period of transition and cultural need. If you break with romanticism and mysticism, you will be more of a servant to humanity, highly appreciated by the forces of progress.[81]

Undaunted by the exhortation, Hanson dismissed it by stating "I am, of course, absolutely 'old hat' in this matter. I am 16th century. Oh, way back—maybe the 15th or 14th."[82] Committing two nearly unforgiveable sins in a row, Hanson continued by admitting that he felt music had little to do with politics and economics and that, in his opinion, Shostakovich's politically-oriented music was uninteresting.[83] Hanson added that he hoped he wouldn't be thrown out.

Paul Bowles also was not spared leftist gibes. Concerning his all-Bowles Forum in 1936, he has since written that he felt the "leftists were against the music on principle."[84]   One sarcastic question, which Bowles later learned was penned by Henry Brant, was "Do you like sugar with your tea?"[85]

A mischievous audience meant a lively evening and kept composers on their toes; but some returned the punches. When Marion Bauer was asked "do you approve of nationalism in music?" she snapped "it seems an evening would be incomplete without that question."[86]   Bauer continued that she did not "slavishly" believe in nationalism and she herself asked: "What do people expect? What do they want? What is American?"[87]

If social relevance was one *leitmotiv* at Forums, Americanism was another. Bauer was correct in observing the frequent questions pertaining to nationalism and the "American" qualities of American music. Not surprisingly, composers' answers to such questions generally corresponded with their varied compositional outlooks toward Americanism.

When Howard Hanson was asked what was "American" music, he said that it was a mistake to think of it as a single type. Continuing his answer, Hanson seemed to advocate a sort of regional Americanism, although not using this specific term.

> I am a Westerner. Urbane New Yorkers would be out of place in the West and would have no federal certification to compose on this particular premise. On the other hand, if you feel that music should be based on jazz, it is an understandable point, but it would not be anything for those particular composers who are not drawn to that particular type of expression. The present point of view, I think, in this country, is an enormous amount of expression based on many things—the country valley type, folk tunes, pastorals, a cry against social and economic conditions, the urbane type, the political type, etc.   I maintain a belief that it is American music if it is written by Americans.[88]

Hanson's Americanist views toward the performance of native art music were revealed when a questioner asked how contemporary American composers could expect recognition when their predecessors were ignored in the concert halls. Hanson noted:

> I tried to find the works of Loeffler, who died as you know, a comparatively short time ago. None of his works were played in memoriam. . . . I think that the sooner we honor our own composers of the past, the sooner we classify ourselves as an honest and self-respecting (if you will) artistic community.[89]

During his Forum, Daniel Gregory Mason reiterated his anti-nationalist stance, but expressed curiosity about a related issue.

> I am very much interested in trying to find something that is typical to us here in America.   There is something different in the American temperament. . . . Cheerfulness and sympathy—which is characteristically American. I think many of

us are interested in trying to find that, but like everything else in life, that is experimental. I am interested in nationalism in this way. I hope that we shall never become "nationalistic" in the sense of excluding other people.[90]

Roger Sessions responded in a similar vein when he was asked about "American" musical qualities.

I don't believe that at the present time anything can possibly be defined. I think national tendencies insofar as they have any validity at all can only be defined after there is a great deal of music written.[91]

Taking the opposing stance from Mason and Sessions was Lazare Saminsky, who emphatically stated his belief in determinable "American" musical characteristics. When asked if there was such a thing as "American" music, he said:

I am really amazed that someone in New York City in 1938 should ask such a question. . . . I think, certainly, there is no doubt that America has outgrown the naive cultivation of the Negro and Indian songs which were supposed to lead, at a certain stage, to the creation of American music. There are in American music clear characteristics, the same as the characteristics of the American people – a certain snappiness, a certain clear-cut quality of speed and the direct grappling with any problem with every fact of life, a peculiar sense of humor, a certain dash, vivacity, and verve, a certain snap, something which is carefree – perhaps I should say a certain gay and attractive showmanship. Such music is American, just as Mark Twain and Walt Whitman are American. In its broad, epic qualities, all of this is characteristic of the best American music.[92]

On the same subject Aaron Copland noted:

The characteristics of American music are now in the making. Therefore, it is difficult to say with any certainty exactly what they are but one can already see a certain vigor and a certain rhythmic impulse which are recognizably American.[93]

There appears, though, to have been more unanimity in audience concern over "American" music than in composer opinion on the subject. While individual composers' responses are interesting, the very fact that similar questions were recurring is probably more significant. Forum transcripts preserve on-the-spot listener commentary not readily found in other sources. They reveal an audience actively pressing composers for a particular type of music. It is impossible to conclude how representative were the tastes of listeners. Surely audiences varied from city to city, from concert to concert, and from year to year. Yet the demand was fairly consistent for music with an "American" sound, with contemporary societal relevance – music which appealed to the participants as twentieth-century Americans.

The impact of Forum lobbying for "American" music cannot readily be determined. Pettis has noted that William Schuman was one composer deeply affected by the Forum experience. As a result of poor audience response, Schuman shelved two early works and immediately embarked upon his *Second String Quartet* and *Second Symphony*. These were premiered at the Forum with great success, and the symphony was performed shortly thereafter by the Boston Symphony Orchestra under Koussevitzky.[94] Yet Schuman, though changed by his first Forum, really did not move toward compositional Americanism as a result.

Still, it seems fair to suggest that regular appeals by listeners for "American" music might have had some influence during a period in which many composers were more concerned with pleasing the American people than at any other time. At his Forum, Roger Sessions remarked that "just now there is a great tendency to demand something very definitely American."[95] Perhaps Forum demand for "American" music was but one more catalyst in the developing Americanist outlook of many composers in the late 1930s who participated in these programs.

The general attitude of Forum audiences may have had the reverse effect upon some composers. One who seems to have reacted negatively was Elliott Carter, whose comments about the question period have already been cited. Although Carter found the discussions irritating, they were not his chief objection to the Forum program. Carter complained that the Forums did little to secure performances of American works by private professional organizations. "The famous remain famous and the obscure men obscure," wrote Carter; "the concerts appear to have done nothing more than to give a small group of friends and others a chance to hear their works."[96] Pettis, in an article written the year before the Forum was founded, had expressed concern over this very problem, albeit with an overlay of leftist ideology.

> As long as our creative musical minds are confined to development in the atmosphere of clinical, musical laboratories, without coming in contact with the reactions of groups, or the masses of our people, so long will they continue to create music which will fail to attain great significance, or to catch the changing spirit of mankind in its struggles to escape the straitjacket of the past.[97]

Pettis, in response to Carter, admitted that the carryover from the WPA Forums to major musical institutions was not as great as could be hoped.

> It is true, at the immediate moment, that a large American public is not clamoring for frequent performances of new and unfamiliar native works or repetitions of

compositions already performed at the concerts of the Composers' Forum-Laboratory.[98]

However, Pettis cited some further performances of major works premiered in the Forums by other WPA units, and noted that private musical groups sympathetic to contemporary music had sought information about Forum pieces.[99]

Furthermore, Pettis recalled that the purpose of the Forums was to perform new works before a responsive audience and to provide composers with suggestions about their music—not to present polished works for the examination of well-known performers and conductors.

> The record of the Composers' Forum-Laboratory contains numerous eloquent tributes, both from individuals and educational institutions, acclaiming the value of appearances and performances and its stimulating and inspiring influence upon creative activity. The accent in these written statements is upon the "incentive" hitherto unknown to the native composer.[100]

Pettis seems to have regarded the forums as but one facet of a campaign necessary for the recognition of American art music. While he acknowledged inadequacies in the WPA Forum program, he was enthusiastic about its future.[101]

The potential of the Composers' Forum-Laboratories and the WPA music projects as a whole was never realized to the extent that Pettis, Sokoloff, Hopkins and others envisioned in the program's early years. The reasons were inherent in the very nature of the WPA. Though many hoped that the cultural programs would be retained permanently, the WPA was first and foremost a re-employment system whose *raison d'être* diminished with each improvement in the economy. The first employee decreases were rumored in fall, 1936 and carried out in December, less than two years after the inception of the WPA. Many federal artists were rudely reminded that the projects in which they invested great hope were still tied to the fragile whim of Congress. Picketing, fasting, and all-night vigils could not deter the next cuts in July, 1937, when funding was reduced by one-quarter.[102] In fact, while peak WPA employment was not reached until 1939, that of the controversial Arts Projects was achieved in 1936.[103] Although the cultural programs continued, the first blows had been dealt early in their development. As the 1930s progressed, more reductions and frequent changes of administrative personnel drained the original visionary spirit from those associated with Federal Project Number One.

A further reason why the WPA music projects did not accomplish as much as had been hoped, particularly for American composers, was due to their means of organization. Unlike the Writers' and Art Projects, the FMP and WPA Music Program did not directly sponsor creative activity by individual artists, in this case composers. Musicians were hired as teachers, performers, conductors, and in a few instances as arrangers, but not as composers.[104]   The WPA emphasis upon the performance of American art music, as practiced by the Forums and less rigorously by other FMP and WPA Music Program units, was to some extent a compensation for the lack of funding for new American music.

The non-sponsorship of American composers was a source of considerable embarrassment to music program officials because provision for such employment had been made by the Division of Service Projects, the administrative heading including the FMP.[105]   The neglected composers themselves, represented by the American Composers' Alliance, lobbied vigorously for recognition by the WPA. Under pressure from the Alliance in 1938, FMP Director Sokoloff proposed that FMP funds, specifically those generated by sponsors' groups, be used for commissions to composers.[106] An agreement was reached in 1939 to have the concept included in the reorganization of the WPA in 1940, but no program was ever initiated.

Precisely why American composition was not directly encouraged by the FMP and WPA Music Program only may be speculated. That the subject was much-discussed and troublesome is apparent from George Foster's lengthy and apologetic consideration of it.[107] Foster indicated that logistical problems were paramount. How to document work from individuals following their own schedules away from Project offices was not an easy task for a huge bureaucracy continually justifying itself to the President, Congress and the American people. Yet the Art and Writers' Projects overcame the problem,[108] and other governmental agencies employed composers at the very time the FMP declined to do so. The Resettlement Administration, in addition to its folksong project, commissioned music for documentary films.   Virgil Thomson, in collaboration with Pare Lorentz, produced three well-known scores in this manner.[109]   Other composers found similar work,[110] and several were employed by the WPA Federal Theatre Project, a fact Foster overlooked in his discussion. For instance, Herbert Haufrecht, after work with the Resettlement Administration, was hired as a staff composer by the Federal Theatre in 1937;[111] and Aaron Copland, Paul Bowles, and Virgil Thomson were among those commissioned by the Federal Theatre in New York City for incidental music to WPA productions.[112]

Had the WPA Music Program lasted through World War II, it is possible that some project involving composition may have been initiated.

The American Composers' Alliance continued its lobbying, and in November of 1941 WPA assistant commissioner Florence Kerr called together a Special Music Panel to consider the problem.[113] Roy Harris and Howard Hanson participated, and Harris in particular attempted to ensure federal funding for future American composers. Although no program was begun immediately, the Panel recommended that the government provide three means of support to composers: contracts for specific pieces, as was done for artists under PWAP; grants-in-aid for independent work; and establishment of composers-in-residence positions at state universities with federal funds.[114] While none of these proposals was included under the WPA music agencies, each eventually became available through federal or private fellowships and grants, or through private and state university music programs.

Perhaps the emphasis of the WPA music projects—education and performance—merely exemplifies the dominant pursuits of American music historically. In the eyes of most musicians and most of the public, art music in America was something played and taught, not composed. Thus, aside from the composers themselves, few Americans saw urgent need for assuring composers a share of WPA funds.

The chief administrators of the FMP and WPA Music Program demonstrated the primary concerns of American cultivated musical life. In succession they were a conductor (foreign-born, at that) and a music educator, with many lower-level officials of similar backgrounds. Thus the music programs reflected the interests of their leadership. Not until the final two years of the WPA Music Program did a composer, George Foster, taken the helm. Little known as a composer, he assumed the position when the project was in rapid decline, too late to exert any significant influence toward the support of composers. Despite the Americanism promoted by Sokoloff and demonstrated by WPA reports, at least one high-level administrator saw it as a facade. Charles Seeger, who became Assistant FMP Director in 1937 following the termination of the Resettlement Administration music program, felt that Sokoloff was primarily interested in travelling about the country to conduct WPA orchestras. A staunch Americanist, Seeger surmised that Sokoloff actually disliked American music.[115] In essence, though the WPA was Americanist toward the performance of native music, it was still primarily an institution for the perpetuation of cultivated music in America, not American cultivated music, and thus reflected the general American conception of art music at this time.

The WPA music programs attempted to impose a musical culture upon the United States which, if not completely foreign, was previously limited to large cities and experienced by small portions of American society. According to WPA records, the reception was warm. Sokoloff remarked that the WPA had

> disclosed a vast and unsuspected hunger for music among great masses of our people, and . . . brought to light an unlooked for richness both in creative and executant talent.[116]

Sokoloff, a bureaucrat justifying his agency, undoubtedly was biased. Yet in some cases, the cultural grafting took hold in specific ways. Several performing groups, notably the Buffalo Philharmonic, were begun under the WPA and then maintained privately after 1943,[117] and the Composers' Forum-Laboratories have continued, if on a much reduced scale from those under the WPA.

Rather than deterring support for private musical institutions, the WPA encouraged an overall interest in art music. John Tasker Howard, in a study of American musical activities between 1929 and 1937, concluded that American musical life had expanded to an unprecedented degree despite the Depression, and cited the WPA as partially responsible.[118] Virgil Thomson has credited the WPA orchestras with firmly establishing the popularity of symphonic music in the United States.[119]

The FMP and WPA Music Program had enormous potential at their outset. Had their existence not been clouded by politics and continual employee reductions, especially from 1937 on, their impact upon American culture might have been immense. Also, had American composers been more fully integrated into WPA music programs as a whole, a greater societal awareness of American cultivated music might have resulted; despite the Forums and the Americanist slant of the projects toward performance, the WPA was somewhat disappointing to American composers. Even the Forums tended to isolate them from the rest of the WPA, thus mirroring and continuing the isolation of American composers from American musical life in general.

Canon concluded his discussion of the place of American composers in the WPA as follows:

> Although there were no composers employed by the Federal Music Projects as composers, many were employed in other capacities as conductors, performers, arrangers and administrators. In this respect, the Federal Music Project reflects the normal pattern of the composer in the United States. It has been said that the number of composers in the United States supported solely through the fruits of their compositions could be counted on one hand.[120]

Canon's assessment is one way of looking at it. Americanists such as Pettis, Harris, and Seeger, however, viewed the WPA's tacit acceptance of the status quo as a missed opportunity for American composers. Had the

WPA been stronger, better-coordinated, and longer-lived, the separation between American cultivated music and the institutions for cultivated music in America might have been overcome once and for all.

VIII

Musical Americanism and World War II

In a study of patriotism in the United States, the historian John J. Pullen observed that Americans have willingly supported wars in which they felt moral issues were at stake, and in which they perceived their cause "just and right."[1]   World War II was such a war. Even before America's official participation, many Americans believed that Nazism and the Axis powers threatened democracy, and conversely that the Allies were the upholders of democratic ideals. The Japanese bombing of Pearl Harbor on December 7, 1941 only cemented American resolve toward the War.

Such unanimity of outlook replaced a strong isolationism pervading America in the early and mid-1930s. Pullen has written that "to be a patriot in the thirties was in most cases to be an isolationist," a position that transcended political boundaries.[2] Those on the right preached nonintervention. Those on the left insisted that war itself was the invention of capitalist profiteers who cruelly benefitted from man's darker side. But it was the left that first encouraged American participation in the European war in the late 1930s. Many left-wing Americans themselves joined the Loyalist side of the Spanish Civil War after 1936.[3] Furthermore, American Communist sympathizers echoed Russia's nervousness about its proximity to the spreading Nazi empire. By the late 1930s the *Daily Worker, New Masses*, and liberal publications had launched a vigorous campaign against the fascist governments. If not urging American entry into the War, those on the left believed such action was inevitable.

Most Americans' feelings about the necessity of an active role in the war took longer to coalesce. One historian of World War II described the turning from isolationism toward participation in the late 1930s in this manner:

> The ruthless bombing of helpless Chinese all through the spring of 1938, the almost incredible barbarities of Japanese infantrymen, the increasing severity of Nazi persecutions of Jews in Germany, the repeated ruthless aggressions of Hitler and Mussolini—all these had forced millions of formerly isolationist Americans to

conclude that something (opinions varied as to what) must be done to thwart the insatiable ambitions of the Japanese militarists, the Nazi-Fascist dictators. Many who had theretofore accepted the simple view that wars are caused by commercial rivalries and interests, and by those alone, began to recognize other causative factors — factors having little or nothing to do with economics. A paranoid megalomania, a perverted sexuality expressed through ruthless power lusts, the profound moral outrage joined to an "instinct" of self-preservation which such evil inevitably provoked — these, too, were causative. Thousands of Americans who had been most vehemently pacifist in the early 1930s now realized that their pacifism stemmed from a yet deeper commitment, a commitment to human freedom and humane values. The same moral energies that had fed it now fed their anti-fascism.[4]

Some Americans questioned the very meaning of the word "fascism."[5] They observed that the evils the term had come to describe were merely symptoms of a disease of civilization to which any country – even the United States – was susceptible.[6] To many, this realization was the most frightening aspect of the war. Recognizing the potentialities within themselves for all that "fascism" then represented made fighting it imperative.

Today, it may not be easy to recapture the single-mindedness that dominated the American perspective toward World War II throughout its duration. Even more difficult to recollect, and perhaps to embrace, is that single-mindedness translated into art. A recent review of a new recording of Marc Blitzstein's *The Airborne Symphony* (1943) faulted the work's heavy-handed propaganda and called all patriotic music of the 1940s "a national embarrassment."[7] Truly, the same criticism often leveled at the leftist pieces of the 1930s can be made of some patriotic pieces of the 1940s: primarily, the blatant predominance of "message." If such music is sometimes questionable as art, however, and if it is no longer viable as propaganda, it remains worthy of historical consideration. That artists, traditionally society's skeptics and critics, so willingly devoted their abilities to the aims of the country at war indicates an unusual national unity.

More American composers expressed concern over World War II than had commented upon the American Depression. In an issue of *Modern Music* appearing after Pearl Harbor, two composers wrote gravely about the war. Lehman Engel compared it to the crisis faced by the nation's founders:

> The trials ahead have never been equalled in our history, except perhaps in the experience of those robust souls who helped establish the country.[8]

Roger Sessions viewed the war as a test of American resolve:

The United States is engaged in a desperate struggle which involves the ultimate conditions of our existence. . . . Our hour is at hand, and either we must begin to live seriously as heirs of a great civilization, or we must, in refusing this role, face destruction.[9]

Elsewhere, Sessions confessed frustration at being too old for active military duty,[10] an experience shared by several other composers. William Schuman was also ineligible, although for a physical difficulty and not age. When he volunteered for the army and was turned down, he determined to serve his country through his special abilities, and that decision led to the composition of his *Prayer in Time of War* (1943).[11]

Although the gravity of the conflict was unanimously recognized, there was less agreement about the usefulness of art music for a nation at war. Henry Cowell summed up the pertinent issues: "Is music of use in time of bitter war? Can it 'carry on'? In what form, and how?"[12] The music historian studying American composers' answers to these questions is greatly aided by the work of Ross Lee Finney. In 1942, Finney wrote to fifty American composers asking for their views about music during wartime. He then read a paper presenting many of the responses at the annual meeting of the M.T.N.A.[13] Finney's report is a valuable account of American composers' attitudes toward their place in American society; it reveals a fundamental division in how composers assessed their purpose.

For composers, as for Americans, the war kindled and intensified patriotism. While most American composers wrote at least one piece related in some way to the war, the degree to which patriotism was reflected directly in their music varied widely. Yet a pattern is discernible. Generally, the manifestation of patriotism in a composer's works corresponded to his previous creative response to social or sociopolitical events. For instance, the music of Roger Sessions had not reflected the Americanism or obvious social concern common in the 1930s. His works of the 1940s, except for a *Dirge* commissioned by the League of Composers (see below, pp. 194–95), made little reference to patriotism, Americanism, or the war. In fact, in an open letter to his colleagues, Sessions maintained that the crisis took precedence over everything, including the arts and special abilities of artists. Taking time to compose might literally impede the salvation of civilization.

Can any of us . . . . do less than try to fulfill with credit and without complaint whatever task is assigned us? Are you and I, really, as individuals, so indispensible that we can with any possible justification ask for exceptional treatment? I feel passionately that, should any of us do so, we would be advertising ourselves and our art as a mere commodity capable of possible minor utilization in the war effort, or as a curiosity to be kept going as part of a kind of fluid "time capsule" – one of the articles of no intrinsic value to be preserved for posterity as a curious survival of a superseded civilization.[14]

Elsewhere, Sessions wrote that music had little to do with "morale," and that "wars are won, not by 'morale,' but by people possessed of guts and imagination."[15]

The opposite extreme from Sessions's views can be found in the comments of Earl Robinson. Like that of other leftists, Robinson's music consistently had manifested a social concern in the 1930s. Joining the left's "united front" against fascism, Robinson in the 1940s became a fervent patriot and maintained his conviction for the need of social relevance in music. To Robinson, art music was as vital to the war effort as it had been to the Depression.

> I believe it is the function of the composer during wartime to compose, in addition, of course, to whatever patriotic wartime activities such as air-raid warden work, he may be doing. However, I think most emphatically that it cannot be *just* composing "as usual." Any more than "business as usual" can be tolerated during the fighting of a world-wide People's War for freedom.
> It is the composer's job and privilege to bend every energy (and every note so to speak) to winning the war, educating the people and building morale both inside and outside of the army. We all agree that music is and can be important not only in peacetime but in war. Then I think we should adopt the slogan "Music as a Weapon" and proceed to make it a weapon.[16]

Several of Robinson's works from this period, such as the *Ballad for Americans* (although dating from 1939), *Battle Hymn* (1942), and *Lonesome Train* (1944) demonstrate his patriotism, as well as his musical Americanism, through the use of national subjects and folk-like musical materials.

The views of Sessions and Robinson, then, while conditioned by the war, represent opposite poles on the place of art music in American society. Sessions believed that music was essentially aloof from societal events, while Robinson maintained that music should be directly related to society. In the 1940s, perhaps more than at any other time in American musical history, composers leaned toward Robinson's view. They wished to be integral and commenting members of American society, especially during the crisis of war. The renewed patriotism and desire to serve, coupled with an already expanded interest in Americana, resulted in a peak of musical Americanism in these years.

Few composers' attitudes toward music during the war were as extreme as Robinson's. Some merely believed that art music should continue to be created. Howard Hanson, for instance, wrote that the composer must continue to write the best music of which he is capable. This is probably more difficult in times of war than in times of peace, but it seems to me that creation and perpetuation of beauty is more important than ever in days like these.[17]

Similarly, Douglas Moore stated that the composer should "above all keep faith with his artistic creed and . . . affirm the validity of music in our national life, now more than ever."[18]

However, many composers, like Robinson, believed that special music should be written in response to the crisis. Isidore Freed explained that the war had caused him to compose in a style different from his previous works.

> Music, being a communal art, can help to keep us balanced as the experience of both Russia and England shows. For myself, I wrote "Appalachian Sketches" (my first venture in American Folk Lore) as a direct result of my consciousness that America is a better way of life than Fascism or Nazism.[19]

Randall Thompson wrote to Finney that a variety of music could be offered to meet different wartime situations.

> The composer might well write music that was as light as eiderdown and do a good deal merely by amusing and entertaining his listeners. Another might write patriotic music and by such a reassessment of values, write music that, war or no war, struck deep in many hearts.[20]

The desire to compose works that would express the deeper emotions caused by the war is echoed by Bernard Rogers. Rogers's ideal was to

> create music that touches the spirit and mood of the times, music of a revealing character, which could interpret the feeling and hopes of humanity, and thus contribute to the cause we all cherish.[21]

As an example of inspirational music growing directly out of the experience of the war, several composers cited the works of Shostakovich, especially his *Seventh ("Leningrad") Symphony.* Aaron Copland noted that Shostakovich had

> made the music of a living composer come fully alive for a world audience. It is not the war fever alone that explains the phenomenon of the *Seventh*. Its success was in large measure due to the consciously adopted music style which is accessible to listeners everywhere. I am not suggesting that Shostakovich has found the solution for our problem—far from it. But all his work, despite its obvious weaknesses, sets that problem before us in an inescapable way. It is the tendency he represents, rather than the music he writes, that makes Shostakovich a key figure of the present time.[22]

Perhaps in writing of Shostakovich, Copland summed up his own goals at this time.

As defined for the purposes of the present study, compositional Americanism means simply a conscious reference to Americana in music. Patriotism expressed in music may be said to be a type of musical Americanism, for it exalts national life. In the 1940s, patriotism was manifested musically in various ways. Most commonly, a patriotic statement was made obvious through choice of title and, in vocal music, of appropriate texts. Therefore, many patriotic works revealed the impact of native materials only on the surface, although some did include American musical elements as well.

The special blend of anti-fascism, patriotism, and musical Americanism in the 1940s is probably best exemplified by a small theatre piece by Elie Siegmeister, *Doodle Dandy of the U.S.A.* Siegmeister added music to the original book by Saul Lancourt for the New York City Junior Programs in 1942.[23] Paralleling the then-current international situation, the story concerns a would-be dictator and the efforts of the American hero–Doodle Dandy–to restrain him. The featured song of the show is Doodle Dandy's and the musical references to the Revolutionary War tune are obvious (see Example 1). The straight-forward plot and musical style are intended for youthful performers but also recall the agit-prop[24] theatre of the 1930s. Fascism has replaced capitalism as the chief enemy, and the United States has replaced Marxism as the purveyor of good.

Many composers wrote pieces focusing on America's basic historical concepts, especially that of freedom. A plethora of works using either the word "freedom" or simply "American" in the title appeared during the war years: Bennett's *"Four Freedoms" Symphony* (1943), Blitzstein's *Freedom Morning* (1943), Carpenter's *Song of Freedom* (1941), Cowell's *American Muse* (1943), Dello Joio's *American Landscape* (1944), Gould's *American Salute* (1942), Gruenberg's *American Suite* (1945), Harris's *American Creed* (1940), Read's *American Circle* (1941), Robinson's *That Freedom Plow* (1942), Siegmeister's *Freedom Train* (1943), and Thompson's *Testament of Freedom* (1943).

Another common way in which composers related their music to the country's fundamental beliefs was to base their works on past American heroes or historical figures, a trend begun in the 1930s which gained ground with the onset of the war. Earl Robinson's cantata, *That Freedom Plow*, was inspired by Thomas Jefferson. A better-known work, Randall Thompson's *Testament of Freedom*, is dedicated to the University of Virginia in memory of Thomas Jefferson, the school's founder. Written for men's voices and orchestra, the vocal writing is frequently in

Example 1
Opening of "Doodle Dandy's Back in Town," *Doodle Dandy of the U.S.A.*, Saul Lancourt and Elie Siegmeister. Copyright 1942 by Saul Lancourt and Elie Siegmeister. Used by permission.

unison, giving the music a solemn, almost chant-like character. Each of the piece's four sections is based on selections from Jefferson's writings, and the texts seem as appropriate to World War II as to the conflict in Jefferson's own time.

Although in the 1940s a looming presence rather than a historical figure, Franklin Delano Roosevelt, by way of Norman Rockwell, inspired Robert Russell Bennett's *"Four Freedoms" Symphony.* Rockwell created a set of paintings representing the "four freedoms" President Roosevelt outlined in an address of January, 1941. Roosevelt's speech, delivered less than a year before our entry into the war, came to symbolize American ideals.[25] Bennett's symphony devoted each of four movements to a different "freedom": freedom of speech, freedom of worship, freedom from want, and freedom from fear. The melodies of the work, while not directly based on pre-existent materials, reflect certain vernacular idioms. In the second movement, for instance, one passage seems clearly influenced by the "blues" through its use of alternating lowered and raised seventh scale degrees. The opening section of the last movement, by contrast, is decidedly march-like (see Examples 2 and 3).[26]

Example 2
Measures 9-12 from Part II, "Freedom of Worship," *"Four Freedoms" Symphony* (Piano Adaptation by Helmy Kresna; New York: Contemporary Publications), Robert Russell Bennett. Used by permission of the composer.

Example 3
Measures 1-10 from Part IV, "Freedom from Fear," *"Four Freedoms" Symphony.*

The national historical figure who inspired the most patriotic Americanist art music was unquestionably Abraham Lincoln. The artistic reverence for Lincoln had begun during the Depression and only intensified during the war. To most Americans, Lincoln represented the archetypical American, the consummate spokesman for democracy. The memory of his leadership and eloquence was no doubt a comfort in these years. Robert E. Sherwood's play *Abe Lincoln in Illinois,* concerning the early years of Lincoln's political career, opened in New York City in 1938. The following year, Carl Sandburg's monumental biography *Abraham Lincoln* was completed with the four-volume study *Lincoln, the War Years.*[27] Simultaneously with the renewed literary and historical interest in Lincoln came a musical one. Elie Siegmeister set Vachel Lindsey's poem *Abraham Lincoln Walks at Midnight* in 1937.[28] Earl Robinson's *Ballad for Americans* of two years later was followed by the composer's *Abraham Lincoln Comes Home* (1942) and *Lonesome Train* (1944). In 1942, Morton Gould's *A Lincoln Legend* appeared and Robert Palmer contributed another setting of the Lindsey poem. Roy Harris's *Sixth Symphony,* based on passages from the Gettysburg Address, was written in 1944 and dedicated to the United States Armed Forces.

The best-known composition inspired by Lincoln is certainly Copland's *A Lincoln Portrait* (1942), mentioned in the preceding section on folksong. This piece and Thompson's *The Testament of Freedom* are among the few patriotic works of the period that are still performed.

Written for narrator and orchestra, *A Lincoln Portrait* was commissioned by André Kostelanetz and premiered by the Cincinnati Symphony Orchestra, Kostelanetz conducting, on May 14, 1942.[29]   The work includes two well-known American tunes from earlier periods, the folksong "The Pesky Sarpent" (now usually known as "Springfield Mountain"), and Stephen Foster's "Camptown Races."   Copland's *A Lincoln Portrait* is a culminating work of musical Americanism from the period between 1939 and 1945.   It well illustrates the combination of artistic and social currents of the times in its use of a technically accessible musical language incorporating pre-existent native materials, its inspiration from an American historical figure, and its direct appeal to American patriotism.

Many younger composers, of course, joined the armed forces. Enlisted composers seemed to want to continue using their special talents in some way.   In an effort to assist the armed services in matching abilities with jobs, Claire Reis and the League of Composers sent out nearly 1,500 questionnaires to American composers to catalogue areas of musical expertise.   Responses were sent to the Joint Army and Navy Committee, but how the information was used was not disclosed to the League.[30]

Many musicians were drafted into military bands, the largest area of musical activity in the armed forces.[31]   Lehman Engel became band leader at the Great Lakes Naval Training Center.   Later he was put in charge of music for Navy films, and wrote several scores during the war.[32]   Gail Kubik also composed film music as a government employee during the war.   According to Kubik, who was the Director of Music for the Office of War Information (domestic) Film Bureau, many military units were involved in filmmaking.[33]   Films were produced for every conceivable purpose, from basic training to propaganda.   According to Kubik, enlisted composers were allowed to write original scores whenever possible.   Often, however, time and expense made stock sound tracks necessary.   Still, Kubik generally was pleased with the treatment of American composers, and believed there was a lesson to be learned from their successful employment by the government.

> It is clear that if the government during war time recognizes the value of the composer, orders three composers in uniform to write music for its service films, believing original music important enough to send a soldier-composer like myself to England in the middle of the war to write a film score—in short, makes clear its faith in original music to do an important military job, then it can, and we hope it will, recognize more clearly than in pre-war days the composer's value to the government's peacetime film program.[34]

The Army Air Force commissioned large works from two well-known enlisted composers, Samuel Barber and Marc Blitzstein — more the exception than the rule for composers in service. Commenting that the Air Force was more progressive in its views toward music than the other military branches, Robert Ward noted that one

> air-minded idea was to fly Samuel Barber around in B-24's for a couple of weeks, presumably to provide inspiration for his *Symphony Dedicated to the Air Forces*.[35]

Just before the premiere of this work, Barber wrote a letter to Walter Damrosch in which he explained the significance and the unusual nature of his commission. Barber believed that his commission was the first of its kind for an American composer of art music. Also, as Ward had suggested, he did make several flights before composing the work.[36] Although it is not a program symphony, Barber's score originally called for an electronic device to simulate the signal of an aviator's radio.[37] The composer also wrote a *Commando March* for the Army Air Force bands.[38]

Marc Blitzstein, like others on the political left, experienced a heightened patriotism and anti-fascism during the war period. Blitzstein, whose 1930s' pieces were notable for their strong criticism of American society, eagerly enlisted in the Army Air Force. While Director of the U.S. Army Negro Chorus, he composed *Freedom Morning*, a cantata premiered in London by this group in 1943.[39] Dedicated to all Negro troops serving in the American armed forces, *Freedom Morning* interspersed spirituals with jazz idioms of the swing era.[40]

Late in 1943, Blitzstein became Director of Music at the American Broadcasting Station in Europe.[41] In London during the worst bombing raids (1943-44), he composed *The Airborne Symphony* mentioned above. Blitzstein recalled to Claire Reis that this was the only American work composed in the zone of military operations on assignment by the armed forces.[42]

Although termed a symphony, *The Airborne* resembles a cantata, calling for two male soloists, male chorus, narrator, and full orchestra. As in his other works, Blitzstein served as librettist as well as composer. The text traces the history of flight from man's dream of being "airborne" through the modern use of aircraft in war.

The Airborne was premiered on April 1, 1946 at the New York City Center with Orson Welles narrating and Leonard Bernstein conducting the New York City Symphony.[43] Olin Downes noted the extremely favorable reception given the work, perhaps as much a comment on the militaristic mood of current audiences as on Blitzstein's achievement.

The instant the last shout of the chorus, and the last word of "Warning" from Mr. Welles with his microphone had sounded, the shouts and applause rent the air, and this went on for minutes, till all the soloists had come back to the stage and acknowledged with the orchestra the plaudits; till Marc Blitzstein, author of the text and composer of the music, had come forth, and Mr. Welles had rushed the length of the footlights and flung his arms around him, and Mr. Bernstein had made a short speech congratulating everyone, including himself, on the composition, the performance, and the taste and perspicacity of his audience.[44]

Yet the text, laden with polemical slang phrases about current events, was not uniformly hailed. Virgil Thomson, for instance, wrote that *The Airborne* contained "good music" but "poor literature," and called its "folksy language . . . . both facile and affected."[45] As with other works by this composer, the libretto and not the music received the harshest criticism.

In 1943, Olin Downes stated:

No situation could be more calculated to take the so-called "serious" composer out of his real or fancied aesthetic seclusion, and force him to stand creatively on his own feet, and address his fellow-man in terms of sincerity and reality. It will be needed in music even after victory and armistice.[46]

The occasion was the announcement of the League of Composers' commissions of eighteen short works by Americans on "martial" subjects.[47] By its commission program, one of only two non-government efforts to tie American art music to the war (the other is discussed subsequently), the League made a substantial contribution to the repertory of patriotic music. The list of works follows:

Nicolai Berezowsky — *Soldiers on the Town*
John Alden Carpenter — *The Anxious Bugler*
Henry Cowell — *American Pipers*
Norman Dello Joio — *To a Lone Sentry*
Howard Hanson — *Fantasy for String Orchestra*
Roy Harris — *March in Time of War*
Bernard Herrmann — *For the Fallen*
Charles Ives — *War Song March (They Are There!)*
Werner Josten — *Before the Battle*
Douglas Moore — *Destroyer Song*
Darius Milhaud — *Introduction et March Funèbre*
Bohuslav Martinu — *Memorial to Lidice*
Quincy Porter — *The Moving Tide*
Walter Piston — *Fugue on a Victory Tune*
Bernard Rogers — *Invasion*
Roger Sessions — *Dirge*
William Grant Still — *In Memoriam: The Colored Soldiers Who Died for Democracy*[48]

The pieces were premiered by the New York Philharmonic under Rodzinski during the 1943-44 and 1944-45 seasons.[49] Additionally, each was recorded at its initial performance by the Office of War Information and broadcast to American troops at home and abroad.

All of the works, with the exception of Ives's, were newly composed and attempted to express some aspect of military life during war. Each composer was asked to contribute a short program note to accompany his piece's premiere. Douglas Moore wrote that his *Destroyer Song* was dedicated to the United States Navy in which he was then serving, and had been inspired by his first-hand experiences on the destroyer U.S.S. Murray.[50] The *War Song March (They Are There!)* by Ives was written during the First World War.

> The War Song March is a kind of reflection and general impression of the old War Brass Band Quicksteps with Fife and Drum Crops — and also of the spirit of both byegone and present days of storm and stress in this country's march on its road of liberty and with the Battle Cry of Freedom — Strains of former war song tunes will be heard throughout, especially in the chorus; these, in former exciting march days would be heard from the Drum Corps even when the Band was shouting out its Quickstep. . . . This was composed during the first World War and scored for orchestra, drum corps and unison chorus — it was also arranged for voice and piano. The last chorus suggests something that even during the first War many were found to be interested in and felt that the world should do — "Then it's build a People's World Nation, Every honest country free to live its own Native Life."[51]

Ives's comments reveal the democratic idealism which we have come to associate with the composer and his works.

Roy Harris wrote that the musical basis of his *March in Time of War* was folksong.

> This work is dedicated to the American composers in the armed services. It is written around the American folk song "True Love, Don't Weep."[52]

Perhaps the most personal and poignant tribute was that by William Grant Still, who wrote:

> When you suggested that I compose something patriotic, there immediately flashed through my mind the press release which announced that the first American in our armed forces to be killed in World War II was a Negro soldier. Then my thoughts turned to the colored soldiers all over the world, fighting under our flag and under the flags of countries allied with us. Our civilization has known no greater patriotism, no greater loyalty than that shown by the colored men who fight and die for democracy. Those who return will, I hope, come back to a better world. I also hope that our tribute to those who die will be to make the

democracy for which they fought greater and broader than it has ever been before.[53]

One other major effort to relate new American works to the war was made by Eugene Goossens and the Cincinnati Symphony Orchestra. Goossens invited composers to help renew an experiment which originated in London during the First World War — the performance of fanfares at each concert following the national anthem. Goossens's request resulted in a series of new pieces even larger than that sponsored by the League of Composers:

> Felix Borowski — *Fanfare for American Soldiers*
> Aaron Copland — *Fanfare for the Common Man*
> Henry Cowell — *To the Forces of Our Latin-American Allies*
> Paul Creston — *Fanfare for Paratroopers*
> Anis Fuleihan — *Fanfare for the Medical Corps*
> Eugene Goossens — *Fanfare for the Merchant Marine*
> Morton Gould — *Fanfare for Freedom*
> Howard Hanson — *Fanfare for the Signal Corps*
> Roy Harris — *Fanfare*
> Daniel Gregory Mason — *Fanfare for Friends*
> Harl McDonald — *Fanfare for Poland*
> Darius Milhaud — *Fanfare de la Liberté*
> Walter Piston — *Fanfare for the Fighting French*
> Bernard Rogers — *Fanfare for the Commandos*
> Leo Sowerby — *Fanfare for Orchestra*
> William Grant Still — *Fanfare for American Heroes*
> Edgar Stillman-Kelly — *Salutation to Our Boys on Land and Sea*
> Deems Taylor — *Fanfare for Russia*
> Virgil Thomson — *Fanfare for France*
> Bernard Wagenaar — *Fanfare for Airmen*[54]

Except for Copland's *Fanfare for the Common Man*, few pieces from either set of commissions are still played today. Excluding several other works by Copland and a few each by Gould, Harris, Thompson, and Robinson, patriotic music from the 1940s has all but disappeared from the concert hall. Perhaps, as Henahan so emphatically stated, some regard this music as a "national embarrassment." Surely much of it has fallen victim to America's different conception of patriotism, as well as of itself. Yet perhaps patriotic music written in the midst of a national and world crisis cannot be judged historically by the same standards as abstract music composed in relatively peaceful periods.

The United States as a nation never suffered the miseries experienced by the Soviet people during World War II. Yet Boris Schwartz, writing of the great quantity of Russian patriotic music composed during the war, makes a point that might be applied to similar American music.

The music of those days was meant to console and uplift, to encourage and exhort; nothing else mattered. Composers did not think of eternal values, not even of tomorrow—only of today, of the moment, of the immediate impact on the listener. . . . Only the survival of body and soul mattered, and the essential element of music was its morale-building force. In detached retrospect one finds shallowness, posturing, hollow heroics; but under fire it all seemed real and very vital. . . . It cannot be judged in a detached, "objective" manner. To do that is to misinterpret its function, and its motivation.[55]

American composers' eagerness to serve the United States and the American people in wartime is revealed from Finney's survey, from enlisted composers' experiences, and from their creative response to commissions and to the war in general. American composers during World War II made a self-conscious attempt to fulfill a constructive role in American society.

Some composers, however, could not help but envy the musical activity generated elsewhere by the war. Composers in the Soviet Union were again most admired it seems. For instance, Henry Cowell thought that the Russians were making "dynamic use of music . . . during the war which now threatens the heart of the country."[56] Cowell noted that all facets of musical life, both related to and detached from the military, were expanding despite the Nazi invasion, and that many new works pertaining to the crisis were being premiered.[57] It was Russia's ability to shape musical creativity to its national purpose that appeared to impress Cowell.[58] By contrast, he believed, the United States' response to the war was more similar to that of Great Britain, where composers not enlisted were looking for ways in which to be useful to the war effort.[59]

Yet many American composers were able to find or create specific channels for their abilities during World War II. Composers such as Kubik, Barber, Engel, and Blitzstein functioned successfully as musicians and composers while enlisted.[60] Those not serving in the armed forces were generally just as eager to contribute appropriately; requests for new works were resoundingly fulfilled and much new non-commissioned patriotic music was composed.

Patriotic music was also performed. Conductors such as Artur Rodzinski and Leopold Stokowski made it their policy during the war years to include a substantial amount of American music on each concert program.[61] Surely more new American art music was heard in concert halls during these years than ever before in the United States. In short, American composers found new recognition from both the government and the institutions of American cultivated music during World War II. The war produced an increased awareness of indigenous American culture by both society and American composers themselves. The doors of opportunity, if not flung wide, at least were pushed farther open.

Part III
Three Composers and Americanism

IX

Marc Blitzstein

Neutrality in culture will no longer work.
You've got to say what you mean; you've
got to say it as directly and as fully as
possible.

Marc Blitzstein, *Daily Worker*,
April 13, 1938

Marc Blitzstein (1905–64) was the most controversial American composer
of his generation. The combination of his political beliefs and intense
personality, and the manner in which these characteristics shaped his
music, are unique in American musical history. From the stormy
premiere of *The Cradle Will Rock* to the announcement of his unfinished
opera on the Sacco and Vanzetti case, Blitzstein's works touched the raw
nerve of American sociopolitical morality and unleashed the fury of those
who mistrusted his views. Even his murder, the details of which have
never been revealed, lent a legendary air to a life that might have been
the basis for one of his own operatic characters. He was tempestuous in
both life and death.[1]

Blitzstein was born into a comfortably affluent family in
Philadelphia that, as one writer has noted, was "committed to the eastern
European Jewish tradition of social democracy."[2] The composer himself
once remarked proudly that "there is a Blitzstein active in every
progressive movement in Philadelphia."[3] Blitzstein's creative talents were
not united with a strong social consciousness until the mid-1930s. From
that time on, however, music and social commentary were never separate
in his works.

Blitzstein's musical ability received early encouragement from his
family. According to his own recollections, he gave his first public
performance as a pianist at age five, and began composing at seven.[4] He
won a scholarship to the University of Pennsylvania but, after a disagree-
ment about a gymnastics requirement, left to attend the Curtis Institute.[5]

Here he studied composition with Rosario Scalero and commuted to New York City to continue piano instruction under Alexander Siloti.

Having decided upon a career in music, Blitzstein, in accordance with the custom of his time, traveled abroad for further training. In 1926, he embarked for Europe, dividing two years of study between Arnold Schoenberg in Berlin and Nadia Boulanger in Paris.[6] Although the impact of Boulanger's advocacy of Stravinsky's music had a temporary effect upon his early works, the influence of neither teacher was ultimately as important to Blitzstein as his contact with three other Europeans. During this trip, Blitzstein met Hanns Eisler and Bertolt Brecht. He also heard Brecht's *Die Dreigroschenoper* to music by Kurt Weill, which was currently playing in Berlin. Many, including the composer himself, have recognized his indebtedness to the artistic concepts of these three Germans.

Blitzstein's early works gave little indication of his later explosive proletarianism. Like many others in the late 1920s and early 1930s, he adopted the neoclassicism then overtaking Europe and America in the wake of Stravinsky.[7]   John Houseman commented that at this time Blitzstein was considered "a sophisticated composer of 'serious,' 'modern music'".[8]   In fact, he acquired the reputation of an experimental composer who dabbled in technical innovations for their own sake. B. H. Haggin found fault with one of Blitzstein's better-known works from these years, the string quartet *Largo, Largo, Largo*. Haggin wrote that with this piece

> Blitzstein got the attention only of a few people interested in the novelty of a string quartet with the three movements written *Largo, Largo, Largo*.[9]

The critic also noted an emotional detachment in Blitzstein's music, stating that he considered the composer incapable of expressing feeling in his works.[10]   After Blitzstein's musical alignment with the left, Haggin interpreted his subsequent change in style as opportunism: "Today he gets the attention of the larger number of people interested in the dramatization of the class struggle."[11]

Blitzstein's move to the left and its impact upon his artistic direction appears to have been sudden. Yet it grew naturally from his family background, his intense social consciousness, the influence of his friends, and the temper of the times. In the mid-1930s, both his father and stepmother became involved with volunteer groups aiding the fight for Spanish democracy, a favorite leftist cause.[12]   In addition, Blitzstein's wife Eva Goldbeck, whom he married in March, 1933, was a noted writer on the radical left. These factors, combined with a recognition of the Depression's severity and the American artist's difficult existence, led Blitzstein to conclude:

> Trying to make a living as a composer, I went through a period of self-criticism – Me in a world of Me's. Then I realized that we were all striving and struggling; that I couldn't make money out of my music; that artists suffer, workers suffer, people suffer. There seemed to be two ways out for the sensitive artist: one to live in a world bounded by g clefs and Bach and the small talk of musicians – a world of half-notes; the other I took.[13]

In 1934, Blitzstein joined the Composers' Collective and was reunited with Hanns Eisler and his compositional philosophy, as well as with American and other immigrant composers of like sociopolitical beliefs. In political leftism Blitzstein found a purpose for his artistic existence, a discovery best told in one of his own works, the radio musical play *I've Got the Tune.*

Both the story and music of *I've Got the Tune* (1937) are by Blitzstein, and the work seems intentionally autobiographical. The hero, Mr. Musiker, is a composer. He had written a melody but cannot find proper words for it. He and his secretary, "Beetzie, the short hand speed queen," wander about the world searching for the correct milieu for Musiker's melody.[14] As they travel, the tune falls into the hands of different types of people, inviting musical parody by the composer. Perhaps in reference to his Berlin days, Blitzstein has the melody first altered to an *avant-garde* Viennese style. It is made more complex, and is given a text concerning the moon and boredom.[15] In another sequence, racial supremacists discover and distort the original tune. Finally, when all hope seems lost, Mr. Musiker and Beetzie come upon a throng of May Day paraders who, it so happens, need a song. The hero offers to give them the tune, but the marchers inform him that it is already theirs. They provide the melody with appropriately meaningful words, and the composer gives it a new setting designed to reveal its innate power and beauty.

Simplistic if not silly by present standards, the work is probably best viewed in light of the 1930s' fervency for art with social purpose and the creative impact of Blitzstein's conversion to Marxism. There is little question that after Blitzstein recognized his calling – composing music for social and political purposes – his compositional style changed drastically. Except for Haggin, few critics have doubted the sincerity of his convictions or of his propagandistic works.[16]

As Blitzstein's political outlook coalesced, he made an artistic decision: a commitment to the musical theatre as his creative medium, and to a straightforward musical and dramatic style. As he once remarked to Aaron Copland, he became "addicted to the theatre."[17] His works from the late 1920s and early 1930s demonstrate simultaneously an intensifying of social criticism and a simplifying of musical language. *Triple Sec* (1928), his first opera, was a brief, relatively light-hearted attack upon social conventions, the music parodying the dissonant harmonies of contemporary music. The composer has described it as

> one of these screwy, modernist things in which, through stage devices, the audience is supposed to get drunk. It had philosophy. I was slamming the smug people and traditions I had been brought up with. It was a philosophy of denial of their values. Actually, it was a process of clearing the fields.[18]

Next came the ballet *Cain* (1930).   Positing that mankind is descended from Cain, not Adam, the work explored the cruelty of human nature. *Cain* was Blitzstein's artistic turning point. He later expanded ideas from the ballet, in which all men were murderers bearing the "Mark of Cain," for his one-act choral opera, *The Condemned* (1932). In the latter work, Blitzstein was "learning to direct the Mark of Cain. Some were murderers, some were the murdered."[19] *The Condemned* was also his first attempt to deal with a contemporary political topic, the Sacco and Vanzetti case. Henry Brant wrote that in *The Condemned* Blitzstein achieved "an austerity and unembarrassed directness of statement suggestive of a kind of neo-Gluck."[20] Yet Brant added that he found Blitzstein's manner of musical expression at odds with his subject matter.

> In *The Condemned*, Blitzstein's work reaches a critical stage where his developing interest in expressing a positive social viewpoint is almost directly in conflict with the rigid, impersonalization of his musical and literary language.[21]

Until this time, Blitzstein maintained a style essentially free from references to American vernacular musical idioms.   With the incorporation of such elements, primarily from popular music, Blitzstein arrived at a musical language suitable to his tastes, his abilities, and his convictions.   Blitzstein wrote no major musical theatre piece for three years after *The Condemned.* His singular voice emerged full blown in 1936 in *The Cradle Will Rock.*

A German Influence

Blitzstein attributes the original idea behind *The Cradle Will Rock* to Bertolt Brecht.

Brecht gave me the germ for the Moll in the *Cradle Will Rock*, which, as you know, is dedicated to him, since it was his ideas which impressed and influenced me so deeply.[22]

The ideas of Brecht and the music of Kurt Weill and Hanns Eisler had a strong impact upon Blitzstein's works beginning with *The Cradle Will Rock*. Blitzstein frequently praised the artistic philosophies of these three in his own writings from the mid-1930s. Not only is Blitzstein best remembered for his English adaptation of the Brecht/Weill *Die Dreigroschenoper*, but the stylistic and conceptual similarity between the music of Weill, in his Brechtian period, and that of Blitzstein has been noted repeatedly by music historians.[23]

Blitzstein's most extended discussion of contemporary music was a three-part series entitled "The Case for Modern Music," published in *New Masses* (July, 1936). In the first two articles, he reviewed the developments of the so-called "revolution" in music beginning around 1890. In the third, he gave a prescription for the future.

Similar to Olin Downes and Roy Welch,[24] Blitzstein noted that changes in twentieth-century art music paralleled those in society. Blitzstein wrote that a new and larger public wanted music that was no longer "art-for-art's-sake" nor geared toward "little excited clubs and societies, all ladies and lions, fomenting some concerts and many teas."[25]

A great new public is born, it storms the gates. It wants culture, it asks for it. A culture, an art that will bring to it a deeper knowledge of itself and of reality, that will show it a possible new reality.[26]

Since the turn of the century, Blitzstein believed, composers had been developing new techniques, and both good and bad trends had evolved. A healthy development was bringing before the public truthful—if unpleasant—sides of life and couching them in appropriately discordant styles. Works such as Schoenberg's *Pierrot Lunaire* and Stravinsky's *Le Sacre du Printemps* shocked the public in the early decades, but exposed painful realities of human nature. Yet composers seemed unable to find a musical language that, while technically an outgrowth of the Euro-American cultivated heritage, could be understood and accepted by general audiences. According to Blitzstein, composers began to realize the need for such a musical language around 1925. He cited the example of *Gebrauchsmusik* as one partly successful attempt to restore communication between composers and the public. Yet

the real lack was that composers were trying to reach a lot of people, but had as a rule only a very vague idea what they wanted to say to them. They used timely subjects, which was good (the earlier moderns went in for fantastic or ancient or metaphysical or exotic ones); but most of them had little political or social education, they were satisfied with merely risible satire or superficial comment or no comment at all. . . . As a movement *Gebrauchsmusik* was important; it was also muddle-headed. It had direction; but it had little content.[27]

At this point, Blitzstein's philosophy diverged from those of Welch and Downes discussed in Chapter IV. Blitzstein cited Weill and Eisler as members of a new generation of contemporary composers who were achieving a communicating style and knew what to communicate. In Blitzstein's opinion, a sociopolitical message was the thing to communicate. He found the texts of Bertolt Brecht especially significant for modern life, and the music of the Marxist Eisler their appropriate vehicle.

> The *Gebrauchsmusik* movement brought forth men who had political education, who saw the possibilities. Brecht, the German poet, was chief among them. He saw the new great public more clearly, more intensely than anyone else. . . . Note that as he became more and more revolutionary in content, Brecht turned more and more to Eisler for musical collaboration. He had made the *Jasager* with Weill, an extraordinary work. Now he became alarmed at certain defeatist interpretations which might be placed on it, and wrote the *Massnahme*, which he called a "concertization" of the same theme; he made this with Eisler.[28]

Elsewhere, Blitzstein praised Eisler's mass songs, a form he believed had evolved with musicians' growing social concern.[29] He called Eisler "the first instance of the real fusion of Marxist and musician."[30]

Clearly, Blitzstein favored Eisler because of this composer's greater political commitment and its effect upon his style. Eisler was direct and powerful, as in a stirring march scene for the movie *Kühle Wampe* described by Blitzstein:

> The workers discover their houses destroyed, [and] are sunk in an abysm of dejection. From somewhere comes music — a street-march — steady, vigorous, and with a certain fury in it; and we see the faces of the workers change, grow stubborn, militant, they draw energy and courage out of the music, they drain the music and strength comes into their faces. Music combats the scene, and pulls everything with it.[31]

Eisler composed purposeful music to uplift the masses. Weill's music, on the other hand, was soft, "velvet propaganda."[32] Of Weill's music to *Die Dreigroschenoper*, Blitzstein wrote:

> Weill's natural sweetness and softness are probably the cause of the *Dreigroschenoper's* enormous and mistaken success. Brecht wanted the middle class audience to shrink in horror at the rotting, callous, spineless underworld characters, saying "This is ourselves!" Instead, they exclaimed with joy, "Why they all have hearts of gold — the *dear* pimps and whores!"[33]

Blitzstein wanted a *Dreigroschenoper* with more bite – politically and musically.

In the early 1930s, before his political conversion, Blitzstein had found fault with Weill's tendency to use popular idioms as a means of simplifying his musical language. At this time, Blitzstein believed that popular music and art music should maintain separate identities.

> One grows to believe in the real worth, wherever it may be in the scale of values, of the untinkered Tin-Pan-Alley "number. . . . " On the whole, popular music (I now use the term literally) has resisted wonderfully the "invasions" of serious music. . . . Serious music might even learn a lesson from this persistently "low" art, in the matter of discovering one's place, and respecting it.[34]

As Blitzstein's social awareness grew and his concern for an artistic connection with the public increased, this attitude changed. By 1936, he considered Weill's use of a "low" style in a different light and retracted his previous remarks. Weill's reworking of popular idioms had become one aspect of his style that Blitzstein could appreciate.

> I have written some harsh things in the past about Kurt Weill and his music. I wish now to write a few good things. He hasn't changed, I have. . . . I have formerly complained about Weill's banality, even his insipidity. I see now that triteness in a work of Weill is curiously not bad, but good. Weill deliberately tries for it – for the familiar turn, for the easy supine harmonies. . . . I think he feels that certain ways of being expressive never die; and I think he believes he can crack open, make plastic, even re-form a mold that has hardened in the memory of other composers. . . . Weill's utter corniness is in a way terribly sophisticated.[35]

Blitzstein's comments appeared in fall of 1936. His description of Weill's use of popular elements may have been close to what he had in mind during the composition of *The Cradle* during the summer of 1936.

There can be little question that Brecht's influence upon Blitzstein was strong, particularly in the conception of *The Cradle Will Rock.* In 1935, Blitzstein played a dramatic sketch for Brecht built around "The Nickel Under the Foot," a song that later became the basis for the street-walker's scene in *The Cradle.* Brecht liked it and encouraged Blitzstein to develop it, noting that prostitution in America was not confined to the literal type. Blitzstein should add "figurative prostitution."[36]

Brecht, according to Dietz, was a powerful personality who guided his collaborators in their use of music instead of being guided by them.[37] Thus he had been able to forge his own musico-dramatic style. Such elements as the use of untrained voices, street vocabulary, and popular idioms – all traits of Brecht's "epic" theatre – can be found in *The Cradle.*

The work also carried a strong political message. Like Brecht, Blitzstein had come to regard music as a vehicle for social commentary in the mid-1930s. Significantly, Blitzstein wrote all his own librettos (actually beginning with *The Harpies* in 1931), and called *The Cradle* not an opera, operetta, or "musical," but a "play-in-music."[38] For Blitzstein in this period, the play was decidedly the thing.

The Cradle Will Rock

Blitzstein wrote *The Cradle* at break-neck speed.

> I wrote the piece during five weeks in June-July 1936, at white heat, as a kind of rebound from my wife's death in May.[39]

The story of the first production of *The Cradle Will Rock* is remarkable.[40] It was *the* musical/theatrical event of the late 1930s; both the play and the event summarized the mood of the times. *The Cradle* first was put into rehearsal by the leftist Actor's Repertory group, but plans were halted when the organization disbanded for lack of funds. Blitzstein's circle of friends in this period included Clifford Odets,[41] Lillian Hellman, Orson Welles, and John Houseman. Welles and Houseman were omnipresent in the contemporary theatrical world, and were associated with many a momentous and innovative dramatic happening of the decade. When they learned of Blitzstein's work and its availability, they took it on.

Welles and Houseman at that time were running the WPA Federal Theatre Project of New York City, and already had been responsible for such mildly controversial productions as a black version of *Macbeth* (actually done with the WPA Negro Theatre) and *Horse Eats Hat*.[42] With *The Cradle*, as Houseman recalled, they acquired a "time-bomb which threatened to bring the entire [Federal Theatre] project tumbling."[43] The project did tumble in 1939, and *The Cradle* was probably one of the causes.

In recalling the mood of spring, 1937, Houseman wrote:

> It is not easy, with a World War, a cold war, Korea, Vietnam and some thirty years of inflation in between, to re-create the world we lived in during the mid-thirties. Nineteen thirty-seven was, in some ways, the most confused and disturbed of those difficult years – a time of transition between the end of the Great Depression and the beginning of the slowly gathering industrial boom that accompanied our preparations for World War II. . . . It was also the year in which labor violence vied for space with the international news on the front pages of the nation's press.[44]

The polemical subject matter, capitalist corruption in "Steeltown, U.S.A." and the labor movement, was downplayed by those involved at first. As the premiere approached, however, more and more attention was drawn to *The Cradle's* political overtones. The producers' growing alarm was fueled by national events — widespread strikes and violent confrontations in steel-producing cities[45] — and the increasing reputation of the New York Federal Theatre Project as a haven for left-wing sympathizers.

It was the policy of the WPA administration in Washington to sanction each production just before opening night. *The Cradle* never received its sanction, however. Instead, in an unprecedented move, armed WPA guards surrounded the theatre (the Maxine Elliott) the day before the scheduled opening, and locked up all costumes, scenery, and props. Houseman, Blitzstein, Welles, Lehman Engel (the conductor), and a few others barricaded themselves in a basement rest room and mapped strategy. Hours of uncertainty followed. The final blow seemed to have been dealt on the morning of the supposed premiere when both the Actors Equity and Musicians Union forbade their members to participate in a production lacking federal approval.[46] As evening approached, no one was sure what would happen. The principal purchaser of opening night's theatre party was the Downtown Music School, an adjunct of the Workers Music League and the Composers' Collective. As curtain time neared, a restless crowd began milling around in front of the building.

Finally, someone suggested another theatre. The vacant Venice was procured, as was an old piano and a truck to haul it. Lehman Engel sneaked the score out under a coat, and, following instructions, the crowd began trekking the nineteen blocks to the newly selected site, gathering new members on the way. Now there was at least a theatre; the sets, costumes, and orchestra could be done without, but what about actors?

Blitzstein appeared on stage, expecting to do a solo performance.

> And there I was alone on a bare stage — myself produced by John Houseman, directed by Orson Welles, lit by Feder and conducted by Lehman Engel. I started, ready to do the whole show myself.[47]

Union regulations only prevented performance onstage, however, and were silent about acting elsewhere. Before Blitzstein could finish the first song, cast members popped up from the audience and carried on the production from all over the theatre. The effect was electric. Copland later recalled: "The opening night of *The Cradle* made history; none of us who were there will ever forget it."[48] Blitzstein, the performers, and the subject had the sympathy of the audience. *The Cradle*, in an austere setting and improvised production, was a huge success.

The Cradle was relocated twice during the 1937-38 season, but was always presented as on opening night.[49]   Each time, its reviews–many of which are cited in the Dietz study–were generally favorable if not raving. Brooks Atkinson was so impressed that he reviewed it twice.[50]   Alistair Cooke, the perennial British commentator on the American scene, devoted an entire broadcast of his weekly New York radio program to *The Cradle*, calling the work "the nearest, most effective equivalent to the form of a Greek tragedy."[51]   Predictably, the Communist *New Masses* gave *The Cradle* flattering notices, praising it for its social realism.

> It is that man with the tune, Marc Blitzstein, who is really breaking new ground, who's bringing American music to grips with reality and proving that musical progressiveness can be entertaining as well as abstractly admirable.[52]

Perhaps the most interesting of all reactions to *The Cradle* is described by Houseman.   Blitzstein intended his work for the unsophisticated masses, with a particular appeal to American laborers and their supporters.   During the period the play was at the Venice Theatre, the WPA group organized a Sunday expedition to a steel capital, Bethlehem, Pennyslvania, to present *The Cradle*.[53]   They hoped for the ideal audience. Houseman wrote of their reception:

> It was a poor turn-out–less than two hundred including stool pigeons and informers, but they seemed grateful to us for coming.   In a letter to Mina [Curtiss] I reported that Marc's sophisticated satire had "left them cold and bewildered but they were moved by the second half and knew all about the corrupt police and press and found Mr. Mister clearly recognizable."[54]

Afterwards, it was discovered that the small attendance resulted from a steel company picnic which the workers had been encouraged to attend. Houseman commented:

> In their embarrassed apology for the poor turnout they gave a more convincing picture of a company-dominated town than Marc with all his satire and drama.[55]

The story of *The Cradle Will Rock* concerns the effect of capitalist control on the residents of Steeltown, U.S.A.   The plot centers on several of the town's leading citizens, members of the Liberty Committee. Mistakenly arrested as union organizers, they wait in night court for Mr. Mister, the employer and embodiment of capitalist evil, to bail them out. A seamy panorama of life spreads before them as they wait.[56]

Beginning with the Moll, an unemployed and desperate young woman who has taken to the streets, Blitzstein explores the many guises of prostitution.   The Moll, the only literal prostitute, turns out to be the play's innocent.   Artists flatter Mrs. Mister for support and social contacts; a college president bows to the wishes of Mr. Mister, the school's most important trustee; a doctor lies about a steel plant murder to receive a research grant. All are forced by circumstances to compromise their principles to survive in Mr. Mister's town. The authentic union leader and the hero of the tale is Larry Foreman, who appears almost as *deus ex machina* in the later part of the work. Foreman unites his newly-organized workers and leads them to victory over Mr. Mister and the Liberty Committee.

In *The Cradle*, Blitzstein consciously created a modern-day morality play, vintage 1937. He has called it

> a middle-class allegory for middle-class people—to shove those into the progressive ranks who stood on the brink; to rescue those who were about to die by joining the "liberty" committees.[57]

Elsewhere, he stated:

> The Cradle is an allegory about people I hate. . . . Its characters are types, not real people. They are symbols of the kinds of people living in our society.[58]

A frequently noted fault of the play, its one-dimensional characters, was actually the intention of the composer.[59] Mr. Mister was not merely a company president, he was capitalism; Larry Foreman was not just a union leader, he was a worker of the world uniting his fellow downtrodden. As a Marxist allegorical play, *The Cradle* resembles agit-prop skits long a part of Marxist rallies and meetings.[60]

The musical language of *The Cradle* is best described as eclectic, mixing American popular music and musical theatre idioms, Kurt Weill's style in *Die Dreigroschenoper*, and certain characteristics of American concert music of the period. Popular music is used largely for parody: Broadway musical style in Sister and Junior Mister's "Croon-Spoon," stylized popular songs about Hawaii in the Honolulu song, and barbershop quartets by the Liberty Committee, all in Act I. "Serious" elements enter the satire as well, however. A motive from Beethoven's *Egmont Overture* serves as the horn of social-climbing Mrs. Mister's "cultured" automobile. The reverent Reverend Salvation spouts religious platitudes to a mixture of Baroque oratorio and Protestant hymn style. Such elements are parodied to reflect the sarcastic treatment Blitzstein has given the characters they represent.

Contrasted with the parodied sections are moments of deadly seriousness, where Blitzstein drives home his message. Three songs stand out: "The Nickel Under the Foot," "Joe Worker," and "The Cradle Will Rock." It is probably no accident that the "message" songs all occur in Act II,[61] which presents the cure for the social ills described in the first act. "Joe Worker" is a strophic ballad telling of the death of a factory worker with unionist inclinations. Presented by Joe's sister, it is at once the simplest and the most powerful song of *The Cradle*, an outcry against social injustice. "The Cradle Will Rock" first is introduced as a solo by Larry Foreman. Transformed to a purposeful mass song in march style, it returns in the finale to accompany the gathering forces of workers mounting their campaign against Mr. Mister.

"The Nickel Under the Foot," around which *The Cradle* was built, is the Moll's plaintive song which opens Act II (see Example 1). After a brief introduction in C minor, "The Nickel Under the Foot" is a strophic song with a 23-measure refrain. Tonally at the level C, the song moves to G♭ major (measure 29) before returning to C major (measure 34). The mode fluctuates between major and minor, and harmonies are almost continually dissonant. Added sevenths and sixths predominate, the latter an adaptation of a current popular song characteristic. A clear C major triad does not occur until the final chord has been sustained for one measure (measure 88). Blitzstein's frequent use of a tonic pedal underpinning dissonances in a chordal, driving accompaniment pattern (as in the Introduction) resembles several songs in *Die Dreigroschenoper*.

The song is tuneful, with a range appropriate for an untrained voice. The refrain opens with two parallel four-measure phrases and, until the sixth measure of the third phrase (measure 33), has the shape and symmetry of a popular song. Yet Blitzstein destroys the symmetry, extending by two measures the third phrase to the brief concluding phrases. The musical content is essentially unchanged throughout the three verses. Although the melody is almost pretty, Blitzstein's continuous dissonant edge and repetitious, propelling accompaniment achieve an ominous quality to match the bitter street vernacular of the text. The Moll bemoans the importance of money; no matter how "sweet" you are, the need for "the nickel" will make you "rotten." The theme of the song is the theme of *The Cradle*.

The issue of *The Cradle's* relevance after the polemical 1930s has arisen with each revival. A decade after its premiere, John Mason Brown remarked that the answer to American working class problems as proposed by Blitzstein then seemed drastically oversimplified.

> A proof of the world's present sorrow is that, as Americans now know, the solution is not that easy. . . . In the presence of the current revival of Mr. Blitzstein's work, those years seem far more than a decade.[62]

In 1960, B. H. Haggin, never a fan of Blitzstein's works, wrote of the New York City Opera production of *The Cradle*:

Example 1
"Nickel Under the Foot," *The Cradle Will Rock*, Marc Blitzstein.
Copyright MCMXXXVIII by Chappell & Co., Inc., N.Y.C. Used by
permission.

live like hearts and flow-ers _____ And ev-'ry

day is a won-der-land tour. _____ O, you can

dream and scheme and hap-pi-ly put and take, Take

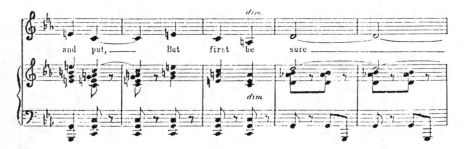

and put, _____ But first be sure

the nick - el's un - der your foot.

Go stand on some - one's neck while you're tak - in',

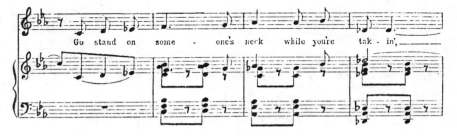

Cut in - to some - bod - y's throat as you put,

For ev - 'ry dream and scheme's de - pend - ing on

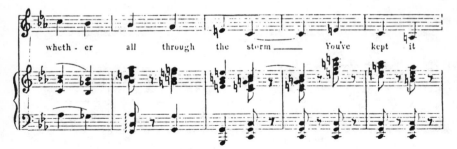

wheth - er   all   through   the   storm ____   You've   kept   it

60

dim.

warm ____   The nick - el   un - der   your

foot. ____   And   if   you're   sweet   then

70

you'll   grow rot - ten, ____   Your pret - ty   heart   cov - ered   o - ver   with

The New York City Opera Company, in its third season of American opera, again ignored distinguished achievement in American opera and added Marc Blitzstein's *The Cradle Will Rock* . . . to its undistinguished repertory. . . . To call this dated today is to imply that it was valid in 1937; whereas actually it was in 1937, as it is now, the crudest agit-prop falsification suited to an audience of readers of the *Daily Worker*.[63]

Whether or not one agrees with his assessment, Haggin does make a point which can be taken in two ways. For *The Cradle* is essentially an allegory of human life and its corruption, as relevant or dated a subject in the present as in 1937. Blitzstein's proposed solution to corruption — Marxism represented by unionism — has attracted few American adherents. Yet the work presents humanity mastering itself and its circumstances. Copland has written that if Blitzstein's agit-prop works fail,

it is not because they are a form of propaganda art but because the propaganda is not couched in terms that make the pieces valid for audiences everywhere. . . . This limits their circulation as works of art and therefore as propaganda.[64]

Perhaps a work so suited to one time cannot, in effect, be timeless.

Blitzstein evidently recognized the narrowness of his musico-dramatic approach in *The Cradle* and its successor, *No for An Answer* (1941).[65] Also, the problems of World War II became overpowering after the latter work. Blitzstein enlisted, and produced two patriotic works while in the Army Air Force (see above, pp. 193–94). Yet he never relinquished the role of social commentator. Unlike others, who seemed to don the stylish cloak of radicalism only to discard it after the Depression, Blitzstein made a life-long commitment to infuse his works with sociopolitical content. While his most blatant agit-prop works were limited to the 1930s and early 1940s, he continued over a period of nearly thirty years to give musical expression to a variety of social ills. *No for an Answer* explored the plight of unemployed Greek immigrants in America. *Native Land* (1942), a film for which he composed music, uncovered the activities of the Ku Klux Klan. *Freedom Morning* (1943) depicted the role of black Americans in World War II. *The Airborne Symphony* (1943) was militantly anti-fascist. *Regina* (1949), based on Lillian Hellman's *The Little Foxes*, revealed capitalist decadence in a southern industrial family.

Nor did Blitzstein reject the language of popular music. In *Regina*, both his message and musical style achieve their highest sophistication and integration. The work is Blitzstein's most operatic, although spoken dialogue is still used. Heavy technical demands are made of the principals; yet Blitzstein incorporates ragtime, jazz, and spiritual idioms. While "good" and "bad" characters are clearly delineated, they are developed as individuals in *Regina* and are no longer stereotypes as in earlier works. In effect, a murder occurs on stage for the sake of money, still the great corruptor, but the message in this work is the individual's recognition of truth. Zan, Regina's daughter, determines to leave her mother's decadent world. It is a more muted and less simplistic statement of hope than found in *The Cradle.*

By the late 1950s and early 1960s, Blitzstein found himself a survivor in a stylistically foreign age. He remained unconvinced by the post-1940s fascination with serialism and did not explore the technique until *Idiots First*, begun in 1963 and left unfinished at his death.[66] Even earlier, Blitzstein had had difficulty visualizing a direction for cultivated music beyond *Gebrauchsmusik* and the proletarian movement. Several of his essays on contemporary music reveal a certain openendedness. The final portion of the three-part essay cited earlier, that comprising the musical forecast, is the weakest. Already in 1936 Blitzstein was troubled with the problem that increasingly plagued him: the balance between comprehensibility and modern techniques in contemporary music.[67] As Minna Lederman wrote in a posthumous tribute to Blitzstein, he was "tormented with the problem of expanding his powers and his idiom without compromising the basic credo of a grand simplicity."[68]

Blitzstein's last major venture also was left unfinished. It was to be an opera based on the Sacco and Vanzetti case that had concerned him from the time of *The Condemned. Sacco and Vanzetti* became, apparently, a compositional Waterloo for Blitzstein.[69] Joan Peyser noted that when the composer reached an impasse in his work on the opera, he placed the score in the trunk of his car and left for Martinique.[70] He never returned, and although the opera eventually was recovered, Blitzstein's final attempt to solve the problem of contemporary music as he saw it remains incomplete.

Blitzstein was both a conceptual and compositional musical Americanist. In 1935 he joined the Composers' Collective, a group attempting to create American music for the American masses.[71] With Aaron Copland and Virgil Thomson in 1937, Blitzstein helped found the American Composers' Alliance, dedicated to economic returns for American music. Through his work with the latter group and the League of Composers, Blitzstein contributed to raising the social status of younger generations of composers in the United States.

Blitzstein's compositional Americanism stemmed directly from his sociopolitical beliefs. As Paul Myers Talley has observed, Blitzstein "insisted that America must live up to its finest principles."[72] To

Blitzstein, music was a tool for improving American society. He was concerned with a direct link between the composer and his audience and, in attempting to find that link, made popular musical idioms a permanent part of his style. Blitzstein never became involved in the folksong movement of the late 1930s and early 1940s that attracted so many American composers, especially those on the left. His subject matter was consistently American, but his interests were the contemporary man-on-the-street and the problems of modern life. The man-on-the-farm and a nostalgia for rural America had little appeal for him. Rather, Blitzstein was an "urban" Americanist. His musico-dramatic language was rooted in American street vernacular.

Blitzstein's artistic direction was forged in the restless mid-1930s. His constant focus on painfully real subjects was an effort to give his audiences reasons to be different from what they observed onstage. Copland, in sympathetic tribute, eloquently stated Blitzstein's position:

> Those composers who are attracted by the immense terrain of new techniques now available to them would do well to consider that humanity's struggle for a fuller life may be equally valid as a moving force in the future history of our music. It was the basic motivation for Marc Blitzstein's art, and resulted in a contribution to American music that is yet to be fully evaluated.[73]

Blitzstein was America's first moralist of the musical theatre.

X

Roy Harris

Harris is, above all, the accepted
one hundred per cent American
composer.

Walter Piston, *Modern Music*, (January–February, 1934)

In the 1930s and early 1940s, no composer was more "American" than
Roy Harris (1898–1979). Nor did the music of any other American
composer—even Aaron Copland's—receive the acclaim of Harris's
symphonic works in this period. Starting with the *Symphony 1933*, which
the conductor Serge Koussevitzky called the "first tragic American
symphony,"[1] Roy Harris's works became synonymous with "American"
when an American label was highly desirable. He was the declared
"white hope of American music."[2]

The inferences of the "white hope" description cannot be
overlooked.[3] Indigenous qualitities in American art music were a matter
of debate in the 1930s, particularly when compared to such an
unquestionably "American" vernacular music as jazz. Unlike some
composers in the 1920s, Harris did not draw upon jazz idioms. Rather,
he emerged from the far West with symphonies, concertos, and string
quartets in a largely self-taught style. In the 1930s, he wrote pieces with
American titles, sometimes including folksong, in an era of national
nostalgia for rural life. Musicians and writers looking for "American"
cultivated music seized upon Harris's example. In an eight-page profile
of the composer published in 1936, Paul Rosenfeld used some derivative
of "American" twenty times in discussing either Harris himself or his
music.[4] Rosenfeld's remarks about Harris are typical of the period.

Roy Harris could rightfully claim a heritage more "American" than
most.[5] His grandfather, a descendant of Scotch-Irish New Englanders,
was a circuit-riding preacher and an early homesteader in the land rushes
after the Civil War. Following family tradition, Harris's parents settled

in the wilderness that became Oklahoma. They built their own house on land they cleared themselves.

Nicolas Slonimsky, a frequent commentator on Harris's career, has written:

> There is something providential about the Americanism of Roy Harris, for he was born in a log cabin on Lincoln's birthday in Lincoln County, Oklahoma in 1898.[6]

Harris's life followed paths that helped to create what Slonimsky has called the "Harris legend."[7] When he was five, his family moved from Oklahoma to California's San Gabriel Valley. In Covina, just east of Los Angeles, they established a farm.

> All my boyhood days were highly romantic with pioneer struggles against nature and market conditions. I came to know the innermost moods of the seasons and the animal and vegetable kingdoms of that region through being a farmer's son with all his attendant chores and work. It was with great heartache and sorrow that I saw the winding dirt roads evolve into boulevards, the family surrey disappear, the cow give way to the milkman, the old schools become antiquated and abandoned, the neighbors forget each other in their absorption of wealth.[8]

Harris's music has often sought to recapture the aura of his rural youth.

At the age of eight, Harris had his first piano lessons with an itinerant music teacher. These continued sporadically throughout his boyhood. In high school, he also learned to play the clarinet and travelled to concerts with music-loving friends. Such experiences comprised his musical education until his twenties. Even then, financial restrictions prevented him from receiving much formal instruction. He enlisted in the Army during World War I and, although never leaving California, was trained for heavy artillery combat. With the war's end, he attended the University of California at Berkeley evenings and drove a dairy truck during the daytime. He studied such diverse subjects as Hindu philosophy and Marxism, even teaching a course in the latter subject for a short time. Music, however, became an increasing preoccupation. Through Fannie Charles Dillon, his music instructor at the University, he learned of Arthur Farwell and began private composition lessons with him.

Farwell, an Americanist of an older generation, was the earliest to recognize Harris's potential. Later Farwell wrote:

> I had the opportunity of seeing his work in California as early as 1924, and I was convinced at that time that he would one day challenge the world. Aside from his manifest talent, my grounds for this belief lay in his mental vitality and breadth, in his insistence upon the subjecting of every accepted musical dictum

and tradition, technical and spiritual, to a searching scrutiny, and a determination to work out a new, vital and creative way in every musical sphere.[9]

Under Farwell's tutelage, Harris composed a one-movement *Andante* for orchestra. Harris played the work on the piano for Farwell and Modeste Altschuler, a Russian conductor with whom he studied orchestration. His mentors were enthusiastic and encouraged him to send the score to Howard Hanson, who as a composer, conductor, and an educator was interested in contemporary American music. Harris was quickly on his way east to hear Hanson conduct the Rochester Philharmonic in the premiere of the work. The *Andante* was then selected for performance by the New York Philharmonic in its 1926 summer concert series at Lewisohn Stadium. In New York City, Harris met Aaron Copland, recently returned from France. Copland highly recommended his teacher, Nadia Boulanger. After managing to secure sufficient funds, Harris embarked for Europe.

Recalling Boulanger, Harris has written:

> She had the patience of an angel. She called me her autodidact and allowed me to go my own way. At the end of the first year I felt quite discouraged. I could not accept the European idea of discipline wherein one learns by exercising a system of formalized studies in harmony, counterpoint and form. It all seemed to leave out the exercise of the most important element in a composer's equipment — the imagination.[10]

Eventually, Harris and Boulanger compromised on methods. Harris proposed that he learn by the examples of past masters, and began studying the works of Beethoven, particularly the string quartets.

> Boulanger cooperated with complete grace and from this point on life unfolded swiftly and with an exciting logic. Days and nights were saturated with Beethoven's exciting forms. I also turned to Bach's rich contrapuntal textures and long, direct musical structures. I learned about the passion and discipline of uninterrupted eloquence — about opulence, fecundity, abundance, clarity and style.[11]

Harris's study of earlier music stretched back to the Renaissance contrapuntalists, especially Josquin. His admiration for older music became life-long, and he considered himself a modern classicist.[12]

For nearly four years, Harris lived and composed in Paris. His financial worries were eased in 1928 when he was given a Guggenheim Fellowship, an award renewed the following year. Although Harris was at first apprehensive about becoming an artistic expatriate while abroad, he found that memories of his American childhood sustained him.[13] In Paris, he charted an artistic course that became the foundation of his

Americanism, for here he wrote his first full-length symphony, *Symphony– American Portrait 1929.*

The *Symphony– American Portrait 1929* was neither performed nor published. Yet it is important, for it established many of Harris's major compositional concerns. First, Harris tied programmatic expression of emotions to formal movements in the *American Portrait*, a trait found in several of his later pieces. Second, he chose an American subject; the symphony illustrates Harris's conception of the dominant characteristics of the American people.[14] Third, the Civil War song "When Johnny Comes Marching Home" is prominent in two movements of the *American Portrait*. Dan Stehman, who has analyzed Harris's symphonies through *Symphony No. 12* (1969), notes that Harris returned often to this tune in his music.[15] "Johnny" is Harris's representatively "American" song.[16]

Finally, Harris's use of "Johnny" in the *American Portrait* set a precedent for his subsequent treatment of quoted American tunes. According to Stehman, Harris left the melody essentially intact, as he did also in the overture *When Johnny Comes Marching Home.*[17] He based his development upon melodic variations, so that even in contrapuntal sections, the original theme or its fragments remain clearly identifiable. As Stehman also has noted, Harris is generally much stricter in his treatment of pre-existent melodic material than of his own, which he varies almost continuously.[18]

Although Harris's *American Portrait* foreshadowed his artistic direction, it did little to further his career. An eight-year hiatus exists between the premiere of the *Andante* and that of *Symphony No. 1*, better known by its subtitle *Symphony 1933*. In part, this gap was caused by an accident that occurred while Harris was still in France. He fractured his spine, and the injury was so serious that he returned to New York for a delicate operation and six months in a cast. During his recuperation he composed, and succeeded in having performed, music for smaller forces. His *String Quartet No. 1* was premiered by the Pro Arte Quartet in 1930 and the *String Sextet* received its first performance at the Yaddo Festival in 1932.

During the late 1920s and early 1930s, Harris's reputation grew. Paul Rosenfeld included a section on Harris in his book of essays *An Hour With American Music* (1929), and Harris's former teacher Arthur Farwell contributed a substantial study (cited above) about the young composer and his music to *The Musical Quarterly* in 1932. Harris was also contributing his own writings to musical publications. In articles such as "Does Music Have to be European?" (1932) and "The Problems of American Composers" (1933), he outspokenly advocated "American" art music.[19]   He called for greater recognition of native composers and criticized the institututions for cultivated music in America, from music schools to orchestras.

By ignoring most American composers, wrote Harris, American musical organizations were not adequately encouraging native musical creativity, and were teaching American audiences to appreciate only European music.   Without sympathetic audiences, an indigenous music could not mature.

> Audiences are the roots of musical culture, interpretative [*sic*] musicians form the professional body of music, and original composition is the final fruit.   And musical culture, that strange plant of civilization, develops in much the same way that a tree develops: roots, body, and fruit are interdependent.   Obviously there can be no body of interpretative [*sic*] musicians until there is already an audience to feed it; nor can there be a growth in musical composition until composers have the necessary experience of hearing their works performed and appraised by capable and sympathetic interpretative [*sic*] musicians.[20]

In these passages, Harris continued a tradition of conceptual Americanism reaching back over the generations to William Henry Fry and George Frederick Bristow.

Harris's Americanist writings also frequently included lengthy discussions of the developing character of American music.   These essays provided commentators with ample reason to label him an "American" composer, because many of his descriptions of native art music seemed to describe his own style.   Thus Harris established a profile for musical Americanism that, intentionally or not, in many ways matched his own. By the time of his next orchestral premiere, the *Symphony 1933*, his "American" reputation was already established.

At a concert sponsored by the Elizabeth Sprague Coolidge Foundation in spring, 1933, Harris met Serge Koussevitzky.   The meeting began a series of collaborations that culminated six years later in Harris's *Third Symphony.*   Koussevitzky was already familiar with Harris's music, and requested a symphony for the following season.[21]   The *Symphony 1933*, premiered by Koussevitzky and the Boston Symphony Orchestra on January 26, 1934, marked Harris's first full public recognition as a symphonic composer.   Unlike his *American Portrait*, the *Symphony 1933* was not programmatic.   Yet the work was hailed as "American" nevertheless.[22]

Harris has written many works that are Americanist because of title or subject choice, or because they quote identifiably American musical materials; he has also composed purely abstract works free from references to Americana.   Harris's symphonies alternate with some

regularity between the two types: *Symphony—American Portrait 1929,
Symphony No. 1 (Symphony 1933), Symphony No. 2* (1934), *Symphony for
Voices* (1935; based on texts by Walt Whitman), *Symphony No. 3* (1938),
Symphony No. 4 (Folksong Symphony) (1940; settings of folksongs for
chorus and orchestra), *Symphony No. 5* (1942), *Symphony No. 6
(Gettysburg)* (1944; setting of the Gettysburg Address for chorus and
orchestra), *West Point Symphony for Band* (1952), *Symphony No. 7*
(1952), *Symphony No. 8 (San Francisco)* (1962), *Symphony No. 9* (1962),
Symphony No. 10 (Abraham Lincoln Symphony) (1965), *Symphony No. 11*
(1967), *Symphony No. 12 (Père Marquette Symphony)* (1969).[23]

Both types of Harris's music have repeatedly been characterized as
"American." His obviously Americanist works are generally straightforward in their incorporation of pre-existent elements. Thus it seems
worthwhile to investigate an abstract piece by Harris to find out what it
is about his music that has led people so consistently to call it "American." Harris's *Third Symphony*, his best-known work, is the obvious
choice for discussion.

**Harris's "Third Symphony":
Music as a National Expression**

Harris began writing his *Third Symphony* during the last months of 1938,
completing it in January, 1939. It was premiered by Koussevitzky and
the Boston Symphony Orchestra on February 24, 1939. Immediately
acclaimed, the *Third Symphony* received an additional nine performances
by the Boston Symphony the same year. Furthermore, within the 1941-
42 season alone, the work was played thirty-three times in the United
States and a number of times abroad as well.[24] Even Arturo Toscanini,
not a noted champion of American music, programmed it, making
Harris's *Third Symphony* the first large American composition that he
conducted.[25]

Reviewing the New York premiere of the *Third Symphony*, Olin
Downes — who was five minutes late for the performance — remarked that

> the last three quarters of Harris's Third Symphony are written more clearly,
> simply, with a greater unity of thought and style than any other work of Mr.
> Harris that we have heard.[26]

The significance of a Harris premiere to the New York musical
world of 1939 is reflected in William Schuman's angry letter to the music
editor of the *Times* following Downes's review:

> An event so important as the first performance of Harris's new work in our city
> deserves some full report in the paper we chose to read. . . .

This symphony seems to me an extraordinary work. Its melodic material reveals once again Harris's remarkable gift.[27]

Schuman's remarks indicate the esteem in which Harris was held by his fellow composers.[28]

The public and critical success of Harris's *Third Symphony* has proven long-lasting. To some commentators, the work is the definitive symphony of its period — an American musical masterpiece.[29] For instance, as recently as 1972 Virgil Thomson has written that the "Third Symphony remains to this day America's most convincing product in that form."[30] Furthermore, the Third may be the only Harris symphony to have achieved a lasting place in the standard orchestral repertory. A study by Kate Hevner Mueller concludes that American symphony orchestras consistently have preferred Harris's *Third Symphony* to his other orchestral works.[31]

Harris's *Third Symphony* is a continuous, one-movement composition in several sections. For the work's premiere, Harris provided the following description:

SECTION I.   Tragic — bow string sonorities.
SECTION II.   Lyric — strings, horns, woodwinds.
SECTION III.   Pastoral — emphasizing woodwind color.
SECTION IV.   Fugue — dramatic.
    A. Brass — percussion predominating
       Canonic development of Section II material
    B. constituting background for further
       development of fugue.
    C. Brass climax. Rhythmic motif derived
       from Fugue subject.
SECTION V.   Dramatic — Tragic.
    Restatement of Violin Theme Section I. *Tutti*
       strings in canon with *tutti* woodwinds.
    Brass and percussion develops rhythmic motif
       from climax of Section IV
Materials:
    1. Melodic Contours — Diatonic — Polytonal.
    2. Harmonic Textures — Consonance — Polytonal.[32]

While Harris's written outline of the *Third Symphony* provides a general idea of the work's sectional plan, it gives no measure numbers. The beginnings of some sections are obvious but others are more difficult to discern. Sections III and IV are distinguished by materials, texture, and tonal centers, as well as other factors. In Section III, the regularity of harmonic rhythm is telling; in Section IV, instrumentation is different from all previous sections (see accompanying chart for details). The beginning of Part II of Section V is marked by a D pedal-point. But the beginnings of Sections II and V (Part I) are less evident. Section II could be said to begin at either m. 139 or m. 151. The rests in m. 138, following what appears to be the climax of Section I (mm. 117-38), make a division there feasible. Yet the principal material of Section II does not enter until m. 152 (in the strings). Furthermore, the reiteration of Section I material in the flute (mm. 140-43) and the anticipatory material in the horns (m. 146 and m. 150, in preparation for principal material of Section II), give the area between m. 139 and m. 151 a transitional character.

The break between Sections IV and V is similarly hazy. The return to duple meter (only Section IV is consistently in triple meter) occurs at m. 554. Also at this point, the fanfare-like motive derived from the fugal subject commences in the brass and tympani, continuing throughout Part I of Section V. Yet the principal unifying device of Part I of Section V – the canon based on Section I materials – does not begin until m. 567 (in the strings). At m. 567 also, the tempo is faster than anywhere else in the symphony ($\downarrow$ = 132-154).

That boundaries between sections are not always clearcut suggests the organic unity of the *Third Symphony*. This unity is underscored on a larger scale by the recurrence of materials throughout the work. Cyclical elements in the various sections of the symphony are indicated in the chart of the Symphony's structural features. While the *Third Symphony* is a continuous one-movement piece, it does retain some of the characteristics of the more standard multimovement symphonic plan. Contrasting tempi, moods, materials, and tonal activity among sections are definitely part of the work. Each section has its own distinct character.

Harris's description of the *Third Symphony* reveals a return at the end of the piece of a mood ("Tragic") and thematic materials from the first section. Several additional elements are also recalled: tempo, tonal centers, tessitura, and to some extent dynamics. For instance, tempo is increased gradually throughout the work to a maximum speed in the "Dramatic" part of Section V (see chart). The tempo then is reduced drastically to nearly the speed of Section I in the very last part of the piece (beginning m. 634; $\downarrow$ = 88-92), also designated "Tragic" by the composer.

This use of tempo in correspondence with specific moods may be explained by what Slonimsky has called Harris's "theory of musical emotion."[33] Harris's theory takes a quarter-note = 80 as its basic speed

Large Structural Features of Harris's *Third Symphony*

	Section I (Tragic)	Section II (Lyric)	Section III (Pastoral)
Measures	1 28 57 75 77 89 91 97	139 159 161	209 272
Meter	$\frac{4}{4}$ $\frac{2}{2}$ $\frac{3}{2}$ $\frac{2}{2}$ $\frac{3}{2}$ $\frac{2}{2}$	$\frac{3}{4}$ $\frac{2}{2}$	
Tempo	♩=81 ♩=120 ♩=72-80 ♩=96-104		♩=104-10 ♩=110-20
Instrumentation	Low strings at first, with gradual addition of low woodwinds, horns, then upper woodwinds; principal melodic material consistently in strings.	Principal melodic material switches between upper woodwinds and upper strings.	Woodwind solos over accompanimental strings
Range	Begins G to g range; upper limit. Gradually rising to a'' (m.125), then returning to B-b (m. 139)	Consistently middle-high tessitura	Consistently middle-high tessitura
Texture	Monodic, becoming contrapuntal, then monodic (mm 131-35)	Sporadically contrapuntal	Consistently melody with accompaniment
Principal Unifying Devices	Predominance of long, sustained lines; much even quarter-note then half-note motion	Melodic material in three Presentations, each varied (m. 151 – upper strings; m-161 – upper strings, m. 169 – upper strings)	Consistent 3-layer texture (double bass, strings, woodwinds); regular, though increasing, harmonic rhythm; ♫ ♩ rhythmic motive in solos
Dynamics	f (m.1)<fff (mm. 131-31)>	P (m.139) f (m.140) < fff (m. 156)>p (m. 20) f (m. 200)	pp < ff > f (m. 209) (mm. 353-54) (m. 412)
Cyclical Elements		Material in flute (mm. 140--43) From section I (mm 92-95), Material in Double Bass (mm. 151-55, 161-64) from section I (mm. 89-91)	
Principal Tonal Centers	G/g (mm.1-12); D/d (mm 16-22); Bb/b (mm 23-27); E/e (mm 28-31); Bb/bb (mm. 32-37); B (mm 41-42)~~~Ab/c(m 59-) A(m 75-) D (m.78-)~~~ No tonal center of lasting significance Eb(m. 109)~~~A/a (mm 129-33)~~~ e(m. 138)	g(m.139)~~~A(m. 152-)~~~ eb/A (mm. 161); A(m. 161-) ~~~D(m. 169-)~~~G(m. 203) ~~~D (mm. 205-)	A/c♯ (m. 209): This section is consistently bitonal mm. 209-68: A as principal tonal center; harmonic rhythm based on 3-measure units mm. 269-326: Ab as tonal center; harmonic rhythm in 1-measure units mm. 329-87: A no principal tonal center; harmonic rhythm in half-measure units mm. 357 D ~~~

Large Structural Features of Harris's *Third Symphony* (cont.)

	Section IV (Fugue)	Section V (Dramatic)	(Tragic)
Measures	416 450 534 554	567	634
Meter	$\frac{36}{24}$ $\frac{2}{2}$		
Tempo	♩=112 ♩=120-128 ♩=132 (♩=132)	𝅝=66-72 Fastest tempo (♩=132-54) of symphony	♩=88-92 Tempo reduced to nearly that of section I
Instrumentation	Emphasis on brass and tympani, although subject first presented in strings	Canon between strings and woodwinds juxtaposed against brass and tympani	Emphasis on low strings, low brass, and low woodwinds
Range	High tessitura in strings and woodwinds against low sounds of tympani	Continued juxtaposition of high tessitura (strings, woodwinds) and low (tympani and low brass)	Range consistently narrowing to G-d' (final triad)
Texture	Contrapuntal, sporadically employing imitation	Juxtaposition of chordal and contrapuntal	Contrapuntal
Principal Unifying Devices	Presence of fugal subject, either in complete statements or in use of derived material	Canon between strings and woodwinds; continuation of materials from section IV in brass and tympani	D pedal; descending ostinato figure; rhythmically even melodic material similar to section I
Dynamics	<ff(m 410); consistently ff>f (m. 553)	f<ff consistently (m. 56) (horns have fff)	Remains ff primarily fff< (m. 710)
Cyclical Elements	♫ ♩ Rhythmic motive from section II in subject and background material; recall of section II material (winds, m. 150) beginning m. 505 (winds)	Canon based on material first used in section I (m. 60, violins) material beginning m. 625 from section I (Beginning m. 89, violins); continuation of section IV materials.	Ostinato based on material used first in section I (m. 60, violins) but also in section II (mm. 151 and 161) and section II (mm. 151 and 161) and section V, Part I (m. 625); material in woodwinds (m. 640) from section II (m. 146)
Principal Tonal Levels	D (mm. 416-72); G (m. 473)~~~ Begins area composed of sequential statements of material derived from subject - no lasting tonal center; beginning m. 529, statement of complete subject in B♭, followed by another in G (m. 507), and a final incomplete statement in A(m. 545); part concludes with g triad, followed by octave E♭'s leading into final part	E♭(m. 567) → g(m.571) → E♭ (m. 577); e♭(m. 584)~~~No tonal center of lasting significance until B(m. 625)	b(m. 634) → D(m.640)~~~ pitch D present continuously in pedal and ostinato, contrapuntal lines create fluctuating harmonies over D pedal; D ostinato becomes d(m. 661-); final progression: G (m. 691) → B(m. 693) → D(m. 694) → double leading tone approach to final g triad (m. 700-)

($\quad$ = 80 is what Harris considers the speed of an average human pulse). Any tempo greater than 80 excites, and any tempo less than 80 depresses. Harris seems to have intended Part I of Section V as the most exciting part—the "Dramatic" climax of the symphony. Therefore, the tempo is fastest at this point. In actuality, however, the last part of Section III well may create the greatest feeling of speed in the piece. The harmonic rhythm of this area of Section III (from m. 327 on), in comparison to Part I of Section V, is markedly faster.

In addition to the return in Part II of Section V of a tempo similar to that in Section I, there is a return of the original tonal center of the piece—level G (mm. 691-92, and finally mm. 700-703). Although level G is not much in evidence in the symphony as a whole (by contrast, levels A and D are of much greater significance), level G may be said to frame the tonal activity of the entire piece. Tonal levels, however, are not established in the traditional sense of functional harmony in this symphony, though each section does have a definite tonal scheme (see chart). Indeed, as is discussed below, the different tonal activity and harmonic language of each of the *Third Symphony's* sections create strong contrasts among them.

The expanding range of the symphony throughout its first four sections and part I of the fifth, followed by the gradually contracting range in Part II of Section V, also contributes to its overall structure.[34] The predominant sound of Section I is that of the lower registers of the strings. By contrast, upper woodwinds consistently carry the melody in Section II. The highest sustained tessitura is in Section V, Part I, in the canon between strings and woodwinds. However, this high tessitura is juxtaposed against the low sounds of the tympani, adding to the climactic effect of this part. The declining tessitura of the second half of Section V, beginning with the D pedal (m. 634), is epitomized by the constantly reiterated descending ostinato figure of the basses.

Example 1
Measures 638-42 from Roy Harris's *Third Symphony* (New York: G. Schirmer, 1940).

The symphony receives coherence from other factors as well. For instance, there is a progressive clarification of tonal activity throughout the work (in the above chart, contrast tonal activity of Sections I and IV particularly). This tendency seems to correspond to the gradual shortening of melodic materials from Section I through Section IV. The motivic, fragmentary character of the fugue subject, strongly in D, hardly could create more of a contrast with the lengthy, wandering melodic lines of Section I, although both have the asymmetric phrase structure typical of Harris's melodic style. Lying between these two poles are the solo phrases of moderate length, interjected over a continuously-shifting bitonal accompaniment, of the "Pastoral" section.

Melodic fragmentation is at its greatest near the end of the fugue (m. 554), where almost no melody is discernible—only brief, repeated rhythmic motives. The juxtaposition beginning in m. 567 of this motivic material against the sustained melodic lines of the canon creates a striking contrast. Dynamics, tempo, and the juxtaposition of extremes in registers, combined with this juxtaposition of materials, make Part I of Section V the "Dramatic" climax of the *Third Symphony*.

Robert Evett, in his article "The Harmonic Idiom of Roy Harris," has described how Harris's emphasis on melody resulted in his rather unusual harmonic practice.[35] Harris's melodies move through various diatonic scales of inconsistent mode. In contrapuntal sections, according to Evett, Harris coordinated these wandering melodies without destroying their individual characters, thus yielding harmonic progressions of a similar wandering quality.[36] It should be remembered that, although Harris did not write within a clearly defined system of functional harmony, his vertical sonorities were almost invariably triads (or two stacked triads); and while the vertical sonorities in Harris's music are primarily consonant, they frequently are not linked by the functional progressions of common-practice harmony. For this reason, perhaps, his music sometimes has been found to resemble that of the Renaissance period.[37]

According to Slonimsky, Harris's harmonic language is based upon the triad.[38] Harris believed that one triad could be extended by others sharing one or two common tones.[39] The vertical results are stacked, overlapping triads. In Section III of the *Third Symphony* nearly every vertical sonority is bitonal, with the two triads almost always having one or two tones in common. Linear progressions in Harris's music also are based on chords related by common tones. For instance, the first part of Section I (the unaccompanied string melody) illustrates the linear exposition of Harris's concept. The first melodic phrases (mm. 1-12) are based on a G diatonic scale, with variable third degree. The melody moves in like fashion through a B scale, then E, then B-flat and so forth. Connections between scale areas are made by using pivotal common tones (between G and D: A; between D and B: F-sharp; between B and E: B, etc.). Harris's harmonic concepts based on common tone relationships do not establish a hierarchy of chords in the traditional tonal scheme, which many account for the lack of urgency in some areas — particularly in Section I — of the work. In the *Third Symphony*, tension and expectation frequently are produced by other than harmonic means through such elements as dynamics, density of texture, register, and rhythmic activity.

Tonal language is the most complex aspect of Harris's *Third Symphony*. As mentioned above, each section of the work seems to have its own harmonic and tonal practice (see chart for specific tonal levels) within a pattern of progressive tonal clarification. For instance, Section I is tonally the most unstable section of the piece. In this section, melody governs vertical simultaneities, and consonant sonorities are not related to any one tonal center. Melodic lines wander in and out of tonal areas with little feeling of direction. For this reason, Section I is best described as one of undefined tonality.[40]

Compared to Section I, Section II has a few fairly lengthy areas of tonal stability (see chart). The presence of tonal centers A and D forecasts the importance that these levels carry in the last three sections of the symphony. In Section II, tonal levels are established by linear presentations of melodic materials derived from triads and diatonic scales, first of A major and then of D major (A: beginning in m. 152 and m. 161; D: beginning in m. 169). Against the principal melodic material in the strings is set a descending scale of the corresponding tonal level in the lowest instruments, also contributing to the feeling of tonal security in these spots. Each of these areas of relative stability is short-lived, however, for the melodic lines wander out of their original scales. In addition, at m. 180 a complex texture of shifting bitonalities predicts the sound continuum of Section III.

In Section III, three separate levels of activity exist in the bass, the strings, and the woodwinds. This section seems organized primarily around the bass line. The bass pattern is stated three times, the first with A as the tonal center, the second with A-flat as the tonal center, and the final part with A again as the tonal center. In each of these three parts the bass does essentially the same thing, moving away from and returning to the tonal center at symmetrical distances of a major third, a fourth, and a fifth above and below this center. In the first part (mm. 209-68), the bass moves at two-measure intervals, merely jumping the distance of the third or fourth or fifth. In the second (mm. 269-326), the distances of the third, fourth, and fifth are filled in by a whole step, thus making the bass line move at one-measure intervals. In the third part (mm. 327-86), the bass line moves chromatically at half-measure intervals (see Example 2).

Example 2
Measures 209-17, 269-77, and 327-35 from the *Third Symphony*.

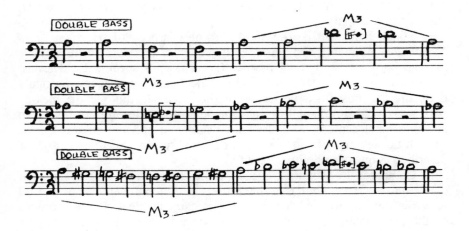

Over this increasingly active bass line, the bitonal harmonies shift accordingly. Thus, the harmonic rhythm is four times as rapid in the last part of the section as in the first part. Corresponding to this increasing harmonic rhythm in Section III is a thickening of texture, reaching its greatest density just before the bass line has finished its final pattern. At this point (mm. 387-88), Harris employs the traditional harmonic device of a deceptive progression. By this spot in the section, the return to a tonal center has been so consistent that the breaking of the pattern through the move to the D major triad with third in the bass is unexpected.

In contrast to the first three sections of the piece, whose harmonic language has been comprised primarily of full triads, Section IV places much greater emphasis on open fourths and fifths. The principal pitches of the fugue subject, other than D, are G and A – those a fourth and a fifth away from the tonal center. The three most important tonal centers of the symphony thus are emphasized by the fugue subject. Accompanimental figures in this section also frequently are comprised of intervals of fourths and fifths (see tympani, mm. 421-25; strings, mm. 423-44).

In Part I of Section V, besides juxtaposing the elements discussed earlier in this chapter (see above, p. 232), Harris also combined both melodic lines of wandering tonality (canon between strings and woodwinds) with concise chordal statements of repeated pitches. Therefore, two extremes of tonal stability are found simultaneously in this part.

The D pedal-point and the D major ostinato figure constantly reiterate the pitch D in the last part of the piece. Of course, D is the dominant level of G, the final resting point of the work. But the dominant function of D to G is not realized. In the final measures of the symphony (beginning at m. 661), the D major ostinato figure changes to D minor, reducing D's strength as a dominant. A G major triad in m. 691, in partial anticipation of the final G minor triad, is approached not by D but by D-flat, a tritone away from G. This progression seems to negate the previous repetition of D. A D major triad returns at m. 694, followed by restatements of the D pedal. However, the final G minor triad is approached by double leading-tones. The effect of this twisting and turning away from expected conclusions is one of increasing tension until the final triad is reached. Harris's individual tonal language, seemingly an admixture of traditional harmonic practice and his own concepts, is well demonstrated by the excitement of this final part.

Harris's outline of the *Third Symphony's* structure (see above, p. 227) reveals at least in part his intentions in the work. He made no overt attempt to incorporate Americana through title, program, or musical quotation. However, the symphony's sectional headings, "Tragic," "Lyric," "Pastoral," etc., demonstrate his grandiose conception of the work.[41] They also indicate his interest in the expressive potential of instrumental music. Through the abstract musical means he describes under each heading, Harris tried to communicate generalized moods or feelings. Communication is an important part of Harris's compositional outlook.

Harris wrote extensively on the communicative aims of music. Although his stress on reaching out to society bears some resemblance to the viewpoints of Blitzstein and other leftists, it does not seem politically motivated. In an essay for the anthology *The Basis of Artistic Creation* (1942), Harris said:

> Born in the present of the strongest physical and emotional rootstocks of the past, creative musicians live to record the emotional gamut and intensities of society.[42]

Harris called creative musicians the "singers of inarticulate humanity."[43] Through the works of composers,

> those uniquely human attributes are intensified, reaffirmed, released and translated into serviceable idioms of culture.[44]

So closely did Harris relate human emotions to artistic expression that he believed American music acquired its qualities from an American national personality. Harris has described what he understood to be the basic elements of "American" character.

> Our subjective moods are naturally being developed to meet the exigencies of our intensely concentrated mechanistic civilization. Our dignity is not pompous, nor are our profoundest feelings suppliant; our gayety is not graceful nor our humor whimsical. Our dignity lies in direct driving force; our deeper feelings are stark and reticent; our gayety is ribald and our humor ironic. These are moods which young indigenous American composers are born with, and from these moods come a unique valuation of beauty and a different feeling for rhythm, melody and form.[45]

It is not certain whether Harris had specifically American "tragedy" or a specifically American "pastoral" scene in mind when he wrote the *Third Symphony*. The evidence does suggest, however, that Harris believed his compositions to be representatively "American" musical expressions.

> The national accent of music springs spontaneously from the deepest unconscious impulses of man. It was bred there and confirmed by environment. I do not think a composer can consciously implant the subjective qualities of a people or a time in his music. He may hope to do so, as I most certainly do, but I am convinced he can do little or nothing about the matter. . . . As Emerson once said: "What you *are* speaks so loudly that I cannot hear your words."[46]

Harris's evocation of Emerson underscores a philosophical similarity to Charles Ives. Harris, like Ives, believed that music was a national expression unconsciously shaped by environment. Unlike Ives, composing specifically "American" music was important to Harris. His prescription for creating "American" music is significant.

> Fortunately for us composers, we *must* accept and live with the gamut and intensities of our subjective impulses. . . . When several authentic talents, bred and nourished from the same background, carry a style forward in natural evolution a new school of music is created. So we must create an authentic school of music.[47]

While Harris's statements could be taken to mean that he believed a work "American" by virtue of being composed by an American, he implied more. A key passage in the above quotation is: "We *must* accept and live with the gamut . . . of our subjective impulses." Harris is saying that composers must accept their nationality before this can be manifested in their music. Harris directed remarks toward those composers and audiences who still looked to Europe for sanction.

> Finally, it must be stated that if we create an indigenous music worthy of our people, it will make its way swiftly and unfalteringly. It seems to be gathering momentum already. Whether it be a little more or less "dissonant" or "original" is of small import—but it must have the pulsing stuff of life in it—creative urge and necessity of continuity. It cannot be a scholarly mosaic of all the materials and forms of the last 200 European years geared to the speed of our present concert public. Give us the originals instead and let us not deceive ourselves with the occasional gesture of sponsoring an innocuous copy made in America.[48]

At a time when the old American dream of a native art music was beginning to be realized in America, Harris found it necessary to reinforce in words his own musical independence.

Harris, however, addressed himself critically to composers who drew upon American vernacular music in their works.

> What has too often been done to native folk songs is a tell-tale evidence that composers can not will to express the emotional qualitites of a people.[49]

Harris made it clear, therefore, that he did not necessarily advocate the quotation of folk or popular music as a means of achieving an "American" style. He seemed to be echoing Paul Rosenfeld in "Variations on the Grass Roots Theme," who told the composer to be "true to his soul . . . for there in his soul lie his ever-greening grass roots and the source of his utility to men."[50]

Yet some of Harris's compositions use musical Americana, such as the *Folksong Symphony*,[51] and many have obviously Americanist titles, such as *American Creed* (1940) and *Sons of the U.S.A.* (1942). Thus a discrepancy exists between Harris's theory about musical Americanism and his practice. This subject will be discussed in the conclusions to this chapter. Regardless of the disparity, it seems evident that Harris considered his abstract works, such as the *Third Symphony*, to be just as "American" as those quoting Americana.

Certainly others have thought Harris's *Third Symphony* to be "American." The following observations appeared in the program notes for the premiere of the work.

> There is indeed an air of the West in his music; whether or not it is everything that it has been called remains to be determined. At any rate, we have another interesting instance of our persisting racial self-consciousness and root-seeking; a quest, it must be added, in which the composer concurs.[52]

Some writers have heard specific types of Americana evidenced in Harris's abstract music. As early as his 1929 essay on Harris, Paul Rosenfeld wrote that Harris's original melodies were definitely related to American folksong, particularly cowboy ballads.[53] Not long after the premiere of the *Third Symphony*, Copland also commented upon the indigenous aspects of Harris's melodic style. Copland noted:

> American, too, is his melodic gift, perhaps his most striking characteristic. His music comes nearest to a distinctly native melos of anything yet done, at least in the ambitious forms. Celtic folksongs and Protestant hymns are its basis, but they have been completely re-worked, lengthened, malleated.[54]

Others have found Harris's rhythmic style to be "American." According to Hitchcock, the *Third Symphony's* "internal cross-rhythms and ambiguous meter . . . stamp it as 'Made in U.S.A.'"[55] As discussed below, there is some evidence for calling Harris's melodic and rhythmic styles "American."

In his essay "Problems of American Composers" (1933), Harris identified rhythmic aspects of American music which he considered indigenously "American."

> Our rhythmic impulses are fundamentally different from the rhythmic impulses of Europeans; and from this unique rhythmic sense are generated different melodic and form values. Our sense of rhythm is less symmetrical than the European sense. European musicans are trained to think of rhythm in its largest common denominator, while we are born with a feeling for its smallest units.[56]

While Harris's statements may or may not apply to American music in general, they illuminate his own rhythmic style in the *Third Symphony*. As has been mentioned, melodic lines are shortened progressively throughout the symphony's first four sections, but these lines are rarely if ever regular. In fact, the essence of Harris's asymmetrical melodic style is found in the fugue subject.

Example 3
Measures 416-21 from the *Third Symphony*.

The fugue subject is 5 1/3 measures in length (2 + 1+ 2 1/3). It consists of two phrases in parallel construction. Because rests occur in every measure, the subject is made up of fragments. Furthermore, accents add ambiguity to the subject's rhythmic organization (the meter is $\frac{36}{24}$). For instance, the first D (m. 416), an elision between melodic material from Section III and the fugue subject of Section IV, could be interpreted as an anacrusis to the following A. This primarily is due to the accent on the A, but also to the brevity of D as compared to A. The D in the fourth measure of the subject acts in a similar way. Also, while the first measure of the subject is a $\frac{3}{2}$ measure, the second appears to be in $\frac{4}{4}$ (the same thing occurs in the second phrase of the subject at the parallel spot). The accents, the dynamic markings, and the entrance of percussion on beat four (in $\frac{6}{4}$) all suggest the $\frac{6}{4}$ interpretation.

Harris's special rhythmic style is found in other sections of the symphony as well, but nowhere as succinctly as in the Fugue. Harris's Fugue actually makes only limited use of imitative counterpoint. The fugue subject does permeate the section, either through complete statements of the subject or through derived material. Imitation, however, does not occur among complete statements, only among fragments of the subject. Frequently these imitative areas are based on sequential statements of fragments of the subject in stretto, such as in mm. 464-73.

The composer's reference to American rhythmic thinking in the "smallest units," instead of larger units which are then broken down into smaller symmetrical units, suggests an additive rather than a divisive concept of rhythm.[57] This concept of additive rhythm is particularly apparent in Section I of the *Third Symphony*, where the quarter-note is the basic unit of the music. Although the music is measured in $\frac{4}{4}$ meter, it is free-flowing, with each phrase observing its own rules of length, accent, and rise and fall. In this way, the opening section bears a similarity to plainchant. Hitchcock's description of Harris's melodic style in the *Third Symphony* as "prose-like" is also appropriate.[58]

If one thinks of the basic melodic unit as the quarter-note and the basic verbal unit as the syllable, further similarities between Harris's melodic style and vocal music are apparent. The basic units (syllables) of prose and some poetry are often stretched or shortened into units of varying lengths. Unlike dance music, which is usually divisive, a divisive framework often seems imposed upon some vocal music, especially traditional songs.

Harris's asymmetrical, unpredictable phrase structure frequently has been associated with Anglo-American folk music, and there is evidence which suggests a resemblance to the performance practices of folksingers.

In *Anglo-American Folksong Style*, Abrahams and Foss state that although Anglo-American folksongs usually are organized by consistent meter and regular phrase structure according to the verse forms of the texts, the rhythm is made less rigid in several ways.

> Many traditional singers, rather than hold a note at the end of a phrase until the metrical value has been filled, will arbitrarily shorten the final note and proceed to the next phrase. . . .
> Traditional singers will sometimes expand or stretch those values expected in a certain meter at the points of relative repose occurring at the end of the phrase. These extensions of the phrase may take the form of a short rest or silence prior to the next phrase or they may be an expansion of note values immediately prior to the phrase ending. Both of these interrupt the constant flow of the metrical background and the latter may even be of such a nature to give the feeling of a new, if temporary, meter.[59]

Transcriptions into regular metered phrases are not always an accurate reflection of the rhythmic structure of folksongs in performance.

Also relating Harris's melodies with folksong style is his consistent use of what Abrahams and Foss call the "singable intervals."[60] These small intervals — seconds and thirds — "are in the great majority both in ascending and descending melodic progressions" in Anglo-American folksongs, while "the slightly larger intervals of fourths, fifths, and sixths are found with less frequency."[61] According to these authors, the other more difficult-to-sing intervals rarely are found. A study of the melodic material in all five sections of Harris's *Third Symphony* reveals the preponderance of the singable intervals. In fact, one of the most interesting features of the *Third Symphony* is the fact that practically any musician can sing through just about all of its melodic materials. Not only are the skips easily manageable, but the degree of floridity is small and the rhythms — while frequently additive — are not tricky except in the last section. Harris has explored the potential of instruments to sing rather than to perform idiomatic acrobatics. The vocal quality of the work's melodies sets it apart from many contemporary symphonies, in which disjunct and chromatic themes are common.

Furthermore, Harris insisted that melody was the most significant aspect of his music. According to Slonimsky, Boulanger once asked Harris to write melodies, and he produced 107 in the time she had given him to devise twenty.[62] Copland's comment about Harris's music very definitely applies to the *Third Symphony*:

> Every piece has melodies in profusion, as if out of his wealth of invention, the composer could afford to be a spendthrift.[63]

In the opening section of the *Third Symphony*, only solo melody is heard initially, with octave punctuation at the ends of phrases. The fourths and fifths are added to the harmonic vocabulary (beginning in m. 24). The first full triad finally is stated at m. 41, producing a strikingly rich effect. Harris affirms the purity of melody alone.

Some evidence suggests that Harris actually simulated a folksong style in his own melodies. In *Composer and Nation*, Sidney Finkelstein stated that in writing the *Third Symphony*, Harris "saturated himself in folksong but did not use specific tunes."[64] Copland has noted, though not specifically concerning the *Third Symphony*, that Harris filled notebooks with melodies based on Anglo-American folksong and hymn style.[65]

It is significant that Harris's exposure to twentieth-century art music as a youngster was extremely limited.

> On his farm as a young man, and later in Los Angeles, he had little opportunity to acquaint himself with the latest trends of modern music. There was no radio; the gramophone industry was undeveloped, and performances of modern works were rare. Harris grew like an American primitive, and his talent was already well formed when he became exposed to the modern music of the 1920's.[66]

The music Harris did hear at home was his mother's singing and instrumental playing of folksongs. He has written:

> Folk music was as natural to our way of life as corn bread and sweet milk. My mother played the guitar and we hummed along with her after supper on the front porch or in the kitchen. We whistled folk songs as we worked on the farm. When I began to study music, I decided that composers were folk singers who had learned to write down the songs that took their fancy; and that therefore folk songs could be recast to suit a composer's purpose, and that they could be legitimately used to generate symphonic forms.[67]

Although these remarks were made in connection with the *Folksong Symphony*, they need not be limited to this work. Folksong was Harris's native tongue.

Roy Harris wrote of his concern for creating an "American" musical style, and in several pieces was consciously Americanist. The foregoing analysis of Harris's *Third Symphony* suggests that connections between the work and identifiably "American" musical elements are tenuous. His *Third Symphony* makes no overt references to native materials, musical or otherwise. Yet the remarkable vocal quality of the symphony's thematic materials and the relationship between Harris's melodies and Anglo-American folksong are evident. The similarity between Harris's music and the melodic characteristics of folksong is the *Third Symphony*'s most tangibly "American" aspect.

What is most striking about the *Third Symphony* is its individuality. In this symphony, Harris brought to fruition his singular melodic and harmonic concepts and rhythmic style. Surely Harris's musical language sounded fresh to audiences in 1939. Certainly it did not sound European. Critical remarks from 1939 to the present indicate that many Americans believe Harris achieved an "American" style in the *Third Symphony*.

The context of Harris's Americanism in the 1930s is significant. He arrived on the musical scene from California at a time when many Americans seemed to hold the West in awe. Even his physical appearance — "tall, lanky, rawboned," as John Tasker Howard described him — added to his appeal.[68] If Americans in the 1930s could have identified with any composer of cultivated music, Harris was the one. His life was a Horatio Alger story. A national poll conducted by the New York Philharmonic in 1935 showed Harris to be the favorite American composer. The following year a similar study undertaken by *Scribner's Magazine* yielded identical results.[69]

There are some who suggest that both Harris and his contemporaries abused the "Harris legend" in a period when composing "American" music was fashionable. Slonimsky has written that Harris helped create his own "American" mystique. To audiences in the 1930s, Harris's *Symphony 1933* was the "first real American symphony."[70] With the work's success, Harris's name was equated with "aggressive musical Americanism."[71] Slonimsky also noted that Harris thereafter seemed to emphasize his "American" background by frequent references to his birth date and rural childhood.[72] Patricia Ashley has gone so far as to imply that Harris consciously sought to be "American" only after he already was being called an "American" composer.

> What happened was that, having been told that his music was like America, Harris worked this idea into his mystique until he was able to believe that America was like his music.[73]

Harris may have sensed the appeal of his own "American" qualities during the 1930s. Having made his reputation as an "American" composer, he did little to discourage the label. His writings and music, in fact, seemed to substantiate it. That Harris's description of American musical qualities delineated his own style already has been noted. Furthermore, most of Harris's overtly Americanist works — those based on folksong or dedicated to American heroes — followed the success of the *Symphony 1933*, after his identity as an "American" composer was established. Surely World War II was influential in the 1940s. Yet Harris's accentuated compositional Americanism, after already being identified as "American," seemed to negate his own prescription for "American" music that was discussed earlier.

Harris himself has provided the most convincing evidence that his musical Americanism in the 1930s and 1940s may have been timely. Musical Americanism was not the dominant trend after World War II. In a statement written for *The New Book of Modern Composers* (1961), Harris discussed those things consistently of concern to him: music as a vehicle for human expression, and the contemporary state of music.[74] Harris reviewed the line of great composers from Josquin through Beethoven, implying that he was a successor to their musical traditions. But nowhere in this article did he mention specifically American music, American musical qualities, or the state of American music. In fact, the word "American" does not appear in the article at all.[75]

What remains signficant, though, is Harris's stated desire in the 1930s and 1940s to be an "American" composer and the willingness of many at the time to accept him as such. The relationship between Harris and Americanist-minded musicians and audiences in this period was apparently symbiotic. Among some music lovers and commentators, a role seems to have been created for an "American" composer. Harris filled that role. Surely Harris should not be indicted for capitalizing on his special appeal. American composers long have searched for means to increase their popularity, and musical Americanism has been one of the methods most commonly used. The difference between Harris and other Americanists is the degree to which Americanism succeeded for Harris in the 1930s and 1940s.

It is also notable that many of Harris's overtly Americanist works have not found as lasting a place in the concert repertory as has his *Third Symphony*, less obviously "American." Commenting on a performance of the *Third Symphony* in 1957, Paul Henry Lang remarked:

> If Mr. Harris had only continued in this vein instead of attempting to naturalize a native-born American, he would have retained the freshness as well as individuality of his gifts; only good and unselfconscious composition is needed to produce genuine American music.[76]

In retrospect, many might agree with Lang's observations, and it is ironic how closely his remarks resemble Harris's own formula for "American" music. However, Harris, like others of his generation, was trying to establish a career as a composer when the very existence of "American" art music was questioned. Harris himself was one of these questioners.

XI

Aaron Copland

In order to create an indigenous music of universal significance three conditions are imperative. First, the composer must be part of a nation that has a profile of its own—that is the most important; second, the composer must have in his background some sense of musical culture and, if possible, a basis in folk or popular art; and third, a superstructure of organized musical activities must exist—that is, to some extent, at least—at the service of the native composer.

Aaron Copland, "Musical Imagination in the Americas," *Music and Imagination*

For decades, Aaron Copland has maintained a position of importance and prestige unprecedented in American musical history. Copland's leadership in creating "an indigenous music of universal significance" has been twofold, stemming both from his recognized excellence as a composer and from his skill as an organizer. The major Americanist trends from the mid-1920s through the mid-1940s are demonstrated by Copland's interest: conceptual Americanism, promotion of Americanist activities, jazz, leftism, folk music, and patriotism. Musical Americanism in this period can be defined by the career of Aaron Copland.

Until the discovery of Charles Ives, Copland usually was thought to be America's "first composer of major significance."[1] Today the plaudits continue to surround him. Leonard Bernstein and Virgil Thomson have both stated that Copland's music is the best America has.[2] He is the "dean" of American composers,[3] the "Moses" of modern music,[4] and a "national asset."[5] Copland has composed for nearly every medium, and his works are frequently performed. As a compositional Americanist, he was not always the first to draw upon native materials, but his treatment of jazz and folksong often came to represent Americanist interest in these sources. Furthermore, he has explored the other musical professions from teaching and performing to writing music history and aesthetics. In the 1930s, he recognized the potential of mass communication and urged his fellow composers to take advantage of it. Then in the 1950s, he grew interested in conducting. With television's expansion, Copland's bespectacled face and lanky figure became familiar to millions. In the eyes of many, he is *the* American composer.

Aaron Copland's life is by now so well known that a brief review will suffice.[6] Born in Brooklyn on November 14, 1900, Copland was a first generation American of Russian Jewish parentage. His father's surname was Kaplan, changed to the English equivalent by an immigration official. The elder Copland entered the dry goods business and for many years lived over a store in which the whole family worked. Music was not an important part of the Copland household. Although Copland's older brother and sister studied instruments, the composer has noted that music as a profession was "original" with him.[7]

> My discovery of music was rather like coming upon an unsuspected city—like discovering Paris or Rome if you had never before heard of their existence. The excitement of discovery was enhanced because I came upon only a few streets at a time, but before long I began to suspect the full extent of this city. The long instinctual drive toward the world of sound must have been very strong in my case, since it triumphed over a commercially minded environment that, so far as I could tell, had never given a thought to art or to art expression as a way of life.[8]

Copland's sister Laurine gave him his first piano lessons. Although showing early promise, he had to beg his parents to allow him to study with a professional teacher, for they had supported the older siblings' musical endeavors to no significant ends. He persuaded them and, at around the age of thirteen, made the arrangements himself with the pianist Leopold Wolfson. The business and artistic worlds were mixed in Copland's youth, perhaps suggesting why he later assumed leadership in both areas of American music.

Copland's musical horizons continued to expand under his own guidance. Taking advantage of New York's musical offerings, he attended concerts as often as possible, usually consulting scores beforehand. The idea of composing began to emerge when Copland learned that the famous Paderewski, then a concert favorite, was a composer as well as a pianist. When Wolfson suggested harmony lessons as a first step toward composing, Copland once again sought his own instructor. In the fall of 1917, Copland began studying with Rubin Goldmark, at that time among the most noted teachers of composition in the United States. His lessons with the German-born teacher lasted four years, and he later sought Goldmark's advice on many issues. Copland has noted his good fortune in finding Goldmark, whom he credits with giving him a solid musical foundation.[9]

Anxious to make music his profession, Copland rejected his parents' plans to send him to college. By chance, he saw an advertisement for a new summer music school opening outside of Paris in 1921. Copland recalls that his enthusiasm was so great and his application so swiftly submitted that his name "headed the list" of students enrolled.[10] Moreover, he was awarded a scholarship. After some family apprehension, Copland embarked for Fontainebleau, France. His intended one year of study became three, largely because of Nadia Boulanger. Copland found Boulanger to be such a good teacher that he simply stayed on.

It cannot be stated unequivocally that Copland's years with Boulanger defined his compositional outlook. Yet surely twentieth-century American music was affected simply by his meeting her, for Copland spread the word about Boulanger's abilities and soon found himself joined by other young American students. Virgil Thomson and Melville Smith, the latter an organist and later director of the French-inspired Longy School of Music in Cambridge, Massachusetts, had found Boulanger independently around the same time.[11] Copland, Thomson, and Smith formed the nucleus of Boulanger's growing number of students.

Studying composition with a woman was virtually unheard of in 1921, and Copland has admitted his apprehension. His private fears were quickly overcome, however, when he realized Boulanger's exceptional abilities as a teacher.

> Two qualities possessed by Mlle. Boulanger make her unique: one is her consuming love for music, and the other is her ability to inspire a pupil with confidence in his own creative powers. Add to this an encyclopedic knowledge of every phase of music past and present, an amazing critical perspicacity, and a full measure of feminine charm and wit.[12]

Boulanger was aware of Schoenbergian atonality, for she familiarized herself with all new trends; but she believed in tonality and was fundamentally a formal classicist. A student of Fauré, she often used his music in classes.[13] Her major interest among contemporary composers, however, was Stravinsky. Many attribute the Stravinskian and neoclassical characteristics of some American music after the mid-1920s to Boulanger's influence.[14]

More significant to the present study is the fact that many of Boulanger's American pupils became the most prominent Americanists.

Copland, Harris, Blitzstein, Thomson, Siegmeister, Douglas Moore, Robert Russell Bennett, and Ross Lee Finney were all students of Boulanger in the 1920s and 1930s, and all composed Americanist music in the 1930s and 1940s. Copland maintains that "Mlle. Boulanger made no particular point about nationalism during my student years or thereafter."[15]   Virgil Thomson, however, has noted that Boulanger believed American music was at a point of development in the 1920s similar to Russian music eighty years earlier — ready to emerge on its own.[16] Boulanger's role in shaping the musical Americanism of the 1930s and 1940s is questionable.   What is certain is her aid in preparing the first generation of American composers sure enough of their skills to follow their own stylistic interests.

Copland's association with Boulanger led to another important development: Serge Koussevitzky's interest in contemporary American music.   Koussevitzky, a Russian double-bass virtuoso and conductor, was then the organizer of a concert series featuring contemporary music at the Paris Opera.   Impressed by Koussevitzky's work, Virgil Thomson wrote an article about him which caught the attention of Americans seeking a new conductor for the Boston Symphony Orchestra.[17] Koussevitzky was chosen.   In 1923, shortly after the appointment was announced, Boulanger took Copland to meet the Russian conductor at his Paris apartment.   Copland played part of his *Cortège Macabre* for him.[18] Koussevitzky was impressed enough that he promised to perform the work during his first season in Boston. A liaison was thus established that benefitted Copland as well as many other American composers, for Koussevitzky made it a policy to perform new American works. In a later tribute to the conductor, Copland wrote:

> Can it be pure chance that the twenty years of Dr. Koussevitzky's leadership — 1924 to 1944 — have coincided with the period during which American symphonic literature has come of age?[19]

In June, 1924 Copland returned to the United States. Here he finished the *Symphony for Organ and Orchestra*, begun when Boulanger requested a new work for her first American tour as an organist. The piece is dedicated to her.[20] Almost from the moment of his return, Copland became recognized as a leader among American composers; but he was not so quickly perceived as an "American" composer.

Copland and Americanism

Copland's statement about the "American" impetus for his jazz-oriented pieces in the mid-1920s is well known.

I was anxious to write a work that would immediately be recognized as American in character. This desire to be "American" was symptomatic of the period.[21]

Elsewhere, Copland has revealed that his concern with writing "American" music began somewhat earlier than the mid-1920s. During his Boulanger years, he was impressed with the way in which French art music appeared to be an integral part of the larger French society. He described how his conceptual Americanism crystallized and led to his compositional Americanism.

> The relation of French music to the life around me became increasingly manifest. Gradually, the idea that my personal expression in music ought somehow to be related to my own back-home environment took hold of me. The conviction grew inside me that the two things that seemed always to have been so separate in America—music and the life about me—must be made to touch. This desire to make the music I wanted to write come out of the life I had lived in America became a preoccupation of mine in the twenties. It was not so very different from the experience of other young American artists, in other fields, who had gone abroad to study in that period; in greater or lesser degree, all of us discovered America in Europe.[22]

In 1845, William Henry Fry had noted a lack of a "national prototype" for American music. Some eighty years later, Copland complained similarly, for, as he sought to make his music "American," he found few antecedents. "American" music and "modern" music were one and the same to Copland and his generation in the 1920s. As he has written, "in those days the example of our American elders in music was not readily at hand."[23] Those American composers with whom he was familiar, such as the Bostonians Paine, Parker, Chadwick, and Foote, were fundamentally different from him in their outlook toward American music.

> Their attitude was founded upon an admiration for the European art work and an identification with it that made the seeking out of any other art formula a kind of sacrilege. The challenge of the Continental art work was not: can we do better or can we also do something truly our own, but merely can we do as well?[24]

Of composers younger than the Boston group, like Loeffler and Griffes, Copland saw much to admire in their music but was uncomfortable with their attitude. The newer composers, according to Copland, were

> in danger of escaping to a kind of artistic ivory tower. As composers, they seemed quite content to avoid contact with the world they lived in.[25]

Among composers interested in achieving an "American" sound, Copland found Henry F. Gilbert most sympathetic. Though a Bostonian like Paine and the others, Gilbert was different. Copland noted that Gilbert believed

> it was better to write a music in one's own way, no matter how modest and restricted its style might be, than to compose large works after a foreign model.[26]

Copland concluded that despite the awkwardness of his music, Gilbert was on the right track. Yet for those of Copland's generation, Gilbert was not to be taken as a model.

> In any event, we in the twenties were little influenced by the efforts of Henry Gilbert, for the truth is that we were after bigger game. Our concern was not with the quotable hymn or spiritual: we wanted to find a music that would speak of universal things in a vernacular of American speech rhythms. We wanted to write music on a level that left popular music far behind—music with a largeness of utterance wholly representative of the country that Whitman envisaged.[27]

Copland's early compositional Americanism yielded three major jazz-oriented works—the *Symphony for Organ and Orchestra* (1924), *Music for the Theatre* (1925), and the *Concerto for Piano and Orchestra* (1927). Jazz was a natural choice upon which Copland could build an "American" music. It was contemporary, fresh, and indigenous to the United States. Yet while Americanism was the primary impetus for the jazz pieces, they seem rather to have been perceived as "ultramodern."[28] The *Symphony for Organ and Orchestra*, premiered by the New York Symphony under the direction of Walter Damrosch, formed the foundation for Copland's reputation as a radical (in the musical sense), one that remained with him in the late 1920s. For after the performance, Damrosch turned to the audience to make a now famous pronouncement:

> Ladies and gentlemen. It seems evident that when the gifted young American who wrote this symphony can compose at the age of 23, a work like this one, it seems evident that in five years he will be ready to commit murder.[29]

Though Damrosch's comments were light-hearted and critics generally praised the work, several noted the difficult rhythms and apparent influence of Stravinsky.[30] For a composer trying to be "American," these were not the desired reactions.

The appropriateness of jazz as a source for cultivated music was debated hotly in the 1920s.[31] Only Gershwin's concert adaptations of popular idioms were well-known. And because Gershwin was considered by some to be from the wrong side of the musical tracks, his example only added to the questionable propriety of using jazz as a basis for art music. Certain aspects of jazz, such as its instrumental combinations and rhythms, were new to American audiences, at least those in concert halls; and it was the rhythmic innovations that particularly interested Copland.

Copland's jazz-influenced works sometimes have been compared with Gershwin's pieces of the same period. At a WPA Composers' Forum-Laboratory in 1937, Copland explained what he believed to be the difference between his own and Gershwin's music. Speaking specifically about *Music for the Theatre*, Copland said:

> Gershwin is serious up to a point. My idea was to intensify it. Not what you get in the dance hall but to use it cubistically—to make it more exciting than ordinary jazz.[32]

Other commentators have noted Copland's ability to integrate elements of jazz with those of contemporary art music, achieving a refined synthesis. Despite the disdain for jazz that his comments reveal, Rosenfeld's observations are worth noting:

> Copland has actually absorbed jazz motives and correlated them with the developments of the past. Hence, the difference between his music and that of the other experimenters. For while they have taken jazz much as they found it, that is, impregnated with a superficial spirit, Copland has driven it far beyond its current uses, and substituted the expression of an almost Rabelaisian irony for its customary parody and blandishment.[33]

Copland distilled jazz idioms, particularly the rhythmic. Yet in the mid-1920s, his displaced accents and alternating meters may have sounded more "modern" than "American."

At the Composers' Forum-Laboratory session in 1937, Copland also remarked:

> My only relation with jazz finished in 1928. I feel I did all I could do with it as a basis for serious composition when I had written my piano concerto. If anyone thinks he can use it interestingly, well and good! I used it when the "Rhapsody in Blue" was new. Since then it has become popular, and used by people here and abroad. However, it is not as fresh as when it was first played.[34]

Although a few later works, notably *Hear Ye! Hear Ye!* (1934) and the *Concerto for Clarinet and Orchestra* (1944), draw upon jazz, Copland did not dwell on the source. The *Symphonic Ode*, written between 1927 and 1929, already manifested a tendency toward greater abstraction of the popular idiom, and is not considered by Copland to be a part of his jazz period. Whether he merely found jazz limiting and tired of it, as he has said, or found the field of cultivated jazz composers overcrowded, as he has hinted, he no longer found jazz the route for him to an "American" music. In his 1929 portrait of Copland, Rosenfeld commented upon Copland's originality, use of jazz, and modernism, and called him an "American" composer; but the emphasis remained upon the former qualities, not the Americanism. The contrast is strong between Rosenfeld's remarks about Copland and those in the same anthology about Harris, who seemed to Rosenfeld the ultimate "American."

Copland's reputation in these years as an Americanist, or at least as a leader of American composers, probably was achieved primarily through his activities in behalf of new American music. Upon his return from Europe, Copland's stature as a force in American music was quickly established. According to Virgil Thomson, it was as if

> he could see already coming into existence an organized body of modernistic American composers with himself at the head of it, taking over the art and leading it by easy stages to higher ground, with himself still at the head of it, long its unquestioned leader, later its president emeritus.[35]

The Koussevitzky connection helped. Several of Copland's works were performed by the Boston Symphony and repeated by other major orchestras shortly after his return. Such achievements by a hitherto unknown American in his mid-twenties were noteworthy indeed. Moreover, Copland received a Guggenheim Fellowship in 1925, the first awarded to a composer. Renewed for the following year, the prize not only provided financial stability but helped to establish his prominence among the crowd of young American composers.

One of Copland's first important organizational accomplishments, according to Thomson, was to assume tacit control of the League of Composers.[36] In the years immediately following its founding in 1923, the League primarily sponsored the performance of European contemporary music. Although the League's goals never became Americanist to the exclusion of other national musics, the increasing numbers of American composers active in the League turned the focus more and more toward developments at home. By the early 1930s, Copland was a member of the Executive Board of the League, and the Advisory Board included others of the younger generation including George Antheil, Henry Cowell, Howard Hanson, and Roger Sessions.[37] Also, through the intervention of Koussevitzky, Copland became the first composer to receive a commission from the League.[38] Many commissions to other composers followed, and in 1933 the League established a fund to support the composition of American music.[39]

With the success of these endeavors, Copland next began to organize concert series of his own. The first were the Copland-Sessions Concerts held in New York City from 1928 through 1931. Copland had met Roger Sessions in Paris in 1921 through Boulanger (although Sessions was not her student). Also interested in increasing an awareness in the United States of contemporary music, Sessions assisted Copland in organizing the series of two programs a year. During their four-year span, the Copland-Sessions Concerts sponsored the premieres of sixteen works by Americans and eleven by Europeans. A total of forty-seven works was performed.[40]

Even before the joint venture with Sessions concluded, Copland contemplated a similar series expressly for American works. He also found what seemed the ideal location. While working on his *Piano Variations* in 1930, he felt the need for seclusion. This problem was solved by an invitation to the Trask estate, better known as "Yaddo," in Saratoga Springs, New York. The beautiful estate and its historical commitment to the arts[41] made it perfect for a music festival. Copland's proposal was accepted, and in April, 1932, the first Yaddo Festival of American Music was held. The works of eighteen composers were performed, including Copland's *Piano Variations* and seven songs by Charles Ives. The second year, eighteen composers again were featured.[42]

Both festivals included conferences as well as concerts. Composers and others in attendance gathered in forums to discuss contemporary American musical life. The first year, a conference for critics and composers was presented although, as Smith noted, few critics attended.[43] The composers took their absence as a signal that they held American music in low esteem. One of the few critics who was there misquoted Copland's speech to the gathering. According to Copland, said the writer, critics were a "menace" to American music. The incorrect remark sparked a furor among composers and critics alike.[44] In an effort to set the record straight, several newspapers printed Copland's entire address, thereby giving considerable publicity to Copland, the Festival, and American composers in general. Also, Copland expanded his views in an article later that spring in *Modern Music*.

In the essay "The Composer and His Critic," Copland sought to make the musical community aware of the importance of its help in creating an indigenous American music. Noting the tremendous power wielded by music critics in the United States, Copland urged the critic to "take his job seriously" and to be "wide awake and intelligent in his attitude toward our native music."[45] He stated that the responsibility of critics in America was greater than ever before because the number of committed American composers was greater than ever before. It was in the power of the critic "to further or to hinder the immediate future of our musical development in no small measure."[46]

The greatest misunderstanding in American musical life, Copland believed, was American society's inability to recognize the composer—not the conductor or the orchestra—as the center of musical culture. It was the composer who reflected and extended the creative life of the nation. "For it is a truism," wrote Copland, that "so long as a country cannot create its own music—and recognize it once it is created—just so long will its musical culture be in a hybrid and unhealthy state."[47] At the time of this essay in 1932, Copland's conceptual Americanism was developed fully.

Following the morale-building and unifying of the early 1930s' efforts, according to Thomson, Copland consolidated his troops into a "commando unit" of the five composers he perceived as the strongest of his generation "both as creators and as allies for combat."[48] In addition to Copland, these were Thomson, Sessions, Harris, and Walter Piston. Their first appearance was at yet another concert series organized by Copland in 1935.[49] This time the location was the New School for Social Research, where he lectured from 1927 to 1937. In this series, each program was devoted to the music of only one man, providing an overview of a composer's output not readily established through normal concert channels.

Copland also featured the music of his four colleagues in "The American Composer Gets a Break," appearing in the *American Mercury* in 1935. In this essay he challenged George Jean Nathan's recently-stated contention that American music was weak because "its hopeful composers are in the aggregate trivial men."[50] To refute this claim, Copland described the music of his fellow composers. Neither the men nor their music was "trivial," believed Copland, and their lack of recognition was the fault of American society.

> All four of these men belong to a larger public. They have suffered in reputation because their profession is music. If they were poets instead of composers, I am convinced that more people would know their names and demand their work. It is worth noting that all are warmly interested in the future of American music and determined to further improve the lot of succeeding composers.[51]

Copland, while noting that the position of the American composer had improved in recent years, stated that

> his real desire is still a long way from fulfillment. His real desire is a genuine and natural place in society: not merely to be tolerated and encouraged, but needed.[52]

Copland's statement expressed the recurring aim of Americanist composers to be identified and appreciated by American society as composers. The difference between Copland and Americanists of previous generations was that Copland, for one, was no longer content to have it any other way.

In 1937, Copland, Thomson, Blitzstein, Lehman Engel, and several others helped to strengthen the financial position of American composers.[53] They were the force behind the formation of the American Composers' Alliance (ACA), of which Copland served as president for seven years. The ACA was created to insure copyright protection for composers of art music in areas not covered by the American Society of Composers, Authors, and Publishers (ASCAP), which was primarily geared toward popular music. The Alliance was formally created on December 19, 1937, when forty-eight composers assembled in New York City, selected an executive board, and drew up a "Proclamation."[54] Appearing in *Modern Music* in 1938, the Proclamation stated the Alliance's two chief objectives:

> first to regularize and collect all fees pertaining to performance of their copyrighted music, in other words, to protect the economic rights of the composer; second, to stimulate interest in the performance of American music, thereby increasing the economic returns.[55]

The Alliance planned to be a "fellow society" of ASCAP, seeking to create consistency in the payment of royalties to composers. At that time, because of the unevenness with which copyright laws were upheld, some composers received payment and others did not; furthermore, only certain types of pieces yielded income at all. The Alliance wished to extend a fee-collecting structure to "symphony orchestras, opera companies, choral societies, chamber music organizations, instrumental soloist recitals, music clubs, schools and colleges, dance recitals, and movies,"[56] in other words, to virtually the entire province of the cultivated composer. Radio, it was noted, was partly covered by ASCAP.[57] With such a long list, however, it is no wonder that the Alliance was necessary. Members of the ACA believed that the collection of royalties initially might hamper the performance of American music, but that eventually "this music will be more valuable in the eyes of the very people who are asked to pay for the privilege of performing it."[58]

The extent of Copland's Americanist activities is vast, going beyond the period included in this study. In 1937, he helped to establish the Arrow Music Press, a cooperative publishing venture for American music that replaced the older Cos Cob Press.[59] He aided the Composers Forum in its transition from the WPA to independence. He served on the boards of the MacDowell Association and the Koussevitzky Foundation, the latter established in 1942 for commissioning American music. Since its founding in 1940, Copland has been associated with the Berkshire Music Center (Tanglewood), where he has shared his abilities with each new generation of America's young people of promise. Additionally, Copland has represented this country for the State Department on "goodwill" tours of South America.[60] Copland has had a personal impact on more areas of contemporary cultivated musical life in the United States than any other American composer.

Simple Gifts

> Question: Is there any discernible and definite trend and aim in today's music?
> Answer: The trend is to get closer to the audience. To write things simpler so that the audience can build it without pulling it down.
> Question: What is your part in it?
> Answer: It is this: to write something that is simple, yet very good.[61]

The above exchange pinpoints one of the most discussed aspects of Copland's compositional career—namely, his striving in the mid-1930s to create a "simple" musical language. Few have been as bothered by the topic as Copland himself, for he apparently has felt the need to explain his "simple" style. Some of the synonyms offered by the *Oxford English Dictionary* for "simple" are "straightforward," "unadorned," and "plain."[62] In a sense, Copland's style always had been "simple" in its clearly delineated forms and economical—even lean—treatment of musical materials.[63]   Yet in the 1930s, consonance and folk-like tunefulness replaced dissonance and disjunct melodies, changes that made his music "simpler" as well as more pleasing to the average listener. As a result, his music exemplified the several goals comprising musical Americanism in this period: directness, accessibility, and an "American" identity.[64]

That Copland felt that need to justify an entire phase of his musical production indicates two things: his concern for the way in which he was perceived by the musical community; and a change in musical climate that made the word "simple" if not an anachronism, at least unfashionable. These topics will be discussed subsequently. At this point, a closer examination of Copland's stylistic direction in the mid-1930s is necessary.

The issue of Copland's style apparently originated with the final paragraphs of his autobiographical sketch appearing in the first edition of *The New Music*, originally *Our New Music*, in 1941. In these frequently-quoted passages, Copland stated that in the mid-1930s he was dissatisfied with the relationship between the public for cultivated music in America and the cultivated composer. The audience for specifically contemporary music had dissipated, and the general concert audience remained uninterested in new music. "It seemed to me that we composers were in danger of composing in a vacuum," he wrote.[65] Furthermore, composers were not taking advantage of nor being sought after by the mass media, in which a fresh and immense public could be reached. Rather than ignoring the new public, he "felt that it was worth the effort to see if I couldn't say what I had to say in the simplest possible terms."[66] His most recent works, he added, were examples of his "imposed simplicity": *El Salón México, The Second Hurricane, Music for Radio, Billy the Kid, The City, Of Mice and Men,* and *Our Town.*[67]

In a postscript to the sketch for the book's 1967 edition, Copland revealed that the passage cited above had done him "considerable harm."[68] Commentators seeking to "pin down" his style for "all time" had "quoted and misquoted" his remarks which, in retrospect, seemed to him an "oversimplification of [his] aims and intentions."[69] Copland explained that his "simpler" works were written in response to two basic stimuli — the Depression and the expansion of the media.

Copland's wish in the 1930s to compose "functional" music, as he called it,[70] surely is understandable. Composers of his generation, committed to making their way primarily as composers, must have viewed the cinema, radio, and phonograph as potential goldmines. Although working in these fields could reduce a composer's creative freedom, as Copland later acknowledged in "Second Thoughts on Hollywood,"[71] they did provide an outlet, a wide audience, and an income for new composition.

Furthermore, Copland wrote that "there was a 'market' especially for music evocative of the American scene — industrialized backgrounds, landscapes of the Far West, and so forth."[72] This statement indirectly acknowledges Copland's other stated impetus for his "simpler" style, the Depression. "In all the arts," noted Copland, "the Depression had aroused a wave of sympathy for and identification with the plight of the common man."[73] Thus composers had not only a reason to compose music for specific purposes, but to compose music of a specific type — namely "American" music. Elsewhere, Copland commented that his goal in the mid-1930s was not very different from that in the mid-1920s:

It seems to me that what I was trying for in the simpler works was only partly the writing of compositions that might speak to a broader audience. More than that they gave me an opportunity to try for a more homespun musical idiom, not so different in intention from what attracted me in more hectic fashion in my jazz-influenced works of the twenties. In other words, it was not only musical functionalism that was in question, but also musical language.[74]

Copland, in the 1930s, still wanted to write "American" music.

Around 1930, Copland's stylistic position was not fundamentally different from Marc Blitzstein's, even though the latter was increasingly attracted to the stage. Both were considered modernists. Copland's jazz phase had given way to what Smith calls his "abstract" period, represented by pieces like *Statements for Orchestra* (1932–35) and the *Short Symphony* (1933).[75] His musical style grew ascetic and dissonant. He experimented with serial techniques in the *Piano Variations* (1930). Yet he was at the same time a confirmed conceptual Americanist, more active in Americanist groups than any other composer. He could not continue in the direction of his most recent works and still easily accommodate recognizable, indigenous vernacular materials.

The sociopolitical atmosphere of the mid-1930s, previously discussed in Chapter V, undoubtedly contributed to Copland's musical Americanism in the later part of the decade. Unlike Blitzstein, Seeger, Siegmeister, and Robinson, Copland does not appear to have been deeply involved in the leftist movement.[76] Even in the 1930s, Copland made an effort to set himself apart from any specific political associations. In his 1937 Composers' Forum-Laboratory presentation, for instance, when asked if he believed it was necessary for a composer to participate in political activity, Copland responded emphatically "no!"[77]

Yet some, including Copland, have hinted at a leftist influence. In accounting for Copland's simplified language, Thomson has written that Copland was surrounded

by left-wing enthusiasts. He wanted populist themes and populist materials and a music style capable of stating these vividly.[78]

In a recent interview published in *The New York Times*, Copland said "I suppose my popular pieces of the late 30s derived from a sympathy with the left."[79]

According to Arthur Berger, Copland had many friends outside the field of music in the 1930s who tended toward the political left.[80] One of these was Harold Clurman, Copland's former roommate from the Boulanger days. Clurman, along with Cheryl Crawford, founded the Group Theatre in 1929. A communal repertory company, the Group

Theatre forsook the "star system" for a non-hierarchical professional structure. The company lived and studied together and shared all theatrical jobs. Moreover, the Group Theatre's primary concern was the contemporary theatre's relationship to modern American life.[81] Much like Copland, they sought a greater integration between the audience and the artist. To achieve this, they frequently chose plays reflecting current sociopolitical issues. The Group Theatre was the home base for the leftist playwright Clifford Odets, whose *Awake and Sing* and *Waiting for Lefty* they premiered. Copland, who maintained his friendship with Clurman through these years, spent a summer with the Group at its holiday location in upstate New York.[82] Berger concluded that

> it was from these associations that he received important impetus for his whole general musical tendency at this point of his career. It seems hardly accidental that his turn towards simplification and a broader audience should coincide with the later depression years, when artists and intellectuals who had formerly been escapist became aware of politics and economics. Liberalism as a means to social recovery became a central topic of discussion among intellectuals. It was important to come out of the shell, to think of the plight of the people. . . . The people were not only to be the source of subject matter for works of art, but these works were to be simple enough in means, direct and immediate enough in appeal, for the common man to recognize himself and his problems.[83]

Perhaps equally important to Copland's Group Theatre association was his relationship with the Composers' Collective. Although apparently not a member, Copland was involved in many of its events. His new stylistic direction, hinted at in the ballet *Hear Ye! Hear Ye!* (1934) and more explicit in *El Salón México* (1933–36) and *The Second Hurricane* (1936), coincided with his activity with the Collective.

Copland's name first is connected with leftist musical organizations in 1934. The Pierre Degeyter Club, parent organization of the Collective, sponsored a recital of Copland's works at its headquarters. Reviewing the concert, "Carl Sands" noted proudly:

> Aaron Copland is one of the three or four most prominent living American composers and certainly the best of the younger men. Yet it has remained for an organization of proletarian musicians to be the first to ask him to give a recital exclusively of his own works![84]

As mentioned above, Copland made an effort to separate himself from specific political philosophies. Before the performance, according to "Sands," Copland told his audience not to view

> his compositions from a revolutionary angle, for, as he said with charming naivete, he had not, at the time of their composition, any ideas of that sort in his head.[85]

Yet "Sands," who found Copland's remarks a challenge to "the very basis upon which the club is organized," discerned a definite progression in Copland's works from the "ivory tower to within hailing distance of the proletariat."[86]   The recital, which included the trio *Vitebsk* and portions of the *Piano Concerto*, culminated with the *Piano Variations*. The last work "Sands" found "one of the most undeniably revolutionary pieces of music ever produced" — evidence that Copland had progressed "further in music development than language development" toward a revolutionary attitude.[87]   It is important to recall that in 1934 the Collective wanted to create a musical language to represent America's new political awareness.   Copland's dissonant, percussive, and intense *Variations* may have come close to what Collective members had in mind at this time.

In the discussion session following the recital, one questioner asked what Copland's music had to do with the proletariat.   A steel-worker, apparently referring to the *Piano Variations*, stated that it seemed to relate to his job and daily life in the city.   Copland then remarked that although he did not intend to portray "riveters and subways" in the piece, he composed it over a noisy New York street, and believed his music was "able to stand up against modern life."[88]   In conclusion, "Sands" commented:

> "Up against!" And with vigor, too — that is the essence of the *Piano Variations*. There [sic] chief shortcomings seems [sic] to be that they are almost too much "against" — against pretty nearly everything.   So some day, Aaaron [sic], write us something "for."   You know what for![89]

The progression from "Sands" statement on March 22, 1934 to Copland's composition of the May Day march "Into the Streets May First!" seems too easy.[90]   Of course it is not certain Copland ever read the *Daily Worker*, let along "Sands's" specific review.   The fact remains, however, that barely one month later Copland's entry won the mass song contest sponsored by the Pierre Degeyter Club, and was printed in the May first edition of *New Masses*.

That Copland wrote a mass song for the Collective is hardly surprising.   Like many others, he apparently was enough disturbed by American problems during the Depression to consider political alternatives.   Several of his friends, such as Cowell and Blitzstein, were active in the Collective, as was Siegmeister, a former member of Copland's Young Composers' Group.[91]   According to Blitzstein's minutes, an effort to solicit Copland's support was discussed.[92]   One need not speculate why.   Copland's prestige, leadership, and organizational abilities would have been an asset to any contemporary musical society.   His youthful interest in Marxism,[93] and the similarity in ethnic and cultural background between himself and many Collective members, further aligned him with the group. Equally important was Copland's consuming interest in the problems of art music in American society, and his willingness to support any organization confronting these issues. The Collective, in its way, was doing just that.

Copland's other activities with leftist musical groups show that music, not politics, was his primary interest. In November, 1935, he offered a scholarship to the winner of a composition contest conducted by the Downtown Music School, the prize being free composition lessons with Copland.[94] Also, he made two brief contributions to leftist magazines. Notably, the theme in both was essentially the composer and his audience. In "A Note on Young Composers," Copland pointed out that by attaching himself to the proletarian movement, a composer solved some problems but created others:

> It is no secret that many of the young composers who had taken one or the other of these two older men [Stravinsky and Schoenberg] as their models have now thrown in their lot with the working class. These young people, at any rate, have settled the problem of the audience. But at the same time they have taken on other problems, new ones, which result from the kind of audience they now wish to reach. These new problems have to do with such broad questions as the style and content of their music, practical possibilities (usually limitations) in performance, sectarian dangers, etc., which do not obtain in the same way in the ordinary bourgeois field of music.
>
> Hence, the young composer who allies himself with the proletarian movement must do so not with the feeling that he has found an easy solution, but with a full realization of what such a step means, if his work is to be of permanent value to the workers and their cause.[95]

In the other article, a review of the Collective's *Workers Song Book, No. 1* for *New Masses*, Copland addressed the issue of the mass song.

> Composers will ask: "what is a good mass song?" In answering this question we must not forget that the opinion of the trained musician will not always coincide with that of the masses. We as musicians will naturally listen to these songs primarily as music, but the workers who sing them will in the first instance decide how they apply to the actualities of the daily struggle. In their eyes the music will not necessarily be of primary importance; if the spirit is right, and the words are right, any music will suffice which does not "get in the way." Composers will want to raise the musical level of the masses, but they must also be ready to learn from them what species of song is most apposite to the revolutionary task.[96]

The appropriate style for mass songs could be learned from the masses, said Copland, but that style must be simple enough not to "get in the way" of the message.

That Copland's own mass song very recently had been criticized as too difficult for untrained voices makes Copland's comments all the more interesting.[97]   Either from his personal experience with the May Day march, or from the Collective's attempts to find a suitable revolutionary style, Copland arrived at a conclusion in the *New Masses* essays later reached by the Collective: music for the masses had to be couched in an understandable, even familiar style.

Surely Copland's well-known concert pieces from the 1930s were not intended to be revolutionary music for the masses.   Yet, in any consideration of Copland's larger stylistic development, the articles just quoted are important.   They reveal Copland's desire to develop a musical language at a variety of technical levels, a premise as applicable to non-political music as to the mass song. The concept, first articulated in the *New Masses* article, was later expanded in Copland's two major discussions of his own career—the autobiographical sketch and "The Composer in Industrial America"—specifically about the "simple" works of the 1930s. In the latter essay, he wrote:

> In my own mind there was never so sharp a dichotomy between the various works I have written. Different purposes produce different kinds of works, that is all.[98]

And in the postscript to the sketch, he stated:

> Those commentators who would like to split me down the middle into two opposing personalities will get no encouragement from me. I prefer to think that I write my music from a single vision; when the results differ it is because I take into account with each new piece the purpose for which it is intended and the nature of the musical materials with which I work.[99]

It seems obvious that Copland's musical development in the mid-1930s was partly shaped by his associations with the sociopolitical left.

The mere wish to simplify did not provide Copland or the Collective with an immediate workable model.   Members of the Collective eventually found a direction for American revolutionary songs in the folk protest songs emerging in the 1930s.   Pure (that is, non-political) folksong itself then was adopted by Collective members, Copland, and others as a means of both simplifying and Americanizing cultivated music as well.   One example for the treatment of folksong in art music, for Copland at least, was the music of Virgil Thomson. Thomson, not associated with any political movement, independently began incorporating folksong before the rush to this material in the late 1930s.   Berger, Smith, and Thomson himself have recognized his influence upon Copland.[100]

According to Copland, Thomson as early as the 1920s criticized what he believed to be the unnecessary complexities and pomposities of some contemporary music.[101]   Copland commented that while many composers are

> busily engaged in inventing all sorts of new rhythmic and harmonic devices, intent upon being as original and different as possible, Thomson goes to the opposite extreme and deliberately writes music as ordinary as possible – so ordinary, in fact, that at first hearing it often strikes one as being merely foolish. But even if we agree that the music is sometimes foolish, the idea behind it is not so foolish. This idea is derived from the conviction that modern music has forgotten its audience almost completely, that the purpose of music is not to impress and overwhelm the listener but to entertain and charm him.[102]

In 1928, years before the composers of his generation grew interested in Anglo-American material, Thomson wrote *Symphony on a Hymn Tune* in which all four movements are based primarily upon two hymn melodies. Although the work was not premiered until 1945, a four-hand piano adaptation by John Kirkpatrick was available in the mid-1930s.[103] Then in 1934 Thomson demonstrated how pure, consonant functional harmony had contemporary relevance. In *Four Saints in Three Acts*, he matched Gertrude Stein's abstract, plotless libretto to melodies rooted in Anglo-American hymnody.

However, the immediate impetus for Thomson's claim to an influence upon Copland were Thomson's films and ballet.   *The Plow That Broke the Plains* (1936) used cowboy tunes, *The River* (1937) drew upon hymns and folksongs, and the ballet *Filling Station* (1937) was based on a variety of musical Americana. Thomson maintains that until he proved that ballets and films could be based on native materials other than jazz, Copland, with the exception of *Hear Ye! Hear Ye!*, did not compose for these media.[104] Thomson wrote:

> My music offered one approach to simplification; and my employment of folk-style tunes was, as Copland was to write me later about *The River*, "A lesson in how to treat Americana."[105]

Thomson's music was only one example, and as he himself has noted, "a simplified harmonic palette was being experimented with everywhere, of course; and a music 'of the people' clearly an ideal of the time."[106]   Copland's familiarity with and admiration for the music of Shostakovich was also influential. Yet another branch of the stream toward simplification was *Gebrauchsmusik*, with which Americans were becoming acquainted in the 1930s.[107]   Copland's opera, *The Second Hurricane*, was written for the Henry Street Settlement music school in

1936 when he was teaching there. Smith notes that the opera appears to be modelled upon Weill's *Der Jasager* and Hindemith's *Wir Bauen Eine Stadt*, both performed shortly before at the school.[108] Yet Copland's work, written to a libretto by Edwin Denby, was American in subject matter and marked Copland's first use of traditional Americana. In Scene 9 of Act II, Copland incorporated the Revolutionary War song "The Capture of General Burgoyne."[109]

Copland's incorporation of "General Burgoyne" in *The Second Hurricane* bears little relationship to his later employment of folksong. The song seems poorly integrated dramatically; the children sing it to alleviate their fear of a hurricane, and it is simply included whole with variation provided by the changing accompaniment of the four verses. On the other hand, the musical language of the opera does create a fitting background for the song. The opera represents a drastic stylistic departure from works such as *Statements for Orchestra* or even the mass song written a few years earlier. In composing for high schoolers, Copland returned to functional harmony, simple rhythmic patterns, and — if not diatonic — at least triadic melodies. Berger has commented that Copland "rehabilitated" the triad in his "simpler" style.[110] Copland's enthusiasm for the triad is clearly demonstrated in the opening measures of *The Second Hurricane* (see Example 1).

Example 1
Opening Measures and Alto Entry of "Choral Overture" from *The Second Hurricane* (Piano-Vocal Score; New York: Boosey and Hawkes, 1957), Aaron Copland.

The first work in which Copland integrated folksong into his style was *El Salón México*, begun before *The Second Hurricane* in 1933 and finished after it in 1936. Its composition coincided with the composer's arrival at his "imposed simplicity." Copland chose Mexican rather than Anglo-American folk melodies for his first real attempt to treat such source material. The choice recalls Copland's later explanation for his developing interest in conducting in the 1950s.[111] Wishing to try his wings where he was not well known, he conducted orchestras everywhere but in the United States, only returning when he had gained confidence. One wonders if a similar motivation may have been involved in *El Salón México*, written and premiered in Mexico before his works on materials from the United States. Copland may have been especially attracted to Mexican folksongs because of their rhythmic liveliness. In *El Salón México*, he expanded the familiar ground of alternating meters and syncopation already developed in the jazz pieces. Yet he also incorporated actual melodies taken from collections of Mexican folklore.[112] For the first time, Copland's music seems tuneful, albeit by virtue of quoted material. Unlike the statement of "General Burgoyne" in the opera, Copland worked over the folksongs by fragmenting them, altering their melodic intervals and time values, and spreading them out in the orchestra as he was to do later in his "cowboy" ballets.

The Second Hurricane and *El Salón México* ushered in a long and productive period in Copland's composing career. Significantly, most of the works — the ballets, film scores, radio and school music, patriotic works, and even later abstract pieces — were commissioned. Having achieved a flexible musical language, sometimes with specific references to Americana, Copland found his music in more demand than ever before. As Oscar Levant commented in 1940:

> Copland was determined to make his talent work for him; and perhaps even to his own surprise discovered that there was a market and an audience for his products. It is a significant thing, too, that the quality of all this music has been very clean and high.[113]

Appalachian Spring

Copland's first ballet was composed while he was still in Paris, but the ballet *Grohg*, to a story by Copland and Clurman, was never performed and was later adapted to become the *Dance Symphony*. His next, not written until 1934, was also his first ballet on American subject matter. *Hear Ye! Hear Ye!* was composed for Ruth Page and the ballet company of the Chicago Grand Opera. Little-known today, the work satirized the American justice system.[114] Copland's jazz-oriented score included references to American popular dances, and parodies of Mendelssohn's "Wedding March" and the "Star-Spangled Banner." The work exemplifies the tone of bitterness toward American life common in the early Depression years.

Copland's next three ballets— *Billy the Kid* (1938), *Rodeo* (1942), and *Appalachian Spring* (1944)—were very well received in their day, and all have become modern American classics. Smith compares Copland's ballet music with Stravinsky's, noting that each composer's works have become popular representations of his own country's folk cultures.[115]

Copland's ballets are also among the best-known Americanist works of any era. Along with his patriotic pieces, they have done the most to identify Copland with things "American." Two of the ballets take the popular theme of the American West, and all three draw upon folksongs. But Copland, unlike Americanists such as Farwell and Seeger, is not a folklorist. His works are not intended to present the quoted melodies as they would be heard in their original surroundings, nor do they necessarily preserve the original character of the tunes. Rather, the composer has used them as materials in building his own "American" sound. And, more than Harris, he transforms his sources. In the postscript to his autobiographical sketch, Copland complained of a mistaken notion that his music from the 1930s and 1940s was

> larded with native materials. A confusion seems to exist between rhythms and melodies that suggest a certain American *ambiente*, often arrived at unconsciously, and specific folk themes, such as those which in my ballets *Billy the Kid* and *Rodeo* are utilized and developed in a way that I like to think is my own.[116]

Of Copland's three major ballets, *Appalachian Spring* draws the least upon pre-existent music. The work is also thought to be among Copland's best.[117] *Appalachian Spring* was composed in 1943 and 1944 at the request of Martha Graham, who choreographed and performed it with her company. Graham had received a commission from the Elizabeth Sprague Coolidge Foundation to have three composers write new ballets for her. She chose Copland, Milhaud, and Hindemith.[118] *Appalachian Spring* was premiered on October 30, 1944 at the Coolidge Auditorium at the Library of Congress, where limited facilities allowed only a chamber orchestra. In its first year, *Appalachian Spring* won the Music Critics' Circle award for the season's most outstanding theatrical production. In 1945, Copland's score for the ballet received the Pulitzer Prize in Music.

Appalachian Spring takes its title from a poem of that name by Vachel Lindsey, although the ballet bears no relation to the literary work. The setting is a rural community in the Pennsylvania mountains in the early nineteenth century. In subject, the ballet is almost abstract; it focuses not upon a narrative but upon the moods and feelings of a young couple about to be married.[119]

The orchestral suite for *Appalachian Spring* consists of eight sections corresponding to the scenes of the original ballet. Despite the sectional nature of the work, Copland's score is unified at several levels. First, cohesion is achieved by the recall of material throughout the piece as a whole and within individual sections. For instance, an abbreviated statement of prelude (Section I) material, including the clarinet solo outline of the triad which opens the piece (mm. 2-4, A major), is recalled to conclude the work (mm. 660-62, C major). On the smaller level of the sections, the same themes open and close Sections I (mm. 1-50) and III (mm. 155-215). Second, the prelude introduces or forecasts much of the important thematic material of the entire work. Copland's rediscovery of the triad was never more effective than in the opening section. By masterful orchestration and pitch placement, the expansion of the tonic triad followed by the dominant creates a tranquil mood appropriate to both the setting and the subject matter.

A motive introduced in m. 9, a rising fourth — in this case to the tonic — followed by a major third, becomes the principal material of the

Example 2
Principal Motive of the Prelude.

work (see Example 2). The motive forms the basis for the accompaniment pattern beginning in m. 13, the rising sequential gestures developed in Section II beginning in m. 55, and the principal theme of *Appalachian Spring*. This theme is first presented in mm. 79-97 as a countersubject to the main material of Section II, a spirited activation of the A major scale (see Example 3). The principal theme is then stated alone, as the basis for Section III (mm. 161-215; see Example 4). It is recalled frequently throughout the work, whenever the quiet, lyrical mood of Section III returns: at the close of Section IV (m. 313), in Section VI (m. 448), and finally in the Coda (m. 644). Furthermore, the motives of Sections II, IV, and V are interrelated, although not as closely as the materials in the lyric sections. The principal motives of IV and V, for instance, recall the opening leap and scalar pattern that characterized the melody of Section II (see Examples 5 and 6).

Equally important to its cyclical function is the principal motive's relation to "Simple Gifts," the Shaker melody on which Copland builds his finale (Section VII).[120] So familiar is the gesture of the melodic rising fourth by this point that "Simple Gifts" seems to grow out of what has come before.   Indeed, the first notes of the melody are really an embellishment of the rising fourth and major third of the principal motive introduced in the prelude (see Example 7).

Example 3
Principal Material of Section II.

Example 4
Recurring Theme from Section III.

Example 5
Principal Material of Section V.

Example 6
Principal Material of Section IV.

Two techniques found throughout *Appalachian Spring* are also introduced in the prelude: the use of pedal points, and the reliance on solo woodwinds to carry principal material. Copland's stress on soloists may have been an effort to maintain some of the intimacy of the original reduced scoring, particularly in the lyric sections. Employing pedals, often in the extreme ranges, heightens anticipation and, in combination with the wind solos, lends a transparency and harmonic sweetness to the work. In fact, the score seems bathed in consonance even when, as in the prelude, the tonic and dominant are superimposed. The consonant feeling is also particularly apparent in the first two variations of "Simple Gifts," where tonic-dominant pedals are sounding almost constantly. The effect, for instance, of the pedal in the upper flute register punctuated by the triangle is magical (see m. 509).

Copland's use of musical Americana in *Appalachian Spring* is limited to the quotation of "Simple Gifts" in the finale. The quotation is not exact, for Copland has smoothed out a few melodic gaps and changed the third phrase to parallel the first (see Example 8). The

Example 7
Opening Gesture of "Simple Gifts."

Example 8
Comparison of Opening of Third Phrase in Copland's Version of "Simple Gifts" with the Original, Taken from Edward Deming Andrew's *The Gift to Be Simple*, p. 136.

Musical examples 2-8 above are taken from *Appalachian Spring* (Full Orchestral Score; London: Boosey and Hawkes, 1945), Aaron Copland.

melody undergoes successive stylistic treatments characteristic of a set of variations, and is transformed from the almost lighthearted initial presentation by the solo clarinet to majesty in the final *tutti* statement. The latter is reminiscent of a Bach chorale, particularly with the strong, slow contrapuntal line in the low register. The five variations are Baroque-like indeed, as Smith has noted, for Copland has preserved the melodic and basic harmonic patterns of the melody while altering the orchestration and rhythmic values.[121] The brilliant fifth variation gives way to a subdued coda in which a quiet melody of limited range is introduced. Copland continues in a neo-Baroque manner of four-part writing, employing three successive deceptive cadences before coming to rest in C major. A final recall of the principal theme and the triadic expansion of the prelude concludes the work.

While Copland has altered his borrowed material, he surely has shaped his score to accommodate it. The principal motive of *Appalachian Spring*, which is discovered to be the head motive of "Simple Gifts," permeates the work. Thus, the pre-existent musical Americana in *Appalachian Spring* penetrates far below the surface level. Furthermore, Copland's own melodies have changed. Compared with *The Second Hurricane*, for instance, *Appalachian Spring* reveals a considerable smoothing out of melodic material from that which characterized the opera. Harmonies are consonant and tonal, even emphasized by the pedals. Also, syncopation and alternating meters are primarily restricted to the climactic portions of the lively dance sequences in *Sections IV and V*. Copland has provided an appropriate and effective musical setting for a rural nineteenth-century American story and hymn.

Musical Americanism is by definition self-conscious. Yet Copland, like some members of the Composers' Collective, may have felt more compelled to prove himself "American" because of his ethnic heritage. A comparison with other composers of Copland's generation who came by their "American" identity more easily adds weight to this idea. Virgil Thomson and Roy Harris, for instance, were both born and bred in the mid- or far-west, idealized as "American" in the 1930s and 1940s. Thomson, who can trace his ancestors to colonial times, has said: "Nobody . . . is more American than I am."[122] His use of Americana, begun considerably before the proletarian movement or the discovery of Ives, seems a natural outgrowth of his upbringing. Harris was also "American" by virtue of birth. Although certainly a musical Americanist, Harris seemed more inclined to forge from the symphony a personal statement to represent America. Urban popular music was the vernacular source closest to Copland's boyhood. It was Copland who delved into the popular dance hall jazz of the 1920s to make his own works "American." However, he received more of a national identity from his later interest in folklore and patriotism, both more readily acceptable than jazz as "American" in the 1930s and 1940s.

That rural music was not a part of Copland's youthful environment has not hampered his assimilation of folk materials. His folk-inspired period culminated in three works, each for a different medium: the film score *The Red Pony* (1948), the opera *The Tender Land* (1952-54), and the *Third Symphony* (1944-46). In *The Red Pony*, Copland demonstrated that his western idiom was not dependent upon quotations. The composer approached a romantic mélange of folk-like materials in *The Tender Land*, which incorporates but one pre-existent song. And the *Third Symphony* is an abstract study of the language Copland developed to embody folk materials in previous works. After *Appalachian Spring*, Copland's use of folksong decreased considerably, with the exception of arrangements like the *Old American Songs* (1950). The folk idiom was by then so well absorbed that specific references were unnecessary.

Also by 1950, Copland was perceived as an "American" composer—by some as "America's No. 1 Composer."[123] His goal of bringing audience and composer closer together was achieved, at least in his own case. The currents of contemporary music were moving away from Americanism, however, away from self-conscious accessibility. Like Blitzstein and Harris, whose fundamental outlooks also were shaped in the 1930s, Copland found himself at odds with dominant stylistic trends. His serial works in the 1950s continued from where he had left off twenty years earlier in the *Piano Variations*. Yet his rate of composing slowed. In a recent interview, Copland commented:

> There's no doubt I've bogged down. . . . That's not to say that tomorrow I might not bog up again. I find it awfully hard after 50 years to feel guilty. I wouldn't want to force myself.[124]

In recent years, few have followed Copland's lead toward the general public. Some have noticed an uneasiness on his part about the altered aesthetic since his own extended "imposed simplicity." Harold Schonberg has written:

> It might be hard for a man who for so long had been the leader of American music to find himself considered an anachronism.[125]

Surely, however, not all consider either his music or his essential attitude an anachronism, as Schonberg also noted. Copland remains the best known and the most performed American composer.[126]   One commentator has written that Copland's "middle way" was

> a cheering sign to all who share his broad vision of music as a comprehensible means of human expression.[127]

If, as Wilfred Mellers has suggested, Copland added a language to the history of music, it is a highly personal and recognizable one.[128] Copland's musical language, perhaps more than any other, also has come to be identified as "American."

XII

Conclusions

The first Yaddo Festival of American Music in 1932 demonstrates several aspects of American cultivated music at the beginning of that decade. American composers organized a festival of their works independent of the major institutions for cultivated music in America. The Festival was not held in New York City. Few besides the composers themselves attended. Some observers noted that the composers appeared self-conscious, even tentative, about the stylistic direction their music should take. Oscar Levant, paraphrasing Pirandello, commented that the Yaddo conferees were like "Six Composers in Search of an Influence."[1]

American cultivated music was at a turning point in the early 1930s. In some ways, Yaddo exemplified the long isolation of American cultivated music from both cultivated music in America and American society in general; but Yaddo also hinted at the future. Excluding the Copland-Sessions concerts, Yaddo was the first significant gathering of the clan of younger American composers. In addition to Copland, those attending (or whose music was performed) included Harris, Blitzstein, Thomson, Bowles, Bennett, Piston, Sessions, Riegger, Levant, and Brant.[2] Many of the same composers figured prominently in Americanist activities and in the formation of Americanist attitudes later in the 1930s and 1940s. Yaddo may have helped unify the group because it was a conference rather than merely a concert series. The misquotation of Copland's speech set off a controversy that marked the Yaddo gathering as an event in the history of musical Americanism. The younger generation of American composers had a banner to rally around; thereafter, they identified themselves with the cause of American music.[3]

The year after the first Yaddo Festival, Henry Cowell's symposium *American Composers on American Music* was published. The composers had decided to criticize themselves in an effort to make up for the lack of astute criticism of new American music. In his introduction to the anthology, Cowell wrote:

> Nationalism in music has no purpose as an aim in itself. Music happily transcends political and racial boundaries and is good or bad irrespective of the

nation in which it was composed. Independence, however, is stronger than
imitation. In the hands of great men independence may result in products of
permanent value. Imitation cannot be expected to produce such significant
achievements.

American composition up to now has been tied to the apron-strings of
European tradition. To attain musical independence, more national consciousness
is a present necessity for American composers. The result of such an awakening
should be the creation of works capable of being accorded international standing.[4]

In the early 1930s, Yaddo and Cowell's symposium set the stage for a
decade and a half of musical Americanism. The younger generation of
like-thinking composers was taking matters into its own hands.

Musical Americanism in the 1930s and 1940s was far different from
what it had been earlier. Surely the century-old complaints of American
composers—lack of performances and recognition for American
cultivated music, lack of social status for American composers, the
preference for European cultivated music in America—continued to be
concerns in these years. Another factor, however, the problem of
"modern" music, was significant as well. In a perceptive paper to
the M.T.N.A. in 1935, Roy D. Welch of Princeton University stated:

> There are in our world two strong opposing social trends affecting every musician.
> The one impels him to preserve his individuality and to address himself to the
> cultivated minority. The other forces him toward a proletarian or nationalistic
> ideal.[5]

American composers in the 1930s seemed to be making a major effort to
attract and keep not just the music-loving public, but the general public
as well. Thus in addition to its usual attractions, Americanism also
offered an alternative to modern, or at least ultramodern, music.

Furthermore, Copland's generation differed significantly from those
of previous American composers. Copland's role as an Americanist
leader was unprecedented. Americanists previously had found
spokesmen, such as Fry, Bristow, early members of the M.T.N.A.,
Farwell, and Gilbert; but until Copland, none could support their
Americanist rhetoric with music of widely-recognized quality. Copland
won respect on both fronts. His combination of skills was perfect for the
moment, and he used them effectively.

There were also more American composers of one generation than
before, most of them living in and around New York City in this period.
Furthermore, more of them were better trained, thanks to the blossoming
of American music education and the abilities of individuals like Arthur
Farwell, Rubin Goldmark, and Nadia Boulanger. Copland's generation
also travelled. Many had been to Paris or Berlin, the major music

capitals of Europe in the 1920s, and some even to Mexico or South America. They counted as friends, teachers or colleagues the foreign leaders of contemporary music. In the 1930s, many European composers visited or emigrated to the United States, reversing the pattern of artistic exchange between Europe and America established in the nineteenth century. American composers could choose from a multitude of European or other foreign stylistic approaches. They did, but not slavishly, for most seemed determined to go their own way. The conviction to create "American" music was apparent in their writings and activities, and in many of their compositions. They were, as Seeger put it, the "blessed generation" of American composers.[6]

A mood of Americanism among the intelligentsia in the 1930s and the heightened patriotism of the World War II period helped foster musical Americanism. Both trends directed the attention of audiences and composers toward America and its own natural musical resources. For the first time in American musical history, others besides the composers themselves took an active interest in American composition. Conductors like Koussevitzky, Goossens, Hanson, and those in the WPA regularly performed native works. Writers like Paul Rosenfeld, Ashley Pettis, and later Virgil Thomson gave close scrutiny to new American music. Claire Reis, then Chairman of the Board of Directors of the League of Composers, befriended several American composers and helped direct the League's activities toward native talent. The League's publication *Modern Music*, a forum for the discussion and criticism of contemporary music, functioned as an artistic barometer of its era (1924–46). In the 1930s, an atmosphere favorable to the creation and evaluation of new music was formed in the United States for the first time. Both American society and American cultivated composers were ready for a period of intense musical Americanism.

If some American composers were floundering about in 1932, as Levant suggested, by 1937 they had found themselves. In that year, Blitzstein's *The Cradle Will Rock* and Copland's *Gebrauchsmusik* opera *The Second Hurricane* were premiered. Harris, having achieved some acclaim for several "American" works, was soon at work on his masterpiece, the *Third Symphony*. Thomson had completed two film scores laden with Americana. Slightly younger composers followed the Americanist suit a few years later. Schuman's *American Festival Overture*, Robinson's *Ballad for Americans*, and Siegmeister's *A Walt Whitman Overture* are each from 1939. Nearly all American composers joined the patriotic bandwagon in the early 1940s with appropriate works. Americanism had emerged as the dominant stylistic trend of the period.

Coincidental with the maturing of Copland's generation came the second significant achievement in American cultivated music in this period: the partial elimination of the barrier which had long existed between the institutions for cultivated music in America and American cultivated music. By 1945, it was no longer rare to hear an American work on a symphony orchestra program. American art music was on the radio, on phonograph recordings, in movie houses, and even occasionally at the Metropolitan Opera.[7] American composer/educators, particularly Hanson, were making American music a normal part of the educational system through its performance, publication, and recording, and through the encouragement of new composition. American composers and their works were recognized by both the government and the prestigious private foundations. The WPA, while not commissioning new American music, sponsored — even insisted upon — its performance. During the War, the O.W.I. instituted a music program and the armed forces employed composers in various ways. Several composers had received Guggenheim Fellowships by 1945, and two had received the Pulitzer Prize in Music.[8] American composers at last had achieved "official" recognition, and their works were gradually being accepted within the realm of cultivated music as a whole.

If, in 1932, Yaddo forecast a direction American music would take for the next decade and a half, the cessation in 1946 of *Modern Music*, a victim of wartime paper shortages, seemed equally prophetic. The end of the War marked the beginning of a new era in American history, and the place of art music in American society again began to change. World War II had demonstrated the sinister ends to which nationalism as both a political and cultural force could be taken. As the historian David D. Van Tassel has written, nationalism was

> challenged at its very foundations by crises in Europe and Asia, by the United States' entry into the Second World War, and by the final unleashing of the atomic bomb. . . . By 1945, it was clear that certain limits of nationalism had been reached.[9]

The United States entered World War II out of self-defense but also, in American eyes at least, as the protector of freedom and humanity. By 1945 these principles, while not forgotten, at least had been compromised by the exigencies of war.

Many organizations established in the atmosphere of political liberalism and Americanism in the 1930s did not survive the exhausted nationalism and growing conservatism of the wartime and post-war years. The WPA Arts Projects, halted in 1943 due to the war, were not revived. The Composers Forum served only New York City after 1940 in relatively infrequent concerts, compared to its WPA years. The

Composers' Collective, most politically left of composers' organizations in New York, did not even last that long. Wartime propaganda films and film scores were no longer needed by the O.W.I., nor did concert halls require as much new patriotic music.

At the same time, composers had grown disillusioned with some of the new creative fields they had embraced so enthusiastically in the 1930s. Despite the monetary rewards, many could not accept the artistic compromises demanded by the film industry, and Hollywood studios more frequently turned to those with a popular music background. With the improvements in recording quality, radio began to rely more heavily upon records as a cheaper and less troublesome alternative to live performance, thus reducing the possibilities for radio commissions or premieres.

Furthermore, the impact of distinguished immigrants began to be felt in the American composers' community, if not the musical community at large. Most important in the late 1940s and 1950s was Arnold Schoenberg. Schoenberg's music was not aimed at the masses. His complex compositional techniques, dissonant atonal music, and uncompromising attitude toward his craft seemed diametrically opposed to the simplicity and social relevance characterizing American musical composition during the 1930s and early 1940s. After World War II, there was a retreat from the meeting ground tenuously established between the general audience and the composer of art music in the pre-war period.

Whether causative or merely symbolic, American composers' turning inward was expressed by their gradual move into academia. The widespread establishment and acceptance of music as an academic field perhaps has been the most significant fact of post-war American musical life for the composer. So strong has this trend been that in the present it is difficult to name more than a few composers after Copland's generation who are not now or have not spent a large part of their professional careers at learning institutions. The academic shelter has provided American composers with their most secure social role, and it has had an enormous effect upon the character and purpose of musical composition in the United States.

However, the post-war decline of musical Americanism as a dominant concern among native composers would seem to have an additional, simpler explanation. To conclude his 1933 discussion of American music, Cowell wrote that when a national consciousness among composers resulted in "the creation of works capable of being accorded international standing, . . . self-conscious nationalism will no longer be necessary."[10] In a dialogue with Lukas Foss in 1974, Aaron Copland was asked about his attempts to be "American" earlier in his career. Copland acknowledged that composing "American" music once had been his and other composers' goal. The present lack of interest in musical Americanism, Copland continued, revealed that being "American" was no longer a pressing problem among younger composers. Perhaps his generation had "accomplished that for them."[11]   In the mid-1920s, Copland had complained that no tradition of American cultivated music was recognizable. By the mid-1940s, he and his generation had created such a tradition.   Americanist music comprises a substantial portion of that American repertory.

Notes

Preface

1. Roger Sessions, *Reflections on the Musical Life in the United States* (New York: Merlin Press, 1956).

2. Virgil Thomson, *American Music Since 1910* (New York: Holt, Rinehart and Winston, 1972), p. 66.

3. See Paul Rosenfeld, "When New York Became Central," *Modern Music,* XX/2 (January–February, 1943), pp. 83-89.

Chapter 1

1. *Oxford English Dictionary*, Vol. V, Part II (Oxford: Clarendon Press, 1933; corr. ed., 1961), p. 505.

2. It should be noted that "Americanism" frequently is placed in quotation marks in this section to denote its use as a term (an ism) alone and not the concepts it represents.

3. *Oxford English Dictionary*, Vol. I, p. 279. A pioneer study of Americanisms is H. L. Mencken's *The American Language* (New York: Alfred A. Knopf, 1919) which has several later editions and supplements. Two others are Mitford M. Mathews, ed., *A Dictionary of Americanisms* (Chicago: University of Chicago, 1951), and Schele De Vere, *Americanisms: The English of the New World* (New York: C. Scribner, 1972).

4. Ibid.

5. Ibid., Vol. VII, p. 560.

6. Ibid., Vol. VII, pp. 31-32; the other definitions offered for "nationalism" are a "national idiom or phrase," which corresponds to a meaning of "Americanism"; "the doctrine that certain nations (as contrasted with individuals) are the object of divine election"; and "a form of socialism based on the nationalizing of all industry." Regarding the second of these alternatives, the historians Louis Hartz and Hans Kohn both have written about America's self-image as a divinely-ordained nation; Hartz, *The Liberal Tradition in America* (New York: Harcourt, Brace, 1955), pp. 11-14, Kohn, *American Nationalism* (New York: Macmillan,

1957), pp. 39-91. On the last, two interesting discussions are Roger Sessions, "Music and Nationalism," *Modern Music,* XI/1 (November–December, 1933), pp. 3-12, and Alfred Ellison, "The Composer under Twentieth Century Political Ideologies" (Ed.D. dissertation, Teacher's College, Columbia University, 1949).

7. See, for instance, Isaiah Berlin, "The Bent Twig: A Note on Nationalism," *Foreign Affairs* 51/1 (October, 1972), pp. 11-30.

8. John J. Pullen, *Patriotism in America* (New York: American Heritage Press, 1971), p. 90.

9. John Tasker Howard, "Our Folk-Music and Its Probable Impress on American Music of the Future," *The Musical Quarterly* VII/2 (April, 1921), p. 167.

10. Paul Rosenfeld, "'Americanism' in American Music," *Modern Music* XVII/4 (May–June, 1940), p. 226. A similar adaptation of the term in a musical context is that of Babette Deutsch, "America in the Arts," *The Musical Quarterly* VII/3 (July, 1921), p. 308.

11. Gilbert Chase, *America's Music* (revised second edition; New York: McGraw-Hill, 1966; original edition 1955), p. 490.

12. Ibid.

13. H. Wiley Hitchcock, *Music in the United States: A Historical Introduction* (second edition; Englewood Cliffs, New Jersey: Prentice-Hall, 1974; original edition 1969), pp. 200, 201, 203.

14. David D. Boyden, *An Introduction to Music* (New York: Alfred A. Knopf, 1956), p. 359; also revised edition, 1969.

15. In fact, Chase has termed the activities of Farwell, et al., at the turn of the century, as American "nationalism," reserving the term "Americanist" for later.

16. Hitchcock, *Music in the United States,* pp. 51-52.

17. Ibid., p. 51.

18. Charles Seeger, "Music and Class Structure in the United States," *American Quarterly* IX/3 (Fall, 1957), pp. 281-94.

19. Ibid., p. 285.

20. Ibid., p. 288.

21. Two articles addressing this subject are: Daniel Gregory Mason, "Democracy and Music," *The Musical Quarterly* III/4 (October, 1917), pp. 641-57; John B. Burk, "The Democratic Ideal in Music," *The Musical Quarterly* V/3 (July, 1919), pp. 316-28.

22. Elie Siegmeister, *Music and Society* (London: Workers' Music Association, 1943; originally published by Critics' Group of New York, 1938), pp. 48-49.

23. *Oxford English Dictionary*, Vol. I, p. 27.

24. Henry F. Gilbert, "The American Composer," in *The American Composer Speaks*, Gilbert Chase, ed. (New York: McGraw-Hill, 1966), pp. 96-97.

25. Henry Cowell, "Roy Harris," in *American Composers on American Music*, Henry Cowell, ed. (orig. 1933; New York: Frederick Ungar, 1962), p. 68.

26. Charles Wakefield Cadman, "Letter to Charles Ives," January 26, 1943, Charles Ives Collection, Yale University.

27. Mordecai M. Kaplan, *Questions Jews Ask* (New York: Reconstructionist Press, 1956), p. 13.

28. Aaron Copland, "Remarks to Lukas Foss," Brooklyn Academy of Music Concert, March 30, 1974.

29. Aaron Copland, "Letter to Barbara Zuck," July 18, 1974.

30. Elie Siegmeister, "Interview with Barbara Zuck," December 14, 1974.

31. Aaron Copland praises both these influential men in "The Critic: Paul Rosenfeld," and "The Conductor: Serge Koussevitzky," *Copland on Music* (New York: W. W. Norton, 1963), pp. 97-100 and 73-83.

32. Béla Bartók, "The Influence of Peasant Music on Modern Music," in *Composers on Music*, Sam Morgenstern, ed. (New York: Pantheon Books, 1956), pp. 425-27.

33. Roger Sessions, in *Reflections on the Musical Life in the United States* (New York: Merlin Press, 1956), pp. 146-53, makes a distinction similar to Bartók's.

34. Curt Sachs, *Our Musical Heritage* (New York: Prentice-Hall, 1955), pp. 318-19.

35. Ibid., p. 323.

36. Ibid.

37. Bruno Nettl, *Folk and Traditional Music of the Western Continents* (Englewood Cliffs, N.J.: Prentice-Hall, 1965), p. 13.

Chapter 2

1. Sidney Smith, in *Edinburgh Review*, Vol. XXXII (1820), pp. 69-80, cited in Hans Kohn, *American Nationalism* (New York: Macmillan, 1957), p. 51; in *American Nationalism*, pp. 47-87, Kohn discusses the origins of American cultural nationalism and European disillusionment with America in the nineteenth century.

2. Ralph Waldo Emerson, "The American Scholar," in *American Poetry and Prose*, Part I, ed. by Norman Foerster (4th ed., Boston: Houghton Mifflin, 1957), p. 489.

3. William Henry Fry, from "Mr. Fry's 'American Ideas' about Music," *Dwight's Journal of Music* II/23 (March 12, 1853), p. 181.

4. William Henry Fry, "Prefatory Remarks," *Leonora* (Philadelphia: E. Ferrett, 1846), p. iv.

5. The development of popular and folk music of the nineteenth century is discussed in George Pullen Jackson's several books on Southern spirituals, Harold Courlander's *Negro Folk Music U.S.A.* (New York: Columbia University Press, 1963), and Hans Nathan's *Dan Emmett and the Rise of Early Negro Minstrelry* (Norman: University of Oklahoma Press, 1962). H. Wiley Hitchcock provides a survey of the subject in Chapter 5 of *Music in the United States* (sec. ed.; Englewood Cliffs, N.J.: Prentice-Hall, 1974).

6. Fry, "Prefatory Remarks," p. iii.

7. Fry, cited in William Treat Upton, *William Henry Fry* (New York: Thomas Y. Crowell, 1954), p. 128.

8. Anthony Philip Heinrich, whose works sometimes drew upon vernacular music, was just becoming known at this time. Heinrich is discussed subsequently.

9. Fry, "Prefatory Remarks," p. v.

10. Upton, *Fry*, p. 136.

11. Irving Lowens, "William Henry Fry: American Nationalist," *Music and Musicians in Early America* (New York: W. W. Norton, 1964), p. 220; various contemporary reviews of *Leonora* are reprinted in Upton, *Fry*, pp. 208-15, and John Tasker Howard, *Our American Music* (third ed.; New York: Thomas Y. Crowell, 1954), pp. 240-42.

12. Lowens, "Fry," p. 220.

13. "Music in New York," *New York Musical Review and Gazette* IX/7 (April 3, 1858), p. 98.

14. Upton, *Fry*, pp. 183-84.

15. The book was by Edward George Earle Lytton Bulwer-Lytton (1803–73), a British novelist, dramatist, and politician, and the libretto was prepared by Fry's brother, Joseph Reese Fry (1811-?).

16. Fry's comments on the importance of his achievement in *Leonora* are scattered through his writings and lectures. See Upton, *Fry*, pp. 128, 138-39.

17. Upton, *Fry*, pp. 305-22.

18. See Howard, *Our American Music*, p. 245, and Upton, *Fry*, pp. 133-35.

19. Upton, in "Composer," *Fry*, surveys and evaluates Fry's major works, and includes contemporary criticism. Not all scores were available to this author. The above

conclusion is therefore based on those of other writers, principally Upton, as well as her own perusal of some of Fry's works.

20. This incident is outlined in Gilbert Chase, *America's Music* (revised sec. ed.; New York: McGraw-Hill, 1966), pp. 327-29, and is discussed in greater detail in the present study in connection with George Frederick Bristow.

21. *Dwight's Journal of Music* I/3 (April 24, 1852), p. 32; a more complete announcement of the lectures is presented in this same journal, I/6 (July 24, 1852), p. 126.

22. Upton, *Fry*, p. 122.

23. Fry's letter to the New York *Musical World and Times* (March 16, 1853) is reprinted in *Dwight's Journal of Music* II/26 (April 2, 1853), pp. 201-2. It was written to correct what Fry felt to be faulty coverage of his final lecture. In this letter he strenuously denied finding fault with the public, saying that his remarks were directed only toward music critics.

24. Oscar George Sonneck, *Early Concert-Life in America* (New York: Musurgia Publishers, 1947; reissue of original 1907 edition).

25. Hitchcock, in *Music in the United States*, p. 91, notes the date of one of the earliest known symphonies by an American as 1831. A *Symphony in D* by William C. Peters was found in Ambridge, Pennsylvania, a town in the western portion of the state which in 1831 would have been frontier. Although Ambridge was settled by Germans, noted for their active musical life, the rural location of the work suggests that more populated areas may have produced symphonic works of an earlier data as yet undiscovered. See Richard D. Wetzel, *Frontier Musicians on the Connoquenessing, Wabash, and Ohio* (Athens: Ohio University Press, 1976), pp. 74-91.

26. Concerning the patriotism of some of Billings's hymns, see David P. McKay and Richard Crawford, *William Billings of Boston* (Princeton University Press, 1975), pp. 62-68, and J. Murray Barbour, *The Church Music of William Billings* (East Lansing: Michigan State University Press, 1960), p. 19. See also Francis Hopkinson's famous remarks about being the first native of the United States to compose in "Dedication to His Excellency George Washington, Esquire," *Seven Songs for Harpsichord or Forte-Piano* (Philadelphia, 1788, facs. ed. by Harry Dichter, Philadelphia: Musical Americana, 1954), cited in Gilbert Chase, ed., *The American Composer Speaks* (Baton Rouge: Louisiana State University Press, 1966), pp. 39-40.

27. Anthony Philip Heinrich, subtitle of the "Finale Brillante" of *The New England Feast of Shells*, an orchestral suite performed at Heinrich's Grand Valedictory Concert in New York, April 21, 1853; cited in William Treat Upton, *Anthony Philip Heinrich* (New York: Columbia University Press, 1939), p. 286.

28. This title originally appeared in the Boston publication *Euterpiad, or Musical Intelligencer* (April 13, 1822) in a review of Heinrich's *The Dawning of Music in*

Kentucky. This entire review and others on Heinrich's works and concerts are reprinted in Upton, *Heinrich,* pp. 66-67 and elsewhere.

29. Upton, *Heinrich,* p. 162.

30. John Hill Hewitt, *Shadows on the Wall* (Baltimore: Trumbull Brothers, 1877), cited in Howard, *Our American Music,* pp. 230-32.

31. Anthony Philip Heinrich, *The Dawning of Music in Kentucky* (Philadelphia: Bacon and Hart, 1820).

32. Upton, *Heinrich,* pp. 261-62; see also Hitchcock, *Music in the United States,* p. 89.

33. Upton, *Heinrich,* p. 163.

34. See also Wilbur Richard Maust, "The Symphonies of Anthony Philip Heinrich Based on American Themes" (Ph.D. dissertation, Indiana University, 1973).

35. Taken from the program to Heinrich's "Grand Musical Festival," New York, June 16, 1842, reprinted in Upton, *Heinrich,* p. 171.

36. Maust, in his discussion of Heinrich's symphonies on Indian subjects, does not note any Indian musical materials; "The Symphonies of Anthony Philip Heinrich," pp. 179-84.

37. See Hitchcock, *Music in the United States,* p. 90.

38. See "List of Compositions of Anthony Philip Heinrich," in Upton, *Heinrich,* pp. 271-315.

39. This work is "Monday" in *The Musical Week* (London: Johanning, [c. 1835]).

40. Heinrich, "Preface" to *The Musical Week.*

41. John Tasker Howard and George Kent Bellows, *A Short History of Music in America* (New York: Thomas Y. Crowell, 1967), p. 127.

42. Heinrich, "Preface" to *The Dawning of Music in Kentucky,* cited in Upton, *Heinrich,* p. 51.

43. John Sullivan Dwight, *Harbinger* (July 4, 1846), reprinted in Upton, *Heinrich,* p. 199.

44. Chase, *America's Music,* p. 326.

45. Delmar Rogers, "Nineteenth Century Music in New York City as Reflected in the Career of George Frederick Bristow" (Ph.D. dissertation, University of Michigan, 1967), p. 175.

46. Ibid., p. 87.

47. *Rip Van Winkle* was revived for performances in both New York and Philadelphia in 1870, and was given in concert version in New York in 1898 (*Annals of Opera, 1597-1940*, Vol. I [2nd ed.; Genève: Societas Bibliographica, 1955], p. 919). Most recently, it was performed at the University of Illinois in winter, 1974.

48. George Frederick Bristow, *Rip Van Winkle; Grand Romantic Opera in Three Acts* (New York: G. Schirmer, 1882).

49. Rogers, "Nineteenth Century Music," p. 176.

50. *Dwight's Journal of Music* VIII/1 (October 6, 1855), p. 6.

51. *The New York Times* (September 28, 1855), p. 4, cited in Rogers, "Nineteenth Century Music," p. 110.

52. George Frederick Bristow, *Niagara* [manuscript, (189?)]).

53. Hitchcock, *Music in the United States*, p. 91.

54. Bristow, *The Great Republic, An Ode to the American Union* (New York: Biglow and Main, 1880).

55. Bourne, prefatory remarks to Bristow, *The Great Republic*, p. 3.

56. Rogers, "Nineteenth Century Music," p. 148; the Bristow-Strong meeting is retold in Rogers's dissertation from George Templeton Strong's *Diary of George Templeton Strong*, Vol. IV, ed. by Allan Nevins and Milton H. Thomas (New York: Macmillan, 1852), p. 327.

57. The Fry-Willis Controversy was carried in *Dwight's Journal of Music*, Vol IV, Nos. 18, 19, 21, 22, 23, 24, and 25 (February 4, 11, 25, March 4, 11, 18, 25, 1854), pp. 138, 140, 145, 163, 171, 173, 182, 186, 195.

58. Chase, *America's Music*, p. 328; Howard and Bellows, *A Short History of Music in America*, p. 130; Rogers, "Nineteenth Century Music," pp. 85-86.

59. Bristow, "Letter," *Dwight's Journal of Music* IV/23 (March 11, 1854), p. 182.

60. Rogers, "Nineteenth Century Music," pp. 87-88.

61. *Dwight's Journal of Music* X/12 (December 20, 1856), p. 93.

62. *Dwight's Journal of Music* XXI/25 (September 20, 1962), p. 196.

63. George M. Fredrickson, *The Inner Civil War* (New York: Harper and Row, 1965), p. 2.

64. *The Musical Review and Musical World* XV/24 (November 19, 1864), p. 373.

65. *New York Weekly Review* XVI/2 (January 14, 1865), p. 6.

   A brief study of Civil War songs is found in the "Introduction" to Richard Crawford's *The Civil War Songbook* (New York: Dover Publications, 1977).

66. *The Musical Review and Musical World* XIV/5 and 12 (February 28 and June 16, 1863), pp. 51 and 30.

67. *The Musical Review and Musical World* XV/15 (July 16, 1864), p. 230.

68. Lanier, from a letter cited in Aubrey H. Starke, "Sidney Lanier as a Musician," *The Musical Quarterly* XX/4 (October, 1934), p. 398; see also: Chase, *America's Music*, p. 341, and Edwin Mims, "Sidney Lanier," *The Dictionary of American Biography*, Vol. 5 (New York: Scribner, [1959-]), pp. 601-5.

69. Starke, "Sidney Lanier," p. 398.

70. Chase, *America's Music*, 340; see also Fannie L. Gwinnen Cole, "Silas Gamaliel Pratt," *The Dictionary of American Biography*, Vol. 8, pp. 177-78.

71. Howard and Bellows, *A Short History of American Music*, pp. 143-44.

72. Robert Offergeld, "Introduction," *Centennial Catalogue of the Published and Unpublished Compositions of Louis Moreau Gottschalk* (New York: Ziff-Davis, 1970), p. 4.

73. Gottschalk, from a letter cited in Chase, *America's Music*, p. 321.

74. Jeanne Behrend, "Prelude," Louis Moreau Gottschalk, *Notes of a Pianist* (New York: Alfred A. Knopf, 1964), p. xxiv.

75. Cited in Howard and Bellows, *A Short History of Music in America*, p. 118.

76. Gottschalk did come in for his share of criticism, however, particularly from the venerable *Dwight's Journal of Music*, whose reviews were a thorn in Gottschalk's side.　See Behrend, "Prelude," p. xxvii.　Among the several discussions of Gottschalk's music found in *Dwight's Journal*, the following comments seem representative: "Liszt and Thalberg and even Chopin, all of whom, particularly the last, have been true tone poets, of decided individuality, which is stamped upon their written works, with which the Gottschalk *Bananiers* and *Dance Ossianiques* bear no more comparison than the slightest magazine verses with the inspired lyrics of the great bards. . . . Could a more trivial and insulting string of musical rigamarole have been offered to an audience of earnest music-lovers than 'American Reminiscences' to begin with!" (IV/3 [October 22, 1853], p. 22). "Mr. Gottschalk has it not in his power to satisfy the true lover and student of music. He lacks the one great essential — *soul*" (XXI/5 [July 12, 1862], pp. 119-20).

77. Used in connection with Gottschalk by Howard, *Our American Music*, p. 205, and then by Lowens, "Our First Matinee Idol: Louis Moreau Gottschalk," *Music and Musicians in Early America*, pp. 223-33.

78. Behrend, "Prelude," pp. xxxii-xxxiii.

79. Gottschalk, *Notes*, p. 50.

80. Ibid., p. 56.

81. Ibid., pp. 94-95.

82. *Dwight's Journal of Music* X/12 (December 20, 1856), p. 93.

83. Behrend, "Postlude," *Notes*, p. 409.

84. Sumner Salter; "The Music Teachers' National Association in its Early Relation to American Composers," *M.T.N.A. Proceedings, 1932*, p. 9.

85. H.S. Perkins, "History of the Music Teachers' National Association," *American Art Journal* 59/12 (July 12, 1892), p. 290. Perkins noted several predecessors to the M.T.N.A. from as early as 1829.

86. In 1908, the M.T.N.A. began to hold its annual meetings with the American branch of the International Music Society. Around this time, there is a noticeable change in the nature of the annual meetings, revealing a more scholarly and historical slant. See *Official Reports* and *Programmes* from 1900-1910.

87. Homer Ulrich, *A Centennial History of the Music Teachers National Association* (Cincinnati: M.T.N.A., 1976), pp. 180-84. On p. 180, Ulrich discusses discrepancies in early data on the number of M.T.N.A. members.

88. Salter, "The Music Teachers' National Association," pp. 11-13.

89. *Official Report* of the Eighth Annual Meeting of the Music Teachers' National Association (Cleveland: M.T.N.A., 1884), pp. 169-77; Perkins, "History of the Music Teachers' National Association," pp. 290-93.

90. Ulrich, *A Centennial History*, p. 12.

91. Frederick Grant Gleason, cited in Salter, "The Music Teachers' National Association," p. 17.

92. Cited in Salter, "The Music Teachers' National Association," pp. 13-14.

93. George E. Whiting, "An American School of Composition," *Official Report* of the Eighth Annual Meeting, pp. 33-37; see Salter, "The Music Teachers' National Association," pp. 17-19.

94. Willard Burr, Jr., "Musical Art-Creation in America," *Official Report* of the Eighth Annual Meeting, p. 14.

95. Calixa Levallée, "President's Address," *Proceedings* of the Tenth Annual Meeting of the Music Teachers' National Association (Boston: M.T.N.A., 1886), p. 9.

96. Salter, "The Music Teachers' National Association," pp. 20-21; see also Burr, "Musical Art-Creation," pp. 10-14.

97. "Petitions of the Honourable Members of the Senate in Congress Assembled," *Official Report* of the Eighth Annual Meeting, pp. 160-61.

98. Alfred M. Shafter, *Musical Copyright* (Chicago: Callaghan and Company, 1939), pp. 448, 454-77.

99. John S. Van Cleve, "American Composition," *Official Report* of the Fourteenth Annual Meeting of the Music Teachers' National Association (Detroit: M.T.N.A., 1890), pp. 46-48.

100. Burr, "Musical Art-Creation," pp. 8-9.

101. Ibid., p. 15.

102. Levallée, "President's Address," p. 9.

103. Emerson, "The American Scholar," p. 489.

104. See pp. 44-46.

105. Salter, "The Music Teachers' National Association," pp. 14-15.

106. Ibid., p. 16.

107. See pp. 50-51.

108. Ulrich, *A Centennial History*, p. 21.

109. Perkins, "History," p. 293.

110. Salter, "The Music Teachers' National Association," pp. 31-34; Ulrich, *A Centennial History*, pp. 20-22.

111. The Manuscript Society also established branches in Chicago and Philadelphia. See Salter, "The Music Teachers' National Association," p. 32.

112. See pp. 51-55.

113. Hitchcock, *Music in the United States*, pp. 130-32. See also Joseph A. Mussulman, *Music in the Cultured Generation* (Evanston: Northwestern University Press, 1971). *Dwight's* ceased publication after 1881.

114. *Dwight's Journal of Music* XXXVI/22 (February 3, 1877), p. 378.

115. Ibid., XXXVI/25 (March 17, 1877), p. 405.

116. *Musical Review* I/11 (December 25, 1879), p. 168.

117. Ibid., I/1 (October 16, 1879), p. 19.

118. L. S. Stavrianos, *The World Since 1500* (Englewood Cliffs, New Jersey: Prentice-Hall, 1966), pp. 264-67; Hans Kohn, *American Nationalism* (New York: Macmillian, 1957).

119. Arthur Foote, "Letter to Sumner Salter," cited in Salter, "The Music Teachers' National Association," pp. 16-17.

120. *The Musical Quarterly* XVIII/1 (January, 1932), pp. 76-105.

121. See John Tasker Howard, "Frank Van der Stucken," *The Dictionary of American Biography*, Vol. 10, pp. 181-82.

122. Compositions by John Knowles Paine, Edward MacDowell, Dudley Buck, George Whiting, Templeton Strong, Van der Stucken, and others were programmed; cited in Salter, "Early Encouragements," p. 80.

123. Charles Darcourt, from *Figaro* (July 12, 1889), cited in Salter, "Early Encouragements," pp. 81-82.

124. Van der Stucken, cited in Salter, "Early Encouragements," pp. 82-83.

125. Cited in Salter, "Early Encouragements," p. 83.

126. Ibid., pp. 84-85.

127. W. J. Henderson, *The New York Times* (December 12, 1890), cited in Salter, "Early Encouragements," p. 88.

128. Henry E. Krehbiel, *The New York Tribune* (December 12, 1890), cited in Salter, "Early Encouragements," p. 88; the above-mentioned American Composers' Choral Association was organized in 1890 by Emilio Argamonte but was discontinued after its first and only season, 1890-91; see Salter, "Early Encouragements," pp. 89-90.

129. *The Musical Record*, No. 347 (December, 1890), p. 3.

130. Salter, "Early Encouragements," pp. 102-5.

131. MacDowell's part in the squabble is presented in detail in Margery M. Lowens, "The New York Years of Edward MacDowell" (Ph.D. dissertation, University of Michigan, 1971), pp. 180-94. See also Salter, "Early Encouragements," pp. 102-5.

132. Letter from Edward MacDowell to Frederick Grant Gleason (April 10, 1891), cited in M. Lowens, "The New York Years," p. 184.

133. The Society of American Musicians and Composers, *Propectus* (September 30, 1899), cited in M. Lowens, "The New York Years," p. 185.

134. M. Lowens, "The New York Years," p. 187.

135. Both Salter and M. Lowens imply but do not substantiate directly that the group's disillusionment was tied to this second concert; see Salter, "Early Encouragements," p. 104, and M. Lowens, "The New York Years," p. 187.

136. M. Lowens, "The New York Years," p. 189.

137. Letter from Edward MacDowell to William Henry Humiston (December 14, 1899), cited in M. Lowens, "The New York Years," p. 189.

138. Letter by Edward MacDowell, cited in Salter, "Early Encouragements," p. 104. M. Lowens states that this letter was addressed to Mrs. Alice Uhl, and dated April 23, 1899; M. Lowens, "The New York Years," p. 187.

139. Letter from Edward MacDowell to Frederick Grant Gleason (April 10, 1891), cited in M. Lowens, "The New York Years," p. 103.

140. *Musical Courier* XL/6 (February 7, 1900), p. 26.

141. Salter, "Early Encouragements," p. 105; M. Lowens, "The New York Years," states that the Manuscript Society continued until 1921.

142. Arthur Farwell revealed a similar disdain for the Manuscript Socity in "Pioneering for American Music," *Modern Music* XII/3 (March-April, 1935), p. 116; Farwell called the group "hopelessly dilettante."

143. Edward MacDowell, in a lecture entitled "Folk-Music," cited by Lawrence Gilman, *Edward MacDowell: A Study* (reprint of 1908 edition; New York: Da Capo Press, 1969), p. 83.

144. Farwell, "Pioneering," p. 117. See also Chase, *America's Music*, pp. 387-92.

145. Among his pupils were: Harvey Worthington Loomis, Rubin Goldmark, and Harry Rowe Shelley; see Paul Rosenfeld, "'Americanism' in American Music," *Modern Music* XVII/4 (May-June, 1940), p. 229.

146. Other works on American themes composed by Dvořák during his visit were: a cantata, *The American Flag* (1893), the *String Quartet in F Major* (sometimes given the unfortunate subtitle "Nigger" [1893]), the *String Quintet in E♭ Major* (the "American" [1895]), and a *Suite for Piano in A Major* ("American Suite" [1893]).

147. Jeannette Thurber, "Dvořák as I Knew Him," *Etude* XXXVII/12 (November, 1919), pp. 693-94.

148. The only scholarly study of Indian music available to Dvořák at this time would have been Theodore Baker's *Über die Musik der nordamerikanischen Wilden* (Leipzig: Breitkopf und Haertel, 1882); *Slave Songs of the United States* by William Francis Allen, Charles P. Ware, and Lucy McKim Garrison (New York: A. Simpson, 1867) was also available, but it is unknown whether Dvořák had any contact with either book.

149. Thurber, "Dvořák," p. 693.

150. Interview with Anton Dvořák, *The New York Herald* (December 12, 1893), cited in John Clapham, "The Evolution of Dvořák's Symphony 'From the New World,'" *The Musical Quarterly* XLIV/2 (April, 1958), p. 169.

151. Clapham, in "Evolution," pp. 175 and 177, discusses Dvořák's themes and their relation to specific spirituals; see also the recollections of Harry T. Burleigh, cited in Chase, *America's Music*, p. 388.

152. *Musical Courier* XXVII/25 (December 20, 1893), pp. 37-38.

153. See *The New York Herald* (May 21, 1893 and December 13, 1893) for interviews with Dvořák, cited in Clapham, "The Evolution," pp. 168-69.

154. Antonin Dvořák, "Music in America," *Harper's* Magazine, XC (February, 1895), pp. 428-34.

155. Ibid., pp. 428-31.

156. Ibid., pp. 432-33.

157. Chase, in *America's Music*, p. 400, coins this term to denote those composers in the early part of this century who were interested in Indian music.

158. M. Lowens, "The New York Years," pp. 100-101.

159. Henry F. Gilbert, cited in Chase, *America's Music*, p. 363.

160. Edward MacDowell, *Second (Indian) Suite*, Op. 48 (reprint of Breitkopf und Härtel edition; New York: Associated Music Publishers, 195?), preface.

161. Edward MacDowell, from a lecture, cited in Gilman. *Edward MacDowell*, p. 84.

162. Ibid., pp. 84-85.

163. The extent is debatable; for one point of view, see Chase, *America's Music*, pp. 354-56.

164. MacDowell, from a lecture, cited in Gilman, *Edward MacDowell*, p. 83.

165. Chase, *America's Music*, p. 364. One should keep in mind here, however, Chase's somewhat disparaging remark about MacDowell in the "Preface" to the second edition (1966) of *America's Music*, p. vii.

166. Gilbert Chase, "The Wa-Wan Press, A Chapter in American Enterprise," *The Wa-Wan Press*, Vol. I, ed. by Vera Brodsky Lawrence (5 vols.; reissue of Wa-Wan series 1901-12, ed. by Arthur Farwell; New York: Arno Press, 1970), pp. ix-xvii.

167. Farwell, "Pioneering," p. 117.

168. Farwell, from the "Introduction" to an Autumn, 1902 issue of the Wa-Wan Press, cited in Edward N. Waters, "The Wa-Wan Press, An Adventure in Musical Idealism," *A Birthday Offering to Carl Engel*, ed. by Gustave Reese (New York: G. Schirmer, 1943), p. 222.

169. Farwell, "Pioneering," p. 117.

170. Farwell, "Introduction" to Autumn, 1903 issue of Wa-Wan Press, cited in Waters, "The Wa-Wan Press," p. 223.

171. Farwell, from a letter to Edward N. Waters, cited in Waters, "The Wa-Wan Press," p. 217.

172. Farwell, "An Affirmation of American Music," *The Musical World* III/1 (January, 1903), cited in Chase, *The American Composer Speaks*, p. 93.

173. Particularly admirable is Gilbert Chase's "The Wa-Wan Press" cited above; see also: Brice Farwell, *A Guide to the Music of Arthur Farwell* (Briarcliff Manor, New York, 1972); and Edgar Lee Kirk, "Toward American Music, A Study of the Life and Music of Arthur Farwell" (Ph.D. dissertation, University of Rochester, 1958).

174. B. Farwell, *A Guide*, p. 2.

175. Farwell, "Introduction," *American Indian Melodies* (Newton Center, Mass.: The Wa-Wan Press, 1901), p. 2.

176. Farwell, "Introduction," *American Indian Melodies*, pp. 11-12.

177. (New York: Moffat, Yard & Co., 1909).

178. (Boston: Maynard & Co., 1915).

179. (New York: Harper & Brothers, 1907).

180. (New York: The Woman's Press, 1926).

181. Farwell, "Pioneering," p. 119.

182. Farwell, "A Letter to American Composers," from an early (1903) issue of the Wa-Wan Press, cited in *The Wa-Wan Press*, Vol. I, p. xvii.

183. Ibid.

184. Waters, "The Wa-Wan Press," pp. 218-19.

185. See Chase, "The Wa-Wan Press," pp. xii-xv, for a brief evaluation of the major Wa-Wan contributors. A list of the contents of the Wa-Wan series is in Waters, "The Wa-Wan Press," pp. 225-28.

186. See B. Farwell, *A Guide*, p. 2, and Chase, "The Wa-Wan Press," p. xii.

187. Farwell, "Introduction," Wa-Wan Press, Vol. V (Spring, 1906), p. 187.

188. The full title of this work as given above, was taken from the Boston: White-Smith, 1918 edition. The opera is usually referred to by its shorter title, *Shanewis*.

189. Howard and Bellows, *A Short History of Music in America*, p. 226.

190. John F. Porte, "Charles Wakefield Cadman," *The Chesterian*, New Series No. 39 (May, 1924), p. 224.

191. Charles Wakefield Cadman, "Foreword," *The Robin Woman (Shanewis)* (Boston: White-Smith, 1918), p. 3.

192. Ibid., p. 5.

193. Virgil Thomson's *The Mother of Us All* (1947) also includes a hodge-podge of American historical figures, but with perhaps more intentional wit.

194. *Musical Courier* LXXVI/13 (March 28, 1918), pp. 5, 8.

195. Denver, Colorado (December 5, 1924) and Los Angeles, California (June 24, 1926); *Annals of Opera*, Vol. I, p. 1343.

196. Charles Wakefield Cadman, "The 'Idealization' of Indian Music," *The Musical Quarterly* I/3 (July, 1915), pp. 387-96.

197. Ibid., p. 387.

198. Ibid., p. 389.

199. Cadman, "The 'Idealization'," p. 389.

200. Representative of this concern are the following: John Alden Carpenter, "Musical Inspiration is Universal," *Musical America* XXXI/2 (November 8, 1919), p. 19; Babette Deutsch, "America in the Arts," *The Musical Quarterly* VII/3 (July, 1921), pp. 303-8; Sidney Grew, "National Music and the Folk-Song," *The Musical Quarterly* VII/2 (April, 1921), pp. 172-85; John Tasker Howard, "Our Folk-Music and Its Probable Impress on American Music of the Future," *The Musical Quarterly* VII/2 (April, 1921), pp. 167-71; Daniel Gregory Mason, "Folk-Song and American Music," *The Musical Quarterly* IV/3 (July, 1918), pp. 323-32; Daniel Gregory Mason, "Artistic Ideals: V. Universality," *The Musical Quarterly* XIII/3 (July, 1927), pp. 345-58; [no author], "Music for America," *Musical Courier* XXI/1 and 2 (July 7 and July 14, 1915), pp. 15-16, 32 and 12-13; Frank Patterson, "Folk Fables," *The League of Composers' Review* II/2 (April, 1925), pp. 25-27; Harold D. Phillips, "The Musical Psychology of America," *The Musical Quarterly* IX/4 (October, 1923), pp. 508-14; Robert Saunders, "National Opera, Comparatively Considered," *The Musical Quarterly* XIII/1 (January, 1927), pp. 72-84; Robert Simon, "Songs of the American Folk" [review of Carl Sandburg's *The American Songbag*], *Modern Music* V/3 (March-April, 1928), pp. 33-34; Francis Toye, "A Case for Musical Nationalism," *The Musical Quarterly* IV/1 (January, 1918), pp. 12-22.

201. Howard, "Our Folk-Music," p. 167.

202. Ibid., p. 168.

203. Ibid.

204. Farwell, "An Affirmation," p. 93.

205. Howard, "Our Folk-Music," pp. 169, 171.

206. Farwell, cited in Chase, "The Wa-Wan Press," p. x.

207. Howard, *Our American Music*, p. 378.

208. (New York: Macmillan, 1904, 1906, 1908, 1918).

209. (New York: Macmillan, 1928); (New York: Alfred A. Knopf, 1931).

210. Mason, "Folk-Song and American Music," pp. 323-32.

211. Ibid., p. 324.

212. Ibid., p. 323.

213. Mason, "Artistic Ideals: V. Universality," p. 356.

214. Ibid., p. 348.

215. Charles Ives, *Essays Before a Sonata*, ed. by Howard Boatwright (New York: W.W. Norton, 1970), pp. 79-81.

216. Mason, "Democracy and Music," *Contemporary Composers*, p. 9.

217. Ibid.

218. Ibid., pp. 15-16.

219. Ives, *Essays*, pp. 75-77.

220. Daniel Gregory Mason, *Contemporary Composers*, cited in Ives, *Essays*, p. 95.

221. Ives, *Essays*, p. 95.

222. Ibid., p. 94.

223. Henry and Sidney Cowell, *Charles Ives and His Music* (New York: Oxford University Press, 1955), p. 148.

224. Frank R. Rossiter, "Charles Ives and American Culture: The Process of Development, 1874-1921" (Ph.D. dissertation, Princeton University, 1970), p. 151. See also Rossiter, *Charles Ives and His America* (New York: Liveright, 1975).

225. Farwell, cited in Waters, "The Wa-Wan Press," p. 223.

226. Charles Seeger, "Tradition and the (North) American Composer," *Music in the Americas*, George List and Juan Orrego-Salas, eds. (The Hague, The Netherlands: Mouton and Co., 1967), p. 198.

227. On this distinction see the discussion of "folk" and "popular" in Chapter I, pp. 14-15, of this study. That much jazz was "popular" in the 1920s and 1930s does not mean that certain artists at this time did not approach the realm of art music in their playing. As jazz developed, particularly after World War II, the distinction between art and popular was lessened. Some musicians consciously moved toward incorporating the sophisticated techniques of composition associated with art music. The arrangements of Gil Evans and Dave Brubeck, and the playing of John Lewis and his Modern Jazz Quartet in the 1950s exemplify this trend.

228. Henry F. Gilbert, who is discussed below, John Powell (1882-1963), and Daniel Gregory Mason represent this interest; see Chase, *America's Music*, pp. 394-99, 401-2, and 379-81. Collections of Negro spirituals became available as early as the 1860s, with the aforementioned *Slave Songs of the United States* the first major contribution. Minstrel tunes, of course, were readily accessible as a staple of the sheet music industry.

229. The Afro-American community had its own native spokesman in the field of art music. This was William Grant Still (b. 1895). Actually of mixed Negroid and Indian background, Still composed works in the traditional genres, freely drawing upon a wide variety of Afro-American musical styles. The principal source dealing with Still is his biography by Verna Arvey, *William Grant Still* (New York: J. Fischer, 1939).

230. The influence of ragtime rhythms is apparent in the music of Charles Ives, perhaps from an even earlier date than in Gilbert's pieces. However, Ives's music was unknown at this time. See David Ross Baskerville, "Jazz Influence on Art Music to Mid-Century" (Ph.D. dissertation, University of California – Los Angeles, 1965), pp. 336-40.

231. Cited in Olin Downes, "An American Composer," *The Musical Quarterly* IV/1 (January, 1918), p. 24.

232. Philip Hale, *Boston Herald* (April 14, 1911), cited in Downes, "An American Composer," p. 24.

233. H. T. Parker, *Boston Transcript* (April 14, 1911), cited in Downes, "An American Composer," p. 24.

234. For a debunking of this commonly accepted notion of the 1920s, see Roderick Nash, *The Nervous Generation: American Thought, 1917-30* (Chicago: Rand McNally, 1970).

235. Taken from the title of Olin Downes's moving tribute to the character of Gilbert, "Henry Gilbert: Nonconformist," *A Birthday Offering to Carl Engel*, pp. 88-94.

236. The two composers carried on a brief correspondence after Ives sent Gilbert a copy of *Essays Before a Sonata*. Gilbert, who also had an intimate knowledge of the writings of Thoreau and Emerson, commented favorably on the book: "I find so much in it which is really mine." Gilbert, "Letter to Charles Ives," May 26, 1920, Ives Collection, Yale University.

237. Based on Downes, "An American Composer," pp. 25-26; see also Elliott Carter, "American Figure, With Landscape," *Modern Music* XX/4 (May–June, 1943), pp. 219-25; and Maud Cuney Hare, "Henry F. Gilbert, A Nationalist in Music," *The Musical Observer* XVIII/6 (June, 1919), pp. 11, 13.

238. For a brief discussion of Gilbert's eclecticism, see Chase, *America's Music*, pp. 396-97.

239. The above quoted passages in this paragraph are all taken from Henry F. B. Gilbert, "The American Composer," *The Musical Quarterly* I/2 (1915), cited in Chase, *The American Composer Speaks*, pp. 95-104. See also Gilbert, "Folk-Music in Art-Music — A Discussion and a Theory," *The Musical Quarterly* III/4 (October, 1917), pp. 577-601.

240. Gilbert, "The American Composer," p. 103.

241. Carter, "American Figure," p. 224.

242. Gilbert originally intended this to be an opera based on Joel Chandler Harris's Uncle Remus tales, but it was never completed. Gilbert cited *Slave Songs of the United States* as his source for both the *Comedy Overture* and *Negro Rhapsody*. See Henry F. Gilbert, "Notes" to *Comedy Overture on Negro Themes* (New York: H. W. Gray, 1912), and *Negro Rhapsody* (New York: H. W. Gray, 1915).

243. See "Note" by Gilbert to *The Dance in Place Congo* (New York: H. W. Gray, 1922).

244. Gilbert, "Letter to Claire Reis," September 13, 1927, Letters File, Music Division, New York Public Library.

245. *The Musical Courier* LXXVI/13 (March 28, 1918), pp. 5, 8.

246. *Boston Post* (August 23, 1914), cited in *Comment and Criticism on the Work of Henry F. Gilbert, Composer* (New York: H. W. Gray, [1926?]), p. 2.

247. Downes, "An American Composer," p. 23.

248. See Copland, *Music and Imagination* (New York: Mentor Books, 1952), pp. 110-11.

249. Carter, "American Figure," p. 225.

250. Adolph Weissman, "A Festival that Failed," *Modern Music* V/1 (November–December, 1927), p. 36.

251. Gilbert, "Letter to Claire Reis," September 13, 1927.

252. Hitchcock, *Music in the United States*, p. 173.

253. The principal Americanist source in the 1920s was surely jazz. But it should be noted that many American composers — traditionalists such as Howard Hanson and experimentalists such as Henry Cowell, for instance — were not particularly interested in jazz, at least from the standpoint of their own works.

254. The jazz historian Marshall Stearns has pointed out that only after Whiteman's Aeolian Hall concert (discussed subsequently) at which both black and white jazz was performed, did the musical intelligentsia as a whole take note of the original. See Marshall W. Stearns, *The Story of Jazz* (New York: Oxford University Press, 1956), pp. 153-78.

255. See Baskerville, "Jazz Influence in Art Music," pp. 3-4.

256. Blitzstein, "Popular Music — An Invasion: 1923-33," *Modern Music* X/2 (January–February, 1933), p. 100.

257. Baskerville, "Jazz Influence on Art Music," pp. 449-50.

258. Ibid.

259. George Gershwin, "The Composer in the Machine Age," in Oliver M. Sayler, ed., *Revolt in the Arts* (New York: Brentano's, 1930), cited in Chase, *The American Composer Speaks*, p. 142; see also Gershwin, "The Relation of Jazz to American Music," *American Composers on American Music*, ed. by Henry Cowell (Stanford: Stanford University Press, 1933), pp. 186-87.

260. Edwin Stringham, "'Jazz' — An Educational Problem," *The Musical Quarterly* XII/2 (April, 1926), p. 195.

261. Ibid.

262. Paul Rosenfeld, "Jazz and Music: Music in America," *An Hour with American Music* (Philadelphia: J. B. Lippincott, 1929), p. 11.

263. Ibid., p. 26.

264. Arthur L. Manchester, "Music Education, A Musical America, The American Composer, A Sequence," *The Musical Quarterly* X/4 (October, 1924), p. 587.

265. Aaron Copland, *The New Music, 1900–1960* (rev. and enlarged ed.; New York: W. W. Norton, 1969), p. 102; see also Copland, "Jazz Structure and Influence," *Modern Music* IV/4 (May-June, 1927), pp. 9-14.

266. Irving Weil, "The American Scene Changes," *Modern Music* VI/4 (May–June, 1929), pp. 6-8.

267. Ibid., p. 8.

268. "Program," Aeolian Hall Concert (February 12, 1924), cited in Isaac Goldberg, *George Gershwin, A Study in American Music* (New York: Frederick Ungar, 1931), pp. 146-47.

269. Hugh C. Ernst, address preceding Aeolian Hall Concert (February 12, 1924), cited in Goldberg, *George Gershwin*, pp. 144-45.

270. Pitts Sanborn, from a review, cited in Goldberg, *George Gershwin*, p. 152.

271. Lawrence Gilman, from a review, cited in Goldberg, *George Gershwin*, p. 152.

272. Olin Downes, from a review, cited in Goldberg, *George Gershwin*, p. 149.

273. W. J. Henderson, from a review, cited in Goldberg, *George Gershwin*, p. 150.

274. George Gershwin, "Rhapsody in Catfish Row," in Merle Armitage, ed., *George Gershwin* (New York: Longmans, Green, 1938), p. 74.

275. The relationship of jazz to works by all of these composers and others is discussed in Baskerville, "Jazz Influence in Art Music," pp. 333-503. Particular attention is paid to Gould, Gershwin, and Copland.

276. Copland, *The New Music*, pp. 56-70.

277. Ibid., p. 158.

278. Ibid., pp. 62-71.

279. Ibid., pp. 64, 70.

280. Armitage, "George Gershwin and His Time," *George Gershwin*, p. 5.

Chapter 3

1. John Mason Brown, *Two On the Aisle* (New York: W. W. Norton, 1938), pp. 194-95.

2. H. Wiley Hitchcock, *Music in the United States* (Englewood Cliffs, N.J.: Prentice-Hall, 1969), p. 198.

3. "The Composers Organize: A Proclamation," *Modern Music* XV/2 (January–February, 1938), pp. 92-95.

4. The Eastman's American Festivals performed the works of over 400 different composers (excluding works by Eastman students in a separate series) from Charles Wakefield Cadman to Chuck Mangione. Howard Hanson's Americanist activities expanded in 1926 to publishing American scores under Eastman auspices. Beginning in 1939, Hanson also recorded American music with several Eastman-Rochester groups for both RCA and Mercury Records. A history of the Americanist activities of Hanson and the Eastman is found in *The Institute of American Music of the University of Rochester; American Composers' Concerts and Festivals of American Music, 1925-1971, Cumulative Report* (Rochester, New York, 1972). See also Howard Hanson, "American Procession at Rochester," *Modern Music* XIII/3 (March–April, 1936), pp. 22-28; Hanson, "The Rochester Group of American Composers," *American Composers on American Music*, ed. by Henry Cowell (originally 1933; New York: Frederick Ungar, 1962), pp. 85-92.

5. Harold Clurman, *The Fervent Years* (originally 1945; New York: Hill and Wang, 1957).

6. Brown, *Two On the Aisle*, p. 194.

Chapter 4

1. Olin Downes, "Music in the Changing Social Order – The Viewpoint of a Critic," *National Federation of Music Clubs: Book of Proceedings, 1933-1935*, ed. by Hazel G. Weaver (Ithaca, N.Y.: National Federation of Music Clubs, 1935), p. 14.

2. Downes, "Music in the Changing Social Order," p. 15.

3. Ibid., p. 16.

4. Ibid., pp. 22-23.

5. Roy Dickinson Welch, "The Musician and Society," *M.T.N.A. Proceedings, 1935*, pp. 75-76.

6. Virgil Thomson, *The State of Music* (New York: Vintage Books, 1962; revised from orginal 1939 edition), pp. 82-125.

7. Oscar Levant, *A Smattering of Ignorance* (New York: Doubleday and Doran, 1940), p. 220. See also Minna Lederman, "No Money for Music," *North American Review* 243 (Spring–Summer, 1937), pp. 124-36.

8. Aaron Copland, *The New Music, 1900–1960* (rev. and enlarged ed.; New York: W. W. Norton, 1969), pp. 160-61.

9. Gilbert Chase, *America's Music* (rev. sec. ed.; New York: McGraw-Hill, 1966), p. 500.

10. Julia Smith, *Aaron Copland* (New York: E. P. Dutton, 1955), p. 163.

11. Paul Hindemith, "Preface," *A Composer's World: Horizons and Limitations* (Cambridge, Mass.: Harvard University Press, 1952), p. viii. See also William W. Austin, *Music in the 20th Century* (New York: W. W. Norton, 1966), pp. 401-2.

12. In fact, the persistent association of the term with his music, despite style, irritated him; Hindemith, "Preface," p. viii.

13. Marc Blitzstein, "Towards a New Form," *The Musical Quarterly* XX/2 (April, 1934), pp. 213-18, and "Coming – the Mass Audience," *Modern Music* XIII/4 (May-June, 1936), pp. 23-29. See also Roger Sessions, *Reflections on the Musical Life in the United States* (New York: Merlin Press, 1956), pp. 164-65.

14. Smith, *Aaron Copland*, p. 165; see also Chapter XI, pp. 263-64, of the present study.

15. Aaron Copland, *The Second Hurricane* (New York: Boosey and Hawkes, 1957).

16. Otto Luening, "Douglas Moore," *Modern Music* XX/4 (May–June, 1943), p. 251; of this work, Luening wrote "this is *Gebrauchsmusik* at its best."

17. Several theatre-music collaborations are discussed in Virgil Thomson, *Virgil Thomson* (London: Weidenfeld and Nicolson, 1967), John Houseman, *Run-Through* (New York: Simon and Schuster, 1972), and Paul Bowles, *Without Stopping* (New York: G. P. Putnam's Sons, 1972).

18. Verna Arvey, *Choreographic Music* (New York: E. P. Dutton, 1941), pp. 287-90.

19. Ibid., p. 297.

20. Davidson Taylor, "Compositions for Radio," *Who is Who in Music, 1941* (Chicago: Lee Stern, 1940), p. 759; see also Arvey, *Choreographic Music*, pp. 294-95.

21. Arvey, *Choreographic Music*, p. 309.

22. Ibid.

23. Smith, *Aaron Copland*, pp. 187-90.

24. Ibid., pp. 190-93.

25. Virgil Thomson, *American Music Since 1910* (New York: Holt, Rinehart and Winston, 1972), pp. 9, 54.

26. Arvey, *Choreographic Music*, p. 310.

27. Arvey, *Choreographic Music*, p. 319; Bowles, *Without Stopping*, p. 192.

28. Irving Kolodin, "American Composers and the Phonograph," *Modern Music* XI/3 (March–April, 1934), p. 128.

29. Ibid., p. 131.

30. *The Institute of American Music of the University of Rochester; American Composers' Concerts and Festivals of American Music, 1925-1971, Cumulative Report* (Rochester, New York, 1972), pp. 67-72.

    The League of Composers also sponsored some recordings of both European and American contemporary music; League of Composers, "Broadcasts and Records" file, Music Division, New York Public Library.

31. Charles C. Alexander, *Nationalism in American Thought, 1930-1945* (Chicago: Rand McNally, 1969), pp. 95-96.

32. Ibid., pp. 77-78.

33. Hans Heinsheimer, "Challenge of the New Audience," *Modern Music* XVI/1 (November–December, 1938), p. 31.

34. League of Composers, "Broadcasts and Records" file, Music Division, New York Public Library; Claire R. Reis, *Composers, Conductors, and Critics* (New York: Oxford University Press, 1955), p. 124.

35. Titles and dates of CBS radio commissions are taken from Taylor, "Compositions for Radio," pp. 759-60. For NBC commissions, see Ernest La Prade, "NBC's Contribution to Music," *Who is Who in Music, 1941*, pp. 760-61. Related sources are: Taylor, "To Order for Radio," *Modern Music* XIV/1 (November–December, 1936), pp. 12-17; Taylor, "Why Not Try the Air?," *Modern Music* XV/2 (January–February, 1938), pp. 86-91; Franklin Dunham, "Music in a Radio-Minded World," *National Federation of Music Clubs Book of Proceedings, 1933-35*, pp. 63-67; Helen Johnson, "Radio Music Education for the Young," *National Federation of Music Clubs Book of Proceedings, 1933-35*, pp. 68-70; Ernest La Prade, *Broadcasting Music* (New York: Rinehart, 1947); and *Music in Radio Broadcasting*, edited by Gilbert Chase (New York: McGraw-Hill, 1946).

36. Reis, *Composers, Conductors, and Critics*, pp. 124-25.

37. See Chapter VI, p. 149, of the present study.

38. Gail Kubik, "Composing for Government Films," *Modern Music* XXIII/3 (Summer, 1946), pp. 189-92.

39. Thomson, *American Music Since 1910*, pp. 53-54, and *Virgil Thomson*, pp. 260, 271-73.

40. Bowles, *Without Stopping*, p. 222; other information about documentaries is taken from Claire R. Reis, *Composers in America* (New York: Macmillan, 1947).

41. Henry Brant, "Marc Blitzstein," *Modern Music* XXIII/3 (Summer, 1946), p. 174.

42. Thomson, "Blitzstein's 'Native Land,'" *The New York Herald Tribune* (May 31, 1942); David Platt, "'Native Land' is Powerful," *Daily Worker* (May 12, 1942), p. 7.

     See also Reis, *Composers, Conductors, and Critics*, pp. 126-27, for comments on evenings of documentary film music in concert versions sponsored by the League of Composers.

43. See Robert F. Nesbett, "Louis Gruenberg: A Forgotten Figure of American Music," *Current Musicology* 18 (1974), pp. 190-95; Smith, *Aaron Copland*, pp. 202-16. Two other studies of filmmaking and music which include material on the

1930s and 1940s are John Huntley and Roger Manvill, *The Technique of Film Music* (London: Focal Press, 1957) and Tony Thomas, *Music for the Movies* (S. Brunswick, N.J.: A. S. Barnes, 1973).

44. Also in 1949, Thomson's *Louisiana Story* became the first film score to receive a Pulitzer Prize; Thomson, *American Music Since 1910*, p. 9.

45. Copland, *The New Music*, p. 161.

46. Thomson, *Virgil Thomson*, p. 279.

47. David Diamond, "The Composer and Film Music," *Decision* I/3 (March, 1941), p. 60.

48. Copland, "Second Thoughts on Hollywood," *Modern Music* XVII/3 (March–April, 1940), pp. 141-47.

Chapter 5

1. Louis Hartz, *The Liberal Tradition in America* (New York: Harcourt, Brace, 1955), pp. 1-34.

2. "Leftism" is defined as "the advocacy of radical or ultraliberal policies," a meaning stemming from the seating arrangements of European legislative bodies with the liberal party on the left side of the aisle; *Standard Dictionary of the English Language* (Chicago: Encyclopedia Britannica, 1958), p. 727; *Oxford English Dictionary, Supplement*, Vol. 2, p. 10. In a discussion of politics during the Depression years, "leftism" is helpfully ambiguous, embracing as it does non-specific ultraliberal philosophies. There were several factions (often warring) active in this period.

3. Throughout the early 1920s, the American Communist Party went through a series of splits, mergers, and name changes before emerging as the somewhat stable Workers Party of America in 1925. This name was again changed, to the Communist Party of the United States of America (CPUSA), when Earl Browder took over leadership in 1929; see Theodore Draper, *American Communism and Soviet Russia* (New York: Viking Press, 1960), pp. 9-28, 160-62.

4. See *The Political Almanac 1952* (New York: B. C. Forbes, 1952), pp. 8-9. Membership estimates of the Communist Party of America at its peak in summer, 1945 are from 75,000 to 80,000. Following this, there were several sharp rises and falls before the steady decline in numbers beginning early in 1948; David A. Shannon, *The Decline of American Communism* (New York: Harcourt, Brace, 1959), pp. 91-107. But, of course, membership numbers alone do not gauge the number of sympathizers with the Party in these years.

5. The first worldwide Socialist organization, which Marx helped found in 1863, was called the International Workingmen's Association, or "First" International. Its successor, established in France in 1884, was the Second Socialist International.

When this dissolved into factions during World War I, it was the Bolsheviks who emerged in control, creating the Third, or "Communist," International, after the 1917 Russian revolution.

6. See Richard Pells, *Radical Visions and American Dreams* (New York: Harper and Row, 1973), pp. 293-95.

7. A "fellow traveler" is "one who sympathizes with the Communist movement without actually being a party member"; *Oxford English Dictionary, Supplement,* Vol. I, p. 1049.

8. Pells, *Radical Visions,* p. 67.

9. About one million total; see *The Political Almanac 1952,* p. 9.

10. Pells, *Radical Visions,* p. 77.

11. See Shannon, *The Decline,* pp. 44-57, 82-112; Melech Epstein, *The Jew and Communism* (New York: Trade Union Sponsoring Committee, 1959); Draper, *American Communism,* pp. 186-202.

12. There were inconsistencies in Party views toward minorities; see, for instance, Draper, *American Communism,* pp. 315-56; Epstein, *The Jew and Communism,* especially pp. 292-381.

13. Pells maintains, for instance, that Granville Hicks, literary editor of *New Masses,* was "less committed to specific doctrines" of Marxism than to "its use as a text in converting an otherwise corrupt world." Pells also notes that Hicks had at one time planned to be a Unitarian minister; *Radical Visions,* p. 172.

14. This phrase is employed, for instance, in a celebration issue of the *Daily Worker* (July 3, 1937), p. 7. On Browder's image, see Shannon, *The Decline,* pp. 10-11.

15. Harold Clurman, *The Fervent Years* (originally 1945; New York: Hill and Wang, 1957), p. 150.

16. Jerre Mangione, *The Dream and the Deal* (Boston: Little, Brown, 1972), p. 160.

17. John Houseman, *Run-Through* (New York: Simon and Schuster, 1972), p. 245.

18. Paul Bowles, *Without Stopping* (New York: G. P. Putnam's Sons, 1972), p. 80.

19. Ibid., p. 222.

20. See Cabell Phillips, *From the Crash to the Blitz* (New York: The Macmillan Co., 1969), pp. 241-48.

21. See Maxwell Geismar, "Introduction," *New Masses Anthology* (International Publishers, 1969), p. 7.

22. Mangione, *The Dream and the Deal*, p. 31.

23. The mural's creator, Diego Rivera, was paid his fee as the work was covered by tar paper; Phillips, *From the Crash*, pp. 403-8. Pictures of the mural are found in *Modern Monthly* VII/4 (May, 1935), pp. 258-60.

24. Brooks Atkinson, cited in Cecil Smith, *Musical Comedy in America* (New York: Theatre Arts Books, 1950), p. 283.

25. Brooks Atkinson, *The New York Times* (October 6, 1932), p. 19.

26. Ibid.

27. Ibid.

28. Ibid.

29. Rome's first Broadway foray into politically-oriented revues was followed by two others: *Sing Out the News* (1938) and *Let Freedom Ring* (1942). Blitzstein's sketch for *Pins and Needles*, no doubt drawn from experience, criticized Federal Theatre officials' hesitancy concerning the performance of a politically controversial work; "Pins and Needles," *The New York Times* (November 29, 1937), p. 18.

30. Geismar, "Introduction," p. 6.

31. Pells, *Radical Visions*, p. 176.

32. Philip Barr, "Opera in the Vernacular," *The Magazine of Art* 32 (June, 1939), p. 356.

33. Bowles, *Without Stopping*, p. 216.

34. Epstein, *The Jew and Communism*, pp. 371-81.

35. See, for instance, John Mason Brown, "Ten Years Later," *The Saturday Review* XXXI/3 (January 17, 1948), pp. 22-24; Gilbert Chase, *America's Music* (rev. sec. ed; New York: McGraw-Hill, 1966), p. 649. Wilfred Mellers, in *Music in a New Found Land* (London: Barrie and Rockliff, 1964), pp. 415-29, on the other hand, analyzes *The Cradle* without emphasis upon its political content. See also H. Wiley Hitchcock's comments in *Music in the United States* (sec. ed.; Englewood Cliffs, N.J.: Prentice-Hall, 1974), pp. 208-9.

36. Alfred Schlee's "Under the Red Flag," *Modern Music* X/3 (March–April, 1932), pp. 108-13 is an early American discussion of the concept of "proletarianism" in music.

37. R. Serge Denisoff, *Great Day Coming* (Urbana: University of Illinois Press, 1971), p. 41; Denisoff has sketched this "quest" principally from the standpoint of the emergence of folksingers as the dominant American proletarian musical spokesmen. Richard A. Reuss, in "American Folklore and Left-Wing Politics: 1927-1957" (Ph.D. dissertation, Indiana University, 1971), has made a similar study with greater attention to Party workings and their influence upon leftist artistic circles.

38. Cornelius B. Canon, "The Federal Music Project of the Works Progress Administration: Music in a Democracy" (Ph.D. dissertation, University of Minnesota, 1963), pp. 226-28.

39. Harrison Kerr, "Creative Music and the New School," *Trend* III/2 (March–April, 1934), pp. 88-89; Virgil Thomson, *American Music Since 1910* (New York: Holt, Rinehart, and Winston, 1972), p. 168.

40. Thomson, *American Music*, p. 134.

41. Canon, "Federal Music Project," pp. 226-28; Kerr, "Creative Music," pp. 88-89.

42. "Music," *Daily Worker* (February 22, 1936), p. 7; "Carl Sands," "World of Music," *Daily Worker* (October 16, 1935), p. 7; "Workers Music League," *Daily Worker* (October 6, 1935), p. 7.

43. "L. E. Swift," "The Return of Hanns Eisler," *Daily Worker* (October 2, 1935), p. 5. The pseudonym "Swift," as well as others, is discussed below.

44. Ibid.

45. Charles Seeger, "Letter to Barbara Zuck," August 9, 1976; "Interview with Barbara Zuck," June 19, 1976.

46. Bowles, *Without Stopping*, p. 222.

47. Robinson, cited in Anita Tilkin, "Singing His Song," *Daily Worker* (October 27, 1938), p. 7.

48. Blitzstein, cited in Charles Glenn, "Hollywood Meets Blitzstein," *Daily Worker* (July 5, 1941), p. 7.

49. The New York Composers' Forum, founded by Ashley Pettis, is discussed in relation to the WPA.

50. "Workers Music League," *New Masses* VII/5 (October, 1931), p. 31; L.[an] A.[dohmyan], "Music," *Daily Worker* (January 9, 1934), p. 5.

51. "Introduction," *Red Song Book* (New York: Workers Library Publications, 1932), p. 3.

52. *Daily Worker* (February 8, 1934), p. 5; *Daily Worker* (March 27, 1935), p. 7; *Daily Worker* (August 23, 1935), p. 5; *Daily Worker* (April 1, 1936), p. 7. The Downtown Music School changed its name to the Metropolitan Music School in 1938; "Unique Among Music Schools," *Daily Worker* (September 21, 1938), p. 7.

53. Elie Siegmeister, *Music and Society* (New York: Critics' Group of New York, 1938).

54. Michael Gold, "Change the World!" *Daily Worker* (April 21, 1934), p. 7.

55. Gold, "Change the World!" *Daily Worker* (January 1, 1936), p. 5.

56. Gold, "Change the World!" *Daily Worker* (November 23, 1934), p. 5.

57. Ibid.

58. Reuss, "American Folklore," p. 52; see also Epstein, *The Jew and Communism,* pp. 210-13.

59. "Carl Sands," "World of Music," *Daily Worker* (March 22, 1935), p. 5.

60. Notices and reviews of these choruses' performances are found in various *Daily Worker* articles: (January 17, 1934), p. 5; (April 21, 1934), p. 7; (April 23, 1935), p. 5; (May 15, 1935), p. 8; (February 10, 1936), p. 7; (February 17, 1936), p. 6; (February 24, 1936), p. 7.

61. Robert Kent, "Singing for the Daily," *Daily Worker* (January 17, 1934), p. 5.

62. "Carl Sands," "World of Music," *Daily Worker* (March 22, 1935), p. 5.

63. Draper, *American Communism,* pp. 188-94; Epstein, *The Jew and Communism.*

64. Copland, "Workers Sing!" *New Masses* XI/10 (June 5, 1934), p. 28.

65. "Music," *Daily Worker* (February 22, 1936), p. 7. Reuss states February as the specific month of the group's founding; Reuss, "American Folklore," p. 47.

66. Although Cowell was an early devotee of the Collective, he soon became too involved with other projects, including some in California, and dropped out; Seeger, "Interview."

67. Seeger, "Interview."

68. Nicolas Slonimsky, "Henry Cowell," Henry Cowell, ed., *American Composers on American Music* (New York: Frederick Ungar, 1962; originally 1933), p. 62; Ashley Pettis, "Proletarian Music," *The Nation* CXXXV/3516 (November 23, 1932), p. 501; Pettis, *Daily Worker* (January 31, 1934), p. 5. Boris Schwartz, in

Music and Musical Life in Soviet Russia, 1917-70 (New York: W. W. Norton, 1973), pp. 54-60, 157, 248, notes Soviet composers' organizations during this period.

69. Charles Seeger, "On Proletarian Music," *Modern Music* XI/3 (March–April, 1934), p. 124.

70. *Baker's Biographical Dictionary of Musicians* (5th ed. rev. by Nicolas Slonimsky; New York: G. Schirmer, 1958), p. 361.

71. "Foreword," *Workers Song Book, No. 1* (New York: Workers' Music League, 1934), p. 3.

72. Seeger, "On Proletarian Music," p. 124.

73. "Carl Sands," "Eisler Farewell Concert," *Daily Worker* (April 23, 1935), p. 5.

74. Seeger, "Interview."

75. Marc Blitzstein, "Notebooks," *Marc Blitzstein Papers*, Wisconsin State Historical Society; *Workers Song Book, No. 1; Workers Song Book, No. 2* (New York: Workers' Music League, 1935). Selected articles containing Collective membership are: George Maynard, "Songs of Struggle," *Daily Worker* (May 12, 1934), p. 7; "Carl Sands," "World of Music," *Daily Worker* (May 16, 1935), p. 5; Marc Blitzstein, "Second Workers Song Book," *Daily Worker* (June 12, 1935), p. 5; "Music," *Daily Worker* (February 22, 1936), p. 7; "Music," *Daily Worker* (March 5, 1936), p. 7; Ashley Pettis, "Marching With a Song," *New Masses* XI/5 (May 1, 1934), p. 15; Anita Garett, "Eisler Praises Chorus Group," *Daily Worker* (February 24, 1936), p. 7.

76. Seeger, "Interview."

77. Pettis, "Marching," p. 15.

78. "L. E. Swift," cited in Michael Gold's "Change the World!" *Daily Worker* (June 4, 1934), p. 5.

79. Seeger, "Interview"; Siegmeister, "Interview with Barbara Zuck," December 14, 1974.

80. George Antheil, *Bad Boy of Music* (Garden City, New York: Doubleday, Doran, 1945), pp. 270-78. Reuss, however, lists Antheil as an active member of the Collective; Reuss, "American Folklore," p. 57.

Blitzstein, in his "Notebooks," also listed several last names of those attending Collective meetings: Heilner, Bennett, Harris, Wechsler, Yates, and "Gross." Although there are several well-known musicians with these same last names, additional sources do not confirm who these people really were. Elsewhere, he has "'Robert Gross' = Gates."

81. Gold, "Change the World!," *Daily Worker* (April 21, 1934), p. 7.

82. "L. E. Swift," in Gold, "Change the World!" *Daily Worker* (June 4, 1934), p. 5.

83. Ibid.

84. Gold, "Change the World!" *Daily Worker* (June 5, 1934), p. 5.

85. Ibid. (October 19, 1933), p. 5. Joe Hill (Joseph Hilstrom [1881-1915], in what leftists always have considered a frame-up, was killed by a firing squad as a convicted murderer. He was the author of several Wobbly songs, such as "Pie in the Sky" and "Casey Jones," and after his death became the subject of numerous others. Alan Lomax, ed., *Hard Hitting Songs for Hard-Hit People* (New York: Oak Publications, 1967), pp. 87-98; N. F., "They Shot Joe Hill," *Daily Worker* (November 20, 1935), p. 5; Pete Seeger, *The Incompleat Folksinger*, ed. by Jo Metcalf Schwartz (New York: Simon and Schuster, 1972), pp. 74, 87-91.

86. Seeger, "Interview."

87. "C.[arl] S.[ands]," "The International Collection," *Daily Worker* (January 31, 1934), p. 7.

88. Pettis, "Proletarian Music," p. 501; see also Pettis, "Musical Flashlights from Moscow," *Modern Music* X/1 (November–December, 1932), pp. 49-52.

89. Pettis, "Proletarian Music," p. 501.

90. Siegmeister, "Musical Life in Soviet Russia," *New Masses* XIII/3 (October 16, 1934), p. 28.

91. Ibid.

92. Ibid.

93. Ibid.

94. "Carl Sands," "Shostakovich's Brilliant Opera," *Daily Worker* (February 18, 1935), p. 5; see also *Daily Worker* (February 10, 1935), p. 5; (February 26, 1935), p. 5, (April 12, 1935), p. 5, (October 8, 1935), p. 5.

95. Cited in Nicolas Slominsky, *Music Since 1900* (third ed.; New York: Coleman-Ross, Co., 1949), p. 402; see also p. 372.

96. Ibid., pp. 402-3. News of the opera's rejection was carried to American leftists in an article by L. F. Boross, "Soviet Music," *Daily Worker* (April 7, 1936), p. 7.

97. In March, 1948, Eisler became a "voluntary deportee" from the United States due to his political beliefs; Slonimsky, *Music Since 1900*, p. 608.

98.   "Comintern" was the first song published by the W.M.L. shortly after the
      organization was founded in 1931; the song appeared in English translation by
      V.J. Jerome; *New Masses* VII/5 (October 31, 1931), p. 31.

99.   "Carl Sands," "World of Music," *Daily Worker* (March 6, 1935), p. 5. See also
      Sergei Radamsky, "Noted Composer," *Daily Worker* (February 18, 1935), p. 5.

100. Seeger, "Interview."

101. Joe Foster, "Hans [*sic*] Eisler," *Daily Worker* (March 1, 1935), p. 5; Austin, *Music
      in the 20th Century*, pp. 499-500.

102. Joe Foster, "Hans [*sic*] Eisler," p. 5.

103. Seeger, "Interview."

104. "L. E. Swift," "The Return," p. 5.

105. M.M., "Music," *Daily Worker* (July 25, 1936), p. 7.

106. "Workers Music League," *Daily Worker* (October 6, 1935), p. 7.

107. The greatest impact of Eisler is probably heard in Marc Blitzstein's music.
      Blitzstein was introduced to the Brecht/Weill/Eisler circle while studying with
      Schoenberg in Berlin in the late 1920s; Paul Myers Talley, "Social Criticism in the
      Original Theatre Librettos of Marc Blitzstein" (Ph.D. dissertation, University of
      Wisconsin, 1965), p. 20.

108. Seeger, "Letter to Barbara Zuck," October 28, 1977.

109. "Carl Sands," "The International Collection," p. 7.

110. Ibid.

111. Ibid.

112. "Sands," "Proletarian Music is a Historical Necessity," *Daily Worker* (March 6,
      1934), p. 5.

113. Charles Seeger, "On Proletarian Music," *Modern Music* XI/3 (March–April, 1934),
      pp. 121-27.

114. Seeger, "On Proletarian Music," pp. 121-22, 126-27.

115. Ibid. p. 127.

116. Ibid., p. 121.

117.　Ibid.

118.　Ibid., p. 124.

119.　Ibid.

120.　Ibid., p. 125.

121.　Ibid.

122.　Ibid.

123.　From *Workers Song Book*, No. 1, p. 12.

124.　Seeger, "On Proletarian Music," p. 125.

125.　"Sands," "Stirring Songs," p. 5.

126.　Ibid., p. 5.

127.　Seeger, "Letter to Barbara Zuck," October 28, 1977.　See also Chapter VI, pp. 141, 143.

128.　See Pete Seeger, *The Incompleat Folksinger*, p. 12.

129.　Michael Gold, "What a World!" *Daily Worker* (August 29, 1933), p. 6.

130.　Ibid.

131.　Michael Gold, "What a World!" *Daily Worker* (August 29, 1933), p. 6., For a discussion of the meaning of "jazz" in the 1920s and 1930s, see Chapter II, pp. 79-85, of the present study.

132.　Michael Gold, "What a World!" *Daily Worker* (September 20, 1933), p. 6.

133.　Siegmeister, cited in Gold, "What a World!" *Daily Worker* (September 20, 1933), p. 6.

134.　Ibid.

135.　Ibid.

136.　Ibid.

137.　Some members wrote other leftist music.　For instance, Siegmeister wrote a *May Day Symphony* (1933) and *Strange Funeral in Braddock* (1933), a solo cantata. Ruth Crawford Seeger composed two vocal works for the Workers Olympiad, a concert sponsored by left-wing groups, in 1933. These were *Sacco-Vanzetti* and *Chinaman Laundryman*. A few other pieces also were published as individual offerings by the Pierre Degeyter Club in the mid-1930s.

138. Three American songs were included: one by Adohmyan, a Negro protest song, and a traditional workers' song: "Sands," "Stirring Songs," p. 5.

139. *Red Song Book*, p. 29; this song is also found in Lomax, ed., *Hard Hitting Songs*, p. 294, with text attributed to Maurice Sugar.

140. The revised edition (also 1934) opens with the "Internationale."

141. *Workers Song Book, No. 1*, p. 3.

142. Ibid., p. 2.

143. Ibid.

144. Maynard, "Songs of Struggle," p. 7.

145. Copland, "Workers Sing!" p. 28.

146. Maynard, "Songs of Struggle," p. 7.

147. "Foreword," *Workers Song Book, No. 2*, p. 3; the editors of this volume are not listed.

148. *Workers Song Book, No. 2.*

149. "Foreword," *Workers Song Book, No. 2*, p. 3.

150. Lawrence Gellert, ed., *Negro Songs of Protest*, collected by Lawrence Gellert, arr. by Elie Siegmeister, foreword by Wallingford Riegger (New York: American Music League, 1936); see *Music Vanguard* I/1 (March–April, 1935), pp. 3-14, and I/2 (Summer, 1935), pp. 68-70. *Music Vanguard* was an attempt at a leftist musical periodical initiated by Max Margulies and Amnon Balber. It produced but two editions, containing articles by Seeger, Copland, Eisler, Gellet, Cowell, Brecht, Siegmeister, and others.

151. "Foreword," *Workers Song Book, No. 2*, p. 3.

152. *New Masses* XI/5 (May 1, 1934), pp. 16-17.

   "Into the Streets May First!" was included as a musical example in the original doctoral dissertation, "Americanism and American Art Music, 1929–1945," in 1978. However, Mr. Copland refused the inclusion of the piece in this edition.

153. Seeger, "Interview." Seeger's own setting of the Hayes poem unfortunately has not survived.

154. See Pettis's remarks to this effect in "Second Worker's Music Olympiad," *New Masses* XI/8 (May 22, 1934), p. 29.

155. Seeger, "Interview."

156. Gold, "Change the World!," *Daily Worker* (January 2, 1936), p. 5.

157. In a letter to the author written after he had read this chapter: "I was never interested in American*ism* nor was the Collective. I felt that composers in Europe had always been brought up to know their local folk music and had an advantage over us *qua* composers in that we were not brought up to know ours. And there was the added factor: did we have a viable folk music?" "Letter to Barbara Zuck," October 28, 1977.

158. Seeger, "Interview."

159. Ibid.

160. Seeger had left the Collective shortly before this refutation appeared and did not read it until many years later; Seeger, "Interview."

161. Reuss, "American Folklore," p. 88.

162. See Gold, "What A World!," *Daily Worker* (October 19, 1933), p. 5.

    An early, indirect attack upon the Collective came in Gold's defense of Jacob Schaefer, calling Schaefer the "father of proletarian music in America." Among other inferences toward the Collective, Gold wrote that Schaefer's compositions were "worth infinitely more than all the splintered and tortuous things evolved by the cerebralists"; "Change the World!" *Daily Worker* (June 14, 1934), p. 5. Schaefer's music from *Workers Song Book No. 1* had received harsh criticism by Collective member George Maynard in "Songs of Struggle," p. 7.

163. See Denisoff, *Great Day Coming*, pp. 68-76.

164. Gold, "Change the World!," *Daily Worker* (November 23, 1934), p. 5.

165. "Sands," "Songs by the Auvilles," *Daily Worker* (January 15, 1935), p. 15.

166. Ibid.

    In a letter to the author, Seeger commented that the Auvilles wrote conservative popular songs and that there was little "folk" about their style. Michael Gold mistook the Auvilles' pieces for folksongs. According to Seeger, however, the Auvilles were much nearer to composing appropriate mass songs, despite their poor quality, than was the Collective; "Letter to Barbara Zuck," October 28, 1977.

167. "Sands," "Songs of the Auvilles," p. 5.

168. Gold, "Change the World!," *Daily Worker* (January 2, 1936), p. 5.

It should be noted that, despite Gold's reference to "Comrade Sands," Seeger was not a member of the Communist Party.   Also, "Sands's" discussion of Schoenberg and Stravinsky did not occur in his review of the Auville collection, but in a separate article, "Schoenberg's Latest Composition," *Daily Worker* (October 23, 1935), p. 5.

169. "Carl Sands," "Music League Plans a New Book," *Daily Worker* (November 18, 1935), p. 5.   According to Reuss, the songbook announced by "Sands" was published in 1937 as *Songs of the People* (New York, January, 1937); Reuss, "American Folklore," p. 102.

170. H.E., "A New Music League," *Daily Worker* (February 10, 1936), p. 7.

171. From *Unison* I/1 (May, 1936), p. 1, cited in Reuss, "American Folklore," p. 154. *Unison* was a shortlived publication sponsored by the A.M.L.

172. Reuss, "American Folklore," p. 94.

Chapter 6

1. See Chapter V, pp. 121 ff., of the present study.

2. Charles Seeger, "On Proletarian Music," *Modern Music* XI/3 (March–April, 1939), pp. 122-23.

3. Charles Seeger, "Grass Roots for American Composers," *Modern Music* XVI/3 (March–April, 1939), pp. 144-45.

4. Seeger, "Grass Roots," pp. 147-59.

5. See Chapter V, pp. 104-5, 110, of the present study.

6. Seeger, "Interview with Barbara Zuck," June 19, 1976.

7. Seeger, "Letter to Barbara Zuck," October 28, 1977.

8. Ibid.

9. Seeger, "Interview."   John and Alan Lomax, *American Ballads and Folk Songs* (New York: Macmillan, 1934).

10. George Pullen Jackson, *White Spirituals in the Southern Uplands* (Chapel Hill, 1933).

11. Seeger, "Letter to Barbara Zuck," October 28, 1977; "Grass Roots," p. 147.

12. Seeger, "Letter to Barbara Zuck," October 28, 1977.

13. Seeger, "Interview." "Herbert Haufrecht" (New York: Broadcast Music, Inc., 195?), p. 1.

14. "Move to Explore Folkways," *The New York Times* (December 26, 1938), p. 28.

15. Harold Spivacke, "The Archive of American Folk Song in the Library of Congress," *M.T.N.A. Proceedings, 1940* (Pittsburgh: The Association), p. 123.

16. Charles Seeger, "Letter to Barbara Zuck," October 28, 1977.

17. Pete Seeger, *The Incompleat Folksinger*, ed. by Jo Metcalf Schwartz (New York: Simon and Schuster, 1972), p. 13. Two other Seegers, Peggy and Mike, also became involved with folk music eventually, Mike primarily as a performer and Peggy as both performer and scholar.

18. Robinson has contributed songs and editing to at least one folksong collection: *Songs of America*, ed. by Miriam Bogorad, Gertrude Burke, D. Huntly McCurdy, and Earl Robinson (New York: Workers Library Publishers, 1939); William Wolff, "The Songs, Dances and Ballads of America," *Daily Worker* (July 1, 1939), p. 7. R. Serge Denisoff, in *Great Day Coming* (Urban: University of Illinois Press, 1971), pp. 71-72, has written of Robinson in relation to folk music.

19. See, for instance, Hugh J. Riddell, "Modern Ballads Come to Life," *Daily Worker* (September 27, 1939), p. 7.

20. Earl Robinson, "Joe Hill," *Daily Worker* (September 4, 1936), p. 7.

21. Louis Reid, "The Song That Stirred a Nation," *The New York Sun* (July 13, 1940), p. 20. Earl Robinson, *Ballad for Americans* (New York: Robbins Music, 1940), p. 1.

22. See, for instance, *Daily Worker* (November 4, 1939), p. 7 and (November 20, 1939), p. 7.

23. Reid, "The Song That Stirred a Nation," p. 20.

24. Elie Siegmeister, as told to Stephen West, "Americans Want American Music!" *Etude* LXII/I (January, 1944), p. 28.

25. Elie Siegmeister, "Composer in Brooklyn," *The Music Lover's Handbook* (New York: William Morrow, 1943), p. 773.

26. Siegmeister, "Interview." Sandburg, *The American Songbag* (New York: Harcourt, Brace, 1927).

27. Siegmeister, "Composer in Brooklyn," p. 771.

28. Along with these and previously-mentioned sources, see Siegmeister's "Social Influences in Modern Music," *Modern Monthly* VII/8 (September, 1933), pp. 472-

79, and "The Class Spirit in Modern Music," *Modern Monthly* VII/10 (November, 1933), pp. 593-98.

29. Siegmeister, "Composer in Brooklyn," p. 773.

30. Elie Siegmeister, *Strange Funeral in Braddock, New Music; A Quarterly Review of Modern Compositions* IX/4 (July, 1936).

31. This group was first called the American Singers; "American Singers on the Air," *Daily Worker* (October 11, 1939), p. 7. The American Ballad Singers premiered in Town Hall on February 18, 1940 with a program entitled "America in Song, 1640-1940"; *Daily Worker* (January 20, 1939), p. 7. The Singers also featured songs representing American ethnic groups and early American music, being one of the first modern ensembles to perform pieces by Billings and Hopkinson; cited in Siegmeister, "Americans Want American Music!" p. 54.

32. Siegmeister, "Interview."
Olin Downes and Elie Siegmeister, eds., *A Treasury of American Song* (New York: Howell, Saskin, 1940).

33. Siegmeister, "Americans Want American Music!," p. 28.

34. Ibid., pp. 28, 54.

35. Ibid., p. 54.

36. Ibid. Siegmeister, *American Legends* (New York: Edward B. Marks, 1940).

37. Siegmeister, "Americans Want American Music!," p. 54. The American Ballad Singers were the first to record the *American Legends; The Gramaphone Shop Encyclopedia of Recorded Music* (third edition; Westport, Conn: Greenwood Publishers, 1970), p. 487.

38. Siegmeister, *Western Suite* (New York: Associated Music Publishers, 1948); *Ozark Set* (New York: E. B. Marks, 1943).

39. Herbert Haufrecht, *Square Set for String Orchestra* (New York: Broadcast Music, Inc., 1942).

40. "Herbert Haufrecht," pp. 1-2.

41. Richard Franko Goldman, "Wallingford Riegger," HiFi/Stereo Review XX/4 (April, 1968), p. 62.

42. Seeger, "Interview."
Henry and Sidney Robertson Cowell, "Our Country Music," *Modern Music* XX/4 (May–June, 1943), pp. 243-47; Sidney Robertson Cowell, "White Spirituals," *Modern Music* XXI/1 (November–December, 1943), pp. 10-14.

43. Siegmeister, "Interview."

44. Several discographies from the period indicate that folk music recordings were available: "The Master Record Catalogue," *Who Is Who in Music, 1941* (New York: Lee Stern, 1940), pp. III-CXXIV; John Hines, Ben Hyam, Helmut Ripaerger, *Record Collector's Guide* (New York: Franklin Watts, 1947). The WPA Writers' Project compiled a *Provisional List of Discs* of folksongs in 1937, and a *Check List of Recorded Songs in the English Language in the Archive of American Folk Song to July, 1940* (D. K. Wilgus, *Anglo-American Folksong Scholarship Since 1898* [New Brunswick, New Jersey: Rutgers University Press, 1959], p. 187).

45. *Talent Files—Radio*, CBS Department of Program Information.

46. Woody Guthrie, *Bound for Glory* (New York: E.P. Dutton, 1968), pp. 391-99.

47. *Talent Files—Radio.*

48. Siegmeister, "Interview." The musical was based upon a book by Walter Kerr and was produced by the Theatre Guild, which also had produced *Oklahoma!*

49. Virgil Thomson, *American Music Since 1910* (New York: Holt, Rinehart, and Winston, 1972), p. 3.

50. John A. Lomax, *Cowboy Songs and Other Frontier Ballads* (New York, 1910); see Wilgus, *Anglo-American Folksong Scholarship*, p. 159.

51. The last of these was compiled and edited posthumously by Maud Karpeles; Cecil J. Sharp, *English Folk-Songs from the Southern Appalachians*, ed. by Maud Karpeles (2 vols.; London: Oxford University Press, 1932).

52. S. Cowell, "White Spirituals," p. 10.

53. Robert Simon, "Songs of the American Folk," *Modern Music* V/3 (March–April, 1928), p. 34.

54. Dan Stehman, "The Symphonies of Roy Harris: An Analytical Study of the Linear Materials and of Related Works" (Ph.D. dissertation, University of Southern California, 1973), p. 266.

55. Virgil Thomson, *Virgil Thomson* (London: Weidenfeld and Nicolson, 1967), pp. 271-72.

56. See John Tasker Howard, *Our American Music* (third edition; New York: Thomas Y. Crowell, 1954), p. 441; Otto Luening, "Douglas Moore," *Modern Music* XX/4 (May–June, 1943), pp. 250-51.

57. Virgil Thomson, *Symphony on a Hymn Tune* (Southern Music Publishing Co., 1954).

58. See Thomson, *Virgil Thomson*, p. 270.

59. Gilbert Chase, *America's Music* (revised second edition; New York: McGraw-Hill, 1966), p. 402.

60. Howard, *Our American Music*, pp. 423-24; David Ewen, ed., *American Composers Today* (New York: H. W. Wilson, 1949), pp. 193-94.

61. Chase, *America's Music*, pp. 401-2; Ewen, *American Composers*, p. 194.

62. Seeger, "Interview."

63. Randall Thompson, "The Contemporary Scene in American Music," *The Musical Quarterly* XVIII/1 (January, 1932), p. 12.

64. Davidson Taylor, "Compositions for Radio," *Who Is Who in Music, 1941*, pp. 159-60.

65. *List of Musical Compositions for Small Orchestra Commissioned for American School of the Air by the Music Library of CBS, 1939–1940 Season*, CBS Department of Program Information.

66. Philip Edward Newman, *The Songs of Charles Ives (1874–1954)*, Vol. II (Ann Arbor, Michigan: University Microfilms, 1967), pp. 279-80.

67. David Wooldridge, *Charles Ives: A Portrait* (London: Faber and Faber, 1975), pp. 262-64.

68. Ferde Grofé's well-known *Grand Canyon Suite* (1932) predates the Thomson work, but is related by geographic region and not by musical content. The suite does not quote folksongs.

69. At least three collections of cowboy songs were available by the late 1930s: John Lomax, *Cowboy Songs*, and *Songs of the Cattle Trail and Cow Camp* (New York: Macmillan, 1919), and John and Alan Lomax, *Cowboy Songs* (New York: Macmillan, 1938).

70. Paul Bowles, arr., *12 American Folk Songs* (New York City: Work Projects Administration Arts Programs, n.d.); see also Bowles, *Without Stopping*, (New York: G. P. Putnam's Sons, 1972), pp. 213-15.

71. William Austin, in *"Susanna," "Jeannie," and "The Old Folks at Home"* (New York: Macmillan, 1975), pp. 317-37, discusses Foster's importance to American composers, especially Ives and Copland.

72. Henry Cowell, "The Flavour of American Music," *The Score and I.M.A. Magazine* No. 12 (June, 1955), p. 8.

73. Otto Luening, "Musical Finds in the Southwest," *Modern Music* XIII/4 (May–June, 1936), p. 18.

74. Paul Rosenfeld, "Folksong and Culture-Politics," *Modern Music* XVII/1 (October–November, 1939), pp. 19-20.

75. Eliott Carter, "Once Again Swing; Also 'American Music,'" *Modern Music* XVI/2 (January–February, 1939), p. 100.

76. Ashley Pettis, "Letter to the Music Editor," *The New York Times* (November 13, 1938), Sec. 9, p. 8; Gian-Carlo Menotti, "Letter to the Music Editor," *The New York Times* (November 20, 1938), Sec. 9, p. 8.

77. Roger Sessions, "On the American Future," *Modern Music* XVII/2 (January–February, 1940), p. 72.

78. Paul Rosenfeld, "Variations on the Grass Roots Theme," *Modern Music* XVI/4 (May–June, 1939), p. 219.

79. Virgil Thomson, "On Being American," *The New York Herald Tribune* (January 25, 1948), cited in *Music Right and Left* (New York: Henry Holt and Company, 1951), p. 189.

80. Roy Harris, "Folksong – American Big Business," *Modern Music* XVIII/1 (November–December, 1940), p. 11.

Chapter 7

1. Harry Hopkins, *Spending to Save* (New York: W. W. Norton, 1936), p. 13.

2. Cabell Phillips, *From the Crash to the Blitz* (London: Macmillan, 1969), p. 35.

3. Hopkins, in *Spending*, pp. 13-14, discusses the disparity in unemployment estimates.

4. Phillips, *From the Crash*, p. 40.

5. Cornelius B. Canon, "The Federal Music Project of the Works Progress Administration: Music in a Democracy," (Ph.D. dissertation, University of Minnesota, 1963), p. 2.

6. Although composers theoretically were protected on the air waves by copyright, it took some time to establish these rights; see John Tasker Howard, *Our American Music* (third edition; New York: Thomas Y. Crowell, 1954), pp. 684-85.

7. Canon, "The Federal Music Project," pp. 4-5.

8. Ibid., pp. 3-4.

9. Charles C. Alexander, *Nationalism in American Thought, 1930-1945* (Chicago: Rand McNally, 1969), p. 76.

10. Canon, "The Federal Music Project," p. 9; Robert J. Dietz, "The Operatic Style of Marc Blitzstein in the American 'Agit-Prop Era'" (Ph.D. dissertation, University of Iowa, 1970), pp. 98-99.

11. Hopkins, *Spending*, pp. 26-27.

12. Ibid., pp. 50-51.

13. The bonus was actually due them, but according to the Congressional act, not until 1945; see Arthur M. Schlesinger, Jr., *The Age of Roosevelt: The Crisis of the Old Order, 1919-1933* (Cambridge, Mass.: The Riverside Press, 1957), pp. 256-65.

14. Phillips, *From the Crash*, p. 107.

15. Milton Crane gave the caption "Roosevelt era" historical validity by his book of that name, *The Roosevelt Era* (New York: Boni and Gaer, 1947).

16. Schlesinger, *The Age of Roosevelt*, pp. 386-95.

17. PWAP was not wholly a relief project; see Richard D. McKinzie, *The New Deal for Artists* (Princeton: Princeton University Press, 1973), pp. 3-20. On other pre-WPA arts projects, see Jerre Mangione, *The Dream and the Deal* (Boston: Little, Brown and Company, 1972), pp. 29-40.

18. See Canon, "The Federal Music Project," pp. 11-33, and *Final Report on the WPA Program, 1935-43* (Washington, 1946), pp. 1-7. Some local music projects under state jurisdiction grew out of FERA.

19. George Foster, "Music," Vol. 7 of *Works Progress Administration, Work Projects Administration: Record of Program Operation and Accomplishment, 1935-43* (n.p., 1943), p. vi.

    Canon has noted that one was not required to be on relief for CWA, as with the later WPA. Therefore, fewer musicians qualified, or were willing to admit their destitution, by coming to WPA offices; Canon, "The Federal Music Project," p. 26.

20. Phillips, *From the Crash*, p. 276.

21. Actually, the WPA never achieved this goal, and its peak employment of 3,300,000 was not reached until November, 1939. However, by the time the entire program was halted after eight years, 8,500,000 people, or one-quarter of all American families, had found temporary support through WPA jobs. Hopkins, *Spending*, p. 167; *Final Report*, pp. iii, 106-7.

22. Hopkins. *Spending*, p. 178.

23. Ibid., p. 174.

24. Ibid., p. 176.

25. Mangione, *The Dream*, pp. 22-49, 107, 200-206.

26. Ibid., pp. 29-30; Canon, "The Federal Music Project," pp. v-vi.

27. John Houseman, *Run-Through* (New York: Simon and Schuster, 1972), p. 252. Houseman headed first the Negro Theatre Project and thereafter Project #891 of New York City's Federal Theatre, the latter being the designation of the classical theatre program; *Run-Through*, pp. 208-16.

28. Earl V. Moore, "The WPA Music Program," *Who Is Who in Music, 1941* (Chicago: Lee Stern, 1940), pp. 388-90.

29. The structure of the WPA FMP is discussed in Canon, "The Federal Music Project"; both WPA music agencies are discussed in Foster, "Music," and William F. MacDonald, assisted by Margaret Kerr and Betty Carr, "Federal Relief Administration and the Arts" (unpublished typescript, 1945) in the possession of the American Council of Learned Societies.

30. "Report on the Music Project," *Government Aid during the Depression to Professional, Technical and Other Service Workers*, prepared by the Division of Professional and Service Projects at the request of Harry L. Hopkins, Federal Administrator of WPA (W.P.A., 1936), p. 19.

31. *Report on Progress of the Works Progress Administration* (Washington, D.C.: U.S. Printing Office, October 15, 1936), p. 40; cited in Dietz, "The Operatic Style," p. 108.

32. Canon, "The Federal Music Project," p. 50.

33. The organizational and following statistical information is taken from WPA Federal Music Project of New York City, *Monthly Report of Activities* (May, 1937), pp. 33-34.

34. The statistical information concerning the Concert and Opera Divisions is taken from WPA FMP of New York City, *Monthy Report*, pp. 1-10, 19, and 37.

35. Ibid., p. 26. All information on the Social Music Education Division is taken from the same report, pp. 20-30.

36. WPA of New York City, *Theatre of Music Pamphlet* ([1937]), p. 4.

37. WPA FMP of New York City, *Monthly Report*, pp. 29-30.

38. Canon, "The Federal Music Project," pp. 53-54.

39. Moore, "The WPA Music Program," pp. 388-89.

40. WPA FMP of New York City, *Monthly Report*, pp. 31-32.

41. Ibid., pp. 31-33.

42. *WPA of New York City Programs File*, Music Division, New York Public Library, "Columbia Concert Orchestra," March 15, 1937.

43. Ibid., "Federal Symphony Orchestra," January 9, 1938.

44. *WPA of New York City Programs File*, "Madrigal Singers," February 14, 1937.

45. WPA FMP of New York City, *Monthly Report*, pp. 17-18.

46. *WPA of New York City Programs File*, "National Music Week, May 2–8, 1937."

47. "Report on the Music Project," p. 21.

48. Foster, "Music," p. 322; see also Moore, "The WPA Music Program," p. 388.

49. Foster, "Music," p. 327.

    A separate survey of musicians was undertaken and published by the Historical Records Survey: *Bio-Bibliographical Index of Musicians in the United States of America from Colonial Times*, foreword by Harold Spivacke (Washington, D.C.: W.P.A. Historical Records Survey, 1941).

50. Cited in Canon, "The Federal Music Project," p. 134.

51. Ibid., pp. 141-42.

52. Ibid., p. 134.

53. Ibid.

54. "Americana Drawer," *Index of American Composers.* The "Americana Drawer" is filed alphabetically by composer.

55. Canon, "The Federal Music Project," pp. 260-63.

56. Ibid., pp. 135-36.

57. William Grant Still, "The American Composers," *The Baton* (California Federal Music Project, April, 1937), *WPA Composers Forum Letters and Press*, The National Archives.

58. Ashley Pettis, "The WPA and the American Composer," *The Musical Quarterly* XXVI/1 (January, 1940), p. 104.

59. Mildred Norton, "A Music Forum is Presented by Federals," *Los Angeles Evening News* (August 19, 1937).

60. *The Composers Forum 25th Anniversary Survey* (New York: The Composers Forum, 1961), pp. 8-9.

61. Ibid.

62. Ashley Pettis, "Two Worlds of Music," *New Masses* VIII/7 (February, 1933), p. 14.

63. Ibid. See also Pettis, "Music," *New Masses* X/2 (January 2, 1934), pp. 29–30; "Music," *New Masses* X/4 (January 23, 1934), pp. 29–30; and "'American' Operas," *New Masses* XII/6 (August 7, 1934), pp. 27–28.

64. Pettis, "Two Worlds of Music," p. 14. See also Pettis, "Proletarian Music," *The Nation* CXXXV/3516 (November 23, 1932), pp. 500–502; "Musical Flashlights from Moscow," *Modern Music* X/1 (November–December, 1932), pp. 49-52; "Music," *New Masses* X/2 (January 9, 1934), p. 28; and "Music," *New Masses* X/10 (March 6, 1934), p. 30.

65. Pettis, "Proletarian Music," pp. 500–501.

66. See, for instance, "Carl Sands," "Workers Audience Applauds Gold's Poem Set to Music," *Daily Worker* (June 26, 1934), p. 5.

67. See "Carl Sands," "Copland's [*sic*] Music Recital at Pierre Degeyter Club," *Daily Worker* (March 22, 1934), p. 5.

68. *The Composers Forum 25th Anniversary Survey*, p. 8.

69. "Carl Sands," "All Copland-Concert," *Daily Worker* (October 16, 1935), p. 5. Other composers featured were Roy Harris, Virgil Thomson, Roger Sessions, and Walter Piston.

70. See Arthur Berger, *Aaron Copland* (New York: Oxford University Press, 1953), pp. 20-21.

71. Canon, "The Federal Music Project," p. 123.

72. Letters to Ashley Pettis in honor of the opening of the third Composers' Forum-Laboratory series, New York City, October 6, 1937. *WPA Composers Forum [sic] Transcripts*, National Archives.

73. Ashley Pettis, *Opening Address*, New York City Composers' Forum-Laboratory (October 30, 1935), *WPA Composers Forum [sic] Transcripts*.

74. Foster, "Music," p. 323.

75. Cited in Pettis, "The WPA," pp. 103-4.

76. More recent Forum transcripts have been preserved at Columbia University; *The Composers Forum 25th Anniversary Survey*, p. 12.

77. Bowles, *Without Stopping*, p. 193.

78. Carter, "Coolidge Crusade; WPA; New York Season," *Modern Music* XVI/1 (November–December, 1938), p. 37.

79. Cited in Foster, "Music," p. 324; cited in another wording and attributed to Henry Holden Huss in *The Composers Forum 25th Anniversary Survey*, p. 10.

80. From Siegmeister, Composers' Forum-Laboratory (October 20, 1937), *WPA Composers Forum [sic] Transcripts*.

81. From Howard Hanson, Composers' Forum-Laboratory (March 17, 1937), *WPA Composers Forum [sic] Transcripts*.

82. Ibid.

83. Ibid.

84. Bowles, *Without Stopping*, p. 193.

85. Ibid.

86. Marion Bauer, Composers' Forum-Laboratory (January 8, 1937), *WPA Composers Forum [sic] Transcripts*.

87. Ibid.

88. Hanson, Composers' Forum Laboratory (March 17, 1937), *WPA Composers Forum [sic] Transcripts*.

89. Ibid.

90. Mason, Composers' Forum-Laboratory (January 15, 1937), *WPA Composers Forum [sic] Transcripts*.

91. Sessions, Composers' Forum-Laboratory (November 29, 1939), *WPA Composers Forum [sic] Transcripts*.

92. Saminsky, Composers' Forum-Laboratory, cited in Pettis, "The WPA," pp. 101-2.

93. Copland, Composers' Forum-Laboratory (February 24, 1937), *WPA Composers Forum [sic] Transcripts.*

94. Pettis, "The WPA," pp. 109-10; see also Flora Rheta Schreiber and Vincent Persichetti, *William Schuman* (New York: G. Schirmer, 1954), pp. 14-20.

95. Sessions, Composers' Forum-Laboratory.

96. Carter, "Coolidge Crusade; WPA; New York Season," p. 37.

97. Pettis, "Music," *New Masses* X/2 (January 2, 1934), p. 29.

98. Pettis, "The WPA," p. 107.

99. Ibid., p. 108.

100. Ibid.

101. For another enthusiastic appraisal of the WPA Forums, see Olin Downes, "Laboratory for Native Composers," *The New York Times* (January 10, 1937), Sec. 10, p. 7, as well as his tribute to Pettis in "Composers' Forum," *The New York Times* (May 21, 1951), Sec. 10, p. 7.

102. See McKinzie, *The New Deal*, pp. 95-102.

103. Canon, "The Federal Music Project," pp. 71-72.

104. A few individuals were given positions as "staff composers" for educational divisions, and performed services such as arranging folk songs for class use. Paul Bowles was one of these; see Canon, "The Federal Music Project," p. 139, and Bowles, *Without Stopping*, pp. 213-16.

105. Foster, "Music," pp. 318 ff.

106. See Canon, "The Federal Music Project," pp. 120-22. Some commissions by private institutions were arranged by Sokoloff in 1936 and 1938.

107. Foster, "Music," pp. 348ff.

108. See McKinzie, *The New Deal*, pp. 105 ff.; Mangione, *The Dream*, pp. 241 ff.

109. Thomson, *Virgil Thomson* (London: Weidenfeld and Nicolson, 1967), pp. 259-74.

110. Paul Bowles, for instance, was hired by the Department of Agriculture for a score to a documentary; Bowles, *Without Stopping*, p. 225.

111. Canon, "The Federal Music Project," p. 140.

112. Houseman, *Run-Through*, pp. 191-93, 212-13, 417-18.

113. Foster, "Music," pp. 353-54.

114. Ibid., pp. 354-56.

115. Seeger, "Interview."

116. Sokoloff, "Text of a Radio Talk," September 22, 1936, *WPA Exhibit No. 2*, Library of Congress.

117. See Foster, "Music," pp. xi-xii.

118. Howard, "Better Days for Music," *Harper's Monthly Magazine* CLXXIV (April, 1937), pp. 483-91.

119. Thomson, *American Music*, p. 59.

120. Canon, "The Federal Music Project," pp. 113-14.

Chapter 8

1. John J. Pullen, *Patriotism in America* (New York: American Heritage Press, 1971), p. 42.

2. Ibid., p. 98.

3. Cabell Phillips, *From the Crash to the Blitz* (London: Macmillan, 1969), pp. 533, 552-53. Leftist artists and musicians sponsored benefits for the Loyalists; see, for instance, *Daily Worker* (February 2, 1939), p. 7.

4. Kenneth S. Davis, *Experience of War* (Garden City, New York: Doubleday, 1965), pp. 5-6. Pullen, in *Patriotism in America*, p. 98, also has claimed that World War II remains the only twentieth-century war Americans still feel was justified. Davis's rhetoric, twenty years after the War, helps substantiate that claim.

5. "Fascism" is "any form of right-wing authoritarianism" *(Oxford English Dictionary, Supplement*, Vol. I, p. 1035), or "a governmental system with strong centralized power, permitting no opposition or criticism, controlling all affairs of the nation . . . and (often) anticommunist" *(The American College Dictionary* [New York: Random House, 1958], p. 438).

6. See, for instance, Roger Sessions's thoughtful essay "No More Business-as-Usual," *Modern Music* XIX/3 (March–April, 1942), pp. 156-62.

7. Donal Henahan, "A Ruptured Duck," *The New York Times* (August 15, 1976), Sec. 2, p. 15.

8. Lehman Engel, "Songs of the American Wars," *Modern Music* XIX/3 (March–April, 1942), p. 151.

9. Sessions, "No More Business-as-Usual," p. 156.

10. Sessions, "Artists and This War," *Modern Music* XX/1 (November–December, 1942), p. 3.

11. Flora Rheta Schreiber and Vincent Persichetti, *William Schuman* (New York: G. Schirmer, 1954), pp. 27–28.

12. Henry Cowell, "In Time of Bitter War," *Modern Music* XIX/2 (January–February, 1942), p. 83.

13. Ross Lee Finney, "The American Composer and the War," *M.T.N.A. Proceedings, 1942*, pp. 31-52. Finney's study also includes a list of new American works composed and premiered since the United States' entry into the war. See also Homer Ulrich, *A Centennial History of the Music Teachers National Association* (Cincinnati, Ohio: M.T.N.A., 1976), pp. 61-65.

14. Sessions, "Artists," pp. 6-7; cited also in Finney, "The American Composer," p. 33.

15. Sessions, "No More Business-as-Usual," p. 157.

16. Earl Robinson, cited in Finney, "The American Composer," pp. 35-36.

17. Howard Hanson, cited in Finney, "The American Composer," pp. 38-39.

18. Douglas Moore, cited in Finney, "The American Composer," p. 39.

19. Isidore Freed, cited in Finney, "The American Composer," p. 37.

20. Randall Thompson, cited in Finney, "The American Composer," p. 32.

21. Bernard Rogers, cited in Finney, "The American Composer," p. 35.

22. Aaron Copland, cited in Finney, "The American Composer," pp. 34-35. See also the remarks of Lehman Engel and Earl Robinson pertaining to Shostakovich, cited in Finney, "The American Composer," pp. 34-36.

    The Soviet Union was temporarily in the good graces of the United States after becoming an ally in 1942 (see Alexander, *Nationalism in American Thought, 1930–1945* [Chicago: Rand McNally, 1971], pp. 174-75), and works by non-leftist composers were dedicated to Russia, such as Roy Harris's *5th Symphony*.

23. Saul Lancourt and Elie Siegmeister, *Doodle Dandy of the U.S.A.* (New York: Musette, 1942), p. 24; also "Interview with Barbara Zuck," December 14, 1974.

24. "Agit-prop" originally referred to a "department . . . . of the Russian Communist Party responsible . . . for 'agitation and propaganda' on behalf of Communism"; *Oxford English Dictionary, Supplement,* Vol. I, p. 43. It has since come to describe plays or skits with an obvious political message.

25. A symbol of Roosevelt and his policies, "four freedoms" was also employed by critics of American entry into the War. Herbert Hoover, objecting to military aid to the Soviet Union, stated: "Now we find ourselves promising aid to Stalin. . . . If we go further and join the war and we win it, then we will have won for Stalin the grip of Communism on Russia. . . . It makes the whole argument of our joining the war to bring the Four Freedoms to mankind a Gargantuan jest." Hoover, cited in Geoffrey Perrett, *Days of Sadness, Years of Triumph* (New York: Coward, McCann & Geoghegan, 1973), p. 169.

    Earl Robinson's *Battle Hymn* (1942) is based upon another speech by Roosevelt.

26. See also Nicolas Slonimsky's brief remarks about this work in *Music Since 1900* (third edition; New York: Coleman-Ross, 1949), p. 535.

27. See Alexander, *Nationalism*, pp. 49, 135.

28. The Lindsey poem was also given a musical setting by Roy Harris in 1953. Perhaps the earliest musical work inspired by Lincoln by a composer from the generation under discussion was Robert Russell Bennett's *Abraham Lincoln Symphony* (1929).

29. Julia Smith, *Aaron Copland* (New York: E.P. Dutton, 1955), p. 224; Kostelanetz had commissioned a series of undesignated musical "portraits" of famous Americans, another of which was Virgil Thomson's piece on Fiorello La Guardia. Smith also includes *Fanfare for the Common Man* and *Preamble for a Solemn Occasion* among Copland's patriotic works; see pp. 222-27.

    A Lincoln Portrait has been the vehicle of statesmen-like actors such as Will Geer and Melvyn Douglas, as well as actual statesmen like the late Adlai Stevenson.

30. Claire R. Reis, "Composers in Wartime," *Composers, Conductors, and Critics* (New York: Oxford University Press, 1955), p. 156.

31. Robert Ward, "Letter from the Army," *Modern Music* XX/3 (March–April, 1943), p. 170.

32. Robert Ward, "Composers In Uniform," *Modern Music* XXIII/2 (Spring, 1946), pp. 108-9.

33. Gail Kubik, "Composing for Government Films," *Modern Music* XXIII/3 (Summer, 1946), pp. 190-91.

34. Ibid., p. 192.

35. Ward, "Composers in Uniform," p. 109.

   For further information about musical activities sponsored by the armed forces, see Richard Franko Goldman, "Bands in Wartime," *Modern Music* XIX/3 (March–April, 1942), pp. 169-72, and Raymond Kendall, "Music for the Armed Services," *The Musical Quarterly* XXXI/2 (April, 1945), pp. 141-56.

36. Samuel Barber, "Letter to Walter Damrosch," February 27, 1944, Letters File, Music Division, New York Public Library.

37. John Tasker Howard, *Our American Music* (third edition; New York: Thomas Y. Crowell, 1954), p. 542. Barber later dropped the radio signal and simplified the work's title to *Second Symphony*.

38. Nathan Broder, *Samuel Barber* (New York: G. Schirmer, 1954), p. 36.

39. *Philadephia Orchestra Program Notes*, April 14-15, 1944.

40. Ibid.

41. Reis, *Composers, Conductors, and Critics*, p. 168.

42. Marc Blitzstein, cited in Reis, *Composers, Conductors, and Critics*, p. 168.

43. Marc Blitzstein, "Notes on the Program," New York City Symphony, Leonard Bernstein, Music Director, Season 1945-46.

44. Olin Downes, "Audience Cheers Blitzstein Work," *The New York Times* (April 2, 1946), p. 23.

45. Virgil Thomson, "Music," *The New York Herald Tribune* (April 2, 1946).

46. Olin Downes, "Composers on War," *The New York Times* (October 10, 1943), Sec. 2, p. 7.

47. Reis, *Composers, Conductors, and Critics*, pp. 163ff.

48. Listed in Downes, "Composers on War." Reis, in *Composers, Conductors, and Critics*, p. 163, wrote that the League commissioned eighteen works in this series, but does not provide a complete list. "Notes on Patriotic Works Written for Dr. Rodzinski with Philharmonic and CBS," from League of Composers "Clippings File," Music Division, New York Public Library, lists only fifteen such works. Downes's listing cited above is the most complete the author has found to date.

49. See Reis, *Composers, Conductors, and Critics*, pp. 163-66.

50. Douglas Moore, cited in "Notes on Patriotic Works."

51. Charles Ives, cited in "Notes on Patriotic Works." The *War Song March* was written in 1917 and originally entitled "He Is There!" The text was revised in 1942; John Kirkpatrick, ed., *Charles E. Ives: Memos* (New York: W. W. Norton, 1972), p. 161.

52. Roy Harris, cited in "Notes on Patriotic Works."

53. William Grant Still, cited in "Notes on Patriotic Works."

54. Howard Hess, "Fanfares by Americans," *Modern Music* XX/3 (March–April, 1943), pp. 189-91; Reis, *Composers in America,* p. 168; Finney, "The American Composer," pp. 41-52.

   Hess, in "Fanfares," pp. 190-91, also lists works in progress by Randall Thompson, Ernest Block, and William Schuman.

55. Boris Schwartz, *Music and Musical Life in Soviet Russia, 1917–1970* (New York: W. W. Norton, 1973), p. 180.

56. Cowell, "In Time of Bitter War," p. 83.

57. Ibid., pp. 85-87. A more complete picture of Russian composers' opportunities and limitations is presented in Schwartz's chapter, "Great Patriotic War," *Music and Musical Life in Soviet Russia,* pp. 175-203.

58. This ability looked quite different in a post-war context. See "Soviet Musical Policy, 1948," Slonimsky, *Music Since 1900,* pp. 684-712.

59. Cowell, "In Time of Bitter War," p. 83; Ernest Chapman, "Britain Calls Music to the Colors," *Modern Music* XIX/2 (January–February, 1942), pp. 117-20. See also Marc Blitzstein, "London: Fourth Winter of the Blackout," *Modern Music* XX/2 (January–February, 1943), pp. 117-20.

60. On the experiences of a few other enlisted composers see Reis, *Composers, Conductors, and Critics,* pp. 154-55, 157, and Finney, "The American Composer," pp. 33-34.

61. Reis, *Composers, Conductors, and Critics,* pp. 163-65, 170.

Chapter 9

1. The murder occurred on the Isle of Martinique early on the morning of January 22, 1964. Blitzstein was found on a sidewalk fatally beaten and robbed. After a long, closed trial, two Portuguese sailors and a local youth were convicted of assault and theft. *Philadelphia Inquirer* (April 1, 1965), p. 8.

2. Joan Peyser, "The Troubled Time of Marc Blitzstein," *Columbia University Forum* IX/1 (Winter, 1966), p. 33.

3. Marc Blitzstein, in an interview with Edith Hale, "Author and Composer Blitzstein," *Daily Worker* (December 7, 1938), p. 7.

4. Ibid.

5. Paul Myers Talley, "Social Criticism in the Original Theatre Librettos of Marc Blitzstein" (Ph.D. dissertation, University of Wisconsin, 1965), p. 18.

6. Paul Moor, in "Tradition of Turbulence," *Theatre Arts* XXXXIV/3 (March, 1950), p. 38, remarked that Schoenberg was impressed enough with Blitzstein to call him his most talented American student.

7. See Henry Brant's remarks on Blitzstein's early works in "Marc Blitzstein," *Modern Music* XXIII/3 (Summer, 1946), p. 170.

8. John Houseman, *Run-Through* (New York: Simon and Schuster, 1972), p. 245.

9. B. H. Haggin, "Music," *The Nation* 152/7 (February 15, 1941), p. 194.

10. Ibid.

11. Ibid.

12. Blitzstein, cited in Hale, "Author and Composer," p. 7.

13. Ibid.

14. Philip Barr, "Opera in the Vernacular," *The Magazine of Art* 32 (June, 1939), pp. 382-83.

15. Robert J. Dietz, "The Operatic Style of Marc Blitzstein in the American 'Agit-Prop' Era" (Ph.D. dissertation, University of Iowa, 1970), pp. 238-39.

16. See Minna Lederman's tribute to Blitzstein's social concern in "Memories of Marc Blitzstein, Music's Angry Man," *Show* IV/6 (June, 1964), p. 18.

17. Blitzstein, cited in Aaron Copland, "In Memory of Marc Blitzstein," *Marc Blitzstein Papers,* Wisconsin State Historical Society, originally published in *Perspectives of New Music* II (Spring, 1964), pp. 6-7.

18. Blitzstein, cited in Charles Glenn, "Hollywood Meets Blitzstein," *Daily Worker* (July 5, 1941), p. 7.

19. Ibid.

20. Brant, "Marc Blitzstein," p. 170.

21.   Ibid., p. 172.

22.   Blitzstein, in Hale, "Author and Composer," p. 7.

23.   See, for instance, William Austin, *Music in the Twentieth Century* (New York: W. W. Norton, 1966), p. 500; Joseph Machlis, *Introduction to Contemporary Music* (New York: W. W. Norton, 1961), p. 568; Aaron Copland, *The New Music, 1900–1960* (New York: W. W. Norton, 1968), p. 140; Moor, "Tradition," p. 38. Dietz, in "The Operatic Style," pp. 152-73, explores in considerable detail the ideas of Brecht, Weill, and Eisler, all prominent in Germany during the 1920s and all immigrants living in America during the 1930s. Only Blitzstein's own views in relation to those of the three Germans are explored in the present study.

24.   See Chapter IV, pp. 93-95, of the present study.

25.   Blitzstein, "The Case for Modern Music," *New Masses* XX/3 (July 14, 1936), p. 27.

26.   Blitzstein, "II. Second Generation," *New Masses* XX/4 (July 21, 1936), p. 28.

27.   Ibid., p. 29.

28.   Ibid.

29.   Blitzstein, "Coming – the Mass Audience!" *Modern Music* XIII/4 (May–June, 1936), p. 29.

30.   Blitzstein, "Music Manifesto," *New Masses* XIX/13 (June 23, 1936), p. 28, cited in Dietz, "The Operatic Style," p. 184.   See also Blitzstein, "Author of Famous 'Cradle Will Rock' Discusses Composer's Task," *Daily Worker* (April 13, 1938), p. 7.

31.   Blitzstein, "On Writing Music for the Theatre," *Modern Music* XV/2 (January–February, 1938), p. 84.

32.   Blitzstein, "Weill Scores for Johnny Johnson," *Modern Music* XIV/1 (November–December, 1936), p. 45.

33.   Blitzstein, "Coming – the Mass Audience!" p. 28.

34.   Blitzstein, "Popular Music – an Invasion: 1923-33," *Modern Music* X/2 (January–February, 1933), p. 102.

35.   Blitzstein, "Weill Scores," pp. 44-45.

36.   Cited in Houseman, *Run-Through*, pp. 245-46.

37.   Dietz, "The Operatic Style," pp. 152ff.

38. Blitzstein, cited in Hale, "Author and Composer," p. 7.

39. Blitzstein, "Letter to John Houseman," November 12, 1959, *Marc Blitzstein Papers*, Wisconsin State Historical Society.

40. For more details, see Houseman, *Run-Through*, pp. 253-74; Dietz, "The Operatic Style," pp. 194-209.

41. John Mason Brown, in "Ten Years Later," *The Saturday Review* XXXI/3 (January 17, 1948), p. 22, stated that *The Cradle* continued to "rank with [Odets's] 'Waiting for Lefty' as the most arresting drama of social protest to have been written in this country."

42. See Houseman, *Run-Through*, pp. 198-295, 218-22.

43. Ibid., p. 254.

44. Ibid., p. 249.

45. John O. Hunter, in "Marc Blitzstein's 'The Cradle Will Rock,' as a Document of America, 1937," *American Quarterly* XVII/2, Part I (Summer, 1966), pp. 231-33, makes a case for Youngstown, Ohio as the model for "Steeltown," although he uses events from 1937, as opposed to 1936 when *The Cradle* was written, as the prototypes.

     On the WPA and the left, see Chapter VII, pp. 160-61 of the present study.

46. According to Houseman, the performers' unions regarded *The Cradle* as "straight CIO propaganda or worse," and had never approved of the production in the first place; *Run-Through*, p. 258.

47. Ibid., pp. 267-68.

48. Copland, "In Memory."

49. It was not until the New York City Opera production in 1960 that *The Cradle* was performed with costumes and scenery. In the 1947 revival, an orchestra replaced Blitzstein at the piano; Talley, "Social Criticism," pp. 81-83.

50. Cited in Dietz, "The Operatic Style," pp. 32 and 221.

51. Alistair Cooke, script from NBC radio broadcast (January 12, 1938), cited in Dietz, "The Operatic Style," p. 224.

52. R. D. Darrell, *New Masses* XXVI/1 (December 28, 1937), p. 27.

53. The *Daily Worker* (June 24, 1937), p. 7, announced that Blitzstein had released *The Cradle* to a road company touring the "labor circuit," including steel-making

centers in Pennsylvania and Ohio. It was to be a continuation of a "Let Freedom Ring" tour organized earlier by Will Geer.

54.   Houseman, *Run-Through*, p. 276.

55.   Ibid.

56.   See also Talley, "Social Criticism," pp. 57-121.

57.   Blitzstein, in Hale, "Author and Composer," p. 7.

58.   Blitzstein, "City College Presents 'Cradle Will Rock' Tonight," *Daily Worker* (November 29, 1940), p. 7.

59.   See, for instance, Mary McCarthy's review of *The Cradle* in *Partisan Review* (April, 1938), cited in Dietz, "The Operatic Style," p. 25.

60.   See, for instance, Richard Pells, *Radical Visions and American Dreams* (New York: Harper and Row, 1973), pp. 33, 252ff.   Pells also discusses the importance of drama to the left.   See also Melech Epstein, *The Jew and Communism* (New York: Trade Union Sponsoring Committee, 1959), , pp. 206-13 for a discussion of Communist club activities.

61.   The opera was originally in one act, but is frequently performed in two; see Dietz, "The Operatic Style," p. 215.

62.   Brown, "Ten Years Later," p. 22.

63.   B. H. Haggin, *Music Observed* (New York: Oxford University Press, 1964), pp. 222-23, originally in the *Hudson Review* (Summer, 1960).

64.   Copland, *The New Music*, pp. 142-43.

65.   See Dietz, "The Operatic Style," pp. 340-58; Wilfred Mellers, "Music, Theatre, and Commerce," *The Score and I.M.A. Magazine* 12 (June, 1955), pp. 69-76; *Music in a New Found Land* (London: Barrie and Rockliff, 1964), pp. 414-29.

66.   See Talley, "Social Criticism," p. 364.

67.   See also Blitzstein's thoughtful essay "The Phenomenon of Stravinsky," *The Musical Quarterly* XXI/3 (July, 1935), pp. 330-47, in which he wrote "Until 1930, Stravinsky held the key position in twentieth-century music.   As yet he has no successor."

68.   Lederman, "Memories of Marc Blitzstein," p. 18.

69.   An uproar occurred when the Ford Foundation announced a grant to Blitzstein for work on this opera.   An obituary in *The New York Times* (January 24, 1964)

noted the controversy stemmed from Blitzstein's alleged membership in the Communist Party from 1938 to 1949; see also Dietz, "The Operatic Style," pp. 8-9; Talley, "Social Criticism," pp. 26-30.

70.   Peyser, "The Troubled Time," p. 32. Peyser also notes (p. 36) that Blitzstein's *Reuben, Reuben* (1955) portrays a hero so incapable of seeing his way that he cannot even locate a subway station.

71.   See Chapter V, pp. 115-21, of the present study.

72.   Talley, "Social Criticism," p. 1.

73.   Copland, "In Memory."

Chapter 10

1.   Serge Koussevitzky, cited in Paul Rosenfeld, *Discoveries of a Music Critic* (New York: Harcourt, Brace, 1936), p. 328.

2.   John Tasker Howard, *Our Contemporary Composers* (New York: Thomas Y. Crowell, 1942), p. 133; see also Oscar Thompson, *Great Modern Composers* (New York: Dodd, Mead, 1941), p. 105.

3.   The significance in the 1930s of Harris's ethnic heritage is underscored by Nicolas Slonimsky in "Music and Musicians," *Boston Evening Transcript* (June 24, 1934), Part 1, p. 1, who wrote that "between the enclosures for European echo-reflectors, and recondite prophets, there is a small acre where an American composer, civilized and free, can meet the unwilling world. Roy Harris of Oklahoma, thirty-five, white, and healthy, is well-equipped to be an American emissary."

4.   Rosenfeld, *Discoveries,* pp. 324-32.

5.   Biographical material is taken from Roy Harris, "Letter to Lawrence Gilman," May 20, 1926, Letters File, Music Division, New York Public Library, and "Perspective at Forty," *The Magazine of Art* 32/11 (November, 1939), pp. 638-39, 667-70; Patricia Ashley, "Roy Harris," *Stereo Review* XXI (December, 1968), pp. 63-72; Nicolas Slonimsky, "Roy Harris," *The Musical Quarterly* XXXIII/1 (January, 1947), pp. 17-37, and "The Story of Roy Harris — American Composer, Parts I and II," *Etude* Nos. 74 and 75 (December, 1956 and January, 1957), pp. 11, 62, and 12, 42.

6.   Slonimsky, "The Story of Roy Harris — Part I," p. 11.

In addition to the material cited in footnote 5, Slonimsky has also written "Roy Harris: Cimarron Composer" (unpublished monograph [c. 1950], at the University of California at Los Angeles Library, noted in Dan Stehman, "The Symphonies of Roy Harris: An Analytical Study of the Linear Materials and of Related Works" (Ph.D. dissertation, University of Southern California, 1973), p. iii.

7.   Ibid.

8.   Harris, "Letter to Lawrence Gilman," May 20, 1926.

9.   Arthur Farwell, "Roy Harris," *The Musical Quarterly* XVIII/1 (January, 1932), p. 18.

10. Harris, "Perspective at Forty," p. 668.

11. Ibid.

12. Harris, cited in David Ewen, ed., *Composers Since 1900* (New York: H. W. Wilson, 1969), p. 263.

13. Harris, "Perspective at Forty," p. 639.

14. In *American Portrait*, the movements correspond to four traits — "Expectation," "Initiative," "Speed," and "Collective Force" — which Harris explains in his program notes; Stehman, "The Symphonies of Roy Harris," p. 5. Extensive explanatory notes are also characteristic of Harris.

15. Stehman, in "The Symphonies of Roy Harris," pp. 41-42, notes that the second movement of the *American Portrait* is the basis for Harris's overture *When Johnny Comes Marching Home* (1934). Harris also set "Johnny" for chorus and orchestra as the last movement of the *Folksong Symphony* (1940), arranged it for *a cappella* chorus, and cited the tune in *Symphony No. 6 (Gettysburg)* (1944).

16. Due to his "providential" birth date and location, Harris always felt "the shadow of Lincoln," as he put it (cited in Slonimsky, "Roy Harris," p. 20). He also said that he remembered his father humming "Johnny" as he came and went in the farm fields (cited in Howard, *Our Contemporary Composers*, p. 139). To Harris, therefore, the tune held a nostalgic fascination representative of both private and collective American experiences.

17. Stehman, "The Symphonies of Roy Harris," pp. 32-33.

18. Ibid., pp. 33-34.

19. Harris, "Does Music Have to be European?," *Scribner's Magazine* XCI/4 (April, 1932), pp. 204-9, and "Problems of American Composers," *American Composers on American Music*, Henry Cowell, ed. (orig. 1933; New York: Frederick Ungar, 1962), pp. 149-55. The earlier article is apparently the basis for the latter, which contains large sections identical to material in the first.

     See also Harris, "American Music Enters a New Phase," *Scribner's Magazine* XCVI/4 (October, 1934), pp. 218-21; "The Growth of a Composer," *The Musical Quarterly* XX/2 (April, 1934), pp. 188-91; "Modern Melody: Its Resources," *MTNA Proceedings*, 1937, pp. 41-47; "Sources of a Musical Culture," *The New York Times* (January 1, 1939), Section 9, pp. 7-8; and "Our Musical Scene in Two Tones," *Twice a Year* 5/6 (Fall–Winter, 1940, Spring–Summer, 1941), pp. 327-37.

20.   Harris, "Problems of American Composers," p. 155.

21.   Slonimsky, in "The Story of Roy Harris — Part II," p. 12, wrote that Koussevitzky said to Harris "I vant a big symphony from the Vest."

22.   H. T. Parker, in the *Boston Evening Transcript* (January 27, 1934), wrote that the *Symphony 1933* was "American, first, in a pervading directness, in a recurring and unaffected roughness of speech"; cited in Howard, *Our Contemporary Composers*, p. 138. See also "An American Work," *The New York Times* (February 11, 1934).

23.   Titles and dates are as found in Stehman, "The Symphonies of Roy Harris," pp. xxv-xxxiv.

24.   Gilbert Chase, *America's Music* (revised second edition; New York: McGraw-Hill, 1966), pp. 507-8.

25.   Peter Yates, *Twentieth Century Music* (New York: Pantheon Books, 1967), p. 281.

Toscanini was at the time conducting the NBC Symphony, an orchestra created especially for him, in regular, nationwide broadcasts.   His lack of interest in American music suggests that some institutions of cultivated music in America were considerably less Americanist than some native composers or even other musicians and music lovers.

26.   Olin Downes, [review of Harris's "Third Symphony"] *The New York Times* (March 12, 1939), Sec. 3, p. 6.

27.   William Schuman, "Letter to the Music Editor," *The New York Times* (March 12, 1939), Sec, 3, p. 6.

28.   It should be noted that Schuman was a close friend and admirer of Harris in these years; see Nathan Broder, "The Music of William Schuman," *The Musical Quarterly* XXXI/1 (January, 1945), pp. 17-28.

29.   See Eric Salzman, *Twentieth Century Music: An Introduction* (Englewood Cliffs, N.J.: Prentice-Hall, 1967), p. 98; Yates, *Twentieth Century Music*, p. 281.

30.   Virgil Thomson, *American Music Since 1910* (New York: Holt, Rinehart and Winston, 1972), p. 9.

31.   Kate Hevner Mueller, *Twenty-Seven Major Symphony Orchestras* (Bloomington: Indiana University Studies, 1973), p. 164.   See also John Tasker Howard and George Kent Bellows, *A Short History of Music in America* (New York: Thomas Y. Crowell, 1967), p. 290; Slonimsky, "The Story of Roy Harris — Part II," p. 12; and Gilbert Chase, *The American Composer Speaks* (Baton Rouge: Louisiana State University Press, 1966), p. 196.

32.   Roy Harris, *Boston Symphony Orchestra Programmes,* February 24, 1939, pp. 777-78.

Spellings are as found in the original.

33. Slonimsky, "Roy Harris," pp. 26-30.

34. Section I also reveals a gradually rising instrumental range. The rise of melodic
     pitch level of Section I climaxes between m. 117 and m. 134, followed by a
     dropping off at the section's end. Also, level G returns at the beginning of the
     transitional area to Section II (m. 139), surrounding the wandering tonalities of the
     section. Because Section I in these ways resembles the symphony as a whole,
     Section I forecasts these aspects of the entire symphony's plan.

35. Robert Evett, "The Harmonic Idiom of Roy Harris," *Modern Music* XXIII/2
     (Spring, 1946), p. 101.

36. Ibid., p. 102.

37. Slonimsky, "Roy Harris," p. 25.

38. Ibid., pp. 28-29.

39. Ibid.

40. According to Rudolf Reti in *Tonality—Atonality—Pantonality* (New York:
     Macmillan, 1958), p. 68, "undefined tonality" refers to sections of music which
     "float in the realm of several keys without deciding, as it were, upon one concrete
     tonic"; the term applies to an area of music in which "actual key relationships
     cannot be determined."

41. One could make a case, perhaps, for a prototype in the late Classic–early
     Romantic period, particularly the semi-programmatic works of Beethoven.

42. Roy Harris, "The Basis of Artistic Creation in Music," in *The Basis of Artistic
     Creation* (New Brunswick, N.J.: Rutgers University Press, 1942), p. 28.

43. Ibid.

44. Ibid.

45. Harris, "Problems of American Composers," p. 150. Harris's description of
     "American" musical character is discussed below.

46. Harris, "Letter to Oscar Thompson," June 7, 1941, cited in Thompson, *Great
     Modern Composers*, pp. 109-10.

47. Ibid., p. 109.

     See Chapter II, pp. 71-73, of the present study for a discussion of Ives and
     Americanism.

48. Harris, "Sources of a Musical Culture," pp. 7-8.

49. Harris, "Letter," cited in Thompson *Great Modern Composers*, p. 109.

50. Paul Rosenfeld, "Variations on the Grass Roots Theme." *Modern Music* XVI/4 (May-June, 1939), p. 219: see Chapter VI, pp. 152-53, of the present study.

51. Slonimsky, "Roy Harris," p. 25. Each of the seven movements of the *Folksong Symphony* is an arrangement of a folksong.

52. John N. Burk, *Boston Symphony Orchestra Programmes,* February 24, 1939, p. 780.

53. Rosenfeld, *An Hour with American Music,* pp. 119-20.

54. Aaron Copland, *The New Music, 1900-1960* (New York: W. W. Norton, 1969), p. 120.

55. H. Wiley Hitchcock, *Music in the United States* (second edition; Engelwood Cliffs, New Jersey: Prentice-Hall, 1974), p. 207.

56. Harris, "Problems of American Composers," p. 151.

57. Curt Sachs, in *Rhythm and Tempo* (New York: W. W. Norton, 1953), pp. 24-25, defined additive and divisive rhythm:

   Divisive rhythm is a "'striding' form of rhythm" in which regular recurrence of a beat is created by the dividing up of a certain duration into equal parts. Additive rhythm is rhythm composed of "aggregates of dissimilar elements." Divisive rhythm may be said to be "regulative" while additive rhythm is "configurative."

58. Hitchcock, *Music in the United States,* p. 206.

59. Roger Abrahams and George Foss, *Anglo-American Folksong Style* (Englewood Cliffs, N. J.: Prentice-Hall, 1968), p. 144.

60. Ibid., p. 159.

61. Ibid.

62. Slonimsky, "The Story of Roy Harris, Part I," p. 62.

63. Copland, *The New Music,* p. 120. In fact, this melodic "profusion" in the *Third Symphony* makes it difficult for the listener to recognize the cyclical elements among sections. Many melodic phrases are presented in the early sections of this piece, and these phrases are not clearly distinguished from one another by striking rhythmic differences or frequent reiteration. Because the composer has not pointed up the significant phrases (in this case, those which will return later in the piece), the ear may not remember them as already having been presented. Harris termed his continuous alteration of melody "autogenetic" development. See Howard, *Our Contemporary Composers,* p. 138.

64. Sidney Finkelstein, *Composer and Nation: The Folk Heritage of Music* (New York: International Publishers, 1960), p. 317.

65. Copland, cited in Slonimsky, "Roy Harris," p. 22.

66. Slonimsky, "Roy Harris," p. 22.

67. Harris, "Notes" for *Folksong Symphony 1940*, Vanguard Everyman Classic recording, SRV 347 SD.

68. Howard, *Our Contemporary Composers*, p. 133.

69. See David Ewen, ed., *The New Book of Modern Composers* (New York: Alfred A. Knopf, 1961), pp. 201-2.

70. Slonimsky, "The Story of Roy Harris, Part II," p. 12.

71. Ibid.

72. Ibid.

73. Ashley, "Roy Harris," p. 68. See also Walter Piston, "Roy Harris," *Modern Music* XI/2 (January–February, 1934), pp. 73-83.

74. Harris, "The Composer Speaks," David Ewen, ed., *The New Book of Modern Composers*, pp. 204-6.

75. Harris's compositional interest in Americana did not disappear altogether after World War II. For instance, his *Abraham Lincoln Symphony* (1965; see above, p. 438) commemorated the centenary of Lincoln's assassination, and other works were based on national subjects.

76. Paul Henry Lang, cited in Howard and Bellows, *A Short History of Music in America*, p. 290.

Chapter 11

1. The above are Copland's words to describe Ives; Copland, "Foreword," Vivian Perlis, *Charles Ives Remembered* (New York: W. W. Norton, 1974), p. xi.

2. Virgil Thomson, *American Music Since 1910* (New York: Holt, Rinehart and Winston, 1972), p. 58.

3. Eric Salzman, "Dean of Our Composers at 60," *The New York Times* (November 13, 1960), p. 51.

4. Donal Henahan, "This Aaron a Musical Moses," *The New York Times* (November 9, 1975), Sec. 4, p. 21.

5. William Schuman, "A Birthday Salute to Aaron Copland," *The New York Times* (October 30, 1960), Sec. 4, p. 7.

6. Unless otherwise stated, biographical information is taken from Julia Smith, *Aaron Copland* (New York: E.P. Dutton, 1955), pp. 11-65.

7. Copland, "Composer from Brooklyn: An Autobiographical Sketch," *The New Music, 1900-1960* (New York: W. W. Norton, 1969), p. 151.

8. Copland, "The Composer in Industrial America," *Music and Imagination* (New York: A Mentor Book, 1952), p. 104.

9. Copland, "Composer from Brooklyn," p. 152.

10. Ibid., p. 154.

11. Thomson, *Virgil Thomson* (London: Weidenfeld and Nicolson, 1967), pp. 43, 53-54. See also Thomson, "'Greatest Music Teacher'—at 75," *The New York Times Magazine* (February 4, 1962), pp. 24, 33, 35.

12. Copland, "Composer from Brooklyn," p. 155. Copland has also written about Boulanger in *Copland On Music* (New York: W.W. Norton, 1963), pp. 83-91.

13. One of Copland's first essays was a tribute to Fauré, "Gabriel Fauré: A Neglected Master," *The Musical Quarterly* X/4 (October, 1924), pp. 574-86.

14. See, for instance, H. Wiley Hitchcock, *Music in the United States* (second edition; Englewood Cliffs, N. J.: Prentice-Hall, 1974), p. 176; Gilbert Chase, *America's Music* (revised second edition; New York: McGraw-Hill, 1966), p. 557.

15. Copland, "Letter to Barbara Zuck," July 18, 1974.

16. Thomson, *Virgil Thomson*, p. 54.

17. Ibid., pp. 59-60.

18. *Cortège Macabre* was a portion of the ballet *Grohg*, Copland's first orchestral work, which later became the basis for the *Dance Symphony*; see Smith, *Aaron Copland*, p. 301.

19. Copland, "Serge Koussevitzky and the American Composer," *The Musical Quarterly* XXX/3 (July, 1944), p. 260. The article lists the American works performed by the Boston Symphony Orchestra under Koussevitzky's direction.

20. Copland, *Copland on Music*, pp. 88-89.

21.   Copland, "Composer from Brooklyn," p. 158.

22.   Copland, "The Composer in Industrial America," pp. 106-7.

23.   Ibid., p. 107. See also Chapter II, pp. 20-21, of the present study.

24.   Ibid.

25.   Ibid., p. 109.

26.   Ibid., p. 110.

27.   Ibid., p. 111.

28.   See Smith, *Aaron Copland*, p. 75.

29.   Damrosch, cited in Smith, *Aaron Copland*, pp. 75-76.

30.   See Smith, *Aaron Copland*, pp. 75-77.

31.   What was meant by "jazz" in the 1920s is discussed in Chapter II, pp. 78-86, of the present study.   Copland's interest in jazz also is mentioned in Chapter II, pp. 84-86.

32.   Copland, WPA Composers' Forum-Laboratory, New York City, February 24, 1937, *WPA Composers [sic] Forum Transcripts*, National Archives.

33.   Paul Rosenfeld, *An Hour with American Music* (Philadelphia: J. B. Lippincott, 1929), pp. 139-40.

34.   Copland, WPA Composers' Forum-Laboratory.

35.   Thomson, *American Music Since 1910*, p. 49.

36.   Ibid., p. 50.

37.   The earliest American composers on the executive board were Louis Gruenberg, Leo Ornstein, and Emerson Whithorne; *The League of Composers Review* I/1 (February, 1924).   See also William Schuman, "A Brief Study of Music Organizations," *Twice A Year* 5/6 (Fall–Winter, 1940, Spring–Summer, 1941), p. 365.

38.   The resulting work was *Music for the Theatre*, which Koussevitzky premiered on November 20, 1925; Claire R. Reis, *Composers, Conductors, and Critics* (New York: Oxford University Press, 1955), pp. 64-65.

39.   *The Composers' Fund*, announcement from the League of Composers, [1933], League of Composers Clippings File, Music Division, New York Public Library.

40. See Smith, *Aaron Copland*, p. 103.

41. See Katrina Trask, *The Story of Yaddo* ([privately printed], 1923).

42. Alfred H. Meyer, "Yaddo — A May Festival," *Modern Music* IX/4 (May-June, 1932), pp. 172-76; Smith, *Aaron Copland*, pp. 126-27, 139-42; Nicolas Slonimsky, *Music Since 1900* (third edition; New York: Coleman-Ross, 1949), pp. 347-48.

43. Smith, *Aaron Copland*, p. 140.

44. Oscar Levant, in *A Smattering of Ignorance* (New York: Doubleday, Doran, 1940), pp. 213-48, recounts the Yaddo episode, as well as others involving Copland. See also Arthur Mendel, "The American Composer," *The Nation* CXXXIV/3489 (May 18, 1932), pp. 578-80.

45. Copland, "The Composer and His Critic," *Modern Music* IX/4 (May–June, 1932), p. 143.

46. Ibid.

47. Ibid., p. 144.

48. Thomson, *American Music Since 1910*, p. 51.

49. Ibid.

50. Cited in Copland, "The American Composer Gets a Break," *American Mercury* XXXIV/136 (April, 1935), p. 489.

51. Ibid., p. 492.

52. Ibid.

53. Thomson, *American Music Since 1910*, p. 50.

54. Smith, *Aaron Copland*, pp. 181-82.

55. "The Composers Organize; A Proclamation," *Modern Music* XV/2 (January–February, 1938), p. 92. See also Schuman, "A Brief Study of Musical Organizations," pp. 363-65.

56. "The Composers Organize," pp. 93-94.

57. Ibid., p. 94.

58. Ibid., p. 93.

59.   See Smith, *Aaron Copland*, p. 107; Arthur Berger, *Aaron Copland* (New York: Oxford University Press, 1953), p. 20; and Thomson, *American Music Since 1910*, p. 50.

60.   See Smith, *Aaron Copland*, p. 142.

61.   Copland and unnamed questioners, WPA Composers' Forum-Laboratory.

62.   *Oxford English Dictionary*, Vol. 18, p. 63.

63.   See Berger, *Aaron Copland*, pp. 39-42; Norman Kay, "Aspects of Copland's Development," *Tempo* 95 (Winter, 1970-71), pp. 23-29.

64.   See also Copland's discussion of "simple" and "complex" music in "The Composer in Industrial America," pp. 114-15.

65.   Copland, "Composer from Brooklyn," p. 160.

It might be well to recall the "economic determinism" of musical style discussed in Chapter IV, p. 95, of the present study.

66.   Copland, "Composer from Brooklyn," p. 160.

67.   Ibid.

68.   Ibid., p. 161.

69.   Ibid.

70.   Ibid.

71.   Copland, "Second Thoughts on Hollywood," *Modern Music* XVII/3 (March–April, 1940), pp. 141-47. See also Chapter IV, pp. 98-101, of the present study.

72.   Copland, "Composer from Brooklyn," p. 162.

73.   Ibid., p. 161.

74.   Copland, "The Composer in Industrial America," p. 115.

75.   See Smith, *Aaron Copland*, pp. 119-60.

76.   At the height of McCarthyism in the early 1950s, Copland, like many others, came in for criticism. His *A Lincoln Portrait* was refused performance at the 1953 Inaugural Concert in Washington, D.C., presumably because of his alleged political leanings. Copland wrote a letter to the Board of Directors of the League of Composers, which jumped to his defense. He stated that the only organizations in which he was a member were those with the cultural life of the United States

as their primary interest, and denied membership in any political party; Aaron Copland, "Letter to the Board of Directors," February 9, 1953, Letters File, Music Division, New York Public Library.

77.   Copland, WPA Composers' Forum-Laboratory.

78.   Thomson, *American Music Since 1910*, p. 55.

79.   Copland, cited in John Rockwell, "Copland, at 75," *The New York Times* (November 12, 1975), p. 48.

80.   Berger, *Aaron Copland*, pp. 26-29.

81.   Harold Clurman, *The Fervent Years* (New York: Hill and Wang, 1957; original edition, 1945), p. 16.

82.   Smith, *Aaron Copland*, p. 149.

83.   Berger, *Aaron Copland*, pp. 28-29.

84.   "Carl Sands," "Copeland's [*sic*] Recital at Pierre Degeyter Club," *Daily Worker* (March 22, 1934), p. 5.

85.   Ibid.

86.   Ibid.

87.   Ibid.

88.   Ibid.

89.   Ibid.

90.   See Chapter V, pp. 131-33, of the present study.

91.   Berger, *Aaron Copland*, pp. 20-21, 28.

92.   Blitzstein, *Marc Blitzstein Papers*, Wisconsin State Historical Society.

93.   See Smith, *Aaron Copland*, p. 29.

94.   "Free Scholarship Prize in Music School Contest," *Daily Worker* (August 23, 1935), p. 5.

95.   Copland, "A Note on Young Composers," *Music Vanguard* I/1 (March–April, 1935), p. 16.

96. Copland, "Workers Sing!," *New Masses* XI/10 (June 5, 1934), p. 28.

97. See Chapter V, p. 133, of the present study.

98. Copland, "The Composer in Industrial America," p. 115.

99. Copland, "Composer from Brooklyn," p. 168.

100. See Berger, *Aaron Copland*, pp. 27, 76, 93; Smith, *Aaron Copland*, pp. 289, 293; Thomson, *American Music Since 1910*, pp. 53-55.

101. Copland, *The New Music*, p. 136.

102. Ibid., pp. 136-37.

103. Kathleen Hoover and John Cage, *Virgil Thomson* (New York: Thomas Yoseloff, 1959), p. 253. Actually, three movements of the *Symphony* were completed in 1926; Hoover and Cage, *Virgil Thomson*, p. 143. Thomson attributes the late premiere of his *Symphony* to Koussevitzky, who apparently disapproved of the last movement; Thomson, *Virgil Thomson*, pp. 72, 131.

104. Thomson, *American Music Since 1910*, pp. 53-54.

105. Ibid., p. 55.

106. Ibid.

107. See Chapters IV and V, pp. 96-97 and pp. 119-120, of the present study.

108. Smith, *Aaron Copland*, p. 165.

109. Copland, *The Second Hurricane* (New York: Boosey and Hawkes, 1957), pp. 98-103. Copland took "The Capture of General Burgoyne" from the *Series of Old American Songs, No. 5*, Brown University Harris Collection of American Poetry and Plays (Providence: Brown University Press, 1936), p. 15. His quotation of the music is literal, although the text is altered.

110. Berger, *Aaron Copland*, pp. 65-71.

111. Copland, "Composer from Brooklyn," pp. 164-65.

112. See Smith, *Aaron Copland*, pp. 175-76; and Hugo Cole, "Popular Elements in Copland's Music," *Tempo*, 96 (Winter, 1970-71), pp. 4-10.

113. Levant, *A Smattering of Ignorance*, p. 243.

114. Smith, *Aaron Copland*, pp. 186-87.

115. Ibid., p. 184.

Both Stravinsky's and Copland's ballets have gained much of their popularity as orchestral suites played in concert halls or recorded.

116. Copland, "Composer from Brooklyn," p. 163.

117. See, for instance, Peter Garvie, "Aaron Copland," *Canadian Music Journal* VI/2 (Winter, 1962), p. 8.

118. In 1945, Copland arranged a suite for full orchestra from the ballet that has become the standard concert version. He cut little from the score, merely a few sections necessary for, as he put it, "choreographic purposes"; the main section eliminated immediately follows the introduction of "Simple Gifts," which in a concert version would seem an interruption. The suite is now available for both full and chamber orchestras, and a recording of the original score has been released; Copland, "A Talk with Philip Ramey," *Copland Conducts Copland: Appalachian Spring,* Columbia M 32736.

On Elizabeth Sprague Coolidge, see Elliott Carter, "Coolidge Crusade; WPA; New York Season," *Modern Music* XVI/1 (November–December, 1938), pp. 33-38. Hindemith's ballet was *Hérodiade;* Milhaud's was *Jeux de Printemps.*

119. Smith, in *Aaron Copland,* pp. 195-98, outlines the action in more detail. See also Thomson, "Two Ballets," *The Art of Judging Music* (New York: Alfred A. Knopf, 1948), pp. 161-64.

120. Copland took "Simple Gifts" from Edward Deming Andrews, *The Gift to Be Simple* (New York: J. J. Augustin, 1940), a history of music within the Shaker religious community; see Smith, *Aaron Copland,* p. 195.

121. Smith, *Aaron Copland,* p. 197.

122. Virgil Thomson, "Virgil Thomson: American Music and Music Criticism," edited by Barbara Zuck, *The Otterbein Miscellany* XII/1 (December, 1976), p. 18.

123. Herbert Kubly, "America's No. 1 Composer," *Esquire* XXIX/4 (April, 1948), pp. 57, 143-45.

124. Copland, cited in Rockwell, "Copland, at 75," p. 48.

125. Harold Schonberg, "He Wanted to Reach Us," *The New York Times* (February 28, 1971), Sec. 2, p. 15.

More than a hint of such a feeling is apparent in a letter from Copland to Claire Reis dated August 2, 1963 (Letters File, Music Division, New York Public Library), in which he remarks how difficult it is to adapt when the attention seems to be on the younger generation.

126. Kate Hevner Mueller, in *Twenty-Seven Major Symphony Orchestras* (Bloomington: Indiana University Studies, 1973), pp. li-lii, lvii, substantiates this claim in the orchestral repertory, at least. Copland's music has been both the American music most played by orchestras and played by the most orchestras since 1945.

127. Peter Evans, "Copland's Middle Way," *The Listener* LXIII/1626 (April 14, 1960), p. 684.

128. Wilfred Mellers, "Language and Function in American Music," *Scrutiny* X/4 (April, 1942), pp. 347-51.

Chapter 12

1. Oscar Levant, *A Smattering of Ignorance* (New York: Doubleday, Doran, 1940), p. 229.

2. Nicolas Slonimsky, *Music Since 1900* (third enlarged edition; New York: Coleman-Ross, 1949), p. 348. Others represented on Yaddo programs were Ives, Gruenberg, Nicolai Berezowsky, Vivian Fine, Israel Citkowitz, and the Mexican composers Carlos Chavez and Silverstro Revueltas.

3. See Chapter XI, pp. 253-54, of the present study.

4. Henry Cowell, "Trends in American Music," *American Composers on American Music* (New York: Frederick Ungar, 1962; originally published in 1933), p. 13.

5. Roy D. Welch, "The Musician and Society," *M.T.N.A. Proceedings, 1935*, p. 75.

6. Charles Seeger, "Interview with Barbara Zuck," June 19, 1976.

7. Aaron Copland, in "The American Composer Gets a Break," *American Mercury* XXXIV/136 (April, 1935), p. 488, noted that on February 28, 1934, three American operas were simultaneously being performed in New York City: George Antheil's *Helen Retires* at the Juilliard School of Music, Virgil Thomson's *Four Saints in Three Acts* on Broadway, and Howard Hanson's *Merry Mount* at the Metropolitan Opera.

8. William Schuman became the first composer to receive the Pulitzer Prize in Music in 1943 for *A Free Song*, a cantata to a text by Walt Whitman. Howard Hanson received the award in 1944 for his *Symphony No. 4;* Claire R. Reis, *Composers in America* (New York: Macmillan, 1947), pp. 164, 319. As mentioned in Chapter XI, p. 266, Copland received the award in 1945 for *Appalachian Spring*.

9. David D. Van Tassel, "Editor's Preface," Charles C. Alexander, *Nationalism in American Thought, 1930-1945* (Chicago: Rand McNally, 1969), p. ix; see also Alexander's discussion of the War's end, pp. 224-29.

10. Cowell, "Trends in American Music," p. 13.

11. Aaron Copland, "Remarks to Lukas Foss, " Brooklyn Academy of Music Concert, March 30, 1974.

Bibliography

Books, Dissertations, Pamphlets

Abrahams, Roger D. and Foss, George. *Anglo-American Folksong Style.* Englewood Cliffs, New Jersey: Prentice-Hall, 1968.

Alexander, Charles C. *Nationalism in American Thought, 1930–1945.* Preface by David D. Van Tassel, Chicago: Rand McNally, 1969.

The American College Dictionary. New York: Random House, 1958.

Andrews, Edward Deming. *The Gift to be Simple.* New York: J. J. Augustin, 1940.

Annals of Opera, 1597–1940. Second Edition. Genève: Societas Bibliographica, 1955.

Antheil, George. *Bad Boy of Music.* Garden City, New York: Doubleday, Doran, 1945.

Armitage, Merle. *George Gershwin.* New York: Longmans, Green, 1938.

Arvey, Verna. *Choreographic Music.* New York: E. P. Dutton, 1941.

_____. *William Grant Still.* New York: J. Fischer, 1939.

Austin, William W. *Music in the 20th Century.* New York: W. W. Norton, 1966.

_____. *"Susanna," "Jeannie," and "The Old Folks at Home."* New York: Macmillan, 1975.

Baker, Theodore. *Über die Musik der nordamerikanischen Wilden.* Leipzig: Breitkopf und Haertel, 1882.

Baker's Biographical Dictionary of Musicians. Fifth edition, revised and edited by Nicolas Slonimsky. New York: G. Schirmer, 1958.

Barbour, J. Murray. *The Church Music of William Billings.* East Lansing: Michigan State University Press, 1960.

Baskerville, David Ross. "Jazz Influence on Art Music to Mid-Century." Ph.D. dissertation, University of California, Los Angeles, 1965.

Berger, Arthur. *Aaron Copland.* New York: Oxford University Press, 1953.

Bernstein, Leonard. *The Joy of Music.* New York: Simon and Schuster, 1965.

Bio-Bibliographical Index of Musicians in the United States of America from Colonial Times. Foreword by Harold Spivacke. Washington, D.C.: WPA Historical Records Survey, 1941.

Birge, Edward Bailey. *History of Public School Music in the United States.* Philadelphia: Oliver Ditson, [1937].

Blitzstein, Marc. "Notebooks." [1934.] *Marc Blitzstein Papers.* Wisconsin State Historical Society.

Borgman, George Allan. "Nationalism in Contemporary American Music." M.M. thesis, Indiana University, 1953.

Bowles, Paul. *Without Stopping.* New York: G. P. Putnam's Sons, 1972.

Boyden, David D. *An Introduction to Music.* New York: Alfred A. Knopf, 1956.

Broder, Nathan. *Samuel Barber.* New York: G. Schirmer, 1954.

Brown, John Mason. *Two On The Aisle.* New York: W. W. Norton, 1938.

Burton, Frederick R. *American Primitive Music.* New York: Moffat, Yard, 1909.

Canon, Cornelius B. "The Federal Music Project of the Works Progress Administration: Music in a Democracy." Ph.D. dissertation, University of Minnesota, 1963.

Chase, Gilbert, ed. *The American Composer Speaks.* Baton Rouge: Louisiana State University Press, 1966.

_____. *America's Music.* Revised second edition. New York: McGraw-Hill, 1966.

_____, ed. *Music in Radio Broadcasting.* New York: McGraw-Hill, 1946.

Clurman, Harold. *The Fervent Years.* Originally 1945. New York: Hill and Wang, 1957.

Comment and Criticism on the Work of Henry F. Gilbert, Composer. New York: H. H. Gray, [1926].

The Composers Forum 25th Anniversary Survey. New York: The Composers Forum, 1961.

"The Composers' Fund." [1933.] League of Composers Clippings File. Music Division, New York Public Library.

Copland, Aaron. *Copland on Music.* New York: W. W. Norton, 1963.

_____. *Music and Imagination.* New York: Mentor Books, 1952.

_____. *The New Music, 1900–1960.* Revised and enlarged edition. New York: W. W. Norton, 1969.

Courlander, Harold. *Negro Folk Music, U.S.A.* New York: Columbia University Press, 1963.

Cowell, Henry, ed. *American Composers on American Music.* Originally 1933. New York: Frederick Ungar, 1962.

_____. and Cowell, Sidney Robertson. *Charles Ives and His Music.* New York: Oxford University Press, 1955.

Crane, Milton. *The Roosevelt Era.* New York: Boni and Gaer, 1947.

Curtis, Natalie. *The Indian's Book.* New York: Harper and Brothers, 1907.

Davis, Kenneth S. *Experience of War.* Garden City, New York: Doubleday, 1965.

Denisoff, R. Serge. *Great Day Coming.* Urbana: University of Illinois Press, 1971.

_____. *Songs of Protest, War and Peace.* Santa Barbara, California: ABC-Clio, 1973.

Densmore, Francis. *The American Indians and Their Music.* New York: The Woman's Press, 1926.

DeVere, Schele. *Americanisms: The English of the New World.* New York: C. Scribner, 1972.

Dietz, Robert J. "The Operatic Style of Marc Blitzstein in the American 'Agit-Prop' Era." Ph.D. dissertation, University of Iowa, 1970.

Downes, Olin. *Olin Downes on Music.* New York: Simon and Schuster, 1957.

Draper, Theodore. *American Communism and Soviet Russia.* New York: Viking Press, 1960.

Einstein, Alfred. *Greatness in Music.* Translated by Cesar Saerchinger. New York: Oxford University Press, 1941.

Ellison, Alfred. "The Composer Under Twentieth Century Political Ideologies." Ed.D. dissertation, Teachers College, Columbia University, 1949.

Engel, Lehman. *Words with Music.* New York: The Macmillan Co., 1972.

Epstein, Melech. *The Jew and Communism, 1919–1941.* New York: Trade Union Sponsoring Committee, 1959.

Ewen, David, ed. *American Composers Today.* New York: H. W. Wilson, 1949.

_____, ed. *Composers Since 1900.* New York: H. W. Wilson, 1969.

_____, ed. *The New Book of Modern Composers.* New York: Alfred A. Knopf, 1961.

Farwell, Arthur, and Denby, W. Dermot. *Music in America.* Vol. IV of *The Art of Music.* Edited by Daniel Gregory Mason. New York: The National Society of Music, 1915.

Farwell, Brice. *A Guide to the Music of Arthur Farwell.* Briarcliff Manor, New York, 1972.

Feather, Leonard. *From Satchmo to Miles.* New York: Stein and Day, 1972.

Final Report on the WPA Program, 1935–43. Washington, 1946.

Finkelstein, Sidney. *Composer and Nation.* New York: International Publishers, 1960.

Fletcher, Alice C. *Indian Story and Song from North America.* Boston: Maynard and Co., 1915.

Foster, George. *Music.* Vol. VII of *Works Progress Administration, Work Projects Administration: Record of Program Operation and Accomplishment, 1935-43.* n.p., 1943.

Frederickson, George M. *The Inner Circle.* New York: Harper and Row, 1963.

Gerson, Robert A. *Music in Philadelphia.* Westport, Connecticut: Greenwood Press, 1970.

Gilman, Lawrence. *Edward MacDowell: A Study.* Reprint of 1908 edition. New York: Da Capo Press, 1969.

Goldberg, Isaac. *George Gershwin, A Study in American Music.* New York: Frederick Ungar, 1931.

Gottschalk, Louis Moreau. *Notes of a Pianist.* Edited by Jeanne Behrend. New York: Alfred A. Knopf, 1964.

The Gramaphone Shop Encyclopedia of Recorded Music. Third edition. Westport, Connecticut: Greenwood Publishers, 1970.

Guthrie, Woody. *Bound for Glory.* New York: E. P. Dutton, 1968. First Published in 1943.

Guttmann, Allen, and Ziegler, Benjamin Munn, eds. *Communism, the Courts and the Constitution.* Boston: D. C. Heath, 1964.

Haggin, B. H. *Music Observed.* New York: Oxford University Press, 1964.

_____. *35 Years of Music.* New York: Horizon Press, 1974.

Hanke, Lewis, ed. *Do the Americans Have a Common History? A Critique of the Bolton Theory.* New York: Alfred A. Knopf, 1964.

Hartz, Louis. *The Liberal Tradition in America.* New York: Harcourt, Brace, 1955.

"Herbert Haufrecht." New York: Broadcast Music, Inc., 195?.

Hindemith, Paul. *A Composer's World: Horizons and Limitations.* Cambridge, Massachusetts: Harvard University Press, 1952.

Hitchcock, H. Wiley. *Music in the United States: A Historical Introduction.* Second edition. Englewood Cliffs, New Jersey: Prentice-Hall, 1974.

Hoover, Kathleen, and Cage, John. *Virgil Thomson.* New York: Thomas Yoseloff, 1959.

Hopkins, Harry. *Spending to Save.* New York: W. W. Norton, 1936.

Houseman, John. *Run-Through.* New York: Simon and Schuster, 1972.

Howard, John Tasker. *Our American Music.* Third edition. New York: Thomas Y. Crowell, 1954.

_____. *Our Contemporary Composers.* New York: Thomas Y. Crowell, 1942.

_____, and Bellows, George Kent. *A Short History of American Music in America.* New York: Thomas Y. Crowell, 1967.

_____, and Lyons, James. *Modern Music.* Revised edition. New York: Mentor Books, 1942.

Huntley, John, and Manvill, Roger. *The Technique of Film Music.* London: Focal Press, 1957.

Index to American Composers. [WPA Federal Music Project, WPA Music Program, 1935-1940.] Music Division, Library of Congress.

The Institute of American Music of the University of Rochester; American Composers' Concerts and Festivals of American Music, 1925–1971, Cumulative Report. Rochester, New York, 1972.

Ives, Charles. *Essays Before a Sonata.* Edited by Howard Boatwright. New York: W. W. Norton, 1970.

_____. *Memos.* Edited by John Kirkpatrick. New York: W. W. Norton, 1972.

Jackson, George Pullen. *White Spirituals in the Southern Uplands.* Chapel Hill, 1933.

Jones, F. O., ed. *A Handbook of American Music and Musicians Containing Biographies of American Musicians, and Histories of the Principal Musical Institutions, Firms and Societies.* Canaseraga, New York: F. O. Jones, 1886.

Kaplan, Mordecai M. *Questions Jews Ask.* New York: Reconstructionist Press, 1956.

Kemp, Ian. *Hindemith.* London: Oxford University Press, 1970.

Kendall, Alan. *The Tender Tyrant.* London: MacDonald and James, 1976.

Kerr, Margaret, and Carr, Betty. "Federal Relief Administration and the Arts." Unpublished typescript, 1945. American Council of Learned Societies.

Kirk, Edgar Lee. "Toward American Music, A Study of the Life and Music of Arthur Farwell." Ph.D. dissertation, University of Rochester, 1958.

Kohn, Hans. *American Nationalism.* New York: Macmillan, 1957.

_____. *The Idea of Nationalism.* New York: Macmillan, 1944.

_____. *Prophets and People.* New York: Macmillan, 1946.

Lang, Paul Henry. *Music in Western Civilization.* New York: W. W. Norton, 1941.

_____. ed. *One Hundred Years of Music in America.* New York: G. Schirmer, 1961.

LaPrade, Ernest. *Broadcasting Music.* New York: Rinehart, 1947.

Leach, Maria, ed. *Standard Dictionary of Folklore, Mythology, and Legend.* New York: Funk and Wagnalls, 1955.

League of Composers. Broadcast and Records File. Music Division, New York Public Library.

Levant, Oscar. *A Smattering of Ignorance.* New York: Doubleday and Doran, 1940.

List of Musical Compositions for Small Orchestra Commissioned for American School of the Air by the Music Library of CBS, 1939-1940 Season. CBS Department of Program Information.

Lomax, Alan, ed. *Hard Hitting Songs for Hard-Hit People.* New York: Oak Publications, 1967.

Lomax, John A. *Adventures of a Ballad Hunter.* New York: The Macmillan Co., 1947.

_____. *Cowboy Songs and Other Frontier Ballads.* New York: 1910.

_____, and Lomax, Alan. *American Ballads and Folksongs.* New York: Macmillan, 1934.

_____. *Folksong U.S.A.* New York: Duell, Sloan, and Pearce, 1947.

Lowens, Irving. *Music and Musicians in Early America.* New York: W. W. Norton, 1964.

Machlis, Joseph. *Introduction to Contemporary Music.* New York: W. W. Norton, 1961.

Mangione, Jerre. *The Dream and the Deal.* Boston: Little, Brown, 1972.

Marc Blitzstein Papers. Wisconsin State Historical Society.

Mason, Daniel Gregory. *Beethoven and His Forerunners.* New York: Macmillan, 1904.

_____. *Contemporary Composers.* New York: Macmillan, 1918.

_____. *The Dilemma of American Music.* New York: Macmillan, 1928.

_____. *From Grieg to Brahms.* New York: Macmillan, 1908.

_____. *The Romantic Composers.* New York: Macmillan, 1906.

_____. *Tune In, America.* New York: Alfred A. Knopf, 1931.

Mathews, Miford M., ed. *A Dictionary of Americanisms.* Chicago: University of Chicago Press, 1951.

Maust, Wilbur Richard. "The Symphonies of Anthony Philip Heinrich Based on American Themes." Ph.D. dissertation, Indiana University, 1973.

May, Henry F. *The End of American Innocence.* New York: Alfred A. Knopf, 1959.

McKay, David P., and Crawford, Richard. *William Billings of Boston.* Princeton: Princeton University Press, 1975.

McKinzie, Richard D. *The New Deal for Artists.* Princeton: Princeton University Press, 1973.

Mellers, Wilfred. *Music in a New Found Land.* London: Barrie and Rockliff, 1964.

_____. *Music and Society.* London: Dennis Dobson Ltd., 1950.

Mencken, H. L. *The American Language.* Fourth edition, corrected, enlarged, and rewritten. New York: Alfred A. Knopf, 1943.

Minogue, K. R. *Nationalism.* Baltimore: Penguin Books, 1970.

Mueller, Kate Hevner. *Twenty-Seven Major Symphony Orchestras.* Bloomington: Indiana University Studies, 1973.

Musselman, Joseph A. *Music in the Cultured Generation.* Evanston: Northwestern University Press, 1971.

Nash, Roderick. *The Nervous Generation: American Thought, 1917–1930.* Chicago: Rand McNally, 1970.

Nathan, Hans. *Dan Emmett and the Rise of Early Minstrelry.* Norman: University of Oklahoma Press, 1962.

Nettl, Bruno. *Folk Music in the United States.* Detroit: Wayne State University Press, 1960.

_____. *Folk and Traditional Music of the Western Continents.* Englewood Cliffs, New Jersey: Prentice-Hall, 1965.

Newman, Philip Edward. *The Songs of Charles Ives, (1874–1954).* 2 volumes. Ann Arbor, Michigan: University Microfilms, 1967.

North, Joseph, ed. *New Masses. An Anthology of the Rebel Thirties.* International Publishers, 1969.

Offergeld, Robert. *Centennial Catalogue of the Published and Unpublished Compositions of Louis Moreau Gottschalk.* New York: Ziff-Davis, 1970.

Oxford English Dictionary. Oxford: Clarendon Press, 1933. Corrected edition, 1961.

Pells, Richard H. *Radical Visions and American Dreams.* New York: Harper and Row, 1973.

Perlis, Vivian. *Charles Ives Remembered.* New York: W. W. Norton, 1974.

Perrett, Geoffrey. *Days of Sadness, Years of Triumph.* New York: Coward, McMann and Geoghegen.

Pettis, Ashley. *Music: Now and Then.* New York: Coleman-Ross, 1955.

Phillips, Cabell. *From the Crash to the Blitz.* New York: The Macmillan Co., 1969.

The Political Almanac 1952. New York: B. C. Forbes, 1952.

Pullen, John J. *Patriotism in America.* New York: American Heritage Press, 1971.

Reis, Claire R. *Composers In America.* New York: Macmillan, 1947.

_____. *Composers, Conductors, and Critics.* New York: Oxford University Press, 1955.

Reti, Rudolf. *Tonality—Atonality—Pantonality.* New York: Macmillan, 1958.

Reuss, Richard A. "American Folklore and Left-Wing Politics, 1927–57." Ph.D. dissertation, Indiana University, 1971.

Rogers, Delmar. "Nineteenth Century Music in New York City as Reflected in the Career of George Frederick Bristow." Ph.D. dissertation, University of Michigan, 1967.

Rosenfeld, Paul. *By Way of Art.* Freeport, New York: Books for Libraries Press, 1967. Reprint of 1928 edition.

_____. *Discoveries of a Music Critic.* New York: Harcourt, Brace, 1936.

_____. *An Hour with American Music.* Philadelphia: J. B. Lippincott, 1929.

_____. *Musical Chronical (1917–1923).* New York: Harcourt, Brace, 1923.

_____. *Musical Impressions: Selections from Paul Rosenfeld's Criticism.* Edited by Herbert A. Leibowitz. New York: Hill and Wang, 1969.

Rossiter, Frank R. "Charles Ives and American Culture: The Process of Development, 1874-1921." Ph.D. dissertation, Princeton University, 1970.

_____. *Charles Ives and His America.* New York: Liveright, 1975.

Sabanyeff, Leonid. *Modern Russian Composers.* Translated by Judith A. Joffe. New York: International Publishers, 19?.

Sachs, Curt. *Our Musical Heritage.* New York: Prentice-Hall, 1955.

_____. *Rhythm and Tempo.* New York: W. W. Norton, 1953.

Salzman, Eric. *Twentieth Century Music: An Introduction.* Englewood Cliffs, New Jersey: Prentice-Hall, 1967.

Saminsky, Lazare. *Music of Our Day: Essentials and Prophecies.* New York: Thomas Y. Crowell, 1932.

Sayler, Oliver. *Revolt in the Arts.* New York: Brentano's, 1930.

Schlesinger, Arthur M., Jr. *The Age of Roosevelt; The Crisis of the Old Order, 1919–1933.* Cambridge, Massachusetts: Riverside Press, 1957.

Schreiber, Flora Rheta, and Persichetti, Vincent. *William Schuman.* New York: G. Schirmer, 1954.

Schwartz, Boris. *Music and Musical Life in Soviet Russia, 1917-1970.* New York: W. W. Norton, 1973.

Seeger, Pete. *The Incompleat Folksinger.* Edited by Jo Metcalf Schwartz. New York: Simon and Schuster, 1972.

Sessions, Roger. *Reflections on the Musical Life in the United States.* New York: Merlin Press, 1956.

Shafter, Alfred M. *Musical Copyright.* Chicago: Callaghan and Company, 1939.

Shannon, David A. *The Decline of American Communism.* New York: Harcourt, Brace, 1959.

Shattuck, Roger. *The Banquet Years, 1885-1918.* Garden City, New York: Anchor Books, 1961.

Siegmeister, Elie. *Music and Society.* London: Workers' Music Association, 1943. Originally published by Critics' Group of New York, 1938.

_____, ed. *Music Lover's Handbook.* New York: William Morrow, 1943.

Slonimsky, Nicolas. *Music Since 1900.* Third edition. New York: Coleman-Ross, 1949.

Smith, Cecil. *Musical Comedy in America.* New York: Theatre Art Books, 1950.

Smith, Julia Frances. *Aaron Copland.* New York: E. P. Dutton, 1955.

Sonneck, Oscar George. *Early Concert Life in America.* New York: Musurgia Publishers, 1949. Reissue of 1907 edition.

Standard Dictionary of the English Language. Chicago: Encyclopedia Britannica, 1958.

Stavrianos, L. S. *The World Since 1500.* Englewood Cliffs, New Jersey: Prentice-Hall, 1966.

Stearns, Marshall W. *The Story of Jazz.* New York: Oxford University Press, 1956.

Strong, George Templeton. *Diary of George Templeton Strong.* Edited by Alan Nevins and Milton H. Thomas. New York: Macmillan, 1952.

Talent Files-Radio. CBS Department of Program Information.

Terkel, Studs. *Hard Times; An Oral History of the Great Depression.* New York: Avon Books, 1970.

Thomas, Tony. *Music for the Movies.* S. Brunswick, New Jersey: A. S. Barnes, 1973.

Thompson, Oscar, ed. *Great Modern Composers.* New York: Dodd, Mead, 1941.

Thomson, Virgil. *American Music Since 1910.* New York: Holt, Rinehart and Winston, 1972.

_____. *The Art of Judging Music.* New York: Alfred A. Knopf, 1948.

_____. *Music Right and Left.* New York: Henry Holt, 1951.

_____. *The Musical Scene.* New York: Alfred A. Knopf, 1945.

_____. *The State of Music.* New York: Vintage Books, 1962. Revised from original 1939 edition.

_____. *Virgil Thomson.* London: Weidenfeld and Nicolson, 1967.

Trask, Katrina. *The Story of Yaddo.* [Privately printed,) 1923.

Ulrich, Homer. *A Centennial History of the Music Teachers National Association.* Cincinnati: M.T.N.A., 1976.

_____. *Symphonic Music; Its Evolution Since the Renaissance.* New York: Columbia University Press, 1952.

Upton, William Treat. *Anthony Philip Heinrich.* New York: Columbia University Press, 1939.

_____. *William Henry Fry.* New York: Thomas Y. Crowell, 1954.

Vaughn Williams, Ralph. *National Music.* New York: Oxford University Press, 1934.

Wetzel, Richard D. *Frontier Musicians on the Connoquenessing, Wabash, and Ohio.* Athens: Ohio University Press, 1976.

Who is Who in Music, 1941. Chicago: Lee Stern, 1940.

Wilgus, D. K. *Anglo-American Folksong Scholarship.* New Brunswick, New Jersey: Rutgers University Press, 1959.

Wooldridge, David. *Charles Ives: A Portrait.* London: Faber and Faber, 1975.

WPA Composers Forum [sic] *Transcripts.* [WPA Federal Music Project, 1935-39.] National Archives.

WPA Federal Music Project of New York City. *Monthly Report of Activities.* May, 1937.

WPA of New York City Programs File. Music Division. New York Public Library.

WPA of New York City. *Theatre of Music Pamphlet.* [1937.]

Yates, Peter. *Twentieth Century Music.* New York: Pantheon, 1967.

Yurchenko, Henrietta. *A Mighty Hard Road; The Woody Guthrie Story.* New York: McGraw-Hill, 1970.

Articles, Periodicals, Letters

A[dohmyan], L[an]. "Music," *Daily Worker* January 9, 1934, p. 5.

"America in Song, 1640-1940." *Daily Worker* January 20, 1939, p. 7.

"American Singers on Air." *Daily Worker* October 11, 1939, p. 7.

"An American Work." *The New York Times* February 11, 1934.

Ashley, Patricia. "Roy Harris." *Stereo Review* XXI/12 (December, 1968), pp. 63-72.

Atkinson, Brooks. Review. *The New York Times* October 6, 1932, p. 19.

Barber, Samuel. "Letter to Walter Damrosch," February 27, 1944. Letters File. Music Division. New York Public Library.

Barker, Virgil. "The Search for Americanism." *The Magazine of Art* 27/2 (February, 1934), pp. 51-52.

Barlow, Samuel L. M. "American Composers, XVII: Virgil Thomson." *Modern Music* XVIII/4 (May-June, 1941), pp. 242-47.

_____. "Blitzstein's Answer." *Modern Music* XVIII/2 (January-February, 1941), pp. 81-83.

Barr, Philip. "Opera in the Vernacular." *The Magazine of Art* 32/6 (June, 1939), pp. 356-57, 382-83.

Bartók, Béla. "The Influence of Peasant Music on Modern Music," and "The Significance of Folk Music." *Composers on Music.* Edited by Sam Morgenstern. New York: Pantheon Books, 1956.

Bauer, Marion, and Reis, Claire. "Twenty-five Years with the League of Composers." *The Musical Quarterly* XXXIV/1 (January, 1948), pp. 1-14.

Berger, Arthur. "Stravinsky and the Younger American Composers." *The American Composer Speaks.* Edited by Gilbert Chase. Baton Rouge: Louisiana State University Press, 1966.

_____. "The Young Composers' Group." *Trend* II/1 (April-May-June, 1933), pp. 26-28.

Berlin, Isaiah. "The Bent Twig: A Note on Nationalism." *Foreign Affairs* LI/1 (October, 1972), pp. 11-30.

Bernstein, Leonard. "Young American – William Schuman." *Modern Music* XIX/2 (January-February, 1942), pp. 97-99.

Blitzstein, Marc.   "Author of Famous 'Cradle Will Rock' Discusses Composer's Tasks."
   Daily Worker April 13, 1938, p. 7.
_____. "The Case for Modern Music," and "Second Generation."   *New Masses*
   XX/3 and 4 (July 14 and 21, 1936), p. 27, p. 38.
_____."Coming – the Mass Audience."   *Modern Music* XIII/4 (May-June, 1936), pp.
   23-29.
_____. "Composers as Lecturers and in Concert."   *Modern Music* XIII/1 (Novem-
   ber–December, 1935), pp. 47-50.
_____. "Letter to John Houseman."   November 12, 1959.   *Marc Blitzstein Papers.*
   Wisconsin State Historical Society.
_____.   "London: Fourth Winter of the Blackout."   *Modern Music* XX/2
   (January–February, 1943), pp. 117-20.
_____. "Music and Theatre–1932." *Modern Music* IX/4 (May–June, 1932), pp. 164-68.
_____. "Notes on the Musical Theatre." *Theatre Arts* XXXIV/6 (June, 1950), pp. 30-31.
_____.   "Notes on the Program."   New York City Symphony, Leonard Bernstein,
   Music Director, Season 1945-46.
_____. "On Music and Words." *Theatre Arts* XXXIV/11 (November, 1950), pp. 52–53.
_____.   "On Writing Music for the Theatre."   *Modern Music* XVI/2 (January–
   February, 1938), pp. 81-85.
_____.   "The Phenomenon of Stravinsky."   *The Musical Quarterly* XXI/3 (July,
   1935), pp. 330-47.
_____.   "Popular Music – An Invasion: 1923–33."   *Modern Music* X/2 (January–
   February, 1933), pp. 96-102.
_____. "Second Workers Song Book." *Daily Worker* June 12, 1935, p. 5.
_____. "Towards a New Form." *The Musical Quarterly* XX/2 (April, 1934), pp. 213–18.
_____.   "Weill Scores for Johnny Johnson."   *Modern Music* XIV/1 (November–
   December, 1936), pp. 44-46.
Borowski, Felix.   "John Alden Carpenter." *The Musical Quarterly* XVI/4 (October, 1930),
   pp. 449-68.
Boross, L. F. "Soviet Music," *Daily Worker* April 7, 1936, p. 7.
Brant, Henry.   "Marc Blitzstein." *Modern Music* XXIII/3 (Summer, 1946), pp. 170-76.
Braudo, Eugen.   "The Russian Panorama."   *Modern Music* X/2 (January–February,
   1933), pp. 79-86.
Bristow, George Frederick.   "Letter."   *Dwight's Journal of Music* IV/23 (March 11,
   1854), p. 182.
Britten, Benjamin.   "England and the Folk-Art Problem."   *Modern Music* XVIII/2
   (January–February, 1941), pp. 71-75.
Broder, Nathan.   "The Music of William Schuman."   *The Musical Quarterly* XXXI/1
   (January, 1945), pp. 17-28.
Brown, John Mason.   "Ten Years Later." *The Saturday Review* XXXI/3 (January 17,
   1948), pp. 22-24.
Buchman, Carl.   "Composers Dedicate Works to the Band."   *Modern Music* XX/1
   (November–December, 1942), pp. 46-48.
Bukofzer, Manfred. "The New Nationalism." *Modern Music* XXIII/4 (Fall, 1946), pp. 243-47.
Burk, John N. *Boston Symphony Orchestra Programmes*, February 24, 1939, p. 780.
_____.   "The Democratic Ideal in Music."   *The Musical Quarterly* V/3 (July, 1919),
   pp. 316-28.
Burke, Kenneth.   "Two Brands of Piety."   *The Nation* 138/3582 (February 28, 1934),
   pp. 256-58.

Burr, Willard, Jr. "Musical Art-Creation in America." *Official Report* of the Eighth Annual Meeting of the M.T.N.A. (Cleveland, Ohio: July 2, 3 and 4, 1884), pp. 8-17.

Cadman, Charles Wakefield. "The 'Idealization' of Indian Music." *The Musical Quarterly* I/3 (July, 1915), pp. 387-96.

_____. "Letter to Charles Ives," January 26, 1943. Charles Ives Collection, Yale University.

Calverton, V. F. "Cultural Barometer." *Current History* XLVIII/4 (April, 1938), pp. 53-55.

Caper, C. L. "Musical Composition in America." *M.T.N.A. Official Report* 14 (1890), pp. 85-89.

Carpenter, John Alden. "Musical Inspiration is Universal." *Musical America* XXXI/2 (November 8, 1919), p. 19.

Carter, Elliott. "American Figure, with Landscape." *Modern Music* XX/4 (May–June, 1943), pp. 219-25.

_____. "Coolidge Crusade; WPA; New York Season." *Modern Music* XVI/1 (November–December, 1938), pp. 33-38.

_____. "Ives Today: His Vision and Challenge." *Modern Music* XXI/4 (May–June, 1944), pp. 199-202.

_____. "Once Again Swing; also 'American Music'." *Modern Music* XVI/2 (January–February, 1939), pp. 99-103.

_____. "Rhythmic Basis of American Music." *Score and I.M.A. Magazine* 12 (June, 1955), pp. 27-32.

Chapman, Ernest. "Britain Calls Music to the Colors." *Modern Music* XIX/2 (January–February, 1942), pp. 117-20.

Chase, Gilbert. "The Wa-Wan Press, A Chapter in American Enterprise." *The Wa-Wan Press*, Vol. I. Edited by Vera Brodsky Lawrence. 5 volumes. New York: Arno Press, 1970. Reissue of original Wa-Wan series, 1901–12, edited by Arthur Farwell.

"City College Presents 'Cradle Will Rock' Tonight." *Daily Worker* November 29, 1940, p. 7.

Clapham, John. "The Evolution of Dvořák's Symphony 'From the New World'." *The Musical Quarterly* XLIV/2 (April, 1958), pp. 167-83.

Clurman, Harold. "Paul Rosenfeld." *Modern Music* XXIII/3 (Summer, 1946), pp. 184-88.

Cole, Fannie L. Gwinner. "Silas Gamaliel Pratt." *The Dictionary of American Biography*, Vol. 8. New York: Scribner, [1959-].

Cole, Hugo. "Popular Elements in Copland's Music." *Tempo* 95 (Winter, 1970-71), pp. 4-10.

The Composer's News-Record, I (February, 1947). Published by the National Composer Members of the League of Composers.

"The Composers Organize: A Proclamation." *Modern Music* XV/2 (January–February, 1938), pp. 92-95.

Copland, Aaron. "The American Composer Gets a Break." *American Mercury* XXXIV/136 (April, 1935), pp. 488-92.

_____. "America's Young Men of Promise." *Modern Music* III/3 (March–April, 1926), pp. 13-20.

_____. "The Composer in America, 1923-1933." *Modern Music* X/2 (January–February, 1933), pp. 87-92.

_____. "The Composers Get Wise." *Modern Music* XVIII/1 (November–December, 1940), pp. 18-21.

_____. "The Composer and His Critic." *Modern Music* IX/4 (May–June, 1932), pp. 143-47.

_____. "From the '20s to the '40s and Beyond." *Modern Music* XX/2 (January–February, 1943), pp. 78-82.

_____. "Gabriel Fauré: A Neglected Master." *The Musical Quarterly* X/4 (October, 1924), pp. 573-86.

_____. "In Memory of Marc Blitzstein." *Marc Blitzstein Papers.* Wisconsin State Historical Society. Originally published in *Perspectives of New Music* II (Spring, 1964), pp. 6-7.

_____. "Jazz Structure and Influence." *Modern Music* IV/4 (May–June, 1927), pp. 9-14.

_____. "Letter to Barbara Zuck," July 18, 1974.

_____. "Letter to the Board of Directors," February 9, 1953. Letters File. Music Division. New York Public Library.

_____. "Letter to Claire R. Reis," August 2, 1963. Letters File. Music Division. New York Public Library.

_____. "Music Since 1920." *Modern Music* V/3 (March–April, 1928), pp. 16-20.

_____. "The Musical Scene Changes." *Twice A Year* 5/6 (Fall–Winter, 1940, Spring–Summer, 1941), pp. 340-43.

_____. "A Note on Young Composers." *Music Vanguard* I/1 (March–April, 1935), p. 16.

_____. "One Hundred and Fourteen Songs." *Modern Music* XI/2 (January–February, 1934), pp. 59-64.

_____. "Our Younger Generation Ten Years Later." *Modern Music* XIII/4 (May–June, 1936), pp. 3-11.

_____. "Remarks to Lukas Foss." Brooklyn Academy of Music Concert. March 30, 1974.

_____. "Second Thoughts on Hollywood." *Modern Music* XVII/3 (March–April, 1940), pp. 141-47.

_____. "Serge Koussevitsky and the American Composer." *The Musical Quarterly* XXX/3 (July, 1944), pp. 255-69.

_____. "A Talk with Philip Ramey." *Copland Conducts Copland: Appalachian Spring.* Columbia M 32736.

_____. "Workers Sing!" *New Masses* XI/10 (June 5, 1934), p. 28.

Cowell, Henry. "American Composers," and "The Development of Modern Music." *Proceedings of the Ohio State Educational Conference, 11th Annual Season.* Edited by Josephine MacLatchy. *Ohio State University Bulletin* XXXVI/3 (September 15, 1931), pp. 375-79.

_____. "The Flavour of American Music." *The Score and I.M.A. Magazine* 12 (June, 1955), pp. 5-8.

_____. "In Time of Bitter War." *Modern Music* XIX/2 (January–February, 1942), pp. 83-87.

_____. "Jazz Today." *Trend* II/4 (October–November, 1934), pp. 162-64.

_____. "New Musical Resources." *The American Composer Speaks.* Edited by Gilbert Chase. Baton Rouge: Louisiana State University Press, 1966.

_____. "Trends in American Music." *American Composers on American Music.* Originally 1933. New York: Frederick Ungar, 1962.

Cowell, Henry and Sidney Robertson. "Our Country Music." *Modern Music* XX/4 (May-June, 1943), pp. 243-47.

Cowell, Sidney Robertson. "White Spirituals." *Modern Music* XXI/1 (November–December, 1943), pp. 10-14.

Daily Worker. January 17, 1934, p. 5.

_____. February 8, 1934, p. 5.

_____. April 21, 1934, p. 7.

_____. February 10, 1935, p. 5.

_____. February 26, 1935, p. 5.

_____. March 23, 1935, p. 5.

_____. April 12, 1935, p. 5.

_____. April 23, 1935, p. 5.

_____. May 16, 1935, p. 5.

_____. August 23, 1935, p. 5.

_____. October 8, 1935, p. 5.

_____. February 10, 1936, p. 7.

_____. February 17, 1936, p. 7.

_____. February 24, 1937, p. 7.

_____. April 1, 1936, p. 7.

_____. June 24, 1937, p. 7.

_____. February 2, 1939, p. 7.

Darrell, R. D. *New Masses* XXVI/1 (December 28, 1937), p. 27.

Deutsch, Babette. "America in the Arts." *The Musical Quarterly* VII/3 (July, 1921), pp. 303-8.

Diamond, David. "The Composer and Film Music." *Decision* I/3 (March, 1941), pp. 57-60.

Downes, Olin. "An American Composer." *The Musical Quarterly* IV/1 (January, 1918), pp. 23-36.

_____. "Audience Cheers Blitzstein Work." *The New York Times* April 2, 1946, p. 23.

_____. "Composers' Forum." *The New York Times* May 21, 1950, Sec. 10, p. 7.

_____. "Composers on War." *The New York Times* October 10, 1943, Sec. 2, p. 7.

_____. "Henry Gilbert: Nonconformist." *A Birthday Offering to Carl Engel.* Edited by Gustave Reese. New York: G. Schirmer, 1943.

_____. "J. A. Carpenter, American Craftsman." *The Musical Quarterly* XVI/4 (October, 1930), pp. 443-48.

_____. "Laboratory for Native Composers." *The New York Times* January 10, 1937, Sec. 10, p. 7.

_____. "Music in the Changing Social Order – The Viewpoint of a Critic." *National Federation of Music Clubs: Book of Proceedings, 1933-35.* Edited by Hazel G. Weaver. Ithaca, New York: National Federation of Music Clubs, 1935, pp. 14-23.

_____. "The Native Essence." *The New York Times* December 31, 1939, Sec. 9, p. 7.

_____. Review of Harris's *Third Symphony.* *The New York Times* March 12, 1939, Sec. 3, p. 6.

Dunham, Franklin. "Music in a Radio-Minded World." *National Federation of Music Clubs: Book of Proceedings, 1933–35.* Edited by Hazel G. Weaver. Ithaca, New York: National Federation of Music Clubs, 1935, pp. 63-67.

Dvořák, Antonín. "Music in America." *Harper's* Magazine, XC (February, 1895), pp. 428-34.

Dwight's Journal of Music, I/3 (April 24, 1852), p. 32.

_____, I/6 (July 24, 1852), p. 126.

_____, II/26 (April 2, 1853), pp. 201-2.

_____, IV/3 (October 22, 1853), p. 22.

_____, IV/18, 18, 21-25 (February 4, 11, 25, March 4, 11, 18, 25, 1854), pp. 138, 140, 146, 163, 171, 173, 182, 186, 195.

_____, VIII/1 (October 6, 1855), p. 6.

_____, X/12 (December 20, 1856), p. 93.

_____, XXI/5 (July 12, 1862), pp. 119-20.

_____, XXI/25 (September 20, 1862), p. 196.

_____, XXXVI/7, 22 and 25 (July 8, 1876, February 3 and March 17, 1877), pp. 226, 378, 405.

Einstein, Alfred. "The Composer, the State and Today." *Modern Music* XIII/1 (November–December, 1935), pp. 3-12.

_____. "National and Universal Music." *Modern Music* XIV/1 (November–December, 1936), pp. 3-11.

_____. "Universality and Music Today." *Modern Music* XVI/3 (March–April, 1939), pp. 150-55.

_____. "War, Nationalism, Tolerance." *Modern Music* CVII/1 (October–November, 1939), pp. 3-9.

E. [isler], H.[ans]. "A New Music League." *Daily Worker* February 10, 1936, p. 7.

Ellsworth, Ray. "Americans on Microgroove, Parts I and II." *High Fidelity* VI/7 and 8 (July and August, 1956), pp. 63-69, 60-66.

Elwell, Herbert. "Harris' Folksong Symphony." *Modern Music* XVIII/2 (January–February, 1941), pp. 113-14.

_____. "Nadia Boulanger: A Tribute." *Modern Music* XV/2 (January–February, 1938), pp. 76-80.

Emerson, Ralph Waldo. "The American Scholar." *American Prose and Poetry*, Part I. Edited by Norman Foerster. Fourth edition. Boston: Houghton Mifflin, 1957, pp. 480-89.

Engel, Lehman. "Music in the Theatre." *Theatre Arts* XXXIV/11 (November, 1950), pp. 49-50.

_____. "Songs of the American Wars." *Modern Music* XIX/3 (March–April, 1942), pp. 147-51.

Etude, III/9 (September, 1885), p. 181.

Evans, Edwin. "Half-Time in England." *Modern Music* III/4 (May–June, 1926), pp. 10-15.

Evans, Peter. "Copland's Middle Way." *The Listener* LXIII/1620 (April 14, 1960), p. 684.

Evett, Robert. "The Harmonic Idiom of Roy Harris." *Modern Music* XXIII/2 (Spring, 1946), pp. 100-107.

Ewen, David. "New Blood in American Music." *Musical Courier* CVII/12 (September 16, 1933), p. 6.

Eyer, Ronald F. "Meet the Composer: Aaron Copland." *Musical America* 63/16 (December 10, 1943), pp. 7, 27.

Farwell, Arthur. "An Affirmation of American Music." *The American Composer Speaks.* Edited by Gilbert Chase. Baton Rouge: Louisiana State University Press, 1966.

_____. "Introduction." *American Indian Melodies.* Newton Center, Massachusetts: The Wa-Wan Press, 1901.

_____. "Introduction." The Wa-Wan Press, Vol. V (Spring, 1906).

_____. "A Letter to American Composers." Originally 1933. *The Wa-Wan Press.* Vol. I, Edited by Vera Brodsky Lawrence, 5 volumes. New York: Arno Press, 1970. Reissue of original Wa-Wan Series, 1901–1912, edited by Arthur Farwell.

_____. "Pioneering for American Music." *Modern Music* XII/3 (March–April, 1935), pp. 116-22.

_____. "Roy Harris." *The Musical Quarterly* XVIII/1 (January, 1932), pp. 18-32.

Finney, Ross Lee. "The American Composer and the War." *M.T.N.A. Proceedings, 1942*, pp. 31-51.

Flanagan, William. "Aaron Copland." *HiFi/Stereo Review* 16 (June, 1966), pp. 43-54.

Foster, Joe. "Hans [*sic*] Eisler." *Daily Worker* March 1, 1935, p. 5.

Fox, Charles Warren. "Rochester's Fall Festival of Americans." *Modern Music* XXIII/1 (Winter, 1946), pp. 62-63.

"Free Scholarship Prize in Music School Contest." *Daily Worker* August 23, 1935, p. 5.

Fried, Alexander. "For the People." *Modern Music* IV/4 (May–June, 1927), pp. 33-37.

Fry, William Henry. "Letter to the New York *Musical World and Times*." March 16, 1853. *Dwight's Journal of Music* II/26 (April 2, 1853), pp. 201-2.

_____. "Mr. Fry's 'American Ideas' About Music." *Dwight's Journal of Music* II/23 (March 12, 1853), p. 181.

_____. "Prefatory Remarks." *Leonora.* Philadelphia: E. Ferrett, 1846.

Fuller, Donald. "Americans to the Fore – New York, 1941–42." *Modern Music* XIX/2 (January-February, 1942), pp. 109-15.

_____. "New York, Spring, '42; Music of the Americas." *Modern Music* XIX/4 (May–June, 1942), pp. 254-60.

_____. "A Symphonist Goes to the Folk Sources." *Musical America* 68 (February, 1948), pp. 29, 256, 397.

"Fugitives," "Inside Germany." *Modern Music* XVI/4 (May-June, 1939), pp. 203-13.

F., N. "They Shot Joe Hill." *Daily Worker* November 20, 1935, p. 5.

Garrett, Anita. "Eisler Praises Chorus Group." *Daily Worker* February 24, 1936, p. 7.

Garvie, Peter. "Aaron Copland." *Canadian Music Journal* VI/2 (Winter, 1962), pp. 3–12.

Geismar, Maxwell. "Introduction." *New Masses Anthology.* International Publishers, 1969.

Gershwin, George. "The Composer in the Machine Age." *The American Composer Speaks.* Edited by Gilbert Chase. Baton Rouge: Louisiana State University Press, 1966. Originally in *Revolt in the Arts.* Edited by Oliver M. Sayler. New York: Brentano's 1930.

_____. "The Relation of Jazz to American Music." *American Composers on American Music.* Edited by Henry Cowell. Originally 1933. New York: Frederick Ungar, 1962.

_____. "Rhapsody in Catfish Row." *George Gershwin.* Edited by Merle Armitage. New York: Longman Green, 1938.

Gilbert, Henry F. "The American Composer." *The American Composer Speaks.* Edited by Gilbert Chase. New York: McGraw-Hill, 1955.

_____. "Folk-Music in Art-Music – A Discussion and a Theory." *The Musical Quarterly* III/4 (October, 1917), pp. 577-601.

_____. "Letter to Charles Ives," May 26, 1920. Charles Ives Collection. Yale University.

_____. "Letter to Claire R. Reis," September 13, 1927. Letters File. Music Division. New York Public Library.

Glanville-Hicks, Peggy. "Paul Bowles: American Composer." *Music and Letters* XXVI/2 (April, 1945), pp. 90-96.

Glenn, Charles. "Hollywood Meets Blitzstein." *Daily Worker* July 5, 1941, p. 7.

Gold, Michael. "Change the World!" *Daily Worker* June 4, 1934, p. 5.

_____. "Change the World!" *Daily Worker* June 5, 1934, p. 5.

_____. "Change the World!" *Daily Worker* June 14, 1934. p. 5.

_____. "Change the World!" *Daily Worker* November 23, 1934, p. 5.

_____. "Change the World!" *Daily Worker* January 1, 1936, p. 5.

_____. "Change the World!" *Daily Worker* January 2, 1936, p. 5.

_____. "What a World!" *Daily Worker* August 29, 1933, p. 6.

_____. "What a World!" *Daily Worker* September 20, 1933, p. 6.

_____. "What a World!" *Daily Worker* October 19, 1933, p. 5.

Goldman, Richard Franko. "Bands in War-Time." *Modern Music* XIX/3 (March–April, 1942), pp. 169-72.

_____. "The Music of Wallingford Riegger." *The Musical Quarterly* XXXVI/1 (January, 1950), pp. 39-61.

_____. "Wallingford Riegger." *HiFi/Stereo Review* XX/4 (April, 1968), pp. 57-67.

Goossens, Eugene. "The Public – Has It Changed?" *Modern Music* XX/2 (January February, 1943), pp. 71-77.

Grew, Sidney. "National Music and the Folk-Song." *The Musical Quarterly* VII/2 (April, 1921), pp. 172-85.

Hale, Edith. "Author and Composer Blitzstein." *Daily Worker* December 7, 1938, p. 7.

Haggin, B. H. "Music." *The Nation* 152/7 (February 15, 1941), p. 194.

Hanson, Howard. "American Procession at Rochester." *Modern Music* XIII/3 (March–April, 1936), pp. 22-28.

_____. "The Rochester Group of American Composers." *American Composers on American Music.* Edited by Henry Cowell. Originally 1933. New York: Frederik Ungar, 1962.

_____. "Twenty Years' Growth in America." *Modern Music* XX/2 (January–February, 1943), pp. 95-101.

Hare, Maud Cuney. "Henry F. Gilbert, A Nationalist in Music." *The Musical Observer* XVIII/6 (June, 1919), pp. 11, 13.

Harris, Johanna. "Personal Note." *The New Book of Modern Composers.* Edited by David Ewen. New York: Alfred A. Knopf, 1961.

Harris, Roy. "American Music Enters a New Phase." *Scribner's Magazine* XCVI/4 (October, 1934), pp. 218-21.

_____. "The Basis of Artistic Creation in Music." *The Basis of Artistic Creation.* New Brunswick: Rutgers University Press, 1942.

_____. *Boston Symphony Orchestra Programmes,* February 24, 1939, pp. 777-78.

_____. "The Composer Speaks." *The New Book of Modern Composers.* Edited by David Ewen. New York: Alfred A. Knopf, 1961.

_____. "Composers and Critics." *The New York Times* December 31, 1939, Sec. 9, p. 8.

_____. "Does Music Have to Be European?" *Scribner's* XCI/4 (April, 1932), pp. 204-9.

_____. "Folksong – American Big Business." *Modern Music* XVIII/1 (November–December, 1940), pp. 8-11.

_____. "Growth of a Composer." *The Musical Quarterly* XX/2 (April, 1934), pp. 188-91.

_____. "Letter to Lawrence Gilman," May 20, 1923. Letters File. Music Division. New York Public Library.

_____. "Modern Melody: Its Resources." *M.T.N.A. Proceedings, 1937,* pp. 41-47.

_____. "Notes." *Folksong Symphony 1940.* Vanguard Everyman Classic Recording, SRV 347-SD.

_____. "Our Musical Scene in Two Tones." *Twice A Year* 5/6 (Fall/Winter, 1940, Spring-Summer, 1941), pp. 327-39.

_____. "Perspective at Forty." *The Magazine of Art* 32/11 (November, 1939), pp. 638-39, 667-70.

_____. "Problems of American Composers." *The American Composer Speaks.* Edited by Gilbert Chase. Baton Rouge: Louisiana State Press, 1966. Originally in *American Composers on American Music.* Edited by Henry Cowell. 1933 Edition.

_____. "Sources of a Musical Culture." *The New York Times* January 1, 1939, Sec. 9, pp. 7-8.

_____. "Statement to N. Slonimsky." *Music Since 1900.* Nicolas Slonimsky. Fourth Edition. New York: Charles Scribner's Sons, 1971, p. 688.

Harrison, Lou. "On Quotation." *Modern Music* XXIII/3 (Summer, 1946), pp. 166-69.

Heinsheimer, Hans. "Challenge of the New Audience." *Modern Music* XVI/1 (November-December, 1938), pp. 28-32.

Henahan, Donal. "A Ruptured Duck." *The New York Times* August 15, 1976, Sec. 2, p. 15.

_____. "This Aaron a Musical Moses." *The New York Times* November 9, 1975, Sec. 4, p. 21.

Hess, Howard. "Fanfares by Americans." *Modern Music* XX/3 (March-April, 1943), pp. 189-91.

Hopkinson, Francis. "Dedication to His Excellency George Washington, Esquire." *Seven Songs for Harpsichord.* Philadelphia: n.p., 1788. Facs. edition by Harry Dichter. Philadelphia: Musical Americana, 1954. *The American Composer Speaks.* Edited by Gilbert Chase. Baton Rouge: Louisiana State University Press, 1966.

Howard, John Tasker. "Better Days for Music." *Harper's Monthly Magazine* 174 (April, 1937), pp. 483-91.
_____. "Changed Conditions for the American Composer." *National Federation of Music Clubs: Books Of Proceedings, 1933-35.* Edited by Hazel G. Weaver. Ithaca, New York: National Federation of Music Clubs, 1935, pp. 36-42.
_____. "Frank Van der Stucken." *The Dictionary of American Biography,* Vol. 10. New York: Scribner, [1959-], pp. 181-82.
_____. "Our Folk-Music and Its Probable Impress on American Music of the Future." *The Musical Quarterly* VII/2 (April, 1921), pp. 167-71.
Hughes, Edwin. "Blackout for the Music Industries." *Modern Music* XIX/4 (May-June, 1942), pp. 251-53.
Hunter, John O. "Marc Blitzstein's 'The Cradle Will Rock' as a Document of America, 1937." *American Quarterly* XVII/2, Part I (Summer, 1966), pp. 227-33.
Ives, Burl. "FolkSongs – BackBone of American Music." *The Music Journal* VIII/1 (January-February, 1950), pp. 5, 28.
Jablonski, Edward. "George Gershwin." *HiFi/Stereo Review* XVIII/5 (May, 1967), pp. 49-61.
Jacobi, Frederick. "WPA Shows with Music." *Modern Music* XIV/1 (November–December, 1936), pp. 42-44.
Johnson, Edward. "The Future of Opera in America." *National Federation of Music Clubs: Book of Proceedings, 1933-35.* Edited by Hazel G. Weaver. Ithaca, New York: National Federation of Music Clubs, 1935, pp. 29-32.
Johnson, Helen. "Radio Music Education for the Young." *National Federation of Music Clubs: Book of Proceedings, 1933-35.* Edited by Hazel G. Weaver. Ithaca, New York: National Federation of Music Clubs, 1935, pp. 68-70.
Kay, Norman. "Aspects of Copland's Development." *Tempo* 95 (Winter, 1970-71), pp. 23-29.
Kendall, Raymond. "Music of the Armed Services." *The Musical Quarterly* XXXI/2 (April, 1945), pp. 141-56.
Kent, Robert. "Singing for the Daily." *Daily Worker* January 17, 1934, p. 5.
Kerr, Harrison. "Contemporary Music in New York." *Trend* II/3 (May–June, 1934), pp. 145-47.
_____. "Creative Music and the New School." *Trend* III/2 (March–April, 1934), pp. 86-91.
_____. "Two Operatic Premieres." *Trend* III/1 (March–April, 1935), pp. 36-37.
Kolodin, Irving. "American Composers and the Phonograph." *Modern Music* XI/3 (March-April, 1934), pp. 128-33.
_____. "The Years of Modern Music Recording." *Modern Music* X/2 (January–February, 1933), pp. 103-6.
Krenek, Ernest. "Opera Between the Wars." *Modern Music* XX/2 (January–February, 1943), pp. 102-11.
_____. "The Survival of Tradition." *Modern Music* XVIII/3 (March–April, 1941), pp. 143-46.
_____. "The Transplanted Composer." *Modern Music* XVI/1 (November–December, 1938), pp. 23-27.
Krueger, John. "Harris." *The New Book of Modern Composers.* Edited by David Ewen. New York: Alfred A. Knopf, 1961.
Kubik, Gail. "Composing for Government Films." *Modern Music* XXIII/3 (Summer, 1946), pp. 189-92.
Kubly, Herbert. "America's No. 1 Composer." *Esquire* XXIX/4 (April, 1948), pp. 57, 143-45.
Labastille, Irma Goebel. "Americanismo Musical." *Modern Music* XIV/1 (November–December, 1936), pp. 76-81.
The League of Composers Review I/1 (February, 1924).
Lederman, Minna. "American Way." *Modern Music* XIX/3 (March–April, 1942), pp. 206-8.

_____. "Memories of Marc Blitzstein, Music's Angry Man." *Show* IV/6 (June, 1964), p. 18ff.

Lederman, Minna. "No Money for Music." *North American Review* 243 (Spring–Summer, 1937), pp. 124-36.

Levallée, Calixa. "President's Address." *Proceedings* of the Tenth Annual Meeting of the M.T.N.A. (Boston: June 30, July 1 and 2, 1886), p. 9.

Lourié, Arthur. "The Approach to the Masses." *Modern Music* XXI/4 (May–June, 1944), pp. 203-07.

_____. "A Tribute to Koussevitsky." *The Musical Quarterly* XXX/3 (July, 1944), pp. 270-76.

Lowens, Margery M. "The New York Years of Edward MacDowell." Ph.D. dissertation, University of Michigan, 1971.

Luening, Otto. "Douglas Moore." *Modern Music* XX/4 (May–June, 1943), pp. 248-53.

_____. "Musical Finds in the Southwest." *Modern Music* XIII/4 (May–June, 1936), pp. 18-22.

Lyle, Watson. "The 'Nationalism' of Sibelius." *The Musical Quarterly* XIII/4 (October, 1927), pp. 617-29.

M., M. "Music." *Daily Worker* July 25, 1936, p. 7.

Manchester, Arthur L. "Music Education, A Musical America, The American Composer." *The Musical Quarterly* X/4 (October, 1924), pp. 587-95.

"Marc Blitzstein." *Current Biography*. New York: H.W. Wilson, 1940.

"Marc Blitzstein, Composer, 58, Killed in Automobile Accident." *The New York Times*, January 24, 1964, pp. 1, 24.

Mason, Daniel Gregory. "Artistic Ideals: V. Universality." *The Musical Quarterly* XIII/3 (July, 1927), pp. 345-58.

_____. "Democracy and Music." *The Musical Quarterly* III/4 (October, 1917), pp. 641-57.

_____. "FolkSong and American Music (A Plea for the Unpopular Point of View)." *The Musical Quarterly* IV/3 (July, 1918), pp. 323-32.

Maynard, George. "Sons of Struggle." *Daily Worker* May 12, 1934, p. 7.

Mellers, W. H. "Language and Function in American Music." *Scrutiny* X/4 (April, 1942), pp. 346-57.

Mellers, W. H. "Music in the Melting Pot." *Scrutiny* VII/4 (March, 1939), pp. 390-403.

_____. "Music, Theatre, and Commerce." *The Score and I.M.A. Magazine* 12 (June, 1955), pp. 69-76.

_____. "New English and American Music." *Scrutiny* XI/2 (December, 1942), pp. 168-79.

Mellquist, Jerome. "Eulogy to Paul Rosenfeld." *Twice A Year* 14/15 (Fall–Winter, 1946-47), pp. 206-7.

Mendel, Arthur. "The American Composer." *The Nation* CXXXIV/3489 (May 18, 1932), pp. 578-70.

_____. "A Change in Structure." *The Nation* CXXXIV/3470 (January 6, 1932), p. 26.

_____. "The Quintet of Roy Harris." *Modern Music* XVII/1 (October–November, 1939), pp. 25-28.

_____. "What is American Music?" *The Nation* CXXXIV/3487 (May 4, 1932), pp. 524-25.

Menotti, Gian-Carlo. "Letter to the Music Editor." *The New York Times* Sec. 9 (November 20, 1938), p. 8.

Meyer, Alfred H. "Yaddo— A May Festival." *Modern Music* IX/4 (May–June, 1932), pp. 172-76.

Mims, Edwin. "Sidney Lanier." *The Dictionary of American Biography*, Vol. 5. New York: Scribner, [1959-], pp. 601-5.

Modern Monthly, VII/4 (May, 1935), pp. 285-60.

Moore, Paul. "Tradition of Turbulence." *Theatre Arts* XXXIV/3 (March, 1950), pp. 36-38.

Moore, Douglas. "The Cause of Native Music." *The Saturday Review* XXX/4 (January 25, 1947), p. 24.

_____. "The Importance of Music in Wartime." *The Saturday Review* XXVI/5 (January 30, 1943), p. 12.

_____. "Young Composers After the War." *Modern Music* XXI/1 (November–December, 1943), pp. 23-26.

Moore, Earl V. "The WPA Music Program." *Who Is Who in Music.* Chicago: Lee Stern, 1940.

Morton, Lawrence. "On the Hollywood Front." *Modern Music* XXI/2 (January–February, 1944), pp. 116-18.

"Move to Explore Folkways." *The New York Times* December 26, 1938, p. 28.

"Music." *Daily Worker* February 22, 1936, p. 7.

_____. *Daily Worker* March 5, 1936, p. 7.

"Music for America." *Musical Courier* XXI/1 and 2 (July 7 and 14, 1915), pp. 15-16, 32, and 12-13.

"Music in New York." *New York Musical Review and Gazette* IX/7 (April 3, 1858), p. 98.

Music Vanguard: A Critical Review, I/1 and 2 (March–April, and Summer, 1935).

Musical Courier, XXVII/25 (December 20, 1893), pp. 37-38.

_____. XL/6 (February 7, 1900), p. 26.

_____. LXXVI/13 (March 28, 1918), pp. 5, 8.

The Musical Record, 347 (December, 1890), p. 3.

Musical Review, I/1 and 11 (October 16, 1879 and December 25, 1879), pp. 19 and 168.

_____. III/10 (December 16, 1880), pp. 151-52.

The Musical Review and Musical World, XIV/5 and 12 (February 28 and June 16, 1863), pp. 51 and 30.

_____, XV/15 and 24 (July 16, 1864 and November 19, 1864), pp. 230 and 373.

Nancarrow, Conlon. "Mexican-Music–A Developing Nationalism." *Modern Music* XIX/1 (November–December, 1941), pp. 67-69.

Nathan, George Jean. "Theater." *Scribner's Magazine* XIII/3 (March, 1938), pp. 7-73.

"Neglected Works: A Symposium." *Modern Music* XXIII/1 (Winter, 1946), pp. 3-12.

Nesbett, Robert F. "Louis Gruenberg: A Forgotten Figure of American Music." *Current Musicology* 18 (1974), pp. 190-95.

Nettl, Paul. "Music as a Weapon of War." *Modern Music* XXI/3 (March–April, 1944), pp. 155-58.

New Masses, XI/5 (May 1, 1934), pp. 16-17.

New York Weekly Review, XVI/2 (January 14, 1865), p. 6.

Norton, Mildred. "A Music Forum is Presented by Federals." *Los Angeles Evening News* August 19, 1937.

"Notes on Patriotic Works Written for Dr. Rodzinski with Philharmonic and CBS." League of Composers Clippings File. Music Division. New York Public Library.

Official Report of the Eighth Annual Meeting of the M.T.N.A. (Cleveland, Ohio: July 2, 3 and 4, 1884), pp. 8-17 and 33-34.

Patterson, Frank. "Folk Fables." *The League of Composers Review* II/2 (April, 1925), pp. 25-27.

Peatman, John. "Non-Militant, Sentimental . . ." *Modern Music* XX/3 (March–April, 1943), pp. 152-56.

Peri, Francis D. "A Half-Century of Opera in America." *Musical America* 50th Anniversary volume. LXVIII/3 (February, 1948), pp. 23, 176, 178, 460.

Perkins, H. S. "History of the Music Teachers' National Association." *American Art Journal* 59/12 (July 12, 1892), pp. 290-93.

Pettis, Ashley. "American Operas." *New Masses* XII/6 (August 7, 1934), pp. 27-28.

_____. "Composers' Forum." *The New York Times* May 21, 1951, Sec. 10, p. 7.

_____. *Daily Worker* January 31, 1934, p. 5.

_____. "Letter to the Music Editor." *The New York Times* November 13, 1938, Sec. 9, p. 8.

_____. "Marching With a Song." *New Masses* XI/5 (May 1, 1934), p. 15.

Pettis, Ashley. "Music." *New Masses* X/1 (January 2, 1934), pp. 29-30.

_____. "Music." *New Masses* X/2 (January 9, 1934), p. 28.

_____. "Music." *New Masses* X/4 (January 23, 1934), pp. 29-30.

_____. "Music." *New Masses* X/10 (March 6, 1934), p. 30.

_____. "Music in Russia Today." *The New Republic* LXXII/926 (August 31, 1932), pp. 73-74.

_____. "Musical Flashlights from Moscow." *Modern Music* X/1 (November–December, 1932), pp. 49-52.

_____. "Opening Address," New York Composers' Forum-Laboratory, October 30, 1935. *WPA Composers Forum [sic] Transcripts* [WPA Federal Music Project, 1935-39], National Archives.

_____. "Proletarian Music." *The Nation* CXXXV/3516 (November 23, 1932), pp. 500-502.

_____. "Second Workers' Music Olympiad." *New Masses* XI/8 (May 22, 1934), pp. 28-29.

_____. "Two Worlds of Music." *New Masses* VIII/7 (February, 1933), pp. 12-14.

_____. "The WPA and the American Composer." *The Musical Quarterly* XXVI/1 (January, 1940), pp. 101-12.

Peyser, Joan. "The Troubled Time of Marc Blitzstein." *Columbia University Forum* IX/1 (Winter, 1966), pp. 32-37.

Philadelphia Inquirer, April 1, 1965, p. 8.

Philadelphia Orchestra Program Notes, April 14-15, 1944.

Philipps, Harold D. "The Musical Psychology of America." *The Musical Quarterly* IX/4 (October, 1923), pp. 408-14.

"Pins and Needles." *The New York Times* November 29, 1937, p. 18.

Piston, Walter. "Roy Harris." *Modern Music* XI/2 (January–February, 1934), pp. 73-83.

Platt, David. "'Native Land' is Powerful." *Daily Worker* May 12, 1942, p. 7.

Polansky, Vyacheslav. "Lenin's View of Art." *Modern Monthly* VII/2 (January, 1934), pp. 738-43.

Porte, John F. "Charles Wakefield Cadman." *The Chesterian* New Series No. 39 (May, 1934), p. 224.

Porter, Quincy. "American Composers, XVIII: Randall Thompson." *Modern Music* XIX/4 (May–June, 1942), pp. 237-41.

Powell, John. "The Value of Our Musical Tradition." *Magazine of Art* 30/5 (May, 1937), pp. 292-93.

"Previously Unpublished Letters As Written to Claire R. Reis." *Musical America* LXXXIII/1 (January, 1963), pp. 14-17.

"Program" of the American Concert, *Official Report* of the Fourteenth Annual Meeting of the M.T.N.A. (Detroit: July 1, 2, 3, 4 and 5, 1890), pp. 152-53.

Radamsky, Sergei. "Noted Composer." *Daily Worker* February 18, 1935, p. 5.

Reid, Louis. "The Song That Stirred a Nation." *The New York Sun* July 13, 1940, p. 20.

"Report of the Committee on American Music for Our Students." *Proceedings* of the Twelfth Annual Meeting of the M.T.N.A. (Chicago: July 3, 4, 5, and 6, 1888), pp. 160-65.

"Report on the Music Project." *Government Aid During the Depression to Professional, Technical and Other Service Workers.* Prepared by the Division of Professional and Service Projects at the Request of Harry L. Hopkins, Federal Administrator of the WPA (WPA, 1936).

Rhodes, Willard. "On the Warpath, 1942." *Modern Music* XX/3 (March–April, 1943), pp. 157-60.

Riddell, Hugh J. "Modern Ballads Come to Life." *Daily Worker* September 27, 1939, p. 7.

Riegger, Wallingford. "To the New Through the Old." *Magazine of Art* 32/8 (August, 1939), pp. 472-92.

Ritter, Frédéric L. "Where We Are in Music." *New York Weekly Review* XVI/14 (April 14, 1865), p. 4.

Rockwell, John. "Copland, at 75." *The New York Times* November 12, 1975, p. 48.

Rosenfeld, Paul. "'Americanism' in American Music." *Modern Music* XVII/4 (May–June, 1940), pp. 226-32.

_____. "Current Chronicle: Copland – Harris – Schuman." *The Musical Quarterly* XXV/3 (July, 1939), pp. 372-81.

_____. "Folksong and Culture-Politics." *Modern Music* XVII/1 (October–November, 1939), pp. 18-24.

_____. "Grand Transformation Scene – 1907–1915." *Twice A Year* 5/6 (Fall–Winter, 1940, Spring-Summer, 1941), pp. 352-60.

_____. "The Newest American Composers." *Modern Music* XV/3 (March–April, 1938), pp. 153-59.

_____. "Variations on the Grass Roots Theme." *Modern Music* XVI/4 (May–June, 1939), pp. 214-19.

_____. "When New York Became Central." *Modern Music* XX/2 (January–February, 1943), pp. 83-89.

Sabin, Robert. "Peaks of Achievement Between Two Wars." *Musical America*, 50th Anniversary volume, LXVIII/3 (February, 1948), pp. 8-9, 228, 392, 395.

_____. "Roy Harris – Still Buoyant as Composer and Teacher." *Musical America* LXXVII/2 (January 15, 1957), pp. 17, 24.

Salazar, Adolfo. "American, North and South." *Modern Music* XVI/2 (January–February, 1939), pp. 75-91.

Salter, Sumner. "Early Encouragments to American Composers." *The Musical Quarterly* XVIII/1 (January, 1932), pp. 76-105.

_____. "The Music Teachers' National Association and Its Early Relation to American Composers." *M.T.N.A. Proceedings, 1932,* pp. 9-34.

Salzedo, Carlos, ed. *Eolus* VI/1 (January, 1927).

Salzman, Eric. "Dean of Our Composers at 60." *The New York Times Magazine* November 13, 1960, p. 51.

Saminsky, Lazare. "The Composer and the Critic." *Modern Music* XIII/2 (January–February, 1936), pp. 12-14.

Samson, Leon. "Americanism: A Substitute for Socialism." *Modern Monthly* VII/2 (July, 1933), pp. 367-72.

Sanborn, Pitts. "All-American On the Air." *Modern Music* IX/4 (May–June, 1932), pp. 176-78.

"Sands, Carl." "All-Copland Concert." *Daily Worker* October 16, 1935, p. 5.

_____. "Copeland's [*sic*] Music Recital at Pierre Degeyter Club." *Daily Worker* March 22, 1934, p. 5.

_____. "Eisler Farewell Concert." *Daily Worker* April 23, 1935, p. 5.

_____. "The International Collection." *Daily Worker* January 31, 1934, p. 7.

_____. "Music League Plans a New Book." *Daily Worker* November 18, 1935, p. 5.

_____. "Proletarian Music as a Historical Necessity." *Daily Worker* March 6, 1934, p. 5.

_____. "Schoenberg's Latest Composition." *Daily Worker* October 23, 1935, p. 5.

_____. "Shostakovich's Brilliant Opera." *Daily Worker* February 18, 1935, p. 5.

_____. "Songs By the Auvilles." *Daily Worker* January 15, 1935, p. 5.

_____. "Workers Audience Applauds Gold's Poem Set to Music." *Daily Worker* June 26, 1934, p. 5.

_____. "World of Music." *Daily Worker* March 6, 1935, p. 5.

_____. "World of Music." *Daily Worker* March 22, 1935, p. 5.

_____. "World of Music." *Daily Worker* May 16, 1935, p. 5.

_____. "World of Music." *Daily Worker* October 16, 1935, p. 7.

Sanger, Hon. A.L. "Address of Welcome." *Official Report* of the Ninth Annual Meeting of the M.T.N.A. (New York: July 1, 2 and 3, 1885), pp. 3-4.

Saunders, William. "National Opera, Comparatively Considered." *The Musical Quarterly* XII/1 (January, 1927), pp. 72-84.

Schlee, Alfredo. "Under the Red Flag." *Modern Music* X/3 (March–April, 1932), pp. 108-13.

Schloezer, Boris de. "The Soviet Fosters A Provincial Art." *Modern Music* III/1 (November–December, 1925), pp. 9-15.

Schonberg, Harold. "He Wanted to Reach Us." *The New York Times* February 28, 1971, Sec. 2, p. 15.

_____. "Virgil Thomson: Parisian from Missouri." *HiFi/Stereo Review* XIV/5 (May, 1965), pp. 43-56.

Schuman, William. "A Birthday Salute to Aaron Copland." *The New York Times* October 30, 1960, Sec. 4, p. 7.

_____. "A Brief Study of Music Organizations Founded in the Interest of the Living Composer." *Twice a Year* 5/6 (Fall–Winter, 1940, Spring–Summer, 1941), pp. 361-67.

_____. "Letter to the Music Editor." *The New York Times* March 12, 1939, Sec. 3, p. 6.

_____. "Letter to the Music Editor." *The New York Times* March 19, 1939, Sec. 11, p. 6.

"Second Worker's Music Olympiad." *New Masses* XI/8 (May 22, 1934), p. 29.

Seeger, Charles. "Charles Ives and Carl Ruggles." *Magazine of Art* 32/7 (July, 1939), pp. 396-437.

_____. "Grass Roots for American Composers." *Modern Music* XVI/3 (March–April, 1939), pp. 143-49.

_____. "Interview with Barbara Zuck," June 19, 1976.

_____. "Letter to Barbara Zuck," August 9, 1976.

_____. "Letter to Barbara Zuck," October 22, 1977.

_____. "Music and Class Structure in the United States." *American Quarterly* IX/3 (Fall, 1957), pp. 281-94.

_____. "Music in America." *Magazine of Art* 31/7 (July, 1938), pp. 411-36.

_____. "On Proletarian Music." *Modern Music* XI/3 (March–April, 1934), pp. 121-27.

_____. "On Style and Manner in Modern Composition." *The Musical Quarterly* IX/3 (July, 1923), pp. 423-31.

_____. "Tradition and the (North) American Composer." *Music in the Americas.* Edited by George List and Juan Orrego-Salas. (The Hague, The Netherlands: Mouton and Co., 1967), pp. 195-212.

Sessions, Roger. "An American Evening Abroad." *Modern Music* IV/1 (November–December, 1926), pp. 33-36.

_____. "American Music and the Crisis." *Modern Music* XVIII/4 (May–June, 1941), pp. 211-17.

_____. "Artists and this War." *Modern Music* XX/1 (November–December, 1942), pp. 3-7.

_____. "Music and Nationalism." *Modern Music* XI/1 (November–December, 1933), pp. 3-12.

_____. "The New Musical Horizon." *Modern Music* XIV/2 (January–February, 1937), pp. 59-66.

_____. "No More Business-As-Usual." *Modern Music* XIX/3 (March–April, 1942), pp. 156-62.

_____. "On the American Future." *Modern Music* XVII/2 (January–February, 1940), pp. 71-75.

Siegmeister, Elie. "Americans Want American Music." *Etude* LXII/1 (January, 1944), pp. 28-54.

_____. "The Class Spirit in Music." *Modern Monthly* VII/10 (November, 1933), pp. 593-98.

_____. "Interview with Barbara Zuck." December 14, 1974.

_____. "Musical Life in Soviet Russia." *New Masses* XIII/3 (October 16, 1934), pp. 27-28.

_____. "Social Influences in Music" and "The Class Spirit in Music." *Modern Monthly* VII/8 and 10 (September and November, 1933), pp. 472-79 and 593-98.

Simon, Robert. "Songs of the American Folk." *Modern Music* V/3 (March–April, 1928), pp. 33-34.

Slonimsky, Nicolas. "Development of Soviet Music." *Research Bulletin on the Soviet Union* II/4 (April 30, 1937), pp. 31-36.

_____. "Henry Cowell." *American Composers on American Music.* Edited by Henry Cowell. Originally 1933. New York: Frederick Ungar, 1962.

_____. "Music and Musicians." *Boston Evening Transcript* June 24, 1934, Part I, p. 1.

_____. "Roy Harris." *The Musical Quarterly* XXXIII/1 (January 1947), pp. 17-37.

_____. "The Story of Roy Harris – American Composer," Parts I and II. *Etude* 74 and 75 (December, 1956 and January, 1957), pp. 11, 62 and 12, 42.

Smith, Cecil. "How Audiences Grew in America, 1900–1948." *Musical America* 50th Anniversary volume. LXVIII/3 (February, 1948), pp. 7, 229.

_____. "League of Composers Program Celebrates Copland Birthday." *Musical America* LXX/14 (December 1, 1950), p. 18.

Smith, Moses. "'The Cradle' Rocks on Records." *The New Republic* XCIX/2 (July 13, 1938), p. 280.

Sokoloff, Nicolai. "Text of a Radio Talk." September 22, 1936. *WPA Exhibit No. 2.* Library of Congress.

"Soldier Songs." *The New York Times Magazine* July 25, 1943, p. 2.

Spalding, Walter R. "The War in Its Relation to American Music." *The Musical Quarterly* IV/1 (January, 1917), pp. 1-11.

Spivacke, Walter. "The Archive of American Folk Song in the Library of Congress." *M.T.N.A. Proceedings, 1940,* pp. 123-27.

Starke, Aubrey H. "Sidney Lanier as a Musician." *The Musical Quarterly* XX/4 (October, 1934), pp. 384-400.

Stehman, Dan. "The Symphonies of Roy Harris: An Analytical Study of the Linear Materials and of Related Works." Ph.D. dissertation, University of Southern California, 1973.

Still, William Grant. "An Afro-American Composer's Point of View." *American Composers on American Music.* Edited by Henry Cowell. Originally 1933. New York: Frederick Ungar, 1962.

_____. "The American Composers." *The Baton.* California Federal Music Project, April, 1937. *WPA Composers Forum Letters and Press.* National Archives.

Stringham, Edwin. "Jazz – An Educational Problem." *The Musical Quarterly* XII/2 (April, 1926), pp. 190-95.

"Swift, L. E." "The Auvilles' Songs." *New Masses* XIV/6 (February 5, 1935), p. 28.

_____. "May Day Song." *New Masses* XV/5 (April 30, 1935), pp. 16-17.

Sykes, James. "Native Notes in Colorado." *Modern Music* XX/1 (November-December, 1942), pp. 49-50.

Talley, Paul Myers. "Social Criticism in the Original Theatre Librettos of Marc Blitzstein." Ph.D. dissertation, University of Wisconsin, 1965.

Taylor, Davidson. "Compositions for Radio." *Who Is Who in Music, 1941.* Chicago: Lee Stern, 1940.

_____. "To Order, For Radio." *Modern Music* XIV/1 (November–December, 1936), pp. 12-17.

Taylor, Davidson. "Why Not Try the Air?" *Modern Music* XV/2 (January–February, 1938), pp. 86-91.

Thompson, Keith. "Opera in America Today." *Modern Music* XXI/1 (November–December, 1943), pp. 18-22.

Thompson, Oscar. "American Creative Art." *National Federation of Music Clubs: Book of Proceedings, 1933-35.* Edited by Hazel G. Weaver. Ithaca, New York: National Federation of Music Clubs, 1935, pp. 43-47.

_____. "An American School of Criticism." *The Musical Quarterly* XXIII/4 (October, 1937), pp. 428-39.

Thompson, Randall. "The Contemporary Scene in American Music." *The Musical Quarterly* XVIII/1 (January, 1932), pp. 9-17.

Thomson, Virgil. "Aaron Copland." *Modern Music* IX/2 (January–February, 1932), pp. 67-73.

_____. "Blitzstein's 'Native Land.'" *The New York Herald Tribune,* May 31, 1942.

_____. "'Greatest Music Teacher'—At 75." *The New York Times Magazine,* February 4, 1962, pp. 24, 33, 35.

_____. "A Little About Movie Music." *Modern Music* X/4 (May–June, 1933), pp. 188-91.

_____. "Music." *The New York Herald Tribune* April 2, 1946.

_____. "Socialism at the Metropolitan." *Modern Music* XII/3 (March–April, 1935), pp. 123-26.

_____. "Transplanted Traditions." As told to Christie Baxter. *Musical America* LXXV/4 (February 15, 1955), pp. 29, 213.

_____. "Virgil Thomson: American Music and Music Criticism." Edited by Barbara Zuck. *The Otterbein Miscellany* XII/1 (December, 1976), pp. 1-23.

Thurber, Jeannette. "Dvořák As I Knew Him." *Etude* XXXVII/12 (November, 1919), pp. 693-94.

Tilkin, Anita. "Singing His Song." *Daily Worker* October 27, 1938, p. 7.

Toye, Francis. "A Case for Musical Nationalism." *The Musical Quarterly* IV/1 (January, 1918), pp. 12-22.

Tuthill, Burnet C. "Fifteen Years of Service to an American Ideal." *Musical America* LIV/16 (August, 1934).

"Unique Among Music Schools." *Daily Worker* September 21, 1938, p. 7.

Upton, William Treat. "Our Musical Expatriates." *The Musical Quarterly* XIV/1 (January, 1928), pp. 143-54.

Van Cleve, John S. "American Composition." *Official Report* of the Fourteenth Annual Meeting of the M.T.N.A. (Detroit: July 1, 2, 3, 4 and 5, 1890), pp. 85-90.

Ward, Robert. "Composers in Uniform." *Modern Music* XXIII/2 (Spring, 1946), pp. 108-10.

_____. "In the Army Now." *Modern Music* XIX/3 (March–April, 1942), pp. 167-68.

_____. "Letter from the Army." *Modern Music* XX/3 (March–April, 1943), pp. 170-74.

Watanabe, Ruth. "Autograph Scores from the American Composers' Concerts, 1925–1930." *University of Rochester Library Bulletin* XVII/3 (Spring, 1962), pp 58-62

Waters, Edward N. "The Wa-Wan Press, An Adventure in Musical Idealism." *A Birthday Offering to Carl Engel.* Edited by Gustave Reese. New York: G. Schirmer, 1943.

Watters, Lorrain E. "The Utilization of Folk Music in Public School Music Education." *M.T.N.A. Proceedings, 1941*, pp. 52-57.

Weil, Irving. "The American Scene Changes." *Modern Music* VI/4 (May–June, 1929), pp. 6-8.

Weill, Kurt. "The Future of Opera in America." *Modern Music* XIV/4 (May–June 1937), pp. 183-886.

Weisgall, Hugo. "The Music of Henry Cowell." *The Musical Quarterly* XV/4 (October 1939), pp. 484-507.

Weissman, Adolph. "Race and Modernity." *The League of Composers Review* I/1 (February, 1924), pp. 3-6.

Welch, Roy Dickinson. "The College, The Composer, and Music." *Modern Music* XIV/1 (November–December, 1936), pp. 18-23.

_____. "The Musician and Society." *M.T.N.A. Proceedings, 1935*, pp. 74-77.

West, Stephan. "Americans Want American Music!" *Etude* LXII/1 (January, 1944), p. 28.

"What Makes a Good War Song? Report from V.O.K.S. on the Moscow Meeting of Composers." *Modern Music* XXI/2 (January–February, 1944), pp. 85-88.

Whiting, George E. "An American School of Composition." *Official Report* of the Eighth Annual Meeting of the M.T.N.A. (Cleveland, Ohio: July 2, 3 and 4, 1884), pp. 33-43.

Wolff, William. "The Songs, Dances and Ballads of America." *Daily Worker* (July 1, 1939), p. 7.

"Workers Music League." *Daily Worker* (October 6, 1935), p. 7.

"Workers Music League." *New Masses* VII/5 (October, 1931), p. 31.

"X – 1941." "The Nazis Draft Music for Total War." *Modern Music* XIX/1 (November–December, 1941), pp. 16-20.

Selected Musical Sources

Allen, William Francis; Ware, Charles; and Garrison, Lucy McKim. *Slave Songs of the United States.* New York: A. Simpson, 1867.

Bennett, Robert Russell. *Abraham Lincoln: A Likeness in Symphony Form.* New York: Harms, 1931.

_____. *"Four Freedoms" Symphony.* Abridged and simplified piano adaptation by Helmy Kresna. New York: Contemporary Publications, 1943.

_____. *Suite of Old American Dances.* New York: Chappell, 1950.

Blitzstein, Marc. *The Cradle Will Rock.* New York: Chappell Music Company, 1938.

_____. *Freedom Morning.* Composer's holograph, 1943.

Bogorad, Miriam; Burke, Gertrude; McCurdy, D. Huntley; and Robinson, Earl, eds. *Songs of America.* New York: Workers Library Publishers, 1939.

Bowles, Paul, arr. *12 American Folk Songs.* New York City: Work Projects Administration Arts Program, n.d.

Bristow, George Frederick. *The Great Republic; An Ode to the American Union.* New York: Biglow and Main, 1880.

_____. *Niagara.* Manuscript, [189?].

_____. *Rip Van Winkle; Grand Opera in Three Acts.* New York: G. Schirmer, 1882.

Cadman, Charles Wakefield. *The Robin Woman (Shanewis).* Boston: White-Smith, 1918.

Carter, Elliott. *Holiday Overture.* New York: Associate Music, 1972.

_____. *Suite from "Pocohontas."* New York: Kalmis, 1941.

Copland, Aaron. *Appalachian Spring.* New York: Boosey and Hawkes, 1945.

_____. *Billy the Kid.* London: Boosey and Hawkes, 1941.

_____. *Rodeo.* New York: Boosey and Hawkes, 1946.

_____. *El Salón México.* New York: Boosey and Hawkes, 1939.

_____. *The Second Hurricane.* New York: Boosey and Hawkes, 1957.

_____. *The Third Symphony.* New York: Boosey and Hawkes, 1947.

Cowell, Henry. *American Melting Pot.* Composer's holograph, n.d.

_____. *American Pipers.* Composer's holograph, n.d.

_____. *Saturday Night at the Firehouse.* New York: Associated Music Publishers, 1949.

_____. *Three Anti-Modernist Songs.* n.p., 1938.

Crawford, Richard. *The Civil War Songbook.* New York: Dover Publications, 1977.

Downes, Olin, and Siegmeister, Elie, eds. *A Treasury of American Song.* New York: Howell, Saskin, 1940.

Eisler, Hanns. "Comintern." *New Masses* VII/5 (October 31, 1931), p. 31.

Fife, Austin E., Alta S., eds. *Cowboy and Western Songs.* New York: Clarkson N. Potter, 1969.

Finney, Ross Lee. *Hymn, Fuging, and Holiday.* New York: Carl Fischer, 1945.

Fry, William Henry. *Leonora.* New York: E. Ferrett and Co., 1846.

Gellert, Lawrence, ed. *Negro Songs of Protest.* Collected by Lawrence Gellert, arranged by Elie Siegmeister, foreword by Wallingford Riegger. New York: American Music League, 1936.

Gilbert, Henry F. *Comedy Overture on Negro Themes.* New York: H. W. Gray, 1912.

_____. *The Dance in Place Congo.* New York: H. W. Gray, 1922.

_____. *Negro Rhapsody.* New York: H. W. Gray, 1915.

Gould, Morton. *American Salute.* New York: Mills Music, 1943.

_____. *Cowboy Rhapsody.* New York: Mills Music, 1940.

_____. *"New" China March.* New York: Mills Music, 1943.

_____. *Spirituals.* New York: Mills Music, 1945.

_____. *Yankee Doodle.* New York: Mills Music, 1945.

Harris, Roy. *Abraham Lincoln Walks at Midnight.* New York: Associated Music Publishers, 1955.

_____. *Cindy.* New York: Carl Fischer, 1951.

_____. *Folksong Symphony.* Composer's holograph, 1940.

_____. *Symphony for Voices.* New York: G. Schirmer, 1939.

_____. *The Third Symphony.* New York: G. Schirmer, 1939.

_____. *When Johnny Comes Marching Home.* New York: G. Schirmer, 1934.

Haufrecht, Herbert. *Square Set for Orchestra.* New York: Broadcast Music, 1942.

Heinrich, Anthony Philip. *The Dawning of Music in Kentucky.* Philadelphia: Bacon and Hart, 1820.

_____. *The Musical Week.* London: Johanning, [1835].

Lancourt, Saul, and Siegmeister, Elie. *Doodle Dandy of the U.S.A.* New York: Musette, 1942.

Lingenfelter, Richard E.; Dwyer, Richard A.; and Cohen, David, eds. *Songs of the American West.* Berkeley and Los Angeles: University of California Press, 1968.

MacDowell, Edward. *Second (Indian) Suite.* Reprint of Breitkopf und Haertel edition. New York: Associated Music Publishers, 195?.

Moore, Douglas. *Down East Suite.* New York: Carl Fischer, 1946.

_____. *The Devil and Daniel Webster.* New York: Boosey and Hawkes, 1943.

_____. *The Headless Horseman.* Boston: E. C. Schirmer, 1937.

_____. *Village Music.* New York: Music Press, 1942.

Phillips, Burrill. *Selections from McGuffey's Reader.* Rochester, New York: Eastman School of Music American Composers' edition, 1937.

Read, Gardner. *American Circle.* Chicago: Clayton F. Summry, 1940.

Red Song Book. New York: Workers Library Publications, 1932.

Robinson, Earl. *Ballad for Americans.* New York: Robbins Music, 1940.

_____. *Giants in the Land.* Piedmont Music, 1952.

_____. "Joe Hill." *Daily Worker,* September 4, 1936, p. 7.

_____. *The Lonesome Train.* New York: Sun Music, 1945.

Sackett, S. J. *Cowboys and the Songs They Sang.* New York: William R. Scott, 1967.

Sandburg, Carl. *The American Songbag.* New York: Harcourt, Brace, 1927. New edition called *New American Songbag.* New York: Broadcast Music, 1950.

Series of Old American Songs. Brown University Harris Collection of American Poetry and Plays. Providence: Brown University Press, 1936.

Sharp, Cecil J. *English Folk-Song from the Southern Appalachians.* Edited by Maud Karpeles. 2 volumes. London: Oxford University Press, 1932.

Siegmeister, Elie. *Abraham Lincoln Walks at Midnight.* New York: Boosey and Hawkes, 1956.

_____. *American Legends.* New York: Edward B. Marks, 1940.

_____. *American Sonata.* New York: Edward B. Marks, 1945.

_____. *Folk Ways U.S.A.* Bryn Mawr, Pennsylvania: Theodore Press, 1954.

_____. *I See A Land.* New York: Lawson-Gould, 1962.

_____. *Ozark Set.* New York: E. B. Marks, 1943.

_____. *Singing Down the Road.* [N.C.]: Ginn and Co., 1947.

_____. *Strange Funeral in Braddock. New Music; A Quarterly Review of Modern Compositions* IX/4 (July, 1936), pp. 2-12.

_____. *Western Suite.* New York: Associated Music Publishers, 1948.

_____. *Wilderness Road.* New York: Leeds Music, 1946.

_____. *Work and Sing.* New York: William R. Scott, 1944.

Silber, Irwin, and Robinson, Earl. *Songs of the Great American West.* New York: Macmillan, 1967.

Slonimsky, Nicolas. *Yellowstone Park Suite.* Providence, R.I.: Axelrod Publications, 1951.

Thompson, Randall. *The American Mercury.* Boston: E. C. Schirmer, 1932.

_____. *Frostiana.* Boston: E. C. Schirmer, 1959.

_____. *The Testament of Freedom.* Boston: E. C. Schirmer, 1943.

Thomson, Virgil. *The Plow That Broke the Plains.* Music Press, 1942.

_____. *Suite from "The River."* New York: Southern Music, 1958.

_____. *Symphony on a Hymn Tune.* New York: Southern Music, 1954.

Workers Song Book, No. 1. New York: Workers' Music League, 1934.

Workers Song Book, No. 2. New York: Workers' Music League, 1935.

Index